D1573101

Handbook of
SEMANTIC WORD NORMS

Michael P. Toglia and **William F. Battig**
University of Colorado

with co-authors:

Kay Barrow   **James W. Pellegrino**
Desmond S. Cartwright   **Thomas J. Moore**
Carla J. Posnansky   **Gregory A. Camilli**

 LAWRENCE ERLBAUM ASSOCIATES, PUBLISHERS
1978   Hillsdale, New Jersey

DISTRIBUTED BY THE HALSTED PRESS DIVISION OF

JOHN WILEY & SONS
New York   Toronto   London   Sydney

Lawrence Erlbaum Associates, Inc., Publishers
62 Maria Drive
Hillsdale, New Jersey 07642

Distributed solely by Halsted Press Division
John Wiley & Sons, Inc., New York

Library of Congress Cataloging in Publication Data

Toglia, Michael P.
     Handbook of semantic word norms.

     Bibliography: p.
     Includes index.
     1.   Meaning (Psychology)   I.   Battig, William F.,
joint author.   II.   Title.
BF778.T63   401'.9   78-6556
ISBN 0-470-26378-4

Printed in the United States of America

Contents

Preface

This volume contains information derived from college-student ratings of a large number and variety of individual words (along with some nonwords) for seven basic semantic characteristics. The primary data consist of rating values for each of 2854 words for the seven dimensions of *concreteness* (CON), *imagery* (IMG), *categorizability* (CAT), *meaningfulness* (MNG), *familiarity* (FAM), *number of attributes* (NOA), and *pleasantness* (PLS). All of these dimensions of verbal materials are of special significance for current research on verbal behavior and related topics, and with the exception of number of attributes, all have been scaled previously for smaller samples of words and/or nonwords.

The first chapter of this book consists of several kinds of descriptive information about the materials and procedure for these ratings, as well as relevant statistical information. Chapter 2 describes the eight groups or clusters in which the actual ratings are presented in Chapter 4, which provides an especially novel and hopefully useful format for this information. To facilitate location of the ratings for any particular word within these clusters, Chapter 3 provides a complete alphabetical listing of all 2854 words along with the number of the cluster in which that word and its ratings are located. Each of these clusters consists of words having a particular pattern of mean ratings across the seven dimensions, as determined from an objective procedure of multivariate classification described in Chapter 2. As a result, investigators searching for any particular type(s) of words should have their work substantially reduced by making reference to the particular cluster(s) containing such words.

No long-term project of this magnitude would be possible without the cooperation of numerous individuals or long-term research support. The latter was provided by a 5-year program grant from the National Science Foundation (BNS 72-02084) for a time period virtually coinciding with that required to carry this project through to completion.

This NSF grant was for collaborative research on "Cognitive Factors in Human Learning and Memory," involving several faculty members of the Institute for the Study of Intellectual Behavior at the University of Colorado. The present project, however, was not even conceived until after this grant had been awarded, and it has represented at best a secondary aspect of the overall NSF-supported research program. Nonetheless, the present word-scaling project undoubtedly represents the longest-term single project conducted under this grant, as well as being the most notable instance of truly collaborative research, which would never have been undertaken, much less completed, had it not been for this NSF grant support.

Appropriate acknowledgments of individual contributions to a project of this magnitude and duration are made especially difficult because of the highly varied and often short-term contributions of many people who are clearly deserving of acknowledgment. In fact, the two primary co-authors, Michael P. Toglia and William F. Battig, are the only individuals who have been centrally involved throughout the entire 5 years of the project. Toglia has unquestionably contributed more than anyone else, taking primary responsibility for data collection and tabulations for all except the first two (CON and IMG) dimensions, as well as for the careful checking and double-checking, which assures the high level of accuracy of all the information in this book, and for numerous other critical aspects of this project. Battig's role has been primarily one of general administration and allocation of necessary research funds and personnel, selection of the dimensions to be scaled, and writing of the textual portion of this book.

Each of the other co-authors has made major contributions to limited parts of the overall project. The actual initiation of these norms, and the selection of the words to be scaled as well as the data collection procedures, were accomplished primarily by Carla J. Posnansky and James W. Pellegrino. Before leaving in 1973 for the universities of Rochester (Posnansky) and Pittsburgh (Pellegrino), they also had supervised the data collection and preliminary analyses for the first two dimensions of CON and IMG. These initial results were presented in a widely distributed technical report dated July 1973, which was intended to make these CON and IMG ratings immediately available to interested researchers. It subsequently became evident, however, that the original tabulating and checking procedures still permitted too many sources of error to yield accurate and reliable rating values. Subsequently, all ratings as presented in this book have been carefully checked and corrected for accuracy, so it is strongly recommended that the values given in the 1973 technical report no longer be used for any purposes.

Two other co-authors, Kay Barrow and Desmond S. Cartwright, both became centrally involved in this project only after the above described initial data collection and reporting had been completed. Barrow is directly responsible for the pleasantness scaling, which was of special significance for her own research, as well as for initiating the cluster and correlational analyses of the present data, which led to the cluster-based format of this book. These initial cluster analyses and their interpretation also led directly to the central involvement in this project of Cartwright, an authority on multivariate analysis, who has taken responsibility for most of the advanced statistical analyses of these data, including the aforementioned cluster analyses and computation of reliabilities (which turned out to be an especially difficult and time-consuming job because of the ways the present data were originally obtained and recorded).

Co-authors Thomas J. Moore and Gregory A. Camilli both made especially significant contributions that call for special mention. During the final 2 years of the project, Moore worked very closely with Toglia, devoting countless hours to checking the words and scale values for accuracy and organizing them according to clusters. Camilli's special contribution was to develop a completely computerized technique whereby the norms as presented in this book were obtained directly from the original raw data without human intervention.

Of the 21 other individuals who made notable contributions to this project, Terry R. Barrett, Catherine S. Brown, Shu-in Huang, Louis C. Oswald, Susan E. Stahl, and Colleen Tovani are also deserving of special mention. The remaining 15 contributors (in alphabetical order) are Janice E. Blaz, Clara Chapman, Deborah Davis, Gilles O. Einstein, Mark E. Fetler, Margaret Graves, Leslie Hamilton, William G. Maier, Michele S. Mondani, Paul G. Neumann, Barbara Pellegrino, Philip M. Salzberg, Jean M. Schab, Cathleen J. Toglia, and James N. West.

Last, but far from least, this project required extensive use of the computing facilities of the University of Colorado Computing Center, as well as of the Computer Laboratory for Instruction in Psychological Research in the Department of Psychology. Special appreciation is due to Sally E. Battig, data processing manager of the Daily Camera (Boulder's newspaper), for assistance in printing out the final results as they appear in this book.

Boulder, Colorado   MICHAEL P. TOGLIA
                                                      WILLIAM F. BATTIG

General Procedural and Statistical Information

1

This book consists primarily of information about several semantic properties of English words, which should be of interest especially to researchers concerned with linguistics and/or verbal behavior for use in selecting or calibrating verbal materials. A total of 2854 individual items, which are listed in alphabetical order in Chapter 3, were all rated for each of seven different semantic dimensions by 54 to 65 students at the University of Colorado providing ratings for each word on each dimension (although a few ratings were made by as many as 69 students). These seven dimensions, which are described in more detail later in this chapter (pp. 3–8) are: (1) *Concreteness* (CON); (2) *Imagery* (IMG); (3) *Categorizability* (CAT); (4) *Meaningfulness* (MNG); (5) *Familiarity* (FAM); (6) *Number of attributes or features* (NOA); and (7) *Pleasantness* (PLS).

Chapter 4 (pp. 35–146) constitutes the major portion of this book, including nearly 20,000 mean ratings (along with their standard deviations) for each individual word on each of the seven dimensions. In an effort to improve upon the usual listing of all words in alphabetical order, which unnecessarily complicates the task of the typical researcher trying to find words at one or more specified levels on one or more dimensions, a new and hopefully more useful format has been adopted for presentation of this rating information herein.

This format is based upon the results of a cluster analysis performed upon the seven mean ratings for each of the individual words, using the BC TRY system (Tryon & Bailey, 1970). The remarkable outcome of this cluster analysis was to partition the present words into eight distinct clusters, with only six of the 2854 words not fitting into any of these

eight clusters. Consequently, the eight clusters have been reproduced in this book, with all words that belong to a particular cluster being listed together in alphabetical order in one of the eight sections of Chapter 4. In addition to the mean rating and its standard deviation for each word on each of the seven dimensions, the magnitude and direction of any difference between the individual word and cluster means are given for each dimension in parentheses below each of the rating values.

A complete alphabetical listing of the 2854 words in Chapter 3 precedes the eight clusters, including the number of the cluster to which each word belongs in a column to the right of the words. As a further aid to finding words with specified values on any of the present dimensions, Tables 6 through 12 (pp. 20–23) present separately for each dimension the numbers of words falling within specified half-unit intervals of mean ratings, which are included in each of the eight clusters. Through this combination of alphabetical ordering of all 2854 words along with separate clusters containing all rating information for mutually similar words, it is hoped that the present rating information has been made maximally accessible with minimal space and cost for users of this book.

The following sections of this first chapter include descriptions of the types of word materials included in this scaling project, separate descriptions of each of the seven rating dimensions, and a general procedural description. Subsequent sections contain relevant statistical information, including reliabilities, intercorrelations between dimensions, and comparison of our ratings with other ratings.

DESCRIPTIONS OF MATERIALS

When this project was initiated in October 1972, its purpose was simply to provide a larger and more varied set of verbal materials scaled for IMG, CON, and MNG, than was provided by the 925 nouns scaled for these variables by Paivio, Yuille, and Madigan (1968). Consequently, the process by which the present 2854 items were selected consisted primarily of inviting faculty and student researchers at the University of Colorado to submit lists of words that they wanted to have scaled for purposes of future research.

The resulting word sample thus represents a wide-ranging but somewhat idiosyncratic collection of items that has little systematic relationship to any single specifiable population of verbal materials. Moreover, the several specific sources from which these items were selected led to sufficient overlap that an estimated 25–30% of the words represent at least two of these sources. Furthermore, the format of presentation of these materials as eight empirically based "clusters" bears little resemblance to the original sources from which they were selected, except that the 100 nonword CVCVC paralogs taken from Locascio and Ley (1972) constitute a large portion of Cluster 1. A special effort was also made to include words representing all parts of speech, including articles, prepositions, and adverbs, most of which can be found in Cluster 2.

Nonetheless, a brief description of the major sources of these words may be of some interest. Over one-half of the words were selected on the basis of particular kinds of structural or semantic characteristics, or relationships between words. Pairs of rhyming words represent the largest single subset (almost 20%), followed by homophones (almost

16%), conceptual category members (13%), and synonyms and/or antonyms (9%). Also included are all but two of Phebe Cramer's 100 homographs (Postman & Keppel, 1970) and 80 of the 109 homographs from Perfetti, Lindsey, and Garson (1971).

In addition to these homographs, many other words were also taken from previous word-association, conceptual-category, or other specified sources of scaled verbal materials. As noted previously, approximately 13% represent common responses to various conceptual categories, primarily from the Battig–Montague (1969) and Shapiro–Palermo (1970) category norms. Responses from the Underwood–Richardson (1956) sense-impression norms constitute about 5% of the total. Also included are all 96 of Postman's stimulus words representing four frequency levels (Postman & Keppel, 1970), all 200 stimulus words from the Palermo–Jenkins (1964) word-association norms, and Battig's (1964) 300 common four-letter words. Additional smaller and unpublished sets of identifiable words (2% or less) include several lexically simple and complex words obtained from Walter Kintsch, some anxiety-producing words contributed by William F. Hodges, and words representing two or more different solutions for the same anagrams.

SELECTION OF DIMENSIONS

This section contains general information about each of the seven dimensions, how and why they were selected, and the portion of the instructions to subjects that defined each dimension for them. The order of presentation corresponds to the order in which the complete rating information is given in Chapter 4, which in turn was determined by magnitude of interrelationships between dimensions (as shown in Table 1 and described later in this chapter).

Concreteness (CON) and Imagery (IMG)

The need for a larger number and wider range of words scaled for CON and IMG was directly responsible for the initiation of the present project; hence, these were the first two dimensions to be rated. Our instructions and procedure for CON and IMG ratings was patterned very closely after those of Paivio et al. (1968), the only major difference being our usage of "low concrete" rather than "high abstract" to characterize the low end of the CON dimension, consistent with Spreen and Schulz (1966). The following instructions for CON and IMG ratings were given to the subjects:

> Concreteness — Words differ in the extent to which they refer to *concrete* objects, persons, places, or things that can be seen, heard, felt, smelled, or tasted, as contrasted with *abstract* concepts that cannot be experienced by our senses. The purpose of this experiment is to rate a list of 480 words with respect to their "concreteness" in terms of sense experience. Any word that refers to objects, materials, or persons should be given a *high concreteness* rating (at the upper end of the numerical scale). Any word that refers to an abstract concept that cannot be experienced by the senses should be given a *low concreteness* rating (at the lower end of the numerical scale). For example, think

of the word "carpet," which can be experienced by our senses and therefore should be rated as high concrete; the word "ambiguous" cannot be experienced by the senses as such and therefore should be rated as low concrete (or abstract). Because words tend to make you think of other words as associates, it is important that your ratings *not* be based on this and that you judge only the concreteness of sense experiences as directly aroused by each word.

Imagery — Words differ in their capacity to arouse mental images of things or events. Some words arouse a sensory experience, such as a mental picture or sound, very quickly and easily, whereas other words may do so only with difficulty (i.e., after a long delay) or not at all. The purpose of this experiment is to rate a list of 480 words as to the ease or difficulty with which they arouse mental images. Any word that in your estimation arouses a mental image (i.e., a mental picture, or sound, or other sensory experience) very quickly and easily should be given a *high imagery* rating (at the upper end of the numerical scale). Any word that arouses a mental image with difficulty or not at all should be given a low imagery rating (at the lower end of the numerical scale). For example, think of the word "buffalo." "Buffalo" would probably arouse an image (e.g. of Ralphie)[1] relatively easily and would be rated as high imagery; "relevant" would probably do so with difficulty and be rated as low imagery. Because words tend to make you think of other words as associates, it is important that your ratings *not* be based on this and that you judge only the ease with which you get a mental image of an object or event in response to each word.

Categorizability (CAT)

This was actually the last of the seven dimensions with respect to data collection, and its inclusion is directly attributable to a report presented by Ruth H. Maki at the 1975 Midwestern Psychological Association meetings, wherein she presented preliminary evidence that words high in IMG and CON typically have "good superordinates." Because of this, along with our previous involvement with conceptual category norms (Battig & Montague, 1969), it was decided to obtain ratings for the present words on ease of finding a superordinate category label, or *categorizability* (CAT). As is demonstrated in subsequent sections, the present data provide especially strong support for Maki's argument that CAT is very closely related to CON and IMG. The following instructions for CAT ratings were given to the subjects:

> Words differ in the ease with which they can be put into some larger category or class. Some words obviously belong to one or more categories, whereas other words may be difficult or impossible to categorize. The purpose of this experiment is to rate a list of 480 words as to how easy or difficult it is to categorize these words. Any word that is very easy to categorize should be given a *high categorizability* rating (at the upper end of the numerical scale). Any word that can be categorized only with difficulty or not at all should be given a *low categorizability* rating (at the lower end of the numerical scale).

[1] For those readers unfamiliar with University of Colorado football, Ralphie is the name of the full-grown female buffalo mascot who is particularly "concrete" for the present subject population.

For example, the word "buffalo" would probably be judged as very easy to categorize, because it belongs to such obvious categories as four-footed and/or wild animals. The word "relevant," on the other hand, would probably be very difficult to categorize in any meaningful way and therefore should be given a low categorizability rating. Because words also differ in many other ways (such as how many other words they make you think of, how easily they can be mentally imaged, or how pleasant they are), it is important that your ratings *not* be based on these other characteristics and that you judge only the ease with which each word can be categorized into some larger group or class.

Meaningfulness (MNG)

Like CON and IMG, MNG values had been included in the Paivio et al. (1968) norms and thus represented the third of the seven dimensions to be scaled in the present project. To maintain consistency with the procedure for the other six dimensions, however, MNG was rated on a 7-point scale rather than being based upon the Noble (1952) production method (number of word associates actually produced by subjects) that had been used by Paivio et al. (1968) and also by Spreen and Schulz (1966). The following instructions for MNG ratings were given to the subjects:

> *Meaningfulness* — Words differ in their capacity to arouse other words as associates to them, or in what is termed their *meaningfulness*. Some words are very strongly associated with other words or are associated with a great many other words, whereas some words are associated only very weakly with only a few other words or cannot be associated with other words at all. The purpose of this experiment is to rate a list of 480 words with respect to the ease with which they can be associated with other words — that is, their *meaningfulness*. Any word that can be associated very easily with other words should be given a *high meaningfulness* rating (at the upper end of the numerical scale). Any word that can be associated with other words only with difficulty or not at all should be given a *low meaningfulness* rating (at the lower end of the numerical scale). For example, think of the word "person," which can very easily be associated with such other words as "people," "man," "woman," and "individual," and which would be rated as highly meaningful; the word "amorphous" would probably be very difficult to associate with any other words and therefore should be rated as of low meaningfulness. Because words sometimes tend to make you think of other things besides words (e.g., mental images or sensory experiences), it is important that your ratings not be based on this and that you judge only the ease with which you can associate each word with other words.

Familiarity (FAM)

Familiarity (FAM) was the fourth dimension to be scaled and the first to be added following completion of the three Paivio et al. (1968) dimensions of CON, IMG, and MNG. Among the primary reasons for including FAM ratings are: (1) the general inclusion of some kind of word-frequency information in scaling projects of this kind, and the ques-

tionable generality of the word-frequency counts that are typically used for such frequency information; (2) the importance of frequency-based interpretations in research in the Colorado laboratories and elsewhere (e.g., Ekstrand, Wallace, & Underwood, 1966; Neumann, 1974); and (3) some evidence (e.g., Galbraith & Underwood, 1973) that abstract words tend to be judged as more frequent or familiar than concrete words, a relationship that could be evaluated in very general terms through inclusion of familiarity or frequency ratings in the present project. That our choice of familiarity rather than frequency makes little if any difference is indicated by the high correlation (0.879) of the present ratings with those obtained by Paivio et al. for printed frequency (see Table 2, p. 16). The following instructions for FAM ratings were given to the subjects:

> *Familiarity* — Words differ in their *familiarity* — that is, in how commonly or frequently they have been experienced or how familiar they appear to be. Some words are very familiar, whereas others may be almost totally unfamiliar. The purpose of this experiment is to rate a list of 480 words with respect to how familiar or common they are — that is, their *familiarity*. Any word that appears very common or familiar should be given a *high familiarity* rating (at the upper end of the numerical scale). Any word that you are unfamiliar with, or that is very new to you, should be given a *low familiarity* rating (at the lower end of the numerical scale). For example, the word "person" should be very familiar to you and would be rated as highly familiar. A word such as "amorphous," on the other hand, is likely to be very unfamiliar to you and therefore should be rated as of low familiarity. Because words also differ in many other ways, such as how many other words they make you think of or how easily they can be mentally imaged, it is important that your ratings *not* be based on these other characteristics and that you judge only how familiar each word is to you.

Number of Attributes or Features (NOA)

This dimension, the sixth for which data were actually collected, is the only one for which there was real uncertainty about whether subjects could give meaningful ratings, leading to preliminary research to evaluate the feasibility of NOA scaling. The potential value of such ratings, however, derives from the existence of influential attribute or feature theories of memory (e.g., Bower, 1967; Underwood, 1969), from a recent attempt to use word frequency as an index of number of meanings (and presumably also attributes) of words (Reder, Anderson, & Bjork, 1974), and most importantly from the Pellegrino–Salzberg (1975) argument that feature sampling as related to total number of features represented by a word constitutes a critical determinant of specificity of encodings. Our preliminary evaluation of the feasibility of rating words for NOA consisted of requiring each of 68 subjects to rate 60 words that varied systematically as to frequency and familiarity (Battig, 1975a). Not only were subjects demonstrably able to make such ratings, but these ratings proved to be only moderately correlated with frequency and

familiarity. Consequently, NOA was added to our list of rated dimensions. The following instructions for NOA ratings were given to the subjects:

> *Number of attributes or features* — Words differ in the number of different features, attributes, and/or properties that are associated with or constitute a part of whatever the word represents. Some words involve several different attributes, whereas other words involve very few. The purpose of this experiment is to rate a list of 480 words with respect to how many different features or attributes they contain — that is, their *number of attributes*. Any word with a very large number of attributes should be given a *high NOA* rating (at the upper end of the numerical scale). Any word that has very few different attributes should be given a *low NOA* rating (at the lower end of the numerical scale). For example, the word "car" would probably be judged as having a great many different attributes, including its various parts (e.g., engine, wheels, fenders, etc.), make and type (e.g., Ford, sedan), color, size, shape, and any number of other attributes. A word such as "triangle," on the other hand, would probably be judged as having few different attributes, because to most people it represents an abstract geometric form with three sides and angles but little else in the way of distinctive features. Because words also differ in many other ways (such as how many other words they make you think of, how easily they can be mentally imaged, or how pleasant they are), it is important that your ratings *not* be based on these other characteristics and that you judge only the number of different attributes involved in each word.

Pleasantness (PLS)

Although PLS was the fifth dimension for which data were collected, it is listed last primarily because of its relative independence of the other six dimensions as shown by the correlations between dimensions in Table 1 (p. 11). This apparent independence may result from both pleasant and unpleasant words representing "emotional" as contrasted with "neutral" words, a characteristic not shared by any of the other six dimensions. Because of the direct relevance of PLS ratings for Kay Barrow's dissertation research (Barrow, 1976), she is directly responsible for the inclusion of the PLS dimension in the present project, as well as for having each word rated by the same numbers of male and female subjects so that the PLS ratings could be compared as a function of sex. These sex comparisons indicated that females tended to give more extreme pleasant and/or unpleasant ratings than did males.[2] As a consequence of these differences, those words

---

[2]Because of the marked sex differences for PLS, which were not found until after all other dimensions except categorizability had been completed, a similar breakdown of separate CAT means for males and females was carried out as a check on the possible generalization of the PLS sex differences to the other dimensions. CAT, however, yielded much smaller and generally nonsignificant discrepancies in mean ratings for the two sexes, indicating that the sizable sex differences in PLS ratings probably do not extend to the other dimensions.

for which males or females gave mean ratings at least 0.5 higher than did the opposite sex are designated in the rating information given in the eight clusters in Chapter 4. More specifically, the letters F and M immediately after the standard deviations for PLS in the final column indicate, respectively, words for which females and males had mean PLS ratings at least half a unit higher than the opposite sex. The following instructions for the PLS ratings were given to the subjects:

> *Pleasantness* — Words differ in their capacity to elicit a feeling of pleasantness. Some words induce a feeling of pleasantness in us, whereas other words evoke an unpleasant feeling. The purpose of this experiment is to rate a list of 480 words with respect to how pleasant or unpleasant they are — that is, their *pleasantness.* Any word that appears very pleasant should be given a *high pleasantness* rating (at the upper end of the numerical scale). Any word that seems unpleasant to you should be given a *low pleasantness* rating (at the lower end of the numerical scale). For example, the word "Christmas" might seem very pleasant to you and would be rated as highly pleasant. A word such as "death," on the other hand, is likely to be very unpleasant to you and therefore should be rated as of low pleasantness. Because words also differ in many other ways, such as how many other words they make you think of or how easily they can be mentally imaged, it is important that your ratings *not* be based on these other characteristics and that you judge only how pleasant each word is to you.

GENERAL PROCEDURE

Except as noted in the preceding section, the same general procedure was used for all of the seven dimensions, except for some refinements resulting from experience with the initially scaled CON and IMG dimensions. The critical procedural characteristics are described briefly in this section.

Subjects were typically run in groups of 15 to 80, with most groups including about 50 subjects and occasional smaller groups especially when the data collection was nearly completed for a particular dimension. A total of over 2500 subjects provided usable data for this project, not counting those who failed to follow instructions and/or made enough errors to cause their data to be discarded. All subjects were undergraduate students enrolled in psychology courses at the University of Colorado, most of whom were fulfilling a course requirement through their participation. Our procedure involved complete compliance with current Federal and university regulations requiring voluntary informed consent, opportunity to withdraw at any time without penalty, and written feedback sheets being given after each rating session.

Each subject was initially given a seven-page booklet containing a cover sheet with the written instructions followed by six pages each containing 80 words to be rated. Thus any single subject typically provided ratings for only one of the seven dimensions, and typically for only 480 of the 2854 words. However, because CON and IMG were scaled concurrently (see p. 3), some subjects did rate one set of 480 words for CON and a dif-

ferent set for IMG. Along with these booklets, each subject was also given six optical scanning forms with 80 10-option spaces (numbered 0–9) for marking their ratings and was instructed to mark ratings for the 80 items in order using No. 2 pencils. In the following paragraphs, these instructions are illustrated for NOA, exactly as they appeared on the cover page; the portions of these instructions that were changed appropriately for each of the other six dimensions are enclosed in brackets:

Your ratings will be made on a 7-point scale, where 1 is the low [number of attributes] end of the scale, and 7 is the high [number of attributes] end of the scale. Make your rating for each word by blackening with your pencil the appropriately numbered space on the answer sheet corresponding to the item number. The words with very high [numbers of attributes] should be given a rating of 7; words that are very low in [number of attributes] should be given a rating of 1. Words that are intermediate in [number of attributes], of course, should be rated appropriately between these two extremes, with a rating of 4 representing what you consider to be [an] average [number of attributes]. You should feel free to use the entire range of ratings from 1 to 7, but don't be concerned about how often you use a particular rating as long as it represents your true judgment. Work as rapidly as you can, but do not be careless in your ratings, and try to give for each word your best judgment as to [how many different attributes the word involves].

It is extremely important that you use the appropriate spaces on the answer sheet to record your ratings for each word. Each page of your booklet containing the words, as well as each page of your answer sheet, is laid out in four numbered columns of 20 each, for a total of 80 numbers on a page. Use a separate answer sheet for each of the six pages in your test booklet. Please be sure that your rating for each numbered word is marked in one of the seven numbered spaces from 1 to 7 for the number on your answer sheet, which corresponds to the word number in the booklet. Also be sure that you use only the spaces numbered from 1 through 7 to make your ratings, the first space (numbered 0) and last two spaces (numbered 8 and 9) should always be left blank. Finally, be sure that you mark one and only one of the spaces from 1 to 7 for each of the 80 words on each page — do not leave any words blank without any of the spaces marked on the answer sheet.

To help you keep straight the meanings of the ratings from 1 through 7, at the top of each of the following pages in the booklet is a rating scale, which shows that 1 represents [a low number of attributes] and 7 represents [a high number of attributes].

The pages in your answer booklet are not consecutively numbered but you should have six pages.

These instructions should be self-explanatory, except for the final sentence. This nonconsecutive numbering of pages in the booklet reflected an effort to counterbalance the order in which the six sets of 80 words were rated by having each set appear with approximately equal frequency across subjects in each of the six page positions in the booklet, as well as being preceded and followed by each of the other five pages with

approximately equal frequency. Moreover, the 80 words on each of the six pages were carefully chosen so that each of the different sources and levels therein (when these were known) were distributed in proper proportions across the 80 positions on each page.

Because each booklet contained only 480 words, it was necessary to use six completely separate 480-word booklets to obtain ratings for all 2854 words. The discrepancy between the total of 2880 words in these six booklets and the 2854 different words in our ratings is because 26 of these words actually were repeated across two different pages or booklets and thus yielded two separate sets of ratings. Further information about these duplicated words and reliability information based thereon appears on p. 14. With the foregoing minor exceptions, however, each booklet contained a different set of 480 words, and the words in each booklet were selected to be comparably representative of all the various types and sources of words in the total 2854-word set. Moreover, all six booklets were always used concurrently for different subjects within each of the group rating sessions.

Complications induced by the usage of several different booklets and of page orders within these booklets did lead to some procedural changes from the first to the last of the seven scaled dimensions. Throughout the first two scaled dimensions (CON and IMG), subjects were also instructed to record identifying numbers from each of their booklet pages on the appropriate answer sheets, and the written cover-page instructions included an additional paragraph describing exactly how this was to be done. Unfortunately, these coding instructions proved to be quite difficult for subjects to comprehend and/or follow, and there was no way to recover the data unless the answer sheets were coded correctly.

For these initial dimensions, there were several instances in which subjects failed to encode their answer sheets correctly, with a consequent loss of data that could not be eliminated (1) even by an expansion of the oral instructions given by the chief experimenter, or (2) by checking the completed answer sheets when these were turned in. Consequently, the six answer sheets for each booklet subsequently were always precoded with the proper identification numbers and were clipped to the back of the booklet in the same order as their corresponding six booklet pages.

For all dimensions and sessions, the booklets were distributed to subjects so that each of the six 480-word sets was represented about equally. Then the chief experimenter explained the coded relationship between the booklet pages and the answer forms, using a specific example on the blackboard at the front of the room. Except for the changes in these coding instructions necessitated by differences between subjects doing their own coding and the aforementioned precoding, the oral instructions at the beginning of a session were comparable for all sessions and dimensions, with special emphasis on marking ratings between one and seven for all of the 80 items in the appropriate spaces on each of the six pages.

Following the verbal instructions, subjects proceeded to rate their 480 words in order at their own pace, which typically required about 30 minutes. Especially for the larger group sessions, several experimenters were present to monitor the subjects and to try to identify and correct those who appeared not to be following instructions. These experimenters also checked each subject's completed response sheets before the sub-

TABLE 1
Correlations Between Pairs of Dimensions, Reliabilities, Means, and Standard Deviations for All Words

	Rating Dimension						
	CON	IMG	CAT	MNG	FAM	NOA	PLS
Concreteness		0.883	0.887	0.425	0.319	0.386	0.215
Imagery			0.905	0.675	0.557	0.543	0.267
Categorizability				0.589	0.488	0.524	0.278
Meaningfulness					0.820	0.749	0.309
Familiarity						0.554	0.267
No. Attributes							0.390
Reliabilities	0.970	0.960	0.970	0.960	0.980	0.920	0.960
Mean Ratings	4.400	4.550	4.330	4.030	5.590	3.560	4.010
Standard Dev.	1.230	1.140	1.190	0.890	1.130	0.730	0.840

ject left the room, which sometimes led to the detection of errors or omissions that could then be corrected by the subject.

GENERAL STATISTICAL INFORMATION

Presented in Table 1 are several kinds of basic statistical information, including: (1) *means and standard deviations* calculated from the mean ratings of the 2854 words, presented in the last two rows of the table; (2) *correlation coefficients* for all possible pairs of dimensions based upon mean ratings for each of the 2854 words; and (3) *reliability* estimates for each dimension, presented in the third row from the bottom of Table 1. Each of these are described in more detail in the following paragraphs.

Means and Standard Deviations

The final two rows of Table 1 are indicative of some differences both in the means and variabilities of ratings across the seven dimensions. Words rated for CON, IMG, CAT, and particularly for FAM, all typically receive ratings above the middle scale value of 4. In contrast, ratings for NOA are somewhat below 4, and both MNG and PLS ratings are relatively close to 4.

The four dimensions with above-average mean ratings also show consistently larger standard deviations and thus greater differences in mean ratings across individual words than the other three dimensions. Unlike the differences in mean ratings, however, these standard deviations are closely comparable across the four dimensions with high mean ratings and differ very little between the three dimensions with lower mean ratings. Thus the difference between these two subsets of dimensions accounts for over 91% of the total variance between these seven standard deviations. More detailed information con-

cerning the distribution of mean ratings for each dimension is given in the last (total) columns of Tables 6 through 12 (pp. 20–23).

These dimensional differences in overall means and standard deviations are sufficiently large to preclude any direct cross-dimensional comparisons in terms of the actual word rating values. This is especially true for comparisons involving FAM, which has a much larger mean (5.59) than any of the other dimensions. That FAM also has one of the largest standard deviations can be attributed to the negative skew and slight bimodality of its distribution, such that most words have very high mean ratings whereas a much smaller number of nonwords and rare words (constituting Cluster 1) show very low familiarity ratings, as shown in Table 10. It is noteworthy that the other seven clusters all show FAM means above 4 and that six of these clusters have means above 5.7. In contrast with familiarity, the other six dimensions all show quite regular distributions of mean word ratings, although CON is shown by Table 6 to be markedly bimodal with relatively few words at intermediate rating levels.

This bimodal distribution for CON is consistent with Cartwright's (1977) claim that concreteness or abstractness of a word represents a selection from a pair of categorical descriptors rather than a unidimensional rating. According to this view, any given interpretation of a word can only be judged as concrete or abstract, and intermediate scale values exist only because of the interpretive ambiguity of English words. For example, the word "felt" may be judged either as concrete or abstract, depending on whether the subject interprets it as a specific concrete cloth object or as the past tense of the abstract word "feel." Thus the mean CON rating of 4.33 for "felt" would reflect the use of both concrete and abstract interpretations by different subjects, as further indicated by its large standard deviation (2.07). That CON has the largest variability, both between mean word ratings (see Table 1) and between individual ratings within a word (see p. 14), also supports Cartwright's view. Hence, our scaled dimension of CON may actually represent a dimension of interpretive doubt.

Correlations Between Dimensions

Presented in the body of Table 1 are the 21 pairwise correlations between individual word ratings on each possible pair of the seven dimensions. There are several points of special interest about these interdimensional correlations that merit some discussion here.

Beginning with the highest correlations in Table 1, the value of 0.883 for CON and IMG is slightly higher than the 0.83 correlation reported by Paivio et al. (1968), and the high MNG–FAM correlation of 0.820 likewise is consistent with previous research (e.g., Underwood & Schulz, 1960). The two highest correlations in Table 1, however, are of CAT with IMG (0.905) and CON (0.887), offering strong support for Maki's (1975) contention that these three dimensions are very closely related. In fact, our results indicate such strong mutual interrelationships between CON, IMG, and CAT that they probably cannot be functionally separated for most words in the English language. This is because 78–82% of the variance in ratings for any one of these three dimensions can be accounted for by its relationship to either of the other two dimensions.

For purposes of the present ratings, the three dimensions of CON, IMG, and CAT perhaps should be viewed as representing a single higher-order semantic dimension. This was indicated by the results of a factor analysis performed upon these data, which showed these three dimensions all to load primarily on the first factor to emerge from this analysis.[3]

The only other correlations that accounted for as much as 45% of the variance for any dimension were those of MNG with NOA (0.749) and IMG (0.675). Nearly one-half (10) of these correlations are in the moderate range between 0.3 and 0.6. Moreover, all of the five lowest correlations involve PLS, which shows its highest correlation of only 0.390 with NOA and its lowest (0.215) with CON. Because none of these correlations below 0.6 encompass more than 35% of the variance, words of differing levels on such pairs of dimensions should be readily obtainable from our data, especially through the use of the clusters in which these ratings are presented. Nonetheless, because all correlations are positive, it generally will be much easier to find subsets of words that covary on two or more dimensions, or vary on one while remaining constant on the other(s), than to find words that are high on one dimension while low on other dimensions.

Reliabilities

Because of technical problems that interfered with preliminary efforts to calculate split-half reliabilities based on all 2854 words and all subjects, the reliability estimates for each of the seven dimensions as given in Table 1 were evaluated on the basis of parts of the data, as described in the following.

Presented in the third row from the bottom of Table 1 are the estimated split-half reliabilities for each dimension, based upon the Kuder–Richardson (1937) 20 formula, but with the usual roles of raters and items reversed so that the resulting reliability estimates represent the expected value of correlation coefficients between two halves of a sample of raters for all possible halves within this sample. More specifically, this procedure was applied to 48 out of 252 possible blocks of 80 words across the seven dimensions, including at least six different blocks for each dimension. The reliabilities given in Table 1 represent the mean correlations based on all blocks that were evaluated for each dimension (mean and median correlations were virtually identical). All dimensions yielded reliabilities by this method that were well above 0.9, with NOA alone being below 0.960 and with FAM the highest at 0.980.

An additional supplementary method of estimating reliabilities was to correlate the two mean ratings obtained for each of the 26 words that were rated twice, which are, in alphabetical order: *brawl, cave, cow, flower, gate, germ, hair, hook, nail, name, needle, night, nose, not, novel, one, only, pawn, pipe, plum, prize, proud, purse, sea, wealth,* and *yoke.* It should be noted that the means and standard deviations presented herein for these 26 words all represent averages based upon both ratings.

---

[3]Because this factor analysis showed little that cannot be seen directly from the correlations in Table 1, it is not discussed further.

The reliability estimates based upon these 26 repeated words were somewhat lower than the reliabilities shown in Table 1, especially for FAM (0.816) and MNG (0.867), but also for NOA (0.895), IMG (0.915), and CAT (0.946). Only PLS (0.953) and CON (0.974) yielded reliability estimates comparable to those in Table 1. These discrepancies probably reflect the predominance of high ratings within this set of 26 words. This is especially true for FAM, where the mean rating for the duplicated words was 6.140 and its standard deviation only 0.38. Because FAM yielded the highest reliability estimate shown in Table 1, its reliability would appear to be at least as impressive as for any other dimension.

In fact, the least reliable of the present dimensions appears to be NOA, which not only shows the lowest value in Table 1 and one of the lowest based upon the 26 repeated words but also is shown by Table 1 to have the lowest mean and standard deviation of ratings for individual words. Thus NOA shows both less reliability and differentiation between words than any of the other dimensions, although by any absolute standards it still appears to be a highly stable and potentially useful dimension.

The Kuder–Richardson (1937) reliability computations also permitted an assessment of changes in reliability estimates as a function of number of subjects in the sample. For all dimensions, consistent negatively accelerated increases in reliabilities were obtained with increasing sample size, asymptoting at or near a sample size of 50. This indicates that our sample sizes, which were always at least 54 for all words, were large enough to provide for maximum reliabilities of the word ratings.

Variability Between and Within Words

The statistical information presented up to this point makes a very ,convincing case for high levels of reliability, validity, and sensitivity of the present norms with respect to scale values for individual words and also differences therein from one word to another. Certainly, the present mean ratings for any word on a given dimension would seem to represent quite accurate estimates of the actual rating for that word by a typical college student.

It is important to note explicitly, however, that any reliability or validity of these mean ratings is *not* indicative of high consistency between individual subjects on the ratings given to any particular word. This is because a common property of such ratings is that the mean values appear quite stable despite marked inconsistencies both between and within subjects in the individual ratings contributing to these apparently stable means, as has been noted by Battig and Spera (1962) and others.

If anything, the present data represent an especially pronounced instance of highly reliable mean ratings that reflect major discrepancies in the individual ratings contributing to these stable means. One obvious indication of such inconsistencies is that the standard deviations given in Table 1, which are based upon variations in mean word ratings for individual words, are only 42–76% as large as the means of the 2854 standard deviation values for the individual words. These mean standard-deviation values proved to be largest for CON (1.90) and IMG (1.87), intermediate in magnitude for CAT (1.76), MNG (1.72), and NOA (1.74), and lowest for FAM (1.48) and PLS (1.41). Clearly, these values are

large enough to demonstrate that the present mean ratings may be relatively inaccurate indications of how a given word would be rated by any individual subject.

Such inconsistencies across individual ratings would be expected even for two or more ratings of the same word by the same individual, in view of the widespread evidence for substantial within-individual inconsistencies that characterize repeated performances on tasks of this kind (Battig, 1975b). Because each word was rated only once for a single dimension by any individual subject, there is no way to evaluate such within-individual differences in the present data. Nonetheless, if a second word rating had been made by a subject, this additional rating would likely be farther from a previous rating of that same word by that same subject than is the group mean. The point of this latter speculation is to emphasize the extent to which reliable and valid group mean ratings may be based upon highly variable and inconsistent ratings by the individual subjects comprising that group.

Comparisons With Other Word Norms

Because the original purpose of the present word-scaling project was to extend the Paivio et al. (1968) norms for CON, IMG, and MNG, the relationship between our and Paivio's ratings for those words included in both sets becomes of particular interest. These comparisons were greatly facilitated by Paivio's provision of IBM cards containing not only the Paivio et al. (1968) data but also some additional unpublished imagery ratings for a large number of other words, as well as ratings of printed familiarity by 47 to 49 subjects for all of these plus some additional new words.

Presented in Table 2 separately for CON, IMG, MNG, and FAM are: (1) the number of overlapping words included both in our (Colorado) and Paivio's norms; (2) the mean ratings based only upon these overlapping words obtained in the Colorado and Paivio norms; (3) the corresponding standard deviations for each; and (4) the correlations between the mean ratings for the individual words contained in both the Colorado and Paivio norms.

As shown in the last column of Table 2, the Colorado and Paivio norms are closely related especially for CON and IMG (r's > 0.91) and also for FAM. The much lower correlation for MNG probably reflects the Paivio et al. (1968) usage of Noble's (1952) pro-

TABLE 2
Comparisons Between Overlapping Words in Colorado and Paivio Norms

Dimension	Number of Words	Means		Standard Deviations		
		Colorado	Paivio	Colorado	Paivio	Correlation
Concreteness	383	4.93	5.44	1.14	1.86	0.918
Imagery	808	4.65	4.58	1.11	1.60	0.912
Meaningfulness	383	4.42	6.21	0.73	1.17	0.529
Familiarity	884	5.98	5.63	0.70	1.09	0.879

duction method, which required subjects to write down as many associates as they could for each word. Thus the Paivio MNG ratings in Table 2 actually represent mean numbers of associates as contrasted with the Colorado MNG ratings on a 7-point scale, so that any comparisons for MNG are at best questionable.

An even higher correlation of 0.936 was obtained between the present CON ratings and those of Spreen and Schulz (1966) for the 170 words included in both sets. In agreement with the Paivio comparisons shown in Table 2, the Spreen–Schulz mean (5.50) and standard deviation (1.62) were both substantially larger than the Colorado mean (5.15) and standard deviation (0.99) for these 170 overlapping words.

In fact, the most consistent difference between the Colorado and the Paivio (and Spreen–Schulz) results is that the present standard deviations are about one-third smaller. This can probably be attributed to the wider range of materials employed in our study and, particularly, our inclusion of nonword paralogs and other rare words, which received the lowest ratings on all four dimensions included in Table 2 (see Cluster 1 in Chapter 4). By contrast, Paivio et al. (1968) included primarily (about 73%) words with Thorndike–Lorge (1944) frequency counts. Moreover, all of the 329 Spreen–Schulz (1966) words had Thorndike–Lorge frequencies of at least 50. Further indicative of a lesser concentration of highly rated words in the Colorado than the Paivio (and Spreen–Schulz) norms are the substantially larger Colorado mean ratings shown in Table 2 than the means based on all 2854 words (see Table 1). Consequently, the much smaller standard deviations shown in Table 2 for the present overlapping words can be attributed to the general finding (e.g., Amster & Battig, 1965) that any given word receives less extreme ratings if rated in a more heterogeneous context that contains more extremely high and/or low words on the rated dimension(s).

Description of Clusters 2

The eight clusters in which the present words and their mean ratings are presented represent the results of a BC TRY cluster analysis (Tryon & Bailey, 1970) of the mean ratings for all words on all dimensions. Except for six words, which are listed in Table 13 and described at the end of this chapter, all of the remaining 2848 words could be specified as members of one of these eight clusters on the basis of this cluster analysis.

More specifically, the criterion for cluster membership was that the square root of the sum of the squared deviations of the seven word-mean ratings from the seven dimension-means for the word's cluster be no larger than 2.744. None of the words in any cluster, however, yielded such a deviation value larger than 2.66, and only seven words exceeded 2.5. Consequently, as is shown more clearly in the subsequent discussion of variabilities and homogeneities for dimensions within these eight clusters, there are a few instances where individual words deviate from their cluster means by as much as 2.0, but the majority of individual words show ratings within one-half a unit of their cluster means.

The numerical ordering of the clusters from 1 to 8 generally corresponds to increasing mean ratings for those words included in the clusters. Consequently, anyone seeking words that are low on any dimension(s) will typically find these in low-numbered clusters, whereas words with high values on any dimension tend to be concentrated in clusters with larger numbers. This is particularly true for IMG and CAT but much less so for PLS and FAM.

Before attempting to describe these eight clusters further, some general statistical information about these clusters must be presented. The mean ratings on each dimension

based upon all words within each of the clusters are presented in Table 3, along with the numbers of words in each cluster (which tend to increase from Clusters 1 through 8 much as the mean ratings do).

Presented in Table 4 are the corresponding standard deviations on each dimension for the mean ratings of words contained in each cluster. Although these are uniformly smaller and in most cases less than one-half as large as the standard deviations shown in Table 1 based on all 2854 words, they are nonetheless large enough to indicate considerable variations in the mean ratings on individual words for at least some cluster—dimension combinations. Of the 16 instances of standard deviations above 0.5, six represent PLS and three each FAM and NOA. Also, the mean standard deviation for all 56 dimension—cluster combinations in Table 4 is 0.464.

TABLE 3
Mean Ratings for Each Cluster—Dimension Combination

Cluster Number	Number of Words	Dimension						
		CON	IMG	CAT	MNG	FAM	NOA	PLS
1	195	2.87	2.30	2.30	1.81	2.20	2.35	3.53
2	255	2.69	2.95	2.76	3.38	5.92	2.95	3.83
3	229	4.11	3.94	3.66	3.13	4.41	3.06	3.74
4	390	3.58	4.17	3.76	4.30	5.84	3.44	3.02
5	330	3.35	4.04	3.68	4.52	6.12	3.94	4.89
6	384	4.55	4.87	4.57	4.41	6.00	3.90	4.11
7	566	5.65	5.49	5.34	4.05	5.74	3.48	3.70
8	499	5.83	5.85	5.76	4.75	6.22	4.21	4.86

TABLE 4
Standard Deviations of Ratings for Each Cluster—Dimension Combination

Cluster Number	Dimension						
	CON	IMG	CAT	MNG	FAM	NOA	PLS
1	.427	.433	.391	.361	.687	.318	.242
2	.430	.454	.386	.500	.625	.433	.502
3	.478	.463	.442	.442	.407	.447	.559
4	.659	.490	.574	.423	.613	.378	.492
5	.423	.505	.443	.421	.381	.569	.504
6	.474	.388	.466	.463	.385	.599	.606
7	.369	.380	.517	.427	.456	.431	.637
8	.394	.313	.437	.470	.334	.638	.524

TABLE 5
Lowest (L) and Highest (H) Word Rating Within Each
Cluster—Dimension Combination

Cluster Number		Dimension						
		CON	IMG	CAT	MNG	FAM	NOA	PLS
1	L	2.03	1.46	1.47	1.26	1.15	1.63	2.75
	H	4.09	3.43	3.42	2.82	4.07	3.21	4.45
2	L	1.54	1.83	1.82	2.10	4.05	1.88	2.23
	H	3.76	3.82	3.90	4.48	6.77	4.22	5.05
3	L	2.84	2.89	2.40	2.05	2.89	2.21	2.41
	H	5.44	5.12	5.43	4.13	5.74	4.03	4.98
4	L	2.40	2.87	2.87	2.98	4.49	2.45	1.81
	H	4.84	5.32	5.55	5.74	6.79	4.93	4.21
5	L	2.10	2.94	2.62	3.59	4.77	2.75	3.84
	H	4.32	5.52	5.40	5.98	6.84	5.52	6.30
6	L	3.43	3.47	3.55	3.15	4.53	2.34	2.17
	H	5.58	6.19	6.09	5.70	6.82	5.90	6.00
7	L	4.35	4.17	3.98	3.03	4.27	2.24	1.73
	H	6.56	6.46	6.62	5.36	6.77	5.02	5.31
8	L	4.31	4.68	4.48	3.42	5.14	2.84	3.24
	H	6.68	6.61	6.68	6.16	6.85	5.98	6.23

Probably more useful to the typical researcher consulting these norms will be the highest and the lowest mean rating values within each cluster for each dimension, which are presented in Table 5. These ranges indicate that a few words can be found in most cluster—dimension combinations that deviate quite substantially from the cluster mean, even by as much as two units. Such deviant words on a single dimension, however, must necessarily be quite close to the cluster mean on all other dimensions, so that these highest and lowest values for most purposes overestimate the magnitude of variability within these clusters. In fact, there are relatively few cases (only 3.5%) in which the mean rating for an individual word differs from the cluster mean by more than one.

Distributional information is presented separately for each of the seven dimensions in Tables 6 through 12, as a further aid to the user seeking words within a specified range of rating values. More specifically, the rows of these tables represent successive half-unit intervals of mean ratings, with the columns representing the eight clusters, and the number of words for each cluster—interval combination in the body of the table. In addition, the total frequencies of such words pooled over all clusters are given in the final column. For example, the second row of Table 6 shows that there are 112 words with concreteness ratings between 2 and 2.49, of which 41, 59, 4, and 8 can be found in Clusters 1, 2, 4, and 5, respectively.

TABLE 6
CONCRETENESS: Distribution of Word Ratings Across Clusters

Rating Interval	Cluster Number								Total
	1	2	3	4	5	6	7	8	
1.5−1.99	——	21	——	——	——	——	——	——	21
2.0−2.49	41	59	——	4	8	——	——	——	112
2.5−2.99	82	107	4	37	56	——	——	——	286
3.0−3.49	56	62	48	136	136	5	——	——	443
3.5−3.99	14	6	56	136	112	45	——	——	369
4.0−4.49	2	——	48	62	18	127	2	2	261
4.5−4.99	——	——	48	15	——	133	22	19	237
5.0−5.49	——	——	25	——	——	71	152	68	316
5.5−5.99	——	——	——	——	——	3	288	234	525
6.0−6.49	——	——	——	——	——	——	99	167	266
6.5−6.99	——	——	——	——	——	——	3	9	12

TABLE 7
IMAGERY: Distribution of Word Ratings Across Clusters

Rating Interval	Cluster Number								Total
	1	2	3	4	5	6	7	8	
1.0−1.49	1	——	——	——	——	——	——	——	1
1.5−1.99	57	5	——	——	——	——	——	——	62
2.0−2.49	74	37	——	——	——	——	——	——	111
2.5−2.99	49	91	2	1	3	——	——	——	146
3.0−3.49	14	89	46	25	44	1	——	——	219
3.5−3.99	——	33	76	119	115	8	——	——	351
4.0−4.49	——	——	71	141	105	51	5	——	373
4.5−4.99	——	——	32	89	54	176	54	2	407
5.0−5.49	——	——	2	15	8	133	221	67	446
5.5−5.99	——	——	——	——	1	14	236	259	510
6.0−6.49	——	——	——	——	——	1	50	168	219
6.5−6.99	——	——	——	——	——	——	——	3	3

TABLE 8
CATEGORIZABILITY: Distribution of Word Ratings Across Clusters

Rating Interval	Cluster Number								Total
	1	2	3	4	5	6	7	8	
1.0–1.49	1	––	––	––	––	––	––	––	1
1.5–1.99	43	6	––	––	––	––	––	––	49
2.0–2.49	92	55	1	––	––	––	––	––	148
2.5–2.99	48	124	29	9	18	––	––	––	228
3.0–3.49	11	64	69	101	98	––	––	––	343
3.5–3.99	––	6	64	168	144	37	1	––	420
4.0–4.49	––	––	47	89	56	146	21	1	360
4.5–4.99	––	––	16	18	13	132	126	31	336
5.0–5.49	––	––	3	4	1	56	203	106	373
5.5–5.99	––	––	––	1	––	12	145	204	362
6.0–6.49	––	––	––	––	––	1	67	143	211
6.5–6.99	––	––	––	––	––	––	3	14	17

TABLE 9
MEANINGFULNESS: Distribution of Word Ratings Across Clusters

Rating Interval	Cluster Number								Total
	1	2	3	4	5	6	7	8	
1.0–1.49	38	––	––	––	––	––	––	––	38
1.5–1.99	96	––	––	––	––	––	––	––	96
2.0–2.49	53	12	17	––	––	––	––	––	82
2.5–2.99	8	44	73	1	––	––	––	––	126
3.0–3.49	––	80	88	6	––	4	53	1	232
3.5–3.99	––	90	49	92	30	70	204	24	559
4.0–4.49	––	29	2	166	130	151	229	130	837
4.5–4.99	––	––	––	102	120	115	69	203	609
5.0–5.49	––	––	––	19	46	37	11	109	222
5.5–5.99	––	––	––	4	4	7	––	27	42
6.0–6.49	––	––	––	––	––	––	––	5	5

TABLE 10
FAMILIARITY: Distribution of Word Ratings Across Clusters

Rating Interval	Cluster Number								Total
	1	2	3	4	5	6	7	8	
1.0–1.49	29	––	––	––	––	––	––	––	29
1.5–1.99	63	––	––	––	––	––	––	––	63
2.0–2.49	42	––	––	––	––	––	––	––	42
2.5–2.99	33	––	4	––	––	––	––	––	37
3.0–3.49	19	––	11	––	––	––	––	––	30
3.5–3.99	8	––	51	––	––	––	––	––	59
4.0–4.49	1	10	58	1	––	––	5	––	75
4.5–4.99	––	15	61	9	2	4	37	––	128
5.0–5.49	––	33	41	76	19	40	113	12	334
5.5–5.99	––	44	3	150	89	126	214	113	739
6.0–6.49	––	119	––	141	166	183	186	262	1057
6.5–6.99	––	34	––	13	54	31	11	112	255

TABLE 11
NUMBER OF ATTRIBUTES: Distribution of Word Ratings Across Clusters

Rating Interval	Cluster Number								Total
	1	2	3	4	5	6	7	8	
1.5–1.99	20	3	––	––	––	––	––	––	23
2.0–2.49	114	37	13	4	––	1	3	––	172
2.5–2.99	54	96	89	59	8	8	56	6	376
3.0–3.49	7	92	99	152	65	100	248	60	823
3.5–3.99	––	24	27	132	124	120	192	137	756
4.0–4.49	––	3	1	36	79	92	57	140	408
4.5–4.99	––	––	––	7	35	40	9	89	180
5.0–5.49	––	––	––	––	18	18	1	52	89
5.5–5.99	––	––	––	––	1	5	––	15	21

TABLE 12
PLEASANTNESS: Distribution of Word Ratings Across Clusters

Rating Interval	Cluster Number								
	1	2	3	4	5	6	7	8	Total
1.5−1.99	−−	−−	−−	5	−−	−−	8	−−	13
2.0−2.49	−−	4	1	78	−−	1	25	−−	109
2.5−2.99	3	13	16	118	−−	10	44	−−	204
3.0−3.49	81	38	56	87	−−	51	95	4	412
3.5−3.99	103	96	81	94	7	91	206	20	698
4.0−4.49	8	90	61	8	78	139	146	99	629
4.5−4.99	−−	13	14	−−	103	59	36	179	404
5.0−5.49	−−	1	−−	−−	103	26	6	140	276
5.5−5.99	−−	−−	−−	−−	32	6	−−	49	87
6.0−6.49	−−	−−	−−	−−	7	1	−−	8	16

DESCRIPTION OF INDIVIDUAL CLUSTERS

In describing each cluster individually, special attention is focused on exceptions to the previously noted general increase in mean ratings on all dimensions from Clusters 1 through 8. Because of the differences between dimensions in overall mean ratings (see Table 1), the present description of cluster means is relative to dimensional averages, so that cluster means characterized as average are close to the dimensional mean value rather than the scale average value of 4.

Cluster 1. This cluster, consisting primarily of nonwords and rare words, is the easiest to describe and the most distinct from all other clusters. Words in Cluster 1 are relatively low on all dimensions, being lower than any other cluster on everything except CON and PLS, where they are second lowest. Relative to other dimensions, they are especially low in MNG and FAM.

Cluster 2. Like Cluster 1, words in Cluster 2 are relatively low in all dimensions except for FAM, where they rank above four of the other clusters. Included in Cluster 2 are many adverbs, function words, and other types of words that tend to be highly abstract but are also highly familiar. Cluster 2 words therefore tend to be the lowest in CON, second only to Cluster 1 as to low IMG, CAT, and NOA, only slightly unpleasant, and relatively low in MNG.

Cluster 3. One of the smallest clusters (only 229 words), Cluster 3 contains words with ratings somewhat but not extremely below average on all dimensions, being particularly low in MNG, FAM, and NOA.

Cluster 4. The most distinguishing characteristic of Cluster 4 is that it represents by far the lowest PLS ratings. These unpleasant words of Cluster 4 tend also to be relatively familiar, somewhat below average in CON, IMG, and CAT, and quite close to average in the remaining dimensions.

Cluster 5.   These words tend to be very much like those of Cluster 4, as described above, except that they have the highest instead of the lowest PLS ratings and are also somewhat higher in FAM and NOA.

Cluster 6.   Words in Cluster 6 are somewhat above average on all dimensions, ranking third from the top on each of the seven dimensions.

Cluster 7.   This cluster contains words that are second from the top in CON, IMG, and CAT but are relatively low in PLS and slightly below average in NOA. They are average or slightly above in MNG and FAM and can also be viewed as slightly lower on all dimensions than words in Cluster 8.

Cluster 8.   Words in Cluster 8 tend to have the highest ratings on all of the seven dimensions, except that the PLS mean is slightly below that for Cluster 3.

NONCLUSTER WORDS

As noted previously, there are six words that failed to meet the criterion for inclusion in any of the eight clusters. None of these words were much above the criterion (which is based upon the square root of the sum of squared deviations from the dimensional means for the cluster), yielding values of 2.77–2.97 as compared with the criterion of 2.744.

Rather than risk unnecessary confusion by including these six words in the clusters to which they could most appropriately be assigned, however, all information for each of these six noncluster words is given in Table 13. In addition to the words in alphabetical order, and their means and standard deviations for each of the seven dimensions, Table 13 also includes in the last two columns both the number of the closest cluster and the deviation value (as described above) with respect to that cluster. It may also be noted that the failure of these words to fit into any of the clusters can be attributed primarily to discrepancies from the cluster means for NOA, MNG, and/or PLS.

TABLE 13
Mean Ratings and Standard Deviations for Six Noncluster Words

Word		Dimension							Cluster No.	Dev.
		CON	IMG	CAT	MNG	FAM	NOA	PLS		
AN	M	2.13	1.78	1.81	1.53	6.22	1.63	3.41	2	2.83
	SD	1.74	1.34	1.30	0.88	1.56	1.38	1.20		
BEAUTIFUL	M	3.89	5.31	4.15	6.17	6.78	5.46	5.97	5	2.97
	SD	2.02	1.80	2.02	1.14	0.50	1.77	1.29		
HAPPINESS	M	3.42	5.27	4.35	5.89	6.58	5.17	6.32	5	2.77
	SD	2.28	1.95	2.01	1.54	1.11	2.01	1.28		
LIFE	M	3.88	5.32	4.68	5.33	6.52	6.00	5.79[F]	6	2.97
	SD	2.21	1.80	2.17	1.84	1.08	1.66	1.43		
LOVE	M	3.55	5.77	4.57	5.48	6.71	5.23	6.07	5	2.87
	SD	2.36	1.81	2.18	2.06	1.09	2.07	1.61		
WAR	M	4.79	5.26	4.65	5.66	6.60	5.37	2.05	6	2.91
	SD	2.17	1.95	1.96	1.71	1.01	1.73	1.56		

Complete Alphabetical Listing of All Words

3

All 2854 words are listed in alphabetical order on pp. 26–34. Following each word is a number from 1 to 8 designating the cluster in Chapter 4 in which the complete rating information for that word can be found. Any word not followed by a cluster number is one of the six words (*an, beautiful, happiness, life, love* and *war*) that did not fit into one of the eight clusters, so that complete rating information is presented instead in Table 13.

As a further aid in locating any particular word(s) in the norms as presented in Chapter 4, Table 14 lists the first and last words appearing on each of the pages of this chapter:

TABLE 14

Words	Page on Which Cluster Is Designated
A – BUTTERFLY	26
BUTTON – DIME	27
DIMPLE – GOOD	28
GOOF – LATHE	29
LATUK – NURSERY	30
OAK – RATION	31
RATTLESNAKE – SOCIAL	32
SOCK – TROMBONE	33
TROOP – ZUREN	34

No	Word	No	Word	No	Word	Word	No	Word	No	Word	No
2	A	7	ALLIGATOR	7	ASPIRIN	BASS	7	BIRTH	8	BRACELET	8
1	ABASEMENT	2	ALLOW	2	ASSIST	BAT	5	BISCUIT	7	BRAIN	8
1	ABBESS	4	ALONE	4	ASTUTE	BATH	2	BISHOP	8	BRAKE	7
1	ABDICATION	2	ALSO	2	AT	BATON	2	BIT	7	BRAMBLE	3
4	ABDUCTION	6	ALTER	2	ATE	BATTLE	5	BITTER	4	BRANDY	8
3	ABHOR	2	ALTHOUGH	6	ATOM	BAWL	6	BLACK	2	BRASS	7
2	ABLE	2	ALUMINUM	4	ATTACK	BE	4	BLACKSMITH	8	BRAT	6
6	ABODE	2	ALWAYS	2	ATTEND	BEACH	5	BLADE	7	BRAVE	5
3	ABORIGINAL	7	AM	4	AUDITION	BEAK	4	BLAND	6	BRAWL	8
2	ABOUT	5	AMBASSADOR	7	AUDITORIUM	BEAM	7	BLANKET	7	BREAD	4
4	ABRUPT	8	AMBITION	8	AUNT	BEAN	8	BLEACH	8	BREAK	8
5	ABUNDANT	7	AMMONIA	1	AURAL	BEAR	1	BLEAK	8	BREAST	6
3	ABYSS	1	AMPERE	5	AUTHENTIC	BEARD	5	BLEW	4	BREATH	3
6	ACADEMY	5	AMUSE	6	AVID	BEAT	6	BLIND	8	BRED	4
3	ACCOMPLICE	7	AN	7	AWARENESS	BEAUTIFUL	2	BLONDE	4	BRIBE	7
2	ACCORD	2	ANCHOR	2	AWAY	BEAUTY	5	BLOOD	1	BRICK	4
7	ACCORDION	1	AND	1	AWEIGH	BEAVER	2	BLOSSOM	7	BRIEF	6
4	ACCOUNT	4	ANELE	4	AWKWARD	BECAME	1	BLOUSE	3	BRIGHT	5
4	ACHE	4	ANGER	6	AWL	BECAUSE	4	BLOW	8	BRILLIANT	3
2	ACKNOWLEDGE	6	ANGLE	8	AXIL	BED	1	BLUE	2	BRISKET	8
8	ACROBAT	8	ANIMALS	1	AXIOM	BEDEL	3	BLUEJAY	8	BROAD	4
5	ACT	1	ANNEAL	5	AXLE	BEE	3	BLUNDER	7	BROADER	6
1	ACUMEN	5	ANSWER	7	AYE	BEECH	7	BLUNDERBUSS	4	BROIL	4
4	ADDING	7	ANT	6	BABY	BEEF	1	BLUSH	1	BROKE	7
5	ADDITION	6	ANTIQUE	2	BACK	BEEN	8	BLUSHING	7	BROKEN	8
2	ADDS	2	ANY	4	BACTERIA	BEER	6	BOAR	3	BROOM	7
4	ADJECTIVE	4	APART	8	BAD	BEET	7	BOARD	8	BROTHER	8
7	ADMIRAL	8	APARTMENT	4	BADGE	BEETLE	4	BOAT	7	BRUSH	7
5	ADMIRE	4	APATHY	8	BAGPIPE	BEFORE	7	BOATING	2	BRUT	3
2	ADMONISH	2	APE	3	BAIL	BEG	6	BODY	4	BRUTAL	4
8	ADORN	8	APEX	2	BALAP	BEGGAR	1	BOIL	7	BRUTE	1
4	ADULT	4	APPEAR	8	BALE	BEING	2	BOLE	2	BUBAL	8
4	ADVERB	8	APPLE	1	BALL	BELIEF	3	BOLL	5	BUBBLE	8
1	ADZE	4	APPRAISE	2	BALLOON	BELL	8	BOLT	8	BUCKET	7
4	AFRAID	2	APT	3	BANALITY	BELLE	8	BOMB	3	BUCKLE	7
2	AFTER	3	ARBOR	3	BANANA	BELLY	1	BONE	7	BUD	6
6	AGE	6	ARC	6	BAND	BELT	8	BOOK	7	BUFFOON	3
2	AGGRESS	2	ARCH	2	BANDAGE	BENEFICIAL	8	BOOT	5	BUILD	5
5	AGILE	5	ARE	5	BANG	BENEFIT	7	BOOTH	5	BUILDING	8
4	AGONY	4	AREA	3	BANK	BERET	4	BORE	7	BUMP	6
2	AH	2	ARID	7	BANKER	BERRY	8	BORED	8	BUNCH	6
5	AID	7	ARK	7	BANNED	BERTH	7	BORN	3	BUNGALOW	7
3	AIL	7	ARM	7	BAR	BEST	4	BORNE	5	BURLAP	6
2	AIM	7	ARMOR	7	BARD	BETEL	8	BOSUN	1	BURN	7
6	AIR	6	ARMY	6	BARE	BHANG	1	BOTANY	1	BURNER	6
3	AIRY	3	ART	4	BARK	BIB	5	BOTH	7	BURRO	2
6	AISLE	6	ARTIFICIAL	8	BARREL	BIBLE	7	BOULDER	8	BURROW	8
3	ALBUMIN	3	ARTIST	2	BASE	BIER	7	BOUQUET	1	BURY	4
8	ALCOHOL	2	AS	7	BASEBALL	BILL	6	BOURBON	7	BUSH	7
7	ALE	7	ASH	4	BASEMENT	BILLED	8	BOW	4	BUSINESS	6
5	ALERT	5	ASHAMED	3	BASIN	BINOCULARS	8	BOWL	7	BUSY	5
4	ALIEN	3	ASHEN	7	BASKET	BIOLOGY	7	BOX	6	BUT	2
5	ALL	7	ASPARAGUS	7	BASKETBALL	BIRCH	7	BOY	8	BUTTER	8
7	ALLEY	7	ASPHALT			BIRD	8	BRA	8	BUTTERFLY	8

Word	#	Word	#	Word	#	Word	#	Word	#	Word	#
BUTTON	7	CATERPILLAR	8	CHINCHILLA	7	COGNITION	2	COURT	6	DANCE	8
BUTYL	1	CATFISH	7	CHIPMUNK	8	COIL	6	COURTEOUS	5	DANCER	8
BUY	5	CATHEDRAL	8	CHISEL	7	COIN	8	COW	8	DANDELION	8
BUYING	5	CAUCUS	3	CHOCOLATE	8	COKE	8	COWARDICE	1	DANDRUFF	7
BY	2	CAUGHT	4	CHOIR	8	COKEM	1	COWARDLY	6	DANGER	4
BYRE	1	CAUL	1	CHOOSE	2	COLD	4	COWL	3	DARE	6
CABBAGE	7	CAULIFLOWER	7	CHOPSTICK	7	COLDER	7	CRABS	7	DARK	8
CABIN	8	CAUSE	2	CHORAL	3	COLLAR	3	CRADLE	8	DATE	8
CABLE	7	CAVE	2	CHUCKLE	6	COLONEL	6	CRANBERRY	7	DAWN	4
CAFE	8	CAWS	7	CHURCH	8	COLONY	8	CRANK	6	DAY	6
CAGE	7	CEDE	1	CHUTE	3	COLOR	3	CRAWL	6	DEAD	6
CAKE	8	CEILING	1	CIGAR	7	COMBINE	7	CRAYONS	8	DEAL	4
CALF	7	CELL	7	CIGARETTE	7	COME	7	CREAM	5	DEAR	5
CALIX	1	CELLAR	7	CINDER	7	COMFORT	7	CRIME	5	DEATH	4
CALL	5	CELOM	1	CINNAMON	8	COMMAND	8	CRITICISM	4	DEBACLE	1
CALM	5	CEMENT	1	CINQUE	1	COMMERCIAL	1	CROAK	4	DEBT	4
CAMEL	2	CENT	7	CIRCLE	7	COMMODE	8	CROCODILE	4	DECAY	4
CAMERA	8	CENTENNIAL	7	CIRCULAR	7	COMPACT	6	CROOKED	7	DECAYED	7
CAMP	8	CENTER	5	CIRCUS	5	COMPLACENT	8	CROQUET	2	DECEIT	7
CAN	2	CENTS	6	CITE	6	COMPLEMENT	2	CROSS	5	DECK	2
CANARY	7	CENTURY	7	CITIZEN	7	COMPLIMENT	3	CROW	5	DECORATE	6
CANCER	7	CEREAL	2	CITY	6	COMPOSURE	6	CROWD	7	DECOY	6
CANDLE	8	CEREBRUM	8	CLAM	8	CONCRETE	8	CROWN	8	DEEP	6
CANDY	8	CEREMONY	7	CLAMMY	7	CONDEMN	7	CRUCIFIX	2	DEER	8
CANNON	7	CHACHA	6	CLAMOR	6	CONDESCENSION	4	CRUEL	4	DEFACE	4
CANOPENER	7	CHAIN	1	CLAMPS	1	CONFERENCE	2	CRUISER	8	DEFEAT	8
CANTEEN	7	CHAIR	7	CLAMS	7	CONFISCATE	4	CRUMB	2	DEFEATED	7
CAPE	7	CHALK	7	CLANG	8	CONJUNCTION	2	CRY	5	DEFICIENT	4
CAPITAL	6	CHAMOIS	8	CLARINET	7	CONSIDERABLE	5	CRYSTAL	8	DEGRADED	4
CAPITOL	8	CHANCE	3	CLEAN	3	CONSPIRATORS	7	CUBE	7	DELIVER	5
CAPSULE	7	CHAOTIC	5	CLEAR	5	CONSTITUTION	5	CUCUMBER	6	DEMOCRACY	5
CAPTAIN	8	CHAPEL	4	CLEAT	4	CONTACT	6	CULLER	6	DEMOLISH	1
CAR	8	CHARLATAN	8	CLEVER	8	CONTRACT	6	CULTURE	7	DENSE	5
CARAT	3	CHARM	3	CLINCH	3	CONVENT	6	CUP	6	DENTIST	4
CARBON	7	CHARMING	5	CLOAK	5	COOK	6	CUPBOARDS	8	DEPICT	7
CARD	7	CHART	8	CLOSER	5	COOKIE	8	CURB	5	DERAY	7
CARDINAL	7	CHEAT	3	CLOSET	6	COOL	5	CURDS	5	DERBY	1
CARE	5	CHEEKS	7	CLOTH	4	COPE	5	CURE	1	DESK	6
CARES	5	CHEERFUL	7	CLOUD	8	COPIOUS	1	CURFEW	7	DESOLATE	7
CARNATION	8	CHEESE	8	CLOVE	5	COPPER	7	CURLER	7	DESPAIR	4
CAROL	7	CHEMISTRY	5	CLOWN	8	CORAL	7	CURSE	7	DESPISE	7
CARP	7	CHERRY	5	CLUB	6	CORD	7	CURVE	7	DESTROY	4
CARPET	1	CHEST	8	CLUE	8	CORK	7	CURVED	8	DESTROYER	6
CARREL	6	CHESTNUT	7	CLUMSY	6	CORN	8	CUSTARD	7	DETONATION	6
CARROT	8	CHEW	7	COACH	4	CORNER	5	CUSTOM	3	DEVICE	7
CARRY	4	CHIC	6	COAL	6	CORNET	3	CUT	4	DIAL	3
CARS	8	CHICKEN	1	COARSE	8	CORPS	4	CYLIX	8	DIAMOND	7
CASE	6	CHICKENPOX	8	COAST	7	COST	4	CYMBAL	8	DIAPERS	7
CASKET	7	CHIEF	4	COAT	6	COTTAGE	6	DAFFODILS	8	DID	8
CAST	6	CHILD	8	COCKPIT	8	COTTON	8	DAGGER	1	DIE	7
CASTE	3	CHILDREN	8	COCKTAIL	8	COUCH	8	DAIS	4	DIFFERENCE	2
CAT	8	CHILI	8	COFFEE	4	COULOMB	7	DAISY	8	DIJON	1
		CHILLY	4	COFFIN	8	COUNT	8	DAMAN	8	DIM	1
		CHINA	8			COUNTRY	8	DAME	5	DIME	8
						COURSE	7				

Word		Word		Word		Word		Word		Word	
DIMPLE	7	DUMB	4	ETERNAL	5	FETISH	3	FOOT	7	GAIT	3
DINNER	8	DUMP	6	ETERNITY	5	FEUDALISM	4	FOOTBALL	8	GALLANT	5
DIRT	6	DUNGEON	7	ETHER	3	FEW	2	FOR	2	GALLERY	8
DISAPPOINT	4	DUSK	6	EVALUATE	4	FIDDLE	7	FORBID	4	GALLON	7
DISAPPOINTED	4	DUST	7	EVEN	2	FIGMENT	2	FORCEPS	7	GAME	8
DISAVOW	2	DUSTY	6	EVER	2	FIGURE	6	FORE	2	GARBAGE	8
DISCOLOR	4	DUTY	5	EVERY	2	FILE	6	FORECAST	5	GARDEN	7
DISCONNECTION	4	DYE	7	EVOLUTION	3	FILL	5	FOREST	7	GARDENIA	7
DISCORD	7	DYNASTY	4	EWE	1	FILM	8	FORK	7	GARLIC	7
DISHWASHERS	4	EACH	2	EXACTITUDE	2	FILTH	4	FORM	4	GARMENT	6
DISOBEDIENT	4	EAGER	5	EXCISE	2	FIND	5	FORMALDEHYDE	3	GAS	8
DISRUPTIVE	2	EAGLE	8	EXCUSE	8	FINE	5	FORTH	5	GASKET	7
DISTINCT	4	EAR	5	EXPANSION	5	FINGERS	8	FOUL	4	GASOLINE	7
DISTORTION	4	EARN	5	EXPOSURE	5	FINITE	4	FOUR	6	GATE	7
DITCH	4	EARRINGS	8	EXPULSION	4	FIR	3	FOURTH	4	GAUNTLET	3
DIVERSITY	5	EARTH	8	EXTRAVAGANT	5	FIRE	8	FOWL	6	GAVEL	7
DIVING	8	EARTHWORM	7	EYE	8	FIRM	5	FOX	8	GEM	8
DIVISION	4	EASEL	7	FABLE	6	FIRST	5	FOXTROT	7	GENDER	3
DO	2	EASIER	5	FACE	8	FISH	8	FRAIL	4	GENERAL	6
DOCILE	3	EAST	6	FACT	5	FISHHOOK	5	FRANC	3	GENEROUS	5
DOCTOR	8	EASY	5	FAIL	4	FISHING	7	FRANK	3	GENES	6
DOE	7	EAT	8	FAILING	4	FIVE	8	FRATERNAL	3	GENTLE	5
DOG	8	EATING	8	FAINT	6	FLAG	7	FRATERNITY	6	GENTLEMAN	6
DOGMA	3	EDGE	4	FAIR	6	FLAIR	5	FRAUD	4	GENUINE	5
DOLL	7	EEL	7	FAIRY	7	FLAME	8	FRAYS	3	GEOGRAPHICAL	6
DOLLAR	8	EERIE	4	FALL	4	FLANNEL	7	FRECKLES	7	GERM	6
DOME	7	EGG	7	FAN	7	FLARE	6	FREE	5	GET	2
DONE	2	EIGHT	2	FANG	6	FLASH	6	FREEDOM	5	GHOST	6
DONOR	5	ELABORATION	5	FANTASY	2	FLASHBULBS	7	FREEZE	6	GIFT	8
DOOR	7	ELEGANT	5	FAR	5	FLAX	3	FREIGHT	7	GILT	3
DOORMAN	7	ELEPHANT	8	FARE	4	FLEA	7	FRIEND	8	GIN	8
DORM	7	ELM	7	FARM	8	FLEAS	4	FRIEZE	1	GINGER	7
DOTAGE	1	ELSE	2	FAROD	2	FLEE	6	FRIGID	4	GIRDLE	5
DOUGH	7	EMANCIPATION	5	FARTHER	5	FLEECE	6	FROCK	3	GIRL	8
DOUGHNUT	8	EMBARRASSED	4	FARTHING	4	FLEET	5	FROG	8	GIST	1
DOWN	4	EMERALD	8	FASHION	8	FLEXIBILITY	3	FROM	2	GIVE	5
DRAB	2	EMERGENCE	3	FAST	3	FLICKER	6	FRONT	6	GLAD	5
DRAMA	6	EMISSION	4	FASTER	4	FLOAT	6	FROST	8	GLASS	8
DRAW	6	EMPIRE	6	FATE	6	FLOOD	8	FROWN	7	GLASSES	8
DREAM	6	EMPTY	6	FATHER	4	FLOOR	7	FRUG	1	GLITTER	6
DREARY	4	ENAMEL	4	FATTER	6	FLOW	5	FRUGAL	8	GLOBE	8
DRESS	8	END	8	FAULT	4	FLOWER	8	FRUIT	8	GLOOM	4
DRESSER	7	ENDURING	7	FAWN	2	FLUSH	6	FRUSTRATE	4	GLORY	5
DRILL	7	ENGINE	2	FAZE	8	FLUTE	8	FUEL	7	GLOVE	8
DRINK	6	ENGINEER	8	FEAR	6	FLUTTERING	4	FULL	5	GLUTTON	4
DRIZZLE	7	ENOUGH	6	FEAT	2	FLY	8	FUNCTIONAL	2	GNAT	7
DROP	4	ENTERTAIN	2	FEEL	5	FOAL	3	FUNCTIONARY	2	GNU	3
DROPPER	3	ENTRANCE	5	FEET	6	FOG	7	FUR	8	GO	5
DRUM	8	ENTREE	6	FEINT	8	FOIL	6	FUSE	6	GOAT	7
DUAL	4	ENVELOPE	3	FELL	1	FOLLOWING	2	FUSELAGE	3	GOD	5
DUCHESS	7	ENVOYS	7	FELT	4	FOLLY	6	FUZZY	6	GOJEY	1
DUCK	8	EONS	3	FENCE	6	FOOD	8	GABLE	8	GOLD	8
DUEL	6	EQUALITY	3	FERRY	3	FOOL	4	GADID	1	GONE	2
DUKE	7	ESTATE	8	FERTILE	8	FOOLISH	4	GAIN	2	GOOD	5

Word	#
GOOF	4
GORAL	1
GORILLA	8
GOT	2
GOWN	8
GRACE	5
GRACEFUL	5
GRAFT	3
GRAMMAR	6
GRANULAR	3
GRAPE	8
GRAPEFRUIT	8
GRAPH	7
GRAPHED	3
GRASS	8
GRASSHOPPER	7
GRATE	3
GRAVE	7
GRAVEL	7
GRAY	3
GRAYS	3
GRAZE	3
GREAT	5
GREEDY	8
GREEN	8
GRIEF	4
GRIND	4
GRISLY	4
GRIZZLY	6
GROAN	4
GROCER	7
GROIN	7
GROUND	6
GROUP	6
GROW	5
GROWN	2
GRUDGE	4
GUARD	6
GUESSED	2
GUEST	6
GUIDE	6
GUILT	4
GULLET	3
GUN	7
GUTTER	7
GYBE	1
GYM	8
HAD	2
HAFIZ	1
HAIL	6
HAILSTONE	7
HAIR	8
HAIRPIN	7
HALE	3

Word	#
HALF	4
HALL	1
HALLWAY	8
HALT	2
HALVE	8
HAM	5
HAMMER	5
HAMSTER	3
HAND	6
HANDGRENADE	3
HANDLEBARS	8
HANDS	8
HANG	7
HAPPINESS	3
HAPPY	8
HARD	7
HARDER	3
HARDLY	7
HARDWARE	7
HARE	3
HAREM	3
HARMONY	3
HARNESS	5
HARPOON	8
HARSH	8
HAS	4
HASTY	4
HAT	4
HATCHET	6
HATE	4
HAUL	7
HAVE	7
HAWK	6
HAZARD	6
HAZE	5
HE	2
HEAD	4
HEADBOARD	6
HEAL	2
HEALTH	6
HEAR	6
HEART	4
HEARTLESS	3
HEAT	7
HEAVY	7
HEEL	1
HEIR	8
HELL	2
HELMET	1
HELP	6
HENCHMAN	7
HER	8
HERB	7
HERE	3

Word	#
HERES	4
HERMIT	7
HERO	7
HEROIN	4
HERRING	3
HEXAGON	8
HIDE	7
HIERARCHY	7
HIGH	8
HIGHER	7
HIGHWAY	7
HIM	8
HIMSELF	4
HINDERS	5
HIRT	6
HIS	5
HOARSE	2
HOCKEY	7
HOE	6
HOG	5
HOLD	7
HOLE	7
HOME	2
HONESTY	8
HONEY	7
HONEYMOON	4
HOOD	8
HOOK	7
HOPE	4
HORIZONTAL	2
HORN	7
HORSE	8
HOSPITAL	4
HOSTAGE	7
HOT	6
HOTEL	8
HOTTER	7
HOUR	5
HOUSE	2
HOW	6
HOWEVER	8
HUE	4
HUMANE	6
HUMANITY	7
HUMBLE	5
HUMILIATION	7
HUMOR	4
HUMP	7
HUNGER	5
HUNGRY	3
HUNT	5
HURRICANE	8
HURT	2

Word	#
HUT	7
HYBRID	3
HYMN	6
HYPNOTIC	6
I	7
ICEBOX	8
ICECREAM	7
ICICLE	5
IDEA	5
IDEAL	4
IDLE	2
IF	6
IGNITION	4
IGNORE	5
IMAGINATION	4
IMITATE	5
IMPARTIAL	2
IMPORT	7
IMPOSSIBILITY	2
IMPOTENCY	3
IMPOVERISHED	2
IMPROPRIETY	2
IN	4
INADEQUATE	4
INANIMATE	7
INCAPABLE	5
INCENSE	5
INCH	6
INCISE	2
INCOMPETENT	7
INDIAN	8
INDIFFERENT	2
INDULGENT	2
INFERIOR	4
INFINITE	5
INHALE	7
INK	2
INNATE	8
INSECT	4
INSOLENT	6
INSTITUTE	6
INSTITUTION	6
INSTRUMENT	4
INSULT	5
INTEGRITY	5
INTENSE	2
INTENTS	5
INTEREST	6
INTIMATE	4
INTO	7
IOTA	6
IRIS	7
IRON	4
IS	8

Word	#
ISLANDER	6
ISLE	6
IT	2
ITCH	4
ITEM	4
ITS	2
IVORY	2
IVY	7
JACK	8
JACKET	7
JAGGED	7
JAIL	8
JALEP	6
JAM	7
JAMB	1
JANGLE	7
JANS	1
JAR	1
JARGON	7
JAW	7
JEEP	8
JELLO	8
JELLY	7
JELLYFISH	7
JERID	1
JERK	4
JET	8
JEWEL	8
JIBE	1
JITTERBUG	7
JOB	6
JOCKEY	7
JOG	2
JOIN	6
JOKE	5
JOURNAL	5
JOY	6
JUBILANT	5
JUDGE	5
JUGGLER	5
JUICE	6
JUMP	7
JUNCTION	2
JUPON	8
JUST	4
JUSTICE	6
JUSTIFY	6
KABOB	2
KALAB	4
KAPOX	6
KARON	1
KEEN	5
KEEP	5
KEPT	2

Word	#
KERNEL	7
KEROSENE	7
KETEL	1
KETTLE	1
KEVEL	1
KEY	8
KID	8
KILL	4
KILOWATTS	3
KIND	5
KINDLE	3
KING	8
KINGDOM	6
KISS	1
KITE	7
KITTEN	1
KNEW	3
KNIFE	1
KNIGHT	1
KNOB	7
KNOLL	8
KNOW	3
KNOWLEDGE	5
KNOWN	7
KNOWS	2
KNUCKLE	2
KULAK	1
KUPOD	1
LABOR	6
LABYRINTH	7
LACE	6
LACK	2
LACKS	6
LAD	5
LADY	5
LAGAN	6
LAID	5
LAIN	5
LAIR	3
LAKE	8
LAMB	8
LAMENT	3
LAMP	8
LANCER	1
LAND	2
LANE	5
LANTERN	2
LAP	3
LAPIN	1
LARD	7
LARK	1
LAST	7
LATE	4
LATHE	3

29

Word	#	Word	#	Word	#	Word	#	Word	#	Word	#
LATUK	1	LIME	8	LYE	3	MEANT	2	MOLECULE	6	NAME	6
LAUD	1	LIMELIGHT	3	LYNX	3	MEASLES	7	MOMENT	5	NAPKIN	7
LAUGH	6	LIMN	1	LYRE	1	MEAT	8	MONAD	1	NARES	1
LAW	6	LIMOUSINE	8	MACARONI	8	MECHANICAL	6	MONASTERY	7	NARROW	4
LAWN	8	LIMP	4	MAD	4	MEDAL	7	MONEY	8	NATION	6
LAWYER	8	LINE	6	MADE	2	MEEK	4	MONKEY	8	NATIVE	7
LAX	2	LINEN	7	MAGAZINE	8	MEET	5	MONSOON	7	NAVAL	1
LAZY	4	LINKS	3	MAGICIAN	8	MEETING	5	MOON	8	NAVE	7
LEAD	6	LINT	7	MAGNATE	3	MELANCHOLY	4	MOOSE	4	NAVEL	5
LEAF	8	LION	8	MAGNET	7	MELT	4	MORBID	7	NEAR	2
LEAL	1	LIPS	1	MAHOGANY	7	MEMORY	5	MORE	8	NEARER	5
LEAN	6	LIQUOR	6	MAIL	6	MEN	8	MORGUE	7	NEAT	8
LEAP	6	LIRE	3	MAIN	2	MENAD	1	MORNING	8	NECK	8
LEARN	5	LISTEN	5	MAIZE	3	MERCURY	7	MORPHINE	7	NECKLACE	5
LEASE	4	LITAS	1	MAKE	5	MERMAID	8	MORTAR	3	NEED	7
LEAST	2	LITER	3	MALE	8	MERRY	5	MORTGAGE	4	NEEDLE	1
LEATHER	8	LITERAL	2	MALLET	7	MESSAGE	6	MOSQUE	3	NELAT	6
LED	4	LITERATURE	6	MAN	8	METAL	7	MOSQUITO	7	NEROL	4
LEFL	1	LITTLE	6	MANE	7	METHOD	5	MOSS	7	NERVE	8
LEES	1	LITTORAL	1	MANNER	2	METIS	1	MOST	2	NERVOUS	7
LEFT	2	LIVE	5	MANOR	6	MICROSCOPE	8	MOTE	3	NEST	2
LEG	8	LIVER	7	MANSION	8	MIEN	1	MOTH	7	NET	5
LEGALITY	4	LIZARD	7	MANURE	7	MIGHT	5	MOTHER	8	NEUTER	8
LEGENDARY	5	LOAD	6	MANUS	1	MILD	5	MOTION	8	NEVER	3
LEGITIMATE	5	LOAFER	4	MANY	5	MILE	7	MOUNTAIN	8	NEW	2
LEMON	8	LOAN	4	MAP	8	MILK	8	MOUSE	7	NEWS	5
LEMONADE	8	LOBSTER	8	MAPLE	8	MIMIC	4	MOUSER	1	NEXT	6
LENIENT	5	LOCKER	7	MAR	3	MINCE	3	MOUSSE	8	NICE	1
LENS	7	LODE	3	MARCH	8	MIND	5	MOUTH	7	NICKEL	7
LESS	2	LOGOS	1	MARE	7	MINE	6	MOUTHPIECE	6	NIDUS	8
LESSEN	6	LONE	4	MARIJUANA	8	MINER	8	MOVE	7	NIGHT	6
LESSON	8	LONG	6	MARK	4	MINISTER	4	MOVIE	8	NIGHTGOWN	1
LETTER	8	LOOK	5	MAROON	7	MINK	7	MUCH	8	NINE	4
LETTERHEAD	3	LOON	3	MARRY	6	MINNOW	6	MUCIN	7	NISUS	3
LETTERS	8	LOOP	6	MARSHALL	8	MINOR	4	MUCUS	4	NITON	2
LETTUCE	8	LOOT	7	MARSHMALLOWS	8	MINSTREL	8	MUD	7	NO	6
LEVEL	4	LOQUACITY	1	MARTIAL	3	MINTS	3	MUG	8	NOEL	2
LEVER	7	LORD	6	MASH	4	MINUTE	4	MUJIK	6	NOLL	8
LIAR	4	LORRY	3	MASS	6	MIRAGE	6	MULE	7	NONE	2
LIBERTY	5	LOSE	4	MAST	7	MIRROR	7	MULTIPLYING	4	NOODLE	6
LIBRARY	8	LOSS	8	MATCH	6	MISCHIEVOUS	7	MURAL	6	NOPE	8
LICE	7	LOTION	6	MATE	6	MISCONCEPTION	2	MURDER	7	NOR	2
LICHEN	3	LOUD	6	MATH	6	MISERY	4	MUSIC	8	NOSE	7
LIE	4	LOVE	6	MATHEMATICAL	4	MISS	5	MUST	2	NOT	8
LIEN	1	LOVELY	5	MATHEMATICS	6	MISSILE	7	MUSTARD	7	NOTE	6
LIEUTENANT	7	LOW	4	MATTRESS	8	MISTER	6	MUTINY	4	NOUN	1
LIFE		LUCES	1	MAUSOR	1	MISUSE	8	MUTTON	4	NOVEL	4
LIFT	4	LUMBER	7	MAY	3	MITE	3	MY	3	NOW	3
LIGHT	8	LUNCH	8	MAYOR	7	MIXER	5	MYSTIC	8	NOWHERE	2
LIGHTER	4	LUNE	4	MAZE	7	MOAT	7	MYTH	3	NUMB	6
LIKEN	5	LUNG	5	ME	6	MOCCASIN	7	NABOB	8	NUMBER	8
LILY	3	LURE	3	MEAL	8	MOHUR	6	NADIR	1	NUN	2
LIMB	8	LUST	8	MEAN	4	MOLD	8	NAG	6	NURSE	7
		LUTE	8			MOLE	4	NAIL	7	NURSERY	6

Word		Word		Word		Word		Word		Word	
OAK	8	OWN	5	PEA	7	PILLOW	8	POUND	6	PUNCH	6
OAR	7	OWNER	6	PEACE	5	PIMPLE	7	POUR	4	PUNISH	4
OAT	7	OXIDE	3	PEACEFUL	5	PINE	7	POWDER	6	PUNY	4
OATMEAL	7	OXYGEN	6	PEACEMAKER	5	PINEAPPLE	8	POWER	5	PUP	8
OBEDIENT	2	OYSTER	7	PEACH	8	PINT	7	PRAISE	5	PUPIL	7
OBESE	7	PACIFISM	2	PEAH	1	PIOUS	4	PRAY	6	PURL	1
OBLIQUE	2	PACKS	6	PEAL	3	PIPE	8	PRAYER	5	PURSE	7
OBLIVIOUS	2	PAEAN	1	PEAR	8	PIQUE	1	PREDICT	4	PUT	2
OBOE	7	PAGE	7	PEARL	8	PITY	4	PREFIX	3	PYTHON	7
OCCASIONAL	2	PAID	5	PEDAL	6	PLACARD	4	PREJUDICE	5	QUACK	4
OCEAN	2	PAIL	7	PEDDLE	3	PLACE	3	PREPOSITION	3	QUAICH	1
ODE	3	PAIN	4	PEEK	4	PLAICE	5	PRESENCE	5	QUAIL	8
OF	2	PAINT	8	PEEL	3	PLAIN	1	PRESIDENT	5	QUAKE	4
OFF	2	PAIR	5	PEER	7	PLAIT	4	PRETTY	2	QUARREL	4
OFFEND	4	PAJAMA	8	PEG	7	PLAN	1	PREVALENT	5	QUART	7
OFFICE	7	PALACE	8	PELT	7	PLANE	5	PREVIEW	6	QUARTER	8
OFFSHOOT	3	PALE	4	PEN	8	PLANT	8	PREY	8	QUEAN	1
OH	2	PALL	1	PENCIL	7	PLATE	7	PRIDE	8	QUEEN	8
OHMS	3	PALM	8	PENICILLIN	8	PLATTER	5	PRIED	7	QUESTION	5
OIL	7	PAN	7	PENNY	3	PLAY	5	PRIEST	5	QUICK	5
OKAY	2	PANE	3	PEON	8	PLAYING	4	PRIME	8	QUICKEN	2
OLD	6	PANIC	4	PEOPLE	7	PLEA	3	PRINCE	8	QUICKLY	5
OLDER	7	PANORAMA	5	PEPPER	4	PLEDGE	8	PRINCESS	5	QUIET	5
OLIVE	4	PANS	7	PERISH	4	PLENTIFUL	4	PRINTS	5	QUIETLY	5
OMEN	4	PANTIES	8	PERJURY	8	PLIABLE	5	PRIVATE	7	QUILL	7
ON	2	PANTS	8	PERMANENT	8	PLIERS	3	PRIZE	8	QUILT	8
ONCE	2	PAPER	7	PERMIT	7	PLOT	7	PROBLEM	7	QUIRE	1
ONE	4	PARADE	8	PERRY	3	PLOW	6	PRODUCE	6	RABBI	7
ONION	7	PARADOX	2	PERSE	1	PLUMB	7	PRODUCTIVE	7	RABBIT	8
ONLY	2	PARAGRAPH	7	PERSONAL	6	POCKET	6	PROFESSOR	8	RACE	6
OPAL	7	PARCEL	2	PESO	6	PODIUM	3	PROFIT	6	RACES	6
OPEN	2	PARDON	7	PESTLE	5	POINT	8	PROHIBIT	7	RACK	3
OPIUM	5	PARE	5	PET	3	POLE	7	PROJECTOR	7	RACQUET	7
OPPONENT	7	PARISH	7	PETAL	6	POLEF	7	PRONOUN	6	RAID	7
OR	2	PARK	4	PEW	8	POLIO	1	PROOF	7	RAIL	8
ORANGE	8	PARRY	2	PEWIT	1	POLITE	6	PROP	1	RAIN	7
ORCHESTRA	8	PART	8	PHANTOM	2	POLL	2	PROPELLER	7	RAINCOATS	7
ORCHID	8	PASS	8	PHASE	5	POLLEN	6	PROPERTY	5	RAINHAT	5
ORDER	4	PASSION	8	PHILOSOPHY	5	POLLUTION	8	PROPHET	6	RAISE	7
ORDERLY	4	PAST	4	PHONE	5	POLO	8	PROSPER	7	RAKE	7
OREGANO	7	PASTE	7	PHOTOGRAPH	7	POMMEL	5	PROTOCOL	6	RAM	3
ORGAN	8	PASTOR	7	PHRASE	4	PONY	8	PROUD	7	RAMP	4
ORIGINATE	2	PAT	8	PHYSICS	7	POOR	6	PROVINCIAL	1	RAMROD	4
ORNATE	3	PATCH	7	PIANO	6	POPE	8	PROXY	8	RANCID	7
OTHER	2	PATH	6	PICK	4	PORE	1	PSALM	4	RAP	5
OUNCE	6	PATHETIC	2	PICKLE	5	PORK	3	PSYCHOLOGY	7	RAPE	7
OUR	2	PATIENCE	6	PICUL	6	PORT	8	PUDDING	3	RAPID	8
OUT	2	PATIENTS	2	PIDGIN	7	PORTRAY	4	PUDDLE	7	RARE	7
OUTFOX	3	PAUL	7	PIE	4	POST	7	PUGH	6	RASH	7
OVEN	7	PAUSE	3	PIECE	2	POT	6	PUIGNE	2	RASPBERRY	8
OVER	5	PAVIS	7	PIER	1	POTATO	8	PULL	7	RAT	7
OWED	2	PAWN	5	PIGEON	6	POTS	8	PULPIT	6	RATAL	1
OWL	8	PAWS	2	PILE	8			PUMMEL	8	RATE	4
		PAX	8	PILL	1			PUMP	7	RATION	4

Word	#	Word	#	Word	#	Word	#	Word	#	Word	#
RATTLESNAKE	7	RETAIN	2	RULE	4	SCAVENGER	6	SHARK	6	SKILLET	7
RAW	4	RETARD	4	RUM	8	SCENE	5	SHAWL	5	SKIN	7
RAZE	1	RETREAT	3	RUMBLE	4	SCENT	6	SHE	6	SKIRT	8
REACH	5	REVERY	3	RUMOR	2	SCHEME	2	SHEAR	2	SKULL	7
READ	6	RHAPSODY	3	RUNNING	6	SCHOLAR	6	SHEEP	6	SKUNK	7
READING	5	RHINESTONES	7	RURAL	4	SCHOOL	8	SHEEPSKIN	8	SKY	8
REAL	5	RHOMBUS	3	RUSH	4	SCIENCE	6	SHEER	6	SKYSCRAPER	3
REALITY	5	RHUMB	1	RUSTY	7	SCISSORS	7	SHEETS	7	SLAG	6
REAP	3	RIB	7	SABLE	3	SCOOTER	7	SHELL	7	SLANG	4
REAPER	3	RICE	8	SACK	7	SCORCHING	4	SHIEK	4	SLAP	4
REAR	4	RICH	5	SAD	4	SCOTCH	8	SHILLING	8	SLAVERY	3
REASON	5	RIDDLE	6	SAFE	5	SCOWL	4	SHINY	4	SLAY	6
REBEC	1	RIDE	4	SAFETY	5	SCREWDRIVER	8	SHIP	8	SLEAVE	4
REBUS	1	RIDICULE	1	SAGACITY	1	SCULL	7	SHIRT	7	SLEEP	3
RECALL	5	RIFLE	5	SAGE	3	SEA	8	SHOE	8	SLEET	6
RECEIVER	6	RIGHT	6	SAID	2	SEAL	7	SHONE	7	SLEEVE	7
RECEPTIVE	2	RIGID	2	SAIL	8	SEALING	3	SHOOT	3	SLEIGH	7
RECOMMEND	2	RIM	2	SAILBOAT	8	SEAM	7	SHOP	7	SLEPT	8
RECRUIT	4	RING	4	SAINT	6	SEAMAN	7	SHOPPER	7	SLICE	5
RECTANGLE	7	RIPE	7	SALE	5	SEAR	3	SHORT	3	SLIDE	6
RED	8	RISE	8	SALEP	1	SEAT	1	SHOT	7	SLIME	7
REEL	7	RITE	5	SALOL	7	SEAWEED	7	SHOULD	7	SLIP	6
REFEREE	7	RIVER	3	SALT	8	SECOND	6	SHOULDER	4	SLIPPER	7
REFINED	2	ROAD	8	SALTY	6	SECRETARY	7	SHOUT	7	SLOE	1
REFRAIN	4	ROBBERY	6	SALUTE	6	SEE	5	SHOVEL	5	SLOPE	8
REFRESH	5	ROBIN	8	SALVE	3	SEED	8	SHOW	8	SLOVENLY	3
REFRIGERATOR	8	ROBUSTNESS	5	SAME	2	SEEK	2	SHOWER	5	SLOW	4
REFUSE	4	ROCK	8	SANCTITY	3	SEEL	3	SHOWN	3	SLOWER	2
REGION	6	ROCKER	7	SANCTUARY	6	SEEM	6	SHRIEK	2	SLOWLY	5
REGULATION	4	ROCKET	8	SAND	8	SEEN	8	SHRIMP	2	SLUGGISH	4
REIGN	5	ROD	7	SANDAL	8	SEER	3	SICK	3	SLUSH	7
REJECTED	4	RODE	4	SANDER	3	SEINE	3	SICKNESS	3	SMACK	6
REJOICE	5	ROE	3	SANDY	6	SELL	6	SIDE	4	SMALL	5
RELAXED	5	ROLE	5	SANE	5	SELLER	5	SIDEWALK	4	SMART	5
RELIC	6	ROLL	5	SAPPHIRE	7	SELLING	7	SIGHED	4	SMEAR	4
RELIGION	6	ROOF	6	SARDINE	7	SELLOUT	7	SIGHT	7	SMELL	6
RELINQUISH	2	ROOM	6	SASH	3	SEMEN	3	SIGIL	1	SMELT	3
RELUCTANT	4	ROOMER	2	SATIN	8	SENATA	8	SIGN	5	SMILE	8
REMEX	1	ROOT	7	SAUCER	7	SEND	7	SILK	7	SMOKE	6
RENOUNCE	2	ROPE	1	SAUERKRAUT	7	SENSE	7	SILOS	5	SMOOTH	5
RENT	4	ROSARY	2	SAVAGE	6	SENT	6	SILVER	2	SMOTHER	4
REPLACEMENT	4	ROSE	4	SAVANT	1	SEQUEL	1	SIMPLE	3	SNAIL	7
REPLETE	1	ROTE	4	SAVE	5	SERF	5	SIN	3	SNAKE	4
REPRESS	4	ROUGH	1	SAVORY	5	SERGEANT	5	SINCE	4	SNAP	7
REPROVE	2	ROUND	4	SAW	6	SERIAL	6	SINE	3	SNEEZE	4
REPTILE	8	ROUTE	8	SAXOPHONE	8	SEVERE	8	SING	4	SNORED	4
REPULSIVE	4	ROWBOAT	7	SCAB	7	SEVERE	7	SINK	7	SNOW	8
REQUIREMENT	2	ROWS	4	SCALE	6	SEWER	4	SISTER	8	SO	2
RESEARCH	6	RUBBLE	3	SCALLOPS	7	SEX	6	SIT	6	SOAP	8
RESORT	6	RUBY	8	SCAPEL	7	SHADY	7	SITE	3	SOAR	5
RESPONSIVE	5	RUDDER	7	SCAR	7	SHALE	3	SIZE	4	SOARED	5
REST	5	RUFF	3	SCARCE	4	SHALLOW	4	SKATE	4	SOB	4
RESTORE	2	RUG	8	SCARLET	7	SHAME	8	SKI	8	SOCCER	8
		RUGGED	5			SHAPE	7	SKIING	6	SOCIAL	5

Word		Word		Word		Word		Word		Word	
SOCK	7	SPRING	8	STRAW	7	TABLE	7	THEME	4	TOASTER	7
SOD	7	SPRUCE	8	STRAWBERRY	8	TAC	1	THEN	2	TOBACCO	7
SODA	8	SPUTTERING	3	STREAMER	6	TACET	1	THEORETICAL	2	TOE	8
SODIUM	8	SQUARE	4	STREET	7	TACK	7	THEORY	5	TOIL	4
SOFA	8	SQUEAK	3	STRING	6	TAIL	2	THERE	2	TOILET	5
SOFT	5	SQUIB	4	STROKE	8	TAKE	8	THEREFORE	2	TOLAN	2
SOFTLY	5	SQUIRREL	8	STUDENT	6	TALE	6	THERMOMETER	7	TOLD	7
SOIL	8	SQUIRT	6	STUDYING	4	TALES	6	THESE	2	TOLERANT	2
SOLD	4	STABLE	6	STUMBLE	6	TALK	4	THEY	2	TOLL	4
SOLDIER	7	STADIUM	7	STUMP	8	TALL	6	THICK	4	TOMATO	8
SOLE	6	STAIR	4	STUNT	6	TALUK	1	THIEF	7	TOMB	7
SOLEMN	4	STAIT	2	STUPID	4	TAME	4	THIMBLE	7	TON	8
SOLEMNITY	2	STAKE	2	STYLE	5	TANG	7	THIN	6	TONGUE	2
SOLIDIFY	4	STALE	3	SUBMARINE	8	TANGERINE	3	THING	5	TOO	8
SOME	2	STALK	3	SUBTRACTING	4	TANK	8	THINK	5	TOOL	5
SONATA	3	STAND	6	SUBTRACTION	4	TAP	5	THINNER	6	TOOTH	6
SONE	1	STANZE	1	SUCCEED	3	TAPE	1	THIRSTY	7	TOP	7
SONG	8	STAR	8	SUCCOR	6	TAPER	2	THIS	2	TORNADO	8
SOON	2	STARCH	2	SUCH	1	TAPIS	4	THOSE	2	TORTOISE	5
SOOT	8	STATE	6	SUCKER	8	TAR	6	THOUGHT	4	TOUGH	6
SORE	2	STATES	5	SUE	4	TARNISH	1	THOUGHTFUL	4	TOURIST	5
SOUL	6	STATION	6	SUEDE	6	TAROP	6	THREAD	1	TOW	7
SOUND	5	STAY	8	SUFFIX	8	TASTE	4	THREAT	4	TOWN	4
SOUP	6	STEAK	6	SUFFOCATE	8	TAX	7	THREE	6	TOY	7
SOUR	8	STEAL	6	SUFFRAGE	2	TEA	5	THREW	7	TRACE	4
SOUTH	6	STEALING	7	SUGAR	8	TEACH	8	THRIFTY	5	TRACTOR	5
SOW	6	STEAM	5	SUIT	8	TEACHER	7	THROAT	7	TRADITION	7
SPACE	7	STEEL	2	SUITE	4	TEAM	7	THROE	8	TRAGEDY	1
SPADE	5	STEEPLE	3	SULPHUR	4	TEAR	7	THRONG	8	TRAIL	3
SPAN	2	STEM	4	SUM	7	TEEM	6	THROUGH	3	TRAILER	2
SPANGLE	3	STEP	6	SUN	7	TEETH	8	THROW	8	TRAIN	6
SPANK	4	STEPPE	8	SUNSET	7	TELEPHONE	8	THUD	4	TRAITOR	3
SPARK	6	STERN	7	SUNTAN	6	TELESCOPE	8	THUNDER	3	TRANCE	3
SPARROW	8	STEW	3	SUPPER	3	TELL	8	THUS	8	TRANQUIL	7
SPATULA	8	STICK	8	SURAL	4	TEMERITY	1	THWART	5	TRANSPORTATION	8
SPAYED	3	STIFLE	6	SURE	8	TEMPERATURE	2	THYME	2	TRAPEZE	6
SPEAK	6	STILE	2	SURF	6	TEMPEST	8	TICKET	3	TRAPEZOID	5
SPEAR	7	STILL	3	SURTAX	7	TEMPLE	3	TICKLE	6	TRASH	7
SPECIMEN	6	STINGY	4	SWAGE	2	TEMPT	1	TIDE	4	TRAVEL	6
SPECK	6	STOCKING	8	SWALLOW	5	TENNIS	6	TIDY	5	TRAWL	3
SPHERE	7	STOLE	6	SWARM	4	TENSE	4	TIE	7	TRAY	7
SPICE	8	STOMACH	7	SWAYED	7	TENT	7	TIED	4	TREASURER	5
SPICY	6	STONE	7	SWEAT	7	TENURE	3	TIGER	8	TREAT	8
SPIDER	7	STOOL	7	SWEEP	6	TERM	4	TIGHT	3	TREE	6
SPIKE	7	STOP	6	SWEET	6	TEST	6	TILL	4	TREND	8
SPINACH	7	STORE	7	SWIFT	8	TESTIMONY	5	TILUS	6	TREY	4
SPOKE	6	STORM	4	SWIM	4	TEST TUBE	7	TIME	5	TRIAL	1
SPONGE	7	STORY	7	SWIMMING	6	THAN	8	TIMEPIECE	7	TRIANGLE	6
SPOOK	4	STOUT	7	SWORD	6	THAT	7	TIP	2	TRIBE	7
SPOOL	7	STOVE	6	SYDAH	6	THAW	1	TIRE	6	TRIP	8
SPOON	7	STRAIGHT	3	SYMBOL	6	THE	5	TITER	4	TRIPOD	1
SPOT	6	STRAND	6	SYMBOLISM	8	THEFT	5	TO	2	TRIUMPH	5
SPOUT	3			SYMPATHETIC	6	THEIR	5	TOAD	2	TROLLEY	7
SPRAY	6			SYNAGOGUE	4	THEM	7	TOAST	2	TROMBONE	7

Word		Word		Word		Word		Word	
TROOP	6	USED	6	WAIT	2	WHIP	7	WRUNG	3
TROUBLE	4	USURP	4	WAIVE	1	WHISKER	7	WYDEN	1
TROUPE	3	UTTER	3	WALK	4	WHISKEY	8	XABIN	1
TROUSER	7	VACANT	7	WALKING	4	WHISTLE	8	XILOS	1
TROUT	8	VACATE	8	WALL	2	WHITE	2	XUBER	1
TRUCKS	8	VAGUE	8	WALLET	4	WHO	5	XYDER	1
TRUE	5	VAIN	5	WALNUT	3	WHOLE	2	XYZAR	1
TRUISM	2	VALE	2	WALRUS	4	WHOM	3	YACHT	8
TRUMPET	8	VALIDATION	8	WALTZ	8	WHY	6	YARD	6
TRUST	5	VALLEY	5	WAMPUM	5	WICKET	6	YAWN	6
TRUTH	5	VALOR	5	WAMUS	3	WIDE	2	YEAR	6
TUBE	7	VANE	7	WANDER	1	WIDER	8	YEARS	5
TUBERCULOSIS	7	VARUR	7	WANT	2	WIFE	7	YELL	6
TUFF	3	VARY	3	WAR	7	WIG	1	YELLOW	8
TULIP	8	VASE	8	WARE	7	WIKOU	5	YET	2
TUMBLE	4	VAULT	7	WARN	7	WILD	1	YOKE	7
TUN	1	VEAL	1	WARY	8	WILER	2	YOLIF	1
TUNE	6	VEGETABLE	6	WAS	7	WILL	8	YOLK	7
TUNIC	7	VEIL	7	WASH	8	WILLOW	6	YONDER	3
TUNNEL	7	VEIN	7	WASTE	4	WIND	8	YOU	5
TURN	2	VELVET	2	WATCH	4	WINDOW	8	YOUNGER	5
TURPENTINE	8	VERB	8	WATER	2	WINE	6	YOUR	2
TURTLE	7	VERTICAL	7	WATTS	7	WING	7	YOUTH	6
TUSK	7	VERY	8	WAVE	3	WINK	2	YUROR	1
TWANG	3	VEST	7	WAX	7	WIRE	4	YUVAL	1
TWEEZER	7	VESTMENT	3	WAY	2	WISDOM	5	ZABER	1
TWIG	7	VET	7	WE	6	WISE	5	ZARAL	1
TWIRLER	7	VIAL	7	WEAK	3	WISH	1	ZEAL	2
TWIST	6	VICE	6	WEALTH	4	WITAN	7	ZEBEL	1
TWO	6	VICTORY	6	WEAR	5	WITCH	2	ZENITH	3
TYPE	6	VIEW	6	WEB	5	WITH	4	ZERO	4
TYPEWRITER	7	VILE	7	WEED	4	WITHER	1	ZESAM	1
TYPICAL	2	VILLAGE	2	WEEK	8	WITHOUT	7	ZIPPER	7
TYRANNY	4	VINEGAR	7	WEEP	7	WIZARD	6	ZIROL	1
UGLY	4	VINIM	4	WEIGH	1	WOLF	1	ZOBEL	1
UMBRELLA	7	VIOLET	7	WEIGHT	8	WOMAN	8	ZOBIT	1
UMPIRE	7	VIOLIN	7	WEIRD	3	WOMB	8	ZOLAR	1
UNCLE	8	VISE	8	WELFARE	5	WON	8	ZONAD	1
UNDER	5	VISION	5	WELL	8	WOOD	5	ZONE	6
UNIQUE	5	VODKA	5	WENT	7	WORK	8	ZONER	1
UNITE	5	VOLCANO	5	WERE	8	WORKING	6	ZOO	8
UNIVERSAL	5	VOLLEYBALL	5	WEST	3	WORLD	5	ZOOLOGY	5
UNIVERSITY	8	VOLT	8	WET	5	WORN	8	ZORON	1
UNJUST	4	VOLUNTARY	4	WHALE	6	WORSE	4	ZUBER	1
UNLIMITED	5	VOTE	5	WHALEBONE	6	WORTH	2	ZUMAP	1
UNREALITY	2	VOTER	2	WHAT	5	WORTHWHILE	5	ZUREN	1
UNREST	4	VOW	4	WHEAT	4	WOULD	2		
UNSUCCESSFUL	4	VULGAR	4	WHEEL	1	WRACK	3		
UP	5	VUMAL	5	WHEET	7	WRAP	6		
UPON	2	VUTAW	2	WHEN	6	WRATH	4		
UPRIGHT	6	WAFER	6	WHERE	4	WRECK	7		
URBAN	6	WAGE	6	WHICH	3	WREST	3		
URN	3	WAIL	3	WHIFF	2	WRITE	6		
US	5	WAIST	5	WHILE	7	WROTE	5		

Clusters With Actual Rating Information 4

As described in Chapter 2, the mean ratings (and standard deviations) for the individual words are presented in the form of eight relatively homogeneous separate clusters, based upon the results of a BC TRY cluster analysis (Tryon & Bailey, 1970). The cluster in which any given word can be found is given in the alphabetical listing of all words in Chapter 3. Detailed information about the properties of each of these clusters can be found in Tables 3 through 12 (in Chapter 2), including means, standard deviations, and ranges for each dimension within each cluster, and frequency distributions of words within specified rating intervals on a given dimension located within each cluster.

For most purposes, these clusters can be used most easily and efficiently by remembering simply that words with lower rating values tend to be concentrated in the lower-numbered clusters and that words with higher rating values are found in higher-numbered clusters, although this is less true for PLS than for any of the other dimensions.

In addition to the mean rating and its standard deviation for each word on each dimension, also given in parentheses below these values are the deviations of the word mean ratings from their cluster mean values. Besides providing an added visual—numerical aid in finding words of a particular type within each cluster, these deviations also can be used to derive directly the cluster means without reference to Table 3 — by simply subtracting the deviation values from the corresponding mean word rating.

As noted in Chapter 1, there is one additional bit of information given only for the PLS dimension. Several of the PLS standard deviation values in the final column are followed by the letters F or M, which are indicative of substantial sex differences in PLS

mean ratings. All words designated by F show a mean PLS rating for females at least 0.5 larger than for males, whereas words designated by M indicate that the male mean PLS rating exceeds that for females by 0.5 or more.

Table 15 lists the number of words in each cluster and the page numbers of each cluster.

TABLE 15

	Cluster Number							
	1	2	3	4	5	6	7	8
Number of Words	195	255	229	390	330	384	566	499
Pages	37—44	45—54	55—63	64—78	79—91	92—106	107—127	128—146

CLUSTER 1

	CON M SD	IMG M SD	CAT M SD	MNG M SD	FAM M SD	NOA M SD	PLS M SD
ABASEMENT	2.55 1.63 (-.32)	2.51 1.92 (.21)	2.32 1.69 (.02)	2.30 1.69 (.49)	3.18 1.86 (.98)	2.91 1.61 (.56)	3.04 1.30 (-.49)
ABBESS	3.49 2.12 (.62)	2.91 2.18 (.61)	2.33 1.67 (.03)	2.18 1.41 (.37)	2.92 2.00 (.72)	2.67 1.42 (.32)	3.72 1.20 (.19)
ABDICATION	2.36 1.55 (-.51)	2.60 1.97 (.30)	2.78 1.80 (.48)	2.77 1.66 (.96)	3.46 2.23 (1.26)	2.74 1.76 (.39)	3.38 1.21 (-.15)
ACUMEN	2.68 1.72 (-.19)	2.23 1.77 (-.07)	2.35 1.81 (.05)	2.10 1.66 (.29)	2.23 1.84 (.03)	3.14 1.50 (.79)	3.59 1.09 (.06)
ADZE	2.79 2.10 (-.08)	2.50 2.07 (.20)	2.38 1.79 (.08)	1.64 1.37 (-.17)	2.12 1.91 (-.08)	2.11 1.46 (-.24)	3.60 1.32 (.07)
AMPERE	3.23 2.40 (.36)	2.98 2.00 (.68)	3.05 1.98 (.75)	2.31 1.76 (.50)	3.46 2.05 (1.26)	2.26 1.44 (-.09)	3.84 1.09M (.31)
ANELE	2.98 2.28 (.11)	1.98 1.72 (-.43)	2.17 1.57 (-.13)	1.84 1.52 (.03)	1.77 1.68 (-.43)	1.97 1.51 (-.38)	3.44 1.48 (-.09)
ANNEAL	2.63 1.70 (-.24)	2.13 1.73 (-.17)	2.33 1.62 (.03)	1.93 1.33 (.12)	2.50 1.80 (.30)	2.11 1.34 (-.24)	3.24 1.21M (-.29)
AURAL	3.05 1.98 (.18)	2.47 2.08 (.17)	2.20 1.60 (-.10)	1.97 1.48 (.16)	2.66 2.03 (.46)	2.81 1.71 (.46)	4.06 1.58 (.53)
AWEIGH	2.27 1.67 (-.60)	2.07 1.77 (-.23)	1.60 .95 (-.70)	1.62 .96 (-.19)	2.41 1.92 (.21)	1.91 1.09 (-.44)	3.50 1.22 (-.03)
AWL	4.09 2.50 (1.22)	2.86 2.27 (.56)	3.19 2.22 (.89)	2.00 1.53 (.19)	3.31 3.23 (1.11)	2.27 1.44 (-.08)	3.51 1.29 (-.02)
AYE	2.29 1.86 (-.58)	2.49 1.92 (.11)	2.41 1.73 (.11)	2.10 1.36 (.29)	4.07 2.08 (1.87)	1.75 1.18 (-.60)	3.81 1.60 (.28)
BALAP	2.76 1.96 (-.11)	1.74 1.55 (-.56)	2.23 1.76 (-.07)	1.56 1.33 (-.25)	1.37 1.08 (-.83)	2.67 1.64 (.32)	3.47 1.23 (-.06)
BANALITY	2.85 1.94 (-.02)	2.38 1.90 (.08)	2.53 1.63 (.23)	2.13 1.52 (.32)	2.42 1.88 (.22)	2.86 1.82 (.51)	3.36 1.39M (-.17)
BARD	3.20 1.88 (.33)	3.16 2.27 (.86)	2.92 1.79 (.62)	2.49 1.78 (.68)	3.17 2.26 (.97)	2.30 1.36 (-.05)	3.53 1.46 (.00)
BEDEL	2.72 1.60 (-.15)	1.71 1.32 (-.59)	2.00 1.44 (-.30)	1.44 .98 (-.37)	1.92 1.46 (-.28)	2.23 1.53 (-.12)	3.36 1.41 (-.17)
BETEL	3.16 2.11 (.29)	2.32 1.95 (.02)	2.23 1.72 (-.07)	2.00 1.68 (.19)	2.03 1.74 (-.17)	2.32 1.47 (-.03)	3.59 1.21 (.06)
BHANG	3.12 2.13 (.25)	2.11 1.74 (-.19)	2.40 1.87 (.10)	1.85 1.56 (.04)	1.90 1.57 (-.30)	2.70 1.69 (.35)	3.83 1.40M (.30)
BIER	4.07 2.22 (1.20)	2.88 2.03 (.58)	3.10 1.89 (.80)	2.42 2.09 (.61)	2.36 1.94 (.16)	2.57 1.79 (.22)	3.50 1.34M (-.03)
BLUNDERBUSS	3.62 2.32 (.75)	3.32 2.48 (1.02)	2.71 2.08 (.41)	2.12 1.50 (.31)	3.39 2.11 (1.19)	2.66 1.58 (.31)	2.99 1.74 (-.54)
BOLE	3.35 2.12 (.48)	2.07 1.64 (-.23)	2.38 1.74 (.08)	1.66 1.28 (-.15)	1.88 1.35 (-.32)	2.05 1.18 (-.30)	3.16 1.48 (-.37)
BOLL	3.46 2.16 (.59)	2.64 1.95 (.34)	2.40 1.93 (.10)	1.87 1.42 (.06)	2.84 2.14 (.64)	2.03 1.24 (-.32)	3.28 1.28 (-.25)
BOSUN	3.80 2.19 (.93)	2.47 1.92 (.17)	2.80 2.05 (.50)	1.81 1.49 (.00)	2.26 1.91 (.06)	2.38 1.62 (.03)	3.57 1.57 (.04)
BUBAL	2.54 1.84 (-.33)	2.27 1.76 (-.03)	2.35 1.76 (.05)	1.74 1.59 (-.07)	1.53 1.20 (-.67)	2.11 1.44 (-.24)	3.66 1.26 (.13)
BUTYL	3.17 1.97 (.30)	2.63 2.17 (.33)	2.73 2.07 (.43)	1.93 1.68 (.12)	2.21 1.79 (.01)	2.55 1.68 (.20)	3.49 1.53M (-.04)
BYRE	2.30 1.67 (-.57)	2.25 1.72 (-.05)	2.24 1.67 (-.06)	1.72 1.42 (-.09)	2.25 1.99 (.05)	2.26 1.41 (-.09)	3.50 1.13 (-.03)
CALIX	3.16 2.15 (.29)	2.42 1.98 (.12)	2.29 1.69 (-.01)	1.58 1.25 (-.23)	1.98 1.79 (-.22)	2.40 1.75 (.05)	3.29 1.14 (-.24)

	CON		IMG		CAT		MNG		FAM		NOA		PLS	
	M	SD	M	SD	M	SD	M	SD	M	SD	M	SD	M	SD
CARREL	3.54	2.23	2.49	2.06	2.37	1.62	2.10	1.64	2.92	2.03	2.77	1.65	3.76	1.40
	(.67)		(.19)		(.07)		(.29)		(.72)		(.42)		(.23)	
CAUL	2.69	1.97	1.82	1.42	1.75	1.38	1.38	.85	1.61	1.16	1.92	1.11	3.43	1.17
	(-.18)		(-.48)		(-.55)		(-.43)		(-.59)		(-.43)		(-.10)	
CAWS	3.71	2.19	2.81	1.90	2.67	1.75	2.18	1.48	2.97	1.93	2.23	1.26	3.31	1.41
	(.84)		(.51)		(.37)		(.37)		(.77)		(-.12)		(-.22)	
CEDE	2.35	1.67	2.34	1.58	2.35	1.56	2.34	1.61	2.67	1.95	2.87	1.68	3.36	1.02
	(-.52)		(.04)		(.05)		(.53)		(.47)		(.52)		(-.17)	
CELOM	2.53	1.96	1.95	1.65	2.00	1.67	1.80	1.49	1.73	1.34	2.36	1.63	3.66	1.04
	(-.34)		(-.35)		(-.30)		(-.01)		(-.47)		(.01)		(.13)	
CHACHA	3.62	1.98	3.14	2.18	3.13	2.11	2.45	1.72	2.40	2.00	2.86	1.84	4.10	1.46
	(.75)		(.84)		(.83)		(.64)		(.20)		(.51)		(.57)	
CINQUE	2.46	1.84	2.33	1.93	3.18	1.89	2.05	1.54	2.35	2.02	2.51	1.65	3.71	1.25
	(-.41)		(.03)		(.88)		(.24)		(.15)		(.16)		(.18)	
COKEM	2.77	1.81	1.83	1.50	2.12	1.74	1.62	1.33	1.35	.99	2.34	1.64	3.51	1.32
	(-.10)		(-.47)		(-.18)		(-.19)		(-.85)		(-.01)		(-.02)	
COPIOUS	2.69	1.96	2.98	1.99	2.62	1.78	2.44	1.67	2.87	2.01	3.19	1.79	3.64	1.48
	(-.18)		(.68)		(.32)		(.63)		(.67)		(.84)		(.11)	
COULOMB	3.13	2.13	2.51	1.92	2.85	2.33	2.22	1.80	2.50	2.01	2.44	1.68	3.32	1.29
	(.26)		(.21)		(.55)		(.41)		(.30)		(.09)		(-.21)	
CULLER	3.12	2.01	2.65	2.09	2.30	1.60	1.79	1.51	2.39	1.94	2.55	1.65	3.31	1.14
	(.25)		(.35)		(.00)		(-.02)		(.19)		(.20)		(-.22)	
CYLIX	3.31	2.16	1.98	1.53	2.26	1.81	1.56	1.24	1.91	1.64	2.30	1.46	3.53	1.15
	(.44)		(-.32)		(-.04)		(-.25)		(-.29)		(-.05)		(.00)	
DAIS	3.29	2.15	2.70	2.00	2.12	1.79	2.03	1.67	2.42	1.77	2.48	1.41	3.78	1.18
	(.42)		(.40)		(-.18)		(.22)		(.22)		(.13)		(.25)	
DAMAN	2.80	1.92	1.84	1.52	2.62	2.06	1.63	1.13	1.87	1.20	2.05	1.49	3.62	1.37
	(-.07)		(-.46)		(.32)		(-.18)		(-.33)		(-.30)		(.09)	
DEBACLE	3.43	2.03	2.91	1.96	2.22	1.37	2.43	1.68	2.92	1.95	2.64	1.61	3.34	1.13
	(.56)		(.61)		(-.08)		(.62)		(.72)		(.29)		(-.19)	
DERAY	2.64	2.03	2.55	2.03	1.88	1.24	2.23	1.57	2.55	1.71	2.56	1.58	3.18	1.20
	(-.23)		(.25)		(-.42)		(.42)		(.35)		(.21)		(-.35)	
DIJON	2.78	1.88	2.18	1.91	2.58	2.06	1.95	1.94	1.95	1.52	2.02	1.31	3.59	1.47
	(-.09)		(-.12)		(.28)		(.14)		(-.25)		(-.33)		(.06)	
DOTAGE	2.89	1.79	2.41	1.82	2.02	1.44	1.90	1.23	2.69	1.93	2.29	1.41	3.03	1.27
	(.02)		(.11)		(-.28)		(.09)		(.49)		(-.06)		(-.50)	
EXACTITUDE	2.50	1.93	3.09	2.19	2.83	1.74	2.65	1.77	3.73	1.90	3.10	1.94	3.42	1.39
	(-.37)		(.79)		(.53)		(.84)		(1.53)		(.75)		(-.11)	
FAROD	2.38	1.67	1.96	1.76	2.22	1.75	1.63	1.25	2.12	1.73	2.03	1.08	3.54	.91
	(-.49)		(-.34)		(-.08)		(-.18)		(-.08)		(-.32)		(.01)	
FARTHING	3.57	2.41	3.43	2.26	3.18	2.07	2.32	1.72	3.00	1.86	2.66	1.36	3.78	1.30
	(.70)		(1.13)		(.88)		(.51)		(.80)		(.31)		(.25)	
FEINT	2.84	1.78	3.07	2.09	2.33	1.49	2.28	1.65	3.08	1.90	2.67	1.47	3.42	1.06
	(-.03)		(.77)		(.03)		(.47)		(.88)		(.32)		(-.11)	
FRIEZE	3.20	1.99	3.09	2.08	2.56	2.00	1.95	1.40	3.70	2.43	2.79	1.78	3.62	1.35F
	(.33)		(.79)		(.26)		(.14)		(1.50)		(.44)		(.09)	
FRUG	3.73	2.34	3.05	2.03	3.02	2.17	2.21	1.49	2.72	2.12	2.25	1.25	3.18	1.34
	(.86)		(.75)		(.72)		(.40)		(.52)		(-.10)		(-.35)	
GADID	2.25	1.53	1.89	1.54	2.00	1.57	1.50	1.36	1.61	1.43	2.20	1.33	3.59	1.15
	(-.62)		(-.41)		(-.30)		(-.31)		(-.59)		(-.15)		(.06)	
GIST	2.91	1.89	2.56	1.98	2.23	1.49	2.53	1.52	3.92	2.30	2.38	1.32	3.46	1.53
	(.04)		(.26)		(-.07)		(.72)		(1.72)		(.03)		(-.07)	
GOJEY	2.03	1.66	1.61	1.59	1.75	1.59	1.26	.87	1.42	1.25	1.63	1.02	3.50	1.39
	(-.84)		(-.69)		(-.55)		(-.55)		(-.78)		(-.72)		(-.03)	

	CON		IMG		CAT		MNG		FAM		NOA		PLS	
	M	SD	M	SD	M	SD	M	SD	M	SD	M	SD	M	SD
GORAL	3.07	2.09	2.00	1.80	2.40	1.78	1.53	1.20	1.77	1.68	1.98	1.36	3.34	1.40
	(.20)		(-.30)		(.10)		(-.28)		(-.43)		(-.37)		(-.19)	
GYBE	2.38	1.79	1.84	1.61	1.73	1.12	1.67	1.11	2.10	1.86	2.37	1.54	3.49	1.26
	(-.49)		(-.46)		(-.57)		(-.14)		(-.10)		(.02)		(-.04)	
HAFIZ	2.16	1.66	1.84	1.45	1.95	1.65	1.38	1.32	1.69	1.55	2.18	1.66	3.67	1.34M
	(-.71)		(-.46)		(-.35)		(-.43)		(-.51)		(-.17)		(.14)	
HERES	2.51	1.78	2.47	1.88	2.25	1.71	2.05	1.36	3.95	2.36	2.39	1.53	3.70	1.37
	(-.36)		(.17)		(-.05)		(.24)		(1.75)		(.04)		(.17)	
HIRT	2.82	2.09	2.94	2.23	2.00	1.55	2.23	1.75	2.67	2.27	2.56	1.48	3.22	1.34
	(-.05)		(.54)		(-.30)		(.42)		(.47)		(.21)		(-.31)	
JALEP	2.91	1.98	1.95	1.43	2.36	1.89	1.56	1.30	1.57	1.24	2.53	1.52	3.42	1.36M
	(.04)		(.06)		(.06)		(-.25)		(-.63)		(.18)		(-.11)	
JAMB	3.22	1.93	2.70	1.91	2.33	1.59	2.05	1.38	3.17	2.26	2.19	1.22	3.42	1.26
	(.35)		(.40)		(.03)		(.24)		(.97)		(-.16)		(-.11)	
JÄNS	2.64	1.87	1.91	1.67	1.47	.96	1.35	.88	1.67	1.31	1.83	1.34	3.35	1.17
	(-.23)		(-.39)		(-.83)		(-.46)		(-.53)		(-.52)		(-.18)	
JERID	2.48	1.77	2.22	1.74	2.28	1.74	1.68	1.32	2.10	2.04	2.10	1.34	3.52	1.08M
	(-.39)		(-.08)		(-.02)		(-.13)		(-.10)		(-.25)		(-.01)	
JIBE	3.33	1.99	3.08	2.11	2.20	1.41	2.51	1.63	2.89	1.75	2.56	1.36	3.53	1.39
	(.46)		(.51)		(-.10)		(.70)		(.69)		(.21)		(.00)	
JUPON	2.34	1.80	2.34	2.06	2.24	1.76	1.41	1.05	1.85	1.87	2.16	1.51	3.73	1.25
	(-.53)		(.04)		(-.06)		(-.40)		(-.35)		(-.19)		(.20)	
KALAB	2.43	1.75	1.98	1.88	2.24	1.78	1.44	.95	1.67	1.47	2.10	1.52	3.61	1.30
	(-.44)		(-.32)		(-.06)		(-.37)		(-.53)		(-.25)		(.08)	
KAPOX	2.64	1.88	2.48	2.06	2.43	1.86	1.42	1.23	1.71	1.64	2.30	1.41	3.55	1.23
	(-.23)		(.18)		(.13)		(-.39)		(-.49)		(-.05)		(.02)	
KARON	2.93	1.82	2.07	1.84	2.72	2.15	1.82	1.70	2.16	2.04	2.34	1.73	4.16	1.54F
	(.06)		(-.23)		(.42)		(.01)		(-.04)		(-.01)		(.63)	
KETEL	3.74	2.45	2.49	2.31	2.97	2.04	2.18	1.93	2.31	2.14	2.08	1.43	3.54	1.50F
	(.87)		(.19)		(.67)		(.37)		(.11)		(-.27)		(.01)	
KEVEL	2.93	2.05	2.25	1.85	1.98	1.72	1.97	1.63	1.86	1.56	2.16	1.27	3.52	1.31
	(.06)		(-.05)		(-.32)		(.16)		(-.34)		(-.19)		(-.01)	
KULAK	3.17	2.17	1.82	1.56	2.37	2.11	1.61	1.45	1.38	1.12	2.46	1.64	3.52	1.33M
	(.30)		(-.48)		(.07)		(-.20)		(-.82)		(.11)		(-.01)	
KUPOD	3.09	2.12	2.44	2.20	1.91	1.49	1.42	1.14	1.93	1.80	2.18	1.48	3.46	1.36
	(.22)		(.14)		(-.39)		(-.39)		(-.27)		(-.17)		(-.07)	
LAGAN	2.42	1.50	1.94	1.55	1.97	1.58	1.35	.95	1.85	1.63	2.18	1.37	3.61	1.11
	(-.45)		(-.46)		(-.39)		(-.46)		(-.35)		(-.17)		(.08)	
LAPIN	3.19	2.14	1.81	1.40	2.37	1.94	1.75	1.58	2.10	1.88	2.54	1.46	3.80	1.19
	(.32)		(-.49)		(.07)		(-.06)		(-.10)		(.19)		(.27)	
LATUK	2.45	1.65	1.75	1.39	1.65	1.08	1.54	1.23	1.43	1.03	1.89	1.45	3.34	1.24
	(-.42)		(-.55)		(-.65)		(-.27)		(-.77)		(-.46)		(-.19)	
LAUD	2.90	1.76	2.82	1.74	3.00	1.97	2.46	1.44	3.61	1.96	2.82	1.54	3.79	1.31
	(.03)		(.52)		(.70)		(.65)		(1.41)		(.47)		(.26)	
LEAL	2.62	1.91	2.74	2.20	2.33	1.76	1.88	1.58	2.03	1.93	2.25	1.59	3.68	1.13
	(-.25)		(.44)		(.07)		(.07)		(-.17)		(-.10)		(.15)	
LEEL	2.93	1.96	2.04	1.79	2.07	1.59	1.66	1.23	1.55	1.38	2.35	1.50	3.30	1.41
	(.06)		(-.26)		(-.23)		(-.15)		(-.65)		(.00)		(-.23)	
LEES	3.02	2.10	2.65	2.02	2.30	1.91	2.03	1.58	3.06	2.11	2.55	1.70	3.84	1.48
	(.15)		(.35)		(.00)		(.22)		(.86)		(.20)		(.31)	
LIEN	3.28	2.24	3.11	2.27	2.74	1.84	1.71	1.33	2.78	2.08	2.50	1.66	3.40	1.31
	(.41)		(.81)		(.44)		(-.10)		(.58)		(.15)		(-.13)	
LIMN	2.71	1.84	2.00	1.53	2.02	1.49	1.27	.61	1.97	1.89	2.08	1.41	3.56	1.19
	(-.16)		(-.30)		(-.28)		(-.54)		(-.23)		(-.27)		(.03)	

	CON (M SD)	IMG (M SD)	CAT (M SD)	MNG (M SD)	FAM (M SD)	NOA (M SD)	PLS (M SD)
LITAS	2.37 1.79 (-.50)	1.87 1.56 (-.43)	1.85 1.15 (-.45)	1.70 1.43 (-.11)	1.57 1.46 (-.63)	2.08 1.55 (-.27)	3.31 1.08 (-.22)
LITTORAL	2.69 1.85 (-.18)	2.18 1.74 (-.12)	2.48 1.69 (.18)	1.63 1.28 (-.18)	2.39 1.89 (.19)	2.23 1.25 (-.12)	3.63 1.35 (.10)
LOGOS	2.95 1.97 (.08)	2.82 2.22 (.52)	2.83 2.00 (.53)	1.87 1.38 (.06)	2.14 1.47 (-.06)	3.16 1.87 (.81)	4.08 1.33 (.55)
LOQUACITY	3.09 1.88 (.22)	2.62 2.10 (.32)	2.24 1.44 (-.06)	2.19 1.68 (.38)	2.39 1.82 (.19)	2.75 1.73 (.40)	3.45 1.59 (-.08)
LUCES	2.85 2.12 (-.02)	2.42 2.04 (.12)	2.34 1.94 (.04)	1.69 1.49 (-.12)	1.93 1.73 (-.27)	2.70 1.71 (.35)	3.66 1.09M (.13)
LUNE	3.24 2.30 (.37)	2.46 1.88 (.16)	2.60 1.90 (.30)	2.02 1.50 (.21)	2.34 1.94 (.14)	2.62 1.54 (.27)	3.62 1.25 (.09)
MANUS	3.11 2.09 (.24)	2.32 2.01 (.02)	2.02 1.55 (-.28)	1.57 1.14 (-.24)	1.87 1.59 (-.33)	2.38 1.70 (.03)	3.49 1.30 (-.04)
MAUSOR	3.33 2.15 (.46)	2.05 1.83 (-.25)	2.60 1.89 (.30)	1.54 1.21 (-.27)	1.59 1.24 (-.61)	2.31 1.69 (-.04)	3.40 1.60M (-.13)
MENAD	2.59 1.86 (-.28)	1.61 1.36 (-.69)	1.77 1.21 (-.53)	1.67 1.49 (-.14)	1.70 1.31 (-.50)	2.08 1.20 (-.27)	3.31 1.46 (-.22)
METIS	2.44 1.86 (-.43)	1.93 1.77 (-.37)	1.67 1.19 (-.63)	1.33 1.07 (-.48)	1.75 1.55 (-.45)	1.82 1.14 (-.53)	3.26 1.38 (-.27)
MIEN	2.79 1.83 (-.08)	2.47 1.89 (.17)	2.52 1.97 (.22)	2.00 1.67 (.19)	2.17 1.88 (-.03)	2.76 1.78 (.41)	3.75 1.23 (.22)
MOHUR	2.62 1.93 (-.25)	1.52 1.21 (-.78)	1.97 1.83 (-.33)	1.28 .73 (-.53)	1.17 .62 (-1.03)	2.03 1.54 (-.32)	3.34 1.18 (-.19)
MONAD	2.43 1.66 (-.44)	1.80 1.43 (-.50)	2.55 1.90 (.25)	1.49 1.37 (-.32)	1.87 1.52 (-.33)	2.60 1.54 (.25)	3.47 1.32 (-.06)
MOUSER	3.43 2.21 (.56)	3.23 2.33 (.93)	3.42 2.08 (1.12)	2.61 1.85 (.80)	2.82 2.17 (.62)	2.98 1.68 (.63)	3.48 1.52M (-.05)
MUCIN	3.00 1.91 (.13)	2.11 1.71 (-.19)	1.96 1.41 (-.34)	1.41 .94 (-.40)	2.02 1.75 (-.18)	2.13 1.50 (-.22)	3.34 1.20 (-.19)
MUJIK	2.39 1.81 (-.48)	1.93 1.81 (-.37)	2.07 1.93 (-.23)	1.48 1.26 (-.33)	1.39 1.06 (-.81)	2.19 1.78 (-.16)	3.46 1.50F (-.07)
NABOB	2.21 1.79 (-.66)	2.07 1.76 (-.23)	2.22 1.54 (-.08)	1.68 1.54 (-.13)	1.57 1.34 (-.63)	2.16 1.51 (-.19)	3.48 1.29 (-.05)
NADIR	2.75 1.84 (-.12)	2.48 2.25 (.18)	2.77 2.05 (.47)	1.84 1.49 (.03)	2.92 2.20 (.72)	2.89 1.76 (.54)	3.69 1.57 (.16)
NARES	3.16 2.13 (.29)	1.63 1.30 (-.67)	2.17 1.84 (-.13)	1.71 1.44 (-.10)	1.68 1.43 (-.52)	2.11 1.40 (-.24)	3.54 1.44 (.01)
NAVE	3.98 2.37 (1.11)	2.76 1.85 (.46)	2.45 1.73 (.15)	2.25 1.69 (.44)	2.77 1.86 (.57)	2.34 1.56 (-.01)	3.70 1.32 (.17)
NELAT	2.75 1.95 (-.12)	1.70 1.53 (-.60)	2.46 2.03 (.16)	1.29 .93 (-.52)	1.37 1.07 (-.83)	2.46 1.65 (.11)	3.55 1.36 (.02)
NEROL	2.39 1.79 (-.48)	1.82 1.60 (-.48)	1.57 1.33 (-.73)	1.42 1.12 (-.39)	1.61 1.27 (-.59)	2.10 1.30 (-.25)	3.51 1.18F (-.02)
NIDUS	2.92 2.16 (.05)	2.07 1.83 (-.23)	1.79 1.42 (-.51)	1.33 .91 (-.48)	1.59 1.30 (-.61)	1.89 1.24 (-.46)	3.31 1.07 (-.22)
NISUS	3.33 2.16 (.46)	2.05 1.75 (-.25)	2.17 1.68 (-.13)	1.60 1.41 (-.21)	1.44 1.20 (-.76)	2.21 1.62 (-.14)	3.38 1.51 (-.15)
NITON	2.80 1.93 (-.07)	1.95 1.69 (-.35)	1.86 1.37 (-.44)	1.35 1.11 (-.46)	1.72 1.50 (-.51)	2.08 1.43 (-.27)	3.48 1.26 (-.05)
NOLL	3.97 2.12 (1.10)	2.91 2.01 (.61)	3.12 2.03 (.82)	2.13 1.72 (.32)	2.95 2.07 (.75)	2.94 1.63 (.59)	3.79 1.63 (.26)
PAEAN	2.77 2.04 (-.10)	2.55 2.13 (.25)	1.98 1.53 (-.32)	1.78 1.33 (-.03)	2.07 1.77 (-.13)	2.69 1.62 (.34)	3.83 1.20 (.30)

	CON M SD	IMG M SD	CAT M SD	MNG M SD	FAM M SD	NOA M SD	PLS M SD
PALL	3.58 2.19 (.71)	2.65 1.83 (.35)	2.43 1.58 (.13)	2.31 1.60 (.50)	3.48 2.19 (1.28)	2.48 1.34 (.13)	3.00 1.26 (-.53)
PARRY	3.07 1.92 (.20)	3.22 2.27 (.92)	2.60 1.56 (.30)	2.13 1.72 (.32)	2.83 2.13 (.63)	2.80 1.81 (.45)	4.08 1.36 (.55)
PAVIS	2.79 2.01 (-.08)	1.88 1.64 (-.42)	2.42 1.92 (.12)	1.39 1.14 (-.42)	1.78 1.64 (-.42)	2.33 1.59 (-.02)	3.51 1.12M (-.02)
PAX	2.70 1.89 (-.17)	2.71 2.07 (.41)	2.43 1.71 (.13)	2.82 2.21 (1.01)	3.38 2.38 (1.18)	2.30 1.46 (-.05)	4.45 1.51 (.92)
PEAH	2.20 1.79 (-.67)	1.98 1.85 (-.32)	2.02 1.73 (-.28)	1.33 1.03 (-.48)	1.40 1.20 (-.80)	1.81 1.26 (-.54)	3.43 1.37 (-.10)
PERSE	3.09 2.04 (.22)	2.65 2.20 (.35)	2.55 1.67 (.25)	2.10 1.54 (.29)	2.61 2.17 (.41)	2.21 1.21 (-.14)	3.66 1.18 (.13)
PEWIT	2.90 1.91 (.03)	2.23 1.68 (-.07)	1.90 1.40 (-.40)	1.34 .71 (-.47)	1.70 1.49 (-.50)	2.02 1.50 (-.33)	3.62 1.21 (.09)
PICUL	3.04 2.24 (.17)	1.68 1.57 (-.62)	2.53 2.13 (.23)	1.61 1.40 (-.20)	1.38 1.16 (-.82)	1.95 1.38 (-.40)	3.49 1.26 (-.04)
PIQUE	3.25 1.94 (.38)	2.87 1.99 (.57)	2.51 1.72 (.21)	1.98 1.27 (.17)	2.74 1.91 (.54)	2.79 1.64 (.44)	3.52 1.17F (-.01)
PLAICE	3.10 2.03 (.23)	2.20 1.75 (-.10)	1.83 1.11 (-.47)	1.65 1.31 (-.16)	2.23 1.88 (.03)	2.22 1.34 (-.13)	3.59 1.26 (.06)
PLAIT	3.49 2.16 (.62)	3.13 2.17 (.83)	3.08 2.04 (.78)	2.23 1.42 (.42)	2.90 2.09 (.70)	2.54 1.46 (.19)	3.69 1.40 (.16)
POLEF	2.59 1.55 (-.28)	1.55 1.31 (-.75)	1.80 1.29 (-.50)	1.46 1.07 (-.35)	1.65 1.54 (-.55)	2.22 1.63 (-.13)	3.31 1.34 (-.22)
POMMEL	3.19 2.02 (.32)	2.74 1.94 (.44)	2.62 1.92 (.32)	2.08 1.42 (.27)	3.02 2.19 (.82)	2.38 1.30 (.03)	3.63 1.33 (.10)
PROTOCOL	2.60 1.75 (-.27)	2.52 1.78 (.22)	2.29 1.50 (-.01)	2.29 1.30 (.48)	3.80 2.02 (1.60)	2.90 1.78 (.55)	3.04 1.32 (-.49)
PUGH	3.32 2.21 (.45)	2.16 1.78 (-.14)	2.66 1.86 (.36)	2.10 1.77 (.29)	2.64 2.29 (.44)	2.52 1.78 (.17)	2.96 1.42 (-.57)
PUIGNE	2.76 1.93 (-.11)	1.74 1.43 (-.56)	2.36 1.98 (.06)	1.53 1.13 (-.28)	1.42 .94 (-.78)	2.43 1.44 (.08)	3.39 1.32 (-.14)
PURL	3.09 2.19 (.22)	3.04 2.30 (.74)	2.22 1.60 (-.09)	1.95 1.43 (.14)	2.40 1.94 (.20)	2.25 1.61 (-.10)	3.79 1.28 (.26)
QUAICH	2.47 1.76 (-.40)	1.95 1.84 (-.35)	1.75 1.30 (-.55)	1.50 1.11 (-.31)	1.59 1.33 (-.61)	2.26 1.44 (-.09)	3.68 1.20 (.15)
QUEAN	3.73 2.34 (.86)	2.57 2.27 (.27)	2.49 2.05 (.19)	1.95 1.73 (.14)	2.00 1.92 (-.20)	3.21 1.99 (.86)	3.83 1.42M (.30)
QUIRE	2.29 1.58 (-.58)	2.34 1.79 (.04)	2.42 1.75 (.12)	1.97 1.43 (.16)	2.53 1.97 (.33)	2.08 1.26 (-.27)	3.62 .97 (.09)
RATAL	2.75 1.90 (-.12)	1.87 1.43 (-.43)	1.74 1.13 (-.56)	1.78 1.45 (-.03)	1.93 1.71 (-.27)	2.44 1.66 (.09)	3.27 1.07 (-.26)
RAZE	3.32 1.97 (.45)	2.65 1.80 (.35)	2.88 1.78 (.58)	2.77 1.78 (.96)	3.55 1.88 (1.35)	2.83 1.61 (.48)	2.75 1.49M (-.78)
REBEC	2.25 1.56 (-.62)	2.18 1.81 (-.12)	1.86 1.41 (-.44)	1.51 1.40 (-.30)	1.66 1.31 (-.54)	2.25 1.60 (-.10)	3.34 1.41 (-.19)
REBUS	2.95 1.94 (.08)	1.95 1.38 (-.35)	2.60 1.90 (.30)	1.74 1.57 (-.07)	2.05 1.55 (-.15)	2.13 1.48 (-.22)	3.19 1.46 (-.34)
REMEX	2.42 1.73 (-.45)	2.16 1.81 (-.14)	2.03 1.72 (-.27)	1.88 1.62 (.07)	1.63 1.30 (-.57)	2.16 1.49 (-.19)	3.89 1.27 (.36)
REPLETE	3.00 1.89 (.13)	2.79 1.91 (.49)	2.80 2.03 (.50)	2.65 1.71 (.84)	3.40 1.97 (1.20)	3.14 1.62 (.79)	3.70 1.41 (.17)
RHUMB	2.81 2.01 (-.06)	1.93 1.66 (-.37)	1.72 1.42 (-.58)	1.50 1.05 (-.31)	2.00 1.63 (-.20)	2.03 1.36 (-.32)	3.44 1.25 (-.09)

	CON		IMG		CAT		MNG		FAM		NOA		PLS	
	M	SD	M	SD	M	SD	M	SD	M	SD	M	SD	M	SD
ROTE	2.91	1.83	2.58	1.90	2.77	1.75	2.35	1.44	3.23	1.88	2.44	1.30	3.21	1.25
	(.04)		(.28)		(.47)		(.54)		(1.03)		(.09)		(-.32)	
SAGACITY	2.07	1.36	2.26	1.74	2.49	1.97	2.26	1.38	2.46	1.77	2.82	1.71	3.75	1.55
	(-.80)		(-.04)		(.19)		(.45)		(.26)		(.47)		(.22)	
SALEP	2.83	2.02	2.05	1.89	2.53	2.03	1.74	1.49	1.63	1.59	2.43	1.56	3.51	1.43M
	(-.04)		(-.25)		(-.23)		(-.07)		(-.57)		(.08)		(-.02)	
SALOL	2.65	1.85	2.00	1.61	1.72	1.23	1.54	1.23	1.60	1.35	2.14	1.47	3.55	1.21
	(-.22)		(-.30)		(-.58)		(-.27)		(-.60)		(-.21)		(.02)	
SAVANT	2.49	1.81	1.89	1.70	1.79	1.54	1.43	1.30	2.13	1.76	1.97	1.25	3.68	1.44
	(-.38)		(-.41)		(-.51)		(-.38)		(-.07)		(-.38)		(.15)	
SENATA	3.48	2.22	2.68	1.98	2.88	1.90	1.78	1.62	2.14	1.84	2.41	1.71	4.27	1.45
	(.61)		(.38)		(.58)		(-.03)		(-.06)		(.06)		(.74)	
SIGIL	2.83	2.12	2.25	2.03	2.27	1.82	1.59	1.25	1.67	1.57	2.45	1.46	3.38	1.06
	(-.04)		(-.05)		(-.03)		(-.23)		(-.53)		(.10)		(-.15)	
SLOE	2.96	2.14	2.70	2.10	2.62	2.00	2.02	1.58	2.59	1.94	2.44	1.44	3.61	1.42
	(.09)		(.40)		(.32)		(.21)		(.39)		(.09)		(.08)	
SONE	2.34	1.69	1.96	1.62	1.68	1.28	1.52	1.13	2.10	1.67	2.02	1.20	3.70	1.04
	(-.53)		(-.34)		(-.62)		(-.29)		(-.10)		(-.33)		(.17)	
STAIT	3.04	1.99	2.45	1.85	2.53	1.76	1.97	1.51	2.81	2.10	2.48	1.59	3.62	1.17
	(.17)		(.15)		(.23)		(.16)		(.61)		(.13)		(.09)	
STANZE	3.09	1.88	2.70	1.97	2.24	1.58	2.12	1.42	3.27	2.11	2.17	1.21	3.55	1.13
	(.22)		(.40)		(-.06)		(.31)		(1.07)		(-.18)		(.02)	
SUCCOR	3.23	1.89	2.78	2.18	2.63	1.76	2.13	1.66	2.73	1.89	3.02	1.77	3.77	1.39M
	(.36)		(.48)		(.33)		(.32)		(.53)		(.67)		(.24)	
SURAL	2.78	1.97	2.25	1.93	2.03	1.66	1.52	.95	2.18	1.60	2.23	1.36	3.63	1.03
	(-.09)		(-.05)		(-.27)		(-.29)		(-.02)		(-.12)		(.10)	
SWAGE	2.88	1.87	2.28	1.90	2.55	1.69	2.03	1.62	2.23	1.64	2.00	1.20	3.31	1.38
	(.01)		(-.02)		(.25)		(.22)		(.03)		(-.35)		(-.22)	
SYDAH	2.98	2.18	2.30	2.02	2.29	1.82	1.55	1.33	1.67	1.54	2.30	1.58	3.40	1.40
	(.11)		(.00)		(-.01)		(-.26)		(-.53)		(-.05)		(-.13)	
TAC	3.04	2.02	2.93	2.32	2.72	1.94	2.32	1.47	3.32	2.22	2.07	1.26	3.34	1.14
	(.17)		(.63)		(.42)		(.51)		(1.12)		(-.28)		(-.19)	
TACET	3.10	1.92	2.28	1.71	2.72	1.84	1.81	1.29	2.25	1.58	2.68	1.69	3.87	1.10
	(.23)		(-.02)		(.42)		(.00)		(.05)		(.33)		(.34)	
TALUK	2.53	1.98	2.24	2.01	2.23	1.92	1.78	1.53	1.59	1.53	2.16	1.42	3.45	1.02
	(-.34)		(-.06)		(-.07)		(-.03)		(-.61)		(-.19)		(-.08)	
TAPIS	3.08	2.18	1.87	1.72	1.93	1.56	1.41	1.28	1.92	1.57	2.17	1.42	3.32	1.33
	(.21)		(-.43)		(-.37)		(-.40)		(-.28)		(-.18)		(-.21)	
TAROP	2.48	1.76	2.34	1.80	2.40	1.87	1.54	1.15	1.68	1.54	2.16	1.28	3.55	1.11
	(-.39)		(.04)		(.10)		(-.27)		(-.52)		(-.19)		(.02)	
TEMERITY	2.88	1.86	2.38	1.93	2.25	1.70	2.30	1.66	3.08	2.14	2.77	1.69	3.23	1.52
	(.01)		(.08)		(-.05)		(.49)		(.88)		(.42)		(-.30)	
THROE	2.36	1.79	2.93	2.18	2.53	1.64	1.98	1.63	2.79	1.83	2.41	1.50	3.29	1.25
	(-.51)		(.63)		(.23)		(.17)		(.59)		(.06)		(-.24)	
TILUS	2.45	1.68	2.41	2.01	2.35	1.88	1.55	1.23	1.62	1.20	2.18	1.40	3.59	1.17
	(-.42)		(.11)		(.05)		(-.26)		(-.58)		(-.17)		(.06)	
TITER	3.18	2.17	2.96	1.99	2.58	1.85	2.48	2.04	2.54	2.18	2.57	1.62	3.85	1.27
	(.31)		(.66)		(.28)		(.67)		(.34)		(.22)		(.32)	
TOLAN	2.33	1.52	2.14	1.74	2.38	1.87	2.00	1.34	1.91	1.56	2.08	1.20	3.49	1.06
	(-.54)		(-.16)		(.08)		(.19)		(-.29)		(-.27)		(-.04)	
TREY	3.85	2.38	2.81	2.02	2.34	1.91	1.64	1.21	3.30	2.38	2.41	1.53	3.42	1.24
	(.98)		(.51)		(.04)		(-.17)		(1.10)		(.06)		(-.11)	
TUN	2.07	1.37	2.29	1.93	1.68	1.33	1.83	1.42	2.15	1.82	1.93	1.14	3.32	1.15
	(-.80)		(-.01)		(-.62)		(.02)		(-.05)		(-.42)		(-.21)	

	CON M	CON SD	IMG M	IMG SD	CAT M	CAT SD	MNG M	MNG SD	FAM M	FAM SD	NOA M	NOA SD	PLS M	PLS SD
USURP	2.56	1.96	2.56	1.70	2.80	2.07	2.26	1.56	2.88	2.15	2.81	1.56	3.10	1.35
	(-.31)		(.26)		(.50)		(.45)		(.68)		(.46)		(-.43)	
VARUR	2.70	1.95	1.64	1.28	2.23	1.91	1.48	1.24	1.27	.97	1.92	1.48	3.55	1.47
	(-.17)		(-.66)		(-.07)		(-.33)		(-.93)		(-.43)		(.02)	
VINIM	2.90	2.16	1.89	1.51	2.73	1.93	1.54	1.30	1.89	1.57	2.68	1.88	3.12	1.50
	(.03)		(-.41)		(.43)		(-.27)		(-.31)		(.33)		(-.41)	
VUMAL	2.63	1.80	2.05	1.81	1.73	1.47	1.52	1.26	1.41	.95	1.97	1.24	3.53	1.11
	(-.24)		(-.25)		(-.57)		(-.29)		(-.79)		(-.38)		(.00)	
VUTAW	2.57	1.99	1.89	1.70	2.03	1.70	1.52	1.39	1.30	1.05	1.95	1.48	3.41	1.57
	(-.30)		(-.41)		(-.27)		(-.29)		(-.90)		(-.40)		(-.12)	
WAMUS	2.72	1.75	2.07	1.72	2.48	1.95	1.54	1.34	1.63	1.30	2.51	1.83	3.63	1.38
	(-.15)		(-.23)		(.18)		(-.27)		(-.57)		(.16)		(.10)	
WHEET	3.84	2.36	2.75	2.09	2.41	1.96	1.90	1.33	2.65	2.31	2.75	1.81	3.80	1.08
	(.97)		(.45)		(.11)		(.09)		(.45)		(.40)		(.27)	
WIKOU	3.11	2.27	1.98	1.78	2.15	1.73	1.73	1.52	1.30	.89	2.53	1.83	3.80	1.29
	(.24)		(-.32)		(-.15)		(-.08)		(-.90)		(.18)		(.27)	
WILER	3.04	1.83	2.20	1.61	2.38	1.62	1.53	.95	2.23	1.61	2.10	1.39	3.63	1.19
	(.17)		(-.10)		(.08)		(-.28)		(.03)		(-.25)		(.10)	
WITAN	2.63	2.04	1.70	1.45	1.78	1.51	1.54	1.27	1.84	1.67	2.22	1.46	3.72	1.27
	(-.24)		(-.60)		(-.52)		(-.27)		(-.36)		(-.13)		(.19)	
WYDEN	2.49	1.76	1.88	1.56	1.72	1.33	1.77	1.38	1.63	1.11	1.98	1.36	4.03	1.09F
	(-.38)		(-.42)		(-.58)		(-.04)		(-.57)		(-.37)		(.50)	
XABIN	2.59	1.95	1.98	1.80	1.61	1.23	1.30	.79	1.42	1.27	1.98	1.41	3.58	1.41
	(-.28)		(-.32)		(-.69)		(-.51)		(-.78)		(-.37)		(.05)	
XILOS	2.95	1.85	1.95	1.65	2.38	2.06	1.50	1.38	1.35	1.09	2.38	1.61	3.97	1.56M
	(.08)		(-.35)		(.08)		(-.31)		(-.85)		(.03)		(.44)	
XUBER	2.25	1.78	2.09	1.84	2.24	1.82	1.44	1.22	1.45	1.39	2.13	1.63	3.61	1.28
	(-.62)		(-.21)		(-.06)		(-.37)		(-.75)		(-.22)		(.08)	
XYDER	2.83	1.95	1.95	1.81	1.79	1.50	1.26	.91	1.45	1.22	2.43	1.73	3.39	1.36
	(-.04)		(-.35)		(-.52)		(-.55)		(-.75)		(.03)		(-.14)	
XYZAR	2.24	1.65	1.46	1.12	2.60	2.32	1.27	1.06	1.15	.68	2.11	1.84	3.34	1.59
	(-.63)		(-.84)		(.30)		(-.54)		(-1.05)		(-.24)		(-.19)	
YOLIF	2.35	1.87	2.18	1.94	1.88	1.73	1.53	1.21	1.38	1.11	2.13	1.56	3.56	1.23F
	(-.52)		(-.12)		(-.42)		(-.28)		(-.82)		(-.22)		(.03)	
YUROR	2.63	1.86	1.95	1.61	1.67	1.29	1.29	.93	1.47	1.31	1.74	1.14	3.35	1.16
	(-.24)		(-.35)		(-.52)		(-.52)		(-.73)		(-.61)		(-.18)	
YUVAL	2.18	1.73	2.17	1.85	2.13	1.68	1.49	1.30	1.55	1.52	2.15	1.54	3.61	1.27M
	(-.69)		(-.13)		(-.17)		(-.32)		(-.65)		(-.20)		(.08)	
ZABER	3.10	2.17	2.77	2.14	1.87	1.40	1.62	1.32	1.82	1.64	2.27	1.32	3.90	1.47
	(.23)		(.47)		(-.43)		(-.19)		(-.38)		(-.08)		(.37)	
ZARAL	2.70	1.88	1.53	1.26	2.03	1.85	1.48	1.32	1.28	.95	2.05	1.68	3.42	1.33
	(-.17)		(-.77)		(-.27)		(-.33)		(-.92)		(-.30)		(-.11)	
ZEBEL	3.04	2.11	2.05	1.62	2.53	1.90	1.69	1.49	1.62	1.37	2.54	1.84	3.85	1.25
	(.17)		(-.25)		(.23)		(-.12)		(-.58)		(.19)		(.32)	
ZESAM	2.72	2.00	2.09	1.80	1.66	1.22	1.43	1.09	1.51	1.34	2.05	1.42	3.84	1.23
	(-.15)		(-.21)		(-.64)		(-.38)		(-.69)		(-.30)		(.31)	
ZIROL	2.66	1.79	1.65	1.44	1.92	1.65	1.33	1.17	1.53	1.39	2.28	1.69	3.58	1.45
	(-.21)		(-.65)		(-.38)		(-.48)		(-.67)		(-.07)		(.05)	
ZOBEL	2.50	1.76	2.49	2.08	2.77	2.09	1.74	1.49	1.43	1.29	2.20	1.55	3.87	1.16
	(-.37)		(.19)		(.47)		(-.07)		(-.77)		(-.15)		(.34)	
ZOBIT	2.89	2.22	2.00	1.68	1.51	1.22	1.92	1.65	1.31	.88	2.36	1.58	3.50	1.28F
	(.02)		(-.30)		(-.79)		(.11)		(-.89)		(.01)		(-.03)	
ZOLAR	2.80	1.75	2.11	1.78	1.71	1.23	1.49	1.04	2.38	2.08	2.21	1.51	3.62	1.39F
	(-.07)		(-.19)		(-.59)		(-.32)		(.18)		(-.14)		(.09)	

	CON		IMG		CAT		MNG		FAM		NOA		PLS	
	M	SD	M	SD	M	SD	M	SD	M	SD	M	SD	M	SD
ZONAD	2.82	2.07	2.28	1.96	2.27	1.71	1.58	1.27	1.57	1.27	2.18	1.70	3.47	1.49M
	(−.05)		(−.02)		(−.03)		(−.23)		(−.63)		(−.17)		(−.06)	
ZONER	3.35	1.95	2.71	2.00	2.62	1.85	1.76	1.13	3.85	2.15	2.58	1.75	3.37	1.21
	(.48)		(.41)		(.32)		(−.05)		(1.65)		(.23)		(−.16)	
ZORON	2.82	1.96	2.04	1.80	2.30	2.03	1.47	1.33	1.57	1.30	2.18	1.64	3.63	1.43
	(−.05)		(−.26)		(.00)		(−.34)		(−.63)		(−.17)		(.10)	
ZUBER	2.76	1.92	1.92	1.58	2.13	1.80	1.80	1.74	1.45	1.23	2.59	1.78	3.69	1.31
	(−.11)		(−.38)		(−.17)		(−.01)		(−.75)		(.24)		(.16)	
ZUMAP	2.30	1.67	1.64	1.24	2.07	1.86	1.52	1.37	1.33	1.06	2.10	1.57	3.28	1.56M
	(−.57)		(−.66)		(−.23)		(−.29)		(−.87)		(−.25)		(−.25)	
ZUREN	2.50	2.02	1.59	1.30	2.02	1.87	1.61	1.54	1.25	.72	2.11	1.74	3.32	1.45
	(−.37)		(−.71)		(−.29)		(−.20)		(−.95)		(−.24)		(−.21)	

CLUSTER 2

	CON		IMG		CAT		MNG		FAM		NOA		PLS	
	M	SD	M	SD	M	SD	M	SD	M	SD	M	SD	M	SD
A	1.97	1.80	2.07	1.69	2.90	2.40	2.60	2.10	6.77	1.00	2.54	2.25	4.03	1.63F
	(-.72)		(-.88)		(.14)		(-.78)		(.85)		(-.41)		(.20)	
ABLE	2.98	1.80	2.79	1.83	2.95	1.69	3.55	1.78	6.27	1.30	3.30	1.75	5.05	1.29
	(.29)		(-.16)		(.19)		(.17)		(.35)		(.35)		(1.22)	
ABOUT	2.23	1.89	2.28	1.44	2.42	1.56	3.00	1.95	6.35	1.42	2.84	1.74	3.42	1.18
	(-.46)		(-.67)		(-.34)		(-.38)		(.43)		(-.11)		(-.41)	
ACCORD	2.95	1.84	2.42	1.66	2.41	1.27	3.07	1.61	5.56	1.67	2.68	1.49	3.94	1.09
	(.26)		(-.53)		(-.35)		(-.31)		(-.36)		(-.27)		(.11)	
ACKNOWLEDGE	2.86	1.92	3.32	2.06	3.20	1.45	4.26	1.61	5.84	1.47	3.21	1.70	4.34	1.52
	(.17)		(.37)		(.44)		(.88)		(-.08)		(.26)		(.51)	
ADDS	2.98	2.02	3.65	2.07	3.40	2.11	3.97	2.05	6.20	1.35	3.11	1.64	4.12	1.32
	(.29)		(.70)		(.64)		(.59)		(.28)		(.16)		(.29)	
ADMONISH	2.65	2.00	2.96	1.76	2.35	1.27	2.92	1.80	4.15	2.07	3.45	1.69	3.34	1.28M
	(-.04)		(.01)		(-.41)		(-.46)		(-1.77)		(.50)		(-.49)	
ADORN	3.35	2.02	3.64	1.87	3.15	1.79	3.55	1.43	5.15	1.70	3.15	1.48	4.27	1.28F
	(.66)		(.69)		(.39)		(.17)		(-.77)		(.20)		(.44)	
AFTER	2.38	1.65	2.11	1.41	2.47	1.67	3.02	1.63	6.49	1.04	2.03	1.08	3.86	1.16
	(-.31)		(-.84)		(-.29)		(-.36)		(.57)		(-.92)		(.03)	
AGGRESS	2.67	1.80	2.64	1.92	2.12	1.42	2.44	1.69	4.25	2.20	2.69	1.91	3.00	1.26
	(-.02)		(-.31)		(-.64)		(-.94)		(-1.67)		(-.26)		(-.83)	
AH	2.49	2.01	3.25	2.37	2.90	2.07	3.22	2.18	5.30	1.99	2.69	2.16	4.77	1.78F
	(-.20)		(.30)		(.04)		(-.16)		(-.62)		(-.26)		(.94)	
AIM	3.40	1.83	3.77	2.01	3.09	1.71	3.83	1.77	5.79	1.52	3.02	1.67	4.16	1.28
	(.71)		(.82)		(.33)		(.45)		(-.13)		(.07)		(.33)	
ALLOW	2.64	1.91	3.67	2.08	2.98	1.41	3.68	1.74	5.78	1.59	2.82	1.42	4.08	1.57F
	(-.05)		(.72)		(.22)		(.30)		(-.14)		(-.13)		(.25)	
ALSO	1.90	1.44	2.58	1.90	2.70	1.85	3.33	1.96	6.26	1.36	2.72	1.88	3.94	1.08
	(-.79)		(-.37)		(-.06)		(-.05)		(.34)		(-.23)		(.11)	
ALTHOUGH	2.14	1.83	2.00	1.60	2.20	1.55	2.70	1.83	6.07	1.35	2.76	1.87	3.57	.94
	(-.55)		(-.95)		(-.56)		(-.68)		(.15)		(-.19)		(-.26)	
ALWAYS	2.45	1.88	3.00	2.10	2.92	2.07	4.21	1.83	6.33	1.34	3.18	2.05	3.79	1.68
	(-.24)		(.05)		(.16)		(.83)		(.41)		(.23)		(-.04)	
AM	2.55	2.06	2.36	1.89	2.10	1.87	2.42	1.64	6.46	1.12	2.60	2.05	4.11	1.63F
	(-.14)		(-.59)		(-.66)		(-.96)		(.54)		(-.35)		(.28)	
AND	2.16	1.79	2.36	1.76	2.63	1.93	2.90	1.93	6.53	1.20	2.61	2.08	3.87	1.12
	(-.53)		(-.59)		(-.13)		(-.48)		(.61)		(-.34)		(.04)	
ANY	2.18	1.69	2.00	1.48	2.05	1.47	2.72	1.69	6.16	1.40	2.48	1.88	3.85	1.15F
	(-.51)		(-.95)		(-.71)		(-.66)		(.24)		(-.47)		(.02)	
APPEAR	2.67	1.64	3.16	1.91	3.42	1.83	3.36	1.71	5.98	1.44	2.95	1.51	4.26	.95
	(-.02)		(.21)		(.66)		(-.02)		(.06)		(.00)		(.43)	
APPRAISE	2.75	1.82	3.00	1.71	2.98	1.59	3.82	1.84	5.33	1.57	3.38	1.50	4.13	1.23
	(.06)		(.05)		(.22)		(.44)		(-.59)		(.43)		(.30)	
APT	1.79	1.36	2.89	1.81	3.07	1.79	3.48	1.82	5.02	1.91	2.33	1.45	4.19	1.47
	(-.90)		(-.06)		(.31)		(.10)		(-.90)		(-.62)		(.36)	
ARE	1.91	1.44	2.56	1.95	2.77	1.93	2.77	1.82	6.38	1.37	2.75	2.01	3.98	1.15
	(-.78)		(-.39)		(.01)		(-.61)		(.46)		(-.20)		(.15)	
AS	1.54	1.24	2.37	1.90	2.20	1.63	2.38	1.79	6.32	1.34	2.28	1.62	3.52	1.05
	(-1.15)		(-.58)		(-.56)		(-1.00)		(.40)		(-.67)		(-.31)	
ASTUTE	2.37	1.57	2.55	1.46	2.57	1.73	2.81	1.62	4.09	2.03	2.87	1.77	4.09	1.37
	(-.32)		(-.40)		(-.19)		(-.57)		(-1.83)		(-.08)		(.26)	
AT	1.90	1.68	2.28	1.88	1.98	1.64	2.58	2.06	6.65	.99	2.10	1.40	3.68	1.32
	(-.79)		(-.67)		(-.78)		(-.80)		(.73)		(-.85)		(-.15)	
AVID	2.71	1.65	2.83	1.71	2.50	1.59	3.03	1.80	4.27	1.95	3.00	1.40	4.15	1.34
	(.02)		(-.12)		(-.26)		(-.35)		(-1.65)		(.05)		(.32)	

	CON		IMG		CAT		MNG		FAM		NOA		PLS	
	M	SD	M	SD	M	SD	M	SD	M	SD	M	SD	M	SD
AWAY	2.53	1.85	2.66	1.81	2.83	1.66	3.84	1.87	6.47	1.07	2.90	1.74	4.25	1.64
	(-.16)		(-.29)		(.07)		(.46)		(.55)		(-.05)		(.42)	
BE	2.21	1.56	2.84	2.36	2.13	1.65	3.25	2.21	6.53	1.23	3.00	2.24	4.25	1.28F
	(-.48)		(-.11)		(-.63)		(-.13)		(.61)		(.05)		(.42)	
BECAME	2.69	1.99	2.56	1.86	2.55	1.89	3.34	1.89	6.05	1.60	3.00	1.91	4.35	1.52F
	(.00)		(-.39)		(-.21)		(-.04)		(.13)		(.05)		(.52)	
BECAUSE	1.92	1.62	2.61	2.12	1.97	1.25	3.10	1.97	6.48	1.20	3.08	2.13	3.70	1.34
	(-.77)		(-.34)		(-.79)		(-.28)		(.56)		(.13)		(-.13)	
BEEN	2.11	1.55	2.16	1.70	1.97	1.29	2.70	1.69	6.41	1.30	2.20	1.59	3.71	1.18
	(-.58)		(-.79)		(-.79)		(-.68)		(.49)		(-.75)		(-.12)	
BEFORE	2.57	1.73	2.66	1.96	2.87	1.69	3.95	1.87	6.23	1.43	2.48	1.57	3.50	1.30
	(-.12)		(-.29)		(.11)		(.57)		(.31)		(-.47)		(-.33)	
BEING	2.30	1.77	3.27	1.81	2.87	1.68	3.61	1.86	6.24	1.28	4.22	2.31	4.56	1.28F
	(-.39)		(.32)		(.11)		(.23)		(.32)		(1.27)		(.73)	
BOTH	3.18	1.96	3.07	2.05	2.62	1.84	3.20	1.56	6.52	.94	2.82	1.64	4.44	1.28F
	(.49)		(.12)		(-.14)		(-.18)		(.60)		(-.13)		(.61)	
BUT	2.23	1.89	1.91	1.67	2.41	1.71	2.25	1.51	6.43	1.32	1.92	1.42	3.09	1.39
	(-.46)		(-1.04)		(-.35)		(-1.13)		(.51)		(-1.03)		(-.74)	
BY	2.04	1.52	2.43	1.77	2.40	1.88	2.74	1.77	6.15	1.56	2.31	1.64	3.61	1.11
	(-.65)		(-.52)		(-.36)		(-.64)		(.23)		(-.64)		(-.22)	
CAME	2.61	1.82	2.82	1.57	2.68	1.82	3.73	1.97	6.37	1.40	3.25	1.69	4.49	1.36
	(-.08)		(-.13)		(-.08)		(.35)		(.45)		(.30)		(.66)	
CAN	3.61	2.37	3.47	2.30	3.47	2.05	3.27	1.74	6.75	.73	2.95	1.81	4.34	1.29F
	(.92)		(.52)		(.71)		(-.11)		(.83)		(.00)		(.51)	
CAUSE	2.90	1.83	2.66	1.78	2.68	1.62	3.67	1.68	6.07	1.30	3.30	1.84	3.94	1.29
	(.21)		(-.29)		(-.08)		(.29)		(.15)		(.35)		(.11)	
CHOOSE	3.04	1.93	2.93	1.84	3.28	1.92	3.61	1.76	6.08	1.33	2.97	1.70	4.00	1.37
	(.35)		(-.02)		(.52)		(.23)		(.16)		(.02)		(.17)	
COGNITION	2.66	1.85	3.15	2.21	2.60	1.24	3.79	1.66	5.06	1.74	3.98	1.90	4.46	1.42
	(-.03)		(.20)		(-.16)		(.41)		(-.86)		(1.03)		(.63)	
COMPLACENT	2.64	1.77	3.59	2.04	2.70	1.71	3.47	1.94	4.56	2.03	3.05	1.70	4.14	1.39M
	(-.05)		(.64)		(-.06)		(.09)		(-1.36)		(.10)		(.31)	
CONDESCENSION	2.81	1.91	2.89	2.12	2.50	1.61	3.00	1.82	4.05	1.87	2.89	1.65	2.93	1.51M
	(.12)		(-.06)		(-.26)		(-.38)		(-1.87)		(-.06)		(-.90)	
CONJUNCTION	2.84	1.92	3.55	1.97	3.90	1.72	3.53	1.97	5.34	1.78	3.39	1.63	3.98	1.06
	(.15)		(.60)		(1.14)		(.15)		(-.58)		(.44)		(.15)	
DECEIT	2.84	1.69	2.93	1.77	2.91	1.49	3.27	1.76	4.97	1.95	3.37	1.77	2.32	1.32M
	(.15)		(-.02)		(.15)		(-.11)		(-.95)		(.42)		(-1.51)	
DEPICT	2.58	1.62	3.10	1.70	3.00	1.66	3.72	1.71	5.15	1.78	3.23	1.54	3.75	1.35
	(-.11)		(.15)		(.24)		(.34)		(-.77)		(.28)		(-.08)	
DID	2.31	1.82	3.23	2.10	2.78	1.98	2.94	1.87	6.16	1.39	2.43	1.55	3.90	1.35
	(-.38)		(.28)		(.02)		(-.44)		(.24)		(-.52)		(.07)	
DIFFERENCE	2.75	1.84	3.02	1.92	2.60	1.63	3.92	1.86	6.29	1.38	3.88	2.05	4.01	1.55F
	(-.06)		(.07)		(-.16)		(.44)		(.37)		(.93)		(.18)	
DISAVOW	2.78	1.75	2.56	1.84	2.35	1.40	2.92	1.85	4.18	2.06	3.02	1.65	3.09	1.34
	(.06)		(-.39)		(-.41)		(-.46)		(-1.74)		(.07)		(-.74)	
DISTINCT	2.43	1.42	3.58	1.89	3.07	1.59	3.97	1.73	5.64	1.64	2.79	1.59	4.47	1.45F
	(-.26)		(.63)		(.31)		(.59)		(-.28)		(-.16)		(.64)	
DO	2.72	1.69	2.70	1.88	2.30	1.78	3.25	1.84	6.58	.93	2.61	1.93	4.37	1.34F
	(.03)		(-.25)		(-.46)		(-.13)		(.66)		(-.34)		(.54)	
DONE	2.67	1.74	3.40	2.32	2.83	1.69	4.48	1.79	6.41	1.19	2.90	1.76	4.41	1.77
	(-.02)		(.45)		(-.07)		(1.10)		(.49)		(-.05)		(.58)	
DRAB	2.77	1.81	3.34	2.05	2.67	1.47	3.97	1.76	5.17	1.91	2.66	1.20	2.23	1.03
	(.08)		(.39)		(-.09)		(.59)		(-.75)		(-.29)		(-1.60)	

	CON		IMG		CAT		MNG		FAM		NOA		PLS	
	M	SD	M	SD	M	SD	M	SD	M	SD	M	SD	M	SD
EACH	2.64	1.77	3.14	2.22	2.85	1.76	3.50	1.84	6.29	1.27	3.10	1.89	3.94	1.37
	(-.05)		(.19)		(.09)		(.12)		(.37)		(.15)		(.11)	
ELABORATION	3.04	1.88	3.51	2.18	3.03	1.63	4.11	1.53	5.36	1.71	3.63	1.96	4.21	1.40
	(.35)		(.56)		(.27)		(.73)		(-.56)		(.68)		(.38)	
ELSE	2.18	1.62	1.83	1.19	2.02	1.35	2.69	1.70	6.20	1.48	2.30	1.35	3.69	1.15
	(-.51)		(-1.12)		(-.74)		(-.69)		(.28)		(-.65)		(-.14)	
ENDURING	3.24	1.77	3.67	1.95	2.90	1.52	3.77	1.39	5.75	1.50	3.52	1.91	4.22	1.53
	(.55)		(.72)		(.14)		(.39)		(-.17)		(.57)		(.39)	
ENOUGH	2.42	1.91	3.39	2.06	3.23	1.87	3.59	1.84	6.19	1.33	3.31	1.78	3.84	1.30
	(-.27)		(.44)		(.47)		(.21)		(.27)		(.36)		(.01)	
EVEN	2.79	1.93	3.25	2.01	3.02	1.98	4.11	1.95	6.47	1.16	3.05	1.76	4.25	1.04
	(.10)		(.30)		(.26)		(.73)		(.55)		(.10)		(.42)	
EVER	2.95	2.22	2.67	1.85	2.60	1.59	3.17	2.03	6.31	1.29	3.10	2.10	4.46	1.43
	(.26)		(-.28)		(-.16)		(-.21)		(.39)		(.15)		(.63)	
EVERY	2.60	1.82	2.82	1.88	2.52	1.50	3.90	1.83	6.36	1.21	3.08	1.94	3.86	1.43
	(-.09)		(-.13)		(-.24)		(.52)		(.44)		(.13)		(.42)	
EXCISE	2.67	1.69	2.81	1.93	2.78	1.68	3.07	1.82	4.30	2.09	2.63	1.10	2.93	1.25M
	(-.02)		(-.14)		(.02)		(-.31)		(-1.62)		(-.32)		(-.90)	
EXCUSF	3.13	2.14	2.93	2.00	3.10	1.76	3.57	1.34	5.76	1.49	3.30	1.96	3.16	1.17
	(.44)		(-.02)		(.34)		(.19)		(-.16)		(.35)		(-.67)	
FAULT	3.03	1.79	3.11	2.01	2.83	1.88	3.72	1.60	6.00	1.39	2.80	1.55	2.56	1.33
	(.34)		(.16)		(.07)		(.34)		(.08)		(-.15)		(-1.27)	
FEW	3.05	1.79	3.42	1.65	3.03	1.51	4.16	1.80	6.28	1.39	2.67	1.49	3.54	1.38M
	(.36)		(.47)		(.27)		(.78)		(.36)		(-.28)		(-.29)	
FIGMENT	3.44	2.11	3.14	1.80	3.15	1.68	3.65	1.62	5.38	1.92	3.16	1.63	3.62	1.50
	(.75)		(.19)		(.39)		(.27)		(-.54)		(.21)		(-.21)	
FOLLOWING	3.11	1.77	3.62	1.80	2.83	1.59	4.08	1.81	6.37	1.10	3.52	1.64	3.70	1.27M
	(.42)		(.67)		(.07)		(.70)		(.45)		(.57)		(-.13)	
FOLLY	2.96	1.79	3.09	1.86	2.57	1.61	3.21	1.44	5.21	1.75	2.85	1.64	3.72	1.53
	(.27)		(.14)		(-.19)		(-.17)		(-.71)		(-.10)		(-.11)	
FOR	2.41	1.91	2.07	1.36	2.34	1.56	2.44	1.65	6.33	1.27	2.39	1.75	3.72	1.11
	(-.28)		(-.88)		(-.42)		(-.94)		(.41)		(-.56)		(-.11)	
FORE	2.96	2.15	3.34	2.15	2.77	1.68	3.08	1.85	4.88	1.80	2.52	1.44	3.75	1.12M
	(.27)		(.39)		(.01)		(-.30)		(-1.04)		(-.43)		(-.08)	
FORTH	3.18	2.06	3.30	2.01	3.42	1.87	2.95	1.63	5.48	1.65	2.68	1.59	4.22	1.04
	(.49)		(.35)		(.66)		(-.43)		(-.44)		(-.27)		(.39)	
FROM	1.93	1.59	2.30	1.54	2.02	1.27	3.05	1.89	6.53	1.19	2.56	1.50	3.80	1.17
	(-.76)		(-.65)		(-.74)		(-.33)		(.61)		(-.39)		(-.03)	
FUNCTIONAL	2.68	1.64	2.82	1.79	3.00	1.74	3.94	1.63	5.82	1.60	3.54	1.80	3.99	1.44
	(-.01)		(-.13)		(.24)		(.56)		(-.10)		(.59)		(.16)	
FUNCTIONARY	2.97	2.00	2.74	1.90	2.92	1.57	3.71	1.70	4.78	2.02	3.21	1.65	4.13	1.37M
	(.28)		(-.21)		(.16)		(.33)		(-1.14)		(.26)		(.30)	
GAIN	3.29	1.79	3.00	1.77	3.03	1.74	3.90	1.58	6.19	1.18	2.70	1.54	4.45	1.22
	(.60)		(.05)		(.27)		(.52)		(.27)		(-.25)		(.62)	
GET	2.86	1.80	2.84	2.08	2.39	1.46	3.18	1.68	6.55	.96	3.03	1.84	3.95	1.31F
	(.17)		(-.11)		(-.37)		(-.20)		(.63)		(.08)		(.12)	
GONE	3.17	2.04	3.07	2.10	2.54	1.46	3.19	1.79	6.20	1.26	2.63	1.65	3.26	1.44M
	(.48)		(.12)		(-.22)		(-.19)		(.28)		(-.32)		(-.57)	
GOT	2.48	1.53	2.80	1.78	2.57	1.66	3.52	1.93	6.39	1.36	2.72	1.60	4.00	1.39
	(-.21)		(-.15)		(-.19)		(.14)		(.28)		(-.23)		(.17)	
GROWN	3.52	1.69	2.86	1.65	3.33	1.73	3.88	1.63	6.26	1.18	3.65	2.00	4.37	1.42
	(.83)		(-.09)		(.57)		(.50)		(.34)		(.70)		(.54)	
GUESSED	3.27	1.86	3.45	2.13	3.12	1.79	4.03	1.64	6.21	1.29	3.13	1.86	3.90	1.79
	(.58)		(.50)		(.36)		(.65)		(.29)		(.18)		(.07)	

	CON M	CON SD	IMG M	IMG SD	CAT M	CAT SD	MNG M	MNG SD	FAM M	FAM SD	NOA M	NOA SD	PLS M	PLS SD
HAD	2.49	2.02	2.90	1.89	2.67	1.87	3.23	1.94	6.44	.99	2.67	1.85	3.40	1.55
	(-.20)		(-.05)		(-.09)		(-.15)		(.52)		(-.28)		(-.43)	
HARDLY	2.19	1.67	2.54	1.94	2.25	1.31	3.00	1.45	5.69	1.69	2.75	1.58	3.28	1.20
	(-.50)		(-.41)		(-.51)		(-.38)		(-.23)		(-.20)		(-.55)	
HAS	2.63	1.84	2.65	1.93	2.37	1.63	2.83	1.71	6.59	1.04	2.34	1.55	3.65	1.12
	(-.06)		(-.30)		(-.39)		(-.55)		(.67)		(-.61)		(-.18)	
HAVE	2.47	1.88	3.02	1.98	2.92	1.97	3.31	1.99	6.20	1.53	2.72	1.77	4.34	1.32
	(-.22)		(.07)		(.16)		(-.07)		(.28)		(-.23)		(.51)	
HERE	2.81	1.99	2.96	1.95	2.60	1.59	3.03	1.80	6.43	1.13	2.61	1.89	4.03	1.35F
	(.12)		(.01)		(-.16)		(-.35)		(.51)		(-.34)		(.20)	
HIMSELF	2.81	1.89	3.11	1.79	3.20	2.15	3.65	2.07	6.43	1.18	2.87	1.71	4.25	1.56F
	(.12)		(.16)		(.44)		(.27)		(.51)		(-.08)		(.42)	
HINDERS	2.84	1.56	3.24	1.93	3.43	1.69	3.67	1.60	5.45	1.59	3.35	1.83	2.90	1.22
	(.15)		(.29)		(.67)		(.29)		(-.47)		(.40)		(-.93)	
HIS	3.16	2.09	3.35	2.13	3.39	2.02	4.23	2.16	6.58	1.03	2.87	1.77	4.37	1.40F
	(.47)		(.40)		(.63)		(.85)		(.66)		(-.08)		(.54)	
HOW	1.91	1.69	2.28	1.78	2.10	1.45	3.21	2.06	6.35	1.45	3.08	2.06	4.00	1.45
	(-.78)		(-.67)		(-.66)		(-.17)		(.43)		(.13)		(.17)	
HOWEVER	1.82	1.36	2.75	2.07	2.63	1.78	2.87	1.70	6.14	1.33	2.36	1.47	3.76	.74
	(-.87)		(-.20)		(-.13)		(-.51)		(.22)		(-.59)		(-.07)	
HYPNOTIC	3.16	1.92	3.61	1.99	3.28	1.67	3.45	1.58	5.41	1.78	3.28	1.58	3.84	1.56F
	(.47)		(.66)		(.52)		(.07)		(-.51)		(.33)		(.01)	
IF	2.00	1.78	2.34	1.96	2.25	1.89	2.78	1.92	6.43	1.26	3.33	2.23	3.46	1.56
	(-.69)		(-.61)		(-.51)		(-.60)		(.51)		(.38)		(-.37)	
IMPARTIAL	3.05	1.83	3.15	1.95	2.90	1.48	4.00	1.57	5.27	1.78	3.28	1.72	4.24	1.23
	(.36)		(.20)		(.14)		(.62)		(-.65)		(.33)		(.41)	
IMPOSSIBILITY	2.86	2.07	3.41	2.09	2.88	1.86	4.28	2.07	6.21	1.10	3.79	2.12	3.47	1.84M
	(.17)		(.46)		(.12)		(.90)		(.29)		(.84)		(-.36)	
IMPROPRIETY	2.42	1.65	3.00	2.02	2.75	1.54	2.98	1.71	4.10	2.11	3.07	1.49	3.48	1.41
	(-.27)		(.05)		(-.01)		(-.40)		(-1.82)		(.12)		(-.35)	
IN	2.74	1.87	3.59	2.14	3.02	2.06	4.13	2.12	6.52	1.07	2.84	1.75	4.48	1.62
	(.05)		(.64)		(.26)		(.75)		(.60)		(-.11)		(.65)	
INCOMPETENT	2.44	1.63	3.53	1.90	2.45	1.62	4.16	1.75	5.77	1.62	3.42	1.85	2.30	1.20M
	(-.25)		(.58)		(-.31)		(.78)		(-.15)		(.47)		(-1.53)	
INDIFFERENT	2.49	1.85	2.84	1.89	3.02	1.51	3.87	1.65	5.76	1.50	2.75	1.52	3.07	1.34
	(-.20)		(-.11)		(.26)		(.49)		(-.16)		(-.20)		(-.76)	
INDULGENT	2.68	1.85	3.11	1.96	3.07	1.76	3.67	1.62	4.87	1.81	3.55	1.88	3.69	1.68M
	(-.01)		(.16)		(.31)		(.29)		(-1.05)		(.60)		(-.14)	
INNATE	3.04	2.15	2.95	1.97	2.83	1.83	2.90	1.63	5.25	1.80	3.56	1.95	4.03	1.36F
	(.35)		(.00)		(.07)		(-.48)		(-.67)		(.61)		(.20)	
INTENTS	2.82	1.90	2.67	1.80	2.70	1.78	3.85	1.70	5.33	1.90	3.98	1.89	4.12	1.43
	(.13)		(-.28)		(-.06)		(.47)		(-.59)		(1.03)		(.29)	
INTO	3.02	2.09	2.61	1.77	2.14	1.43	2.58	1.51	6.18	1.26	2.41	1.66	3.79	1.18
	(.33)		(-.34)		(-.62)		(-.80)		(.26)		(-.54)		(-.04)	
IOTA	2.71	2.16	3.16	2.12	2.68	1.65	3.16	1.99	4.13	1.99	2.40	1.44	3.58	1.41
	(.02)		(.21)		(-.08)		(-.22)		(-1.79)		(-.55)		(-.25)	
IS	2.19	1.77	2.31	1.74	2.22	1.88	3.18	2.22	6.68	1.14	3.25	2.24	4.15	1.57F
	(-.50)		(-.64)		(-.54)		(-.20)		(.76)		(.30)		(.32)	
IT	2.67	2.06	2.88	2.19	2.48	1.95	3.63	2.20	6.69	.89	3.84	2.40	3.31	1.50
	(-.02)		(-.07)		(-.28)		(.25)		(.77)		(.89)		(-.52)	
ITS	2.05	1.56	2.23	1.60	2.58	1.90	2.79	1.78	6.21	1.45	2.93	1.88	3.62	1.24
	(-.64)		(-.72)		(-.18)		(-.59)		(.29)		(.29)		(-.21)	
JUST	2.53	1.87	2.15	1.19	2.19	1.68	2.81	1.71	6.14	1.36	2.68	1.79	4.16	1.43
	(-.16)		(-.80)		(-.57)		(-.57)		(.22)		(-.27)		(.33)	

	CON	IMG	CAT	MNG	FAM	NOA	PLS
	M SD	M SD	M SD	M SD	M SD	M SD	M SD
JUSTIFY	2.85 1.77 (.16)	3.30 2.02 (.35)	2.98 1.60 (.22)	4.00 1.61 (.62)	6.00 1.29 (.08)	3.30 1.83 (.35)	4.36 1.36 (.53)
KEEN	3.32 1.80 (.63)	3.43 1.94 (.48)	3.08 1.75 (.32)	3.72 1.74 (.34)	5.31 1.70 (-.61)	3.05 1.42 (.10)	4.79 1.36 (.96)
KEEP	3.35 2.07 (.66)	2.95 1.79 (.00)	3.07 1.77 (.31)	3.27 1.54 (-.11)	6.30 1.24 (.38)	2.92 1.95 (-.03)	4.25 1.46 (.42)
KEPT	2.60 1.72 (-.09)	2.94 2.07 (-.01)	2.82 1.69 (.06)	3.70 1.67 (.32)	6.05 1.49 (.13)	2.80 1.63 (-.15)	4.06 1.34 (.23)
KNEW	2.87 1.93 (.18)	2.61 1.87 (-.34)	2.41 1.52 (-.35)	3.05 1.69 (-.33)	6.31 1.32 (.39)	2.90 1.77 (-.05)	4.05 1.22 (.22)
KNOWN	2.22 1.62 (-.47)	3.04 1.94 (.09)	2.92 1.63 (.16)	3.53 1.89 (.15)	6.19 1.35 (.27)	3.26 1.72 (.31)	4.17 1.34 (.34)
KNOWS	2.82 1.61 (.13)	2.73 1.83 (-.22)	2.85 1.81 (.09)	3.45 1.80 (.07)	6.51 .99 (.59)	3.51 2.05 (.56)	4.44 1.29 (.61)
LACK	3.07 1.94 (.38)	2.96 2.02 (.01)	2.41 1.50 (-.35)	3.60 1.52 (.22)	6.06 1.31 (.14)	2.56 1.56 (-.39)	2.92 1.20M (-.91)
LACKS	2.60 1.52 (-.09)	3.18 1.90 (.23)	2.42 1.52 (-.34)	2.90 1.76 (-.48)	5.05 2.04 (-.87)	2.38 1.43 (-.57)	2.90 1.11 (-.93)
LAX	3.11 2.00 (.42)	3.57 2.01 (.62)	2.57 1.69 (-.19)	3.41 1.71 (.03)	4.70 2.08 (-1.22)	2.79 1.48 (-.16)	3.64 1.48 (-.19)
LEAST	2.71 1.66 (.02)	2.96 1.89 (.01)	2.85 1.82 (.09)	3.13 1.64 (-.25)	6.03 1.41 (.11)	2.51 1.41 (-.44)	3.08 1.06 (-.75)
LEFT	3.37 2.18 (.68)	3.57 2.07 (.62)	3.74 2.08 (.98)	3.15 1.90 (-.23)	6.33 1.27 (.41)	2.62 1.75 (-.33)	3.99 1.32 (.16)
LESS	2.62 1.50 (-.07)	2.80 1.97 (-.15)	2.80 1.77 (.04)	3.05 1.71 (-.33)	6.15 1.58 (.23)	2.41 1.73 (-.54)	3.00 .82 (-.83)
LESSEN	2.83 1.50 (.14)	2.45 1.87 (-.50)	2.88 1.80 (.12)	3.58 1.79 (.20)	5.31 1.65 (-.61)	3.08 1.92 (.13)	3.46 1.33 (-.37)
LITERAL	2.91 1.89 (.22)	2.55 1.57 (-.40)	2.66 1.63 (-.10)	3.06 1.41 (-.32)	5.42 1.64 (-.50)	2.95 1.81 (.00)	3.81 1.26 (-.02)
MADE	3.23 1.75 (.54)	3.45 2.05 (.50)	2.95 1.59 (.19)	3.83 1.53 (.45)	6.53 .98 (.61)	3.07 1.74 (.12)	4.53 1.25F (.70)
MAIN	2.93 1.79 (.24)	2.95 1.69 (.00)	2.95 1.64 (.19)	3.61 1.63 (.23)	6.18 1.31 (.26)	2.85 1.85 (-.10)	3.91 1.06 (.08)
MANNER	2.93 1.89 (.24)	3.36 1.96 (.41)	3.45 1.65 (.71)	3.67 1.66 (.29)	6.20 1.38 (.28)	3.66 1.61 (.71)	4.23 1.47 (.40)
MEANT	2.22 1.61 (-.47)	2.76 1.92 (-.19)	2.70 1.82 (-.06)	3.03 1.90 (-.35)	5.73 1.61 (-.19)	2.92 1.74 (-.03)	3.81 .97 (-.02)-
MISCONCEPTION	2.46 1.95 (-.23)	2.91 2.00 (-.04)	2.60 1.51 (-.16)	3.80 1.66 (.42)	5.60 1.51 (-.32)	3.39 2.05 (.44)	2.72 1.32 (-1.11)
MORE	2.90 1.92 (.11)	2.48 1.72 (-.47)	2.48 1.70 (-.28)	3.51 1.72 (.13)	6.47 1.13 (.55)	2.92 2.06 (-.03)	4.32 1.37 (.49)
MOST	3.17 1.97 (.48)	3.00 1.98 (.05)	2.75 1.60 (-.01)	3.40 1.91 (.02)	6.34 1.27 (.42)	2.89 1.75 (-.06)	4.31 1.39 (.48)
MUCH	2.38 1.73 (-.31)	3.65 2.08 (.70)	2.92 1.53 (.16)	3.80 1.88 (.42)	6.15 1.31 (.23)	3.40 1.85 (.45)	4.23 1.26 (.40)
MUST	2.93 2.21 (.24)	2.65 1.99 (-.30)	2.70 1.76 (-.06)	3.00 1.81 (-.38)	6.33 1.25 (.41)	2.73 1.82 (-.22)	3.43 1.28 (-.40)
MY	2.49 1.94 (-.20)	3.30 2.03 (.35)	3.28 2.08 (.52)	3.00 1.65 (-.38)	6.50 1.08 (.58)	3.13 2.19 (.18)	4.73 1.23F (.90)
NEARER	2.51 1.59 (-.18)	3.28 1.96 (.33)	2.88 1.70 (.12)	4.13 1.82 (.75)	6.33 1.27 (.41)	2.54 1.57 (-.41)	4.39 1.70F (.56)
NEVER	2.55 1.93 (-.14)	3.45 2.20 (.50)	2.95 1.86 (.19)	3.97 2.05 (.59)	6.46 1.30 (.54)	2.92 1.97 (-.03)	2.44 1.62 (-1.39)

	CON		IMG		CAT		MNG		FAM		NOA		PLS	
	M	SD	M	SD	M	SD	M	SD	M	SD	M	SD	M	SD
NEXT	2.58	1.68	3.80	2.03	3.17	1.86	3.49	1.81	6.22	1.31	2.93	1.64	4.23	1.32
	(-.11)		(.85)		(.41)		(.11)		(.30)		(-.02)		(.40)	
NOPE	2.66	2.17	3.09	1.98	2.73	1.76	3.28	1.83	5.55	1.82	2.19	1.58	3.36	1.49F
	(-.03)		(.14)		(-.03)		(-.10)		(-.37)		(-.76)		(-.47)	
NOR	1.86	1.53	2.37	2.08	2.03	1.45	2.64	1.77	5.03	1.98	1.88	1.20	3.50	1.32F
	(-.83)		(-.58)		(-.73)		(-.74)		(-.89)		(-1.07)		(-.33)	
NOT	2.69	2.05	2.47	1.81	2.31	1.75	2.60	1.60	6.39	1.15	2.34	1.84	2.83	1.25
	(.00)		(-.48)		(-.45)		(-.78)		(.47)		(-.61)		(-1.00)	
NOW	3.05	2.03	3.16	2.07	2.96	1.95	3.39	1.89	6.48	1.07	2.95	2.11	4.26	1.53F
	(.36)		(.21)		(.20)		(.01)		(.56)		(.00)		(.43)	
NOWHERE	2.18	1.82	2.93	1.74	2.43	1.67	3.85	1.98	5.95	1.68	3.22	1.91	3.00	1.54
	(-.51)		(-.02)		(-.33)		(.47)		(.03)		(.27)		(-.83)	
OBEDIENT	3.13	1.82	3.56	1.96	3.69	1.81	3.95	1.74	5.70	1.41	2.92	1.72	4.10	1.58
	(.44)		(.61)		(.93)		(.57)		(-.22)		(-.03)		(.27)	
OBLIQUE	3.47	1.98	3.04	1.83	2.69	1.70	2.80	1.47	4.81	2.00	2.59	1.36	3.83	1.24F
	(.78)		(.09)		(-.07)		(-.58)		(-1.11)		(-.36)		(.00)	
OBLIVIOUS	3.02	2.20	3.41	1.83	2.95	1.67	3.60	1.75	5.42	1.87	3.46	1.88	3.97	1.51
	(.33)		(.46)		(.19)		(.22)		(-.50)		(.51)		(.14)	
OBSCURE	3.16	2.08	3.48	2.04	2.48	1.41	3.62	1.58	5.08	1.65	2.95	1.65	3.27	1.29
	(.47)		(.53)		(-.28)		(.24)		(-.84)		(.00)		(-.56)	
OCCASIONAL	3.11	1.86	2.70	1.72	3.00	1.65	3.50	1.43	5.77	1.67	2.89	1.58	4.22	1.27
	(.42)		(-.25)		(.24)		(.12)		(-.15)		(-.06)		(.39)	
OF	1.76	1.60	2.27	1.76	2.13	1.76	2.17	1.51	6.12	1.75	2.38	1.90	3.71	1.03
	(-.93)		(-.68)		(-.63)		(-1.21)		(.20)		(-.57)		(-.12)	
OFF	2.77	2.02	3.47	2.01	3.50	2.15	4.03	2.08	6.58	1.17	3.05	2.10	3.45	1.48M
	(.08)		(.52)		(.74)		(.65)		(.66)		(.10)		(-.38)	
OH	2.29	1.87	2.74	2.01	2.53	2.09	2.57	2.09	6.07	1.57	2.62	2.12	4.12	1.15F
	(-.40)		(-.21)		(-.23)		(-.81)		(.15)		(-.33)		(.29)	
OKAY	2.41	1.79	2.63	1.80	2.53	1.92	4.14	2.02	6.29	1.26	3.02	2.12	4.52	1.55
	(-.28)		(-.32)		(-.23)		(.76)		(.37)		(.07)		(.69)	
ON	2.58	1.80	2.56	1.82	2.50	1.88	2.90	1.80	6.55	.96	2.63	1.88	3.80	1.34
	(-.11)		(-.39)		(-.26)		(-.48)		(.63)		(-.32)		(-.03)	
ONCE	3.11	2.23	3.16	2.22	3.05	1.94	4.20	2.01	6.13	1.52	2.49	1.79	3.75	1.51
	(.42)		(.21)		(.29)		(.82)		(.21)		(-.46)		(-.08)	
ONLY	2.14	1.77	2.67	2.12	2.25	1.46	3.30	1.90	6.38	1.14	2.32	1.57	3.36	1.47
	(-.55)		(-.28)		(-.51)		(-.08)		(.46)		(-.63)		(-.47)	
OR	2.44	2.02	2.36	1.72	2.45	1.80	2.22	1.66	6.20	1.48	2.41	1.84	3.71	1.15
	(-.25)		(-.59)		(-.31)		(-1.16)		(.28)		(-.54)		(-.12)	
ORIGINATE	2.81	2.02	3.05	1.99	3.08	1.70	4.23	1.81	5.81	1.55	3.22	1.82	4.38	1.37
	(.12)		(.10)		(.32)		(.85)		(-.11)		(.27)		(.55)	
OTHER	2.71	1.84	2.59	1.88	2.12	1.55	3.07	1.94	6.55	.91	3.56	2.25	3.72	1.26
	(-.02)		(-.36)		(-.64)		(-.31)		(.63)		(.61)		(-.11)	
OUR	2.41	1.74	3.09	1.93	3.02	1.99	3.58	2.10	6.31	1.36	3.38	2.18	4.66	1.45F
	(-.28)		(.14)		(.26)		(.20)		(.39)		(.43)		(.83)	
OUT	2.45	1.62	3.37	2.06	3.08	1.99	4.30	2.10	6.53	1.17	3.28	1.93	3.59	1.52F
	(-.24)		(.42)		(.32)		(.92)		(.61)		(.33)		(-.24)	
OWED	2.95	1.71	3.60	2.21	2.72	1.58	3.33	1.92	5.19	1.96	2.60	1.58	2.81	1.35
	(.26)		(.65)		(-.04)		(-.05)		(-.73)		(-1.00)		(-1.02)	
PACIFISM	2.84	1.89	3.48	1.89	3.20	1.83	4.11	1.82	4.60	1.99	3.56	1.91	4.39	1.69
	(.15)		(.53)		(.44)		(.73)		(-1.32)		(.61)		(.56)	
PARADOX	2.53	1.70	3.28	2.05	2.75	1.73	3.15	1.63	4.68	1.71	3.84	1.94	3.75	1.28
	(-.16)		(.33)		(-.01)		(-.23)		(-1.24)		(.89)		(-.08)	
PART	3.17	1.86	3.07	1.69	2.97	1.73	3.37	1.72	6.05	1.51	3.13	2.04	3.58	1.16
	(.48)		(.12)		(.21)		(-.01)		(.13)		(.18)		(-.25)	

	CON		IMG		CAT		MNG		FAM		NOA		PLS	
	M	SD	M	SD	M	SD	M	SD	M	SD	M	SD	M	SD
PAUSE	3.00	1.68	3.34	1.89	3.15	1.57	4.10	1.54	5.80	1.59	2.69	1.27	3.74	1.45F
	(.31)		(.39)		(.39)		(.72)		(-.12)		(-.26)		(-.09)	
PHASE	3.56	1.88	3.13	2.05	3.47	1.67	3.73	1.71	5.90	1.26	3.56	1.69	3.84	1.06
	(.87)		(.18)		(.71)		(.35)		(-.02)		(.61)		(.01)	
PORTRAY	3.33	1.80	3.71	1.83	3.10	1.65	3.49	1.45	5.60	1.69	3.39	1.79	4.31	1.04
	(.64)		(.76)		(.34)		(.11)		(-.32)		(.44)		(.48)	
PREVALENT	2.51	1.83	2.68	1.61	2.48	1.44	3.61	1.84	4.92	1.83	2.80	1.39	4.13	1.30
	(-.18)		(-.27)		(-.28)		(.23)		(-1.00)		(-.15)		(.30)	
PUT	2.83	1.86	2.57	1.55	2.88	1.58	2.97	1.74	6.13	1.41	2.40	1.57	3.55	1.05
	(.14)		(-.38)		(.12)		(-.41)		(.21)		(-.55)		(-.28)	
QUICKEN	3.76	1.78	3.29	1.69	3.21	1.68	3.75	1.74	5.43	1.72	3.06	1.46	4.34	1.29
	(1.07)		(.34)		(.45)		(.37)		(-.49)		(.11)		(.51)	
RECEPTIVE	3.19	1.78	2.96	1.81	3.07	1.62	4.05	1.48	5.61	1.54	3.69	1.53	4.63	1.27
	(.50)		(.01)		(.31)		(.67)		(-.31)		(.74)		(.80)	
RECOMMEND	2.74	1.67	3.07	1.73	2.75	1.28	3.77	1.88	6.03	1.33	3.17	1.67	4.51	1.19
	(.05)		(.12)		(-.01)		(.39)		(.11)		(.22)		(.68)	
REFINED	2.98	1.68	3.47	1.97	3.24	1.71	3.71	1.51	5.62	1.43	3.33	1.89	4.30	1.52
	(.29)		(.52)		(.48)		(.33)		(-.30)		(.38)		(.47)	
RELINQUISH	2.85	1.93	3.31	1.82	2.82	1.85	3.80	1.78	4.93	1.83	3.41	1.77	3.43	1.56
	(.16)		(.36)		(.06)		(.42)		(-.99)		(.46)		(-.40)	
RENOUNCE	2.93	1.61	3.56	2.08	2.90	1.55	3.61	1.42	5.03	1.83	3.15	1.57	3.15	1.30
	(.24)		(.61)		(.14)		(.23)		(-.89)		(.20)		(-.68)	
REPROVE	2.86	2.06	2.95	1.97	2.82	1.67	3.03	1.59	4.38	1.99	2.89	1.59	3.06	1.39
	(.17)		(.00)		(.06)		(-.35)		(-1.54)		(-.06)		(-.77)	
REQUIREMENT	2.96	1.72	3.33	1.94	3.07	1.93	3.93	1.73	5.82	1.76	3.39	1.88	3.00	1.52
	(.27)		(.38)		(.31)		(.55)		(-.10)		(.44)		(-.83)	
RESTORE	2.71	1.63	3.18	1.71	3.34	1.61	3.74	1.69	5.64	1.53	3.46	1.54	4.51	1.27
	(.02)		(.23)		(.58)		(.36)		(-.28)		(.51)		(.68)	
RETAIN	3.04	1.74	3.46	2.05	3.27	1.59	4.10	1.69	5.81	1.39	3.58	1.69	3.85	1.56F
	(.35)		(.51)		(.51)		(.72)		(-.11)		(.63)		(.02)	
RUMOR	3.27	1.97	3.11	2.03	3.36	1.79	3.50	1.53	5.97	1.33	3.76	2.01	2.95	1.48M
	(.58)		(.16)		(.60)		(.12)		(.05)		(.81)		(-.88)	
SAID	3.02	2.02	3.07	2.07	3.19	1.85	3.97	1.80	6.74	.89	3.06	1.88	3.91	1.34
	(.33)		(.12)		(.43)		(.59)		(.82)		(.11)		(.08)	
SAME	2.44	1.78	3.20	2.16	2.62	1.80	4.37	1.81	6.43	1.28	2.30	1.70	3.23	1.21
	(-.25)		(.25)		(-.14)		(.99)		(.51)		(-.65)		(-.60)	
SCHEME	3.09	1.77	3.15	1.94	3.47	1.61	3.63	1.65	5.67	1.55	3.40	1.97	3.58	1.32F
	(.40)		(.20)		(.71)		(.25)		(-.25)		(.45)		(-.25)	
SEEM	2.22	1.63	2.43	1.70	2.77	1.80	3.25	1.90	6.23	1.32	3.37	1.75	4.13	1.24
	(-.47)		(-.52)		(.01)		(-.13)		(.31)		(.42)		(.30)	
SEEN	3.32	1.66	3.45	2.05	2.90	1.66	3.60	1.66	6.50	.92	3.26	1.82	4.14	1.01
	(.63)		(.50)		(.22)		(.22)		(.58)		(.31)		(.31)	
SENT	2.88	1.50	3.80	2.10	3.37	1.53	3.62	1.79	5.97	1.51	2.92	1.43	4.05	1.03
	(.19)		(.85)		(.61)		(.24)		(.05)		(-.03)		(.22)	
SHONE	3.59	1.84	3.78	1.97	2.75	1.53	3.40	1.57	5.56	1.86	2.72	1.42	4.31	1.66F
	(.90)		(.83)		(-.01)		(.02)		(-.36)		(-.23)		(.48)	
SHOULD	2.45	1.90	2.89	1.95	2.47	1.60	3.74	1.92	6.39	1.21	2.62	1.68	3.32	1.37M
	(-.24)		(-.06)		(-.29)		(.36)		(.47)		(-.33)		(-.51)	
SHOWN	3.11	1.80	2.67	1.58	2.84	1.63	2.88	1.62	5.93	1.52	2.82	1.68	4.15	1.06
	(.42)		(-.28)		(.08)		(-.50)		(.01)		(-.13)		(.32)	
SIGHED	3.21	1.92	3.82	1.98	3.30	1.68	3.40	1.54	5.51	1.80	2.84	1.38	4.03	1.18
	(.52)		(.87)		(.54)		(.02)		(-.41)		(-.11)		(.20)	
SINCE	2.43	1.84	2.58	1.76	2.55	1.40	2.83	1.77	6.15	1.42	2.53	1.60	3.93	.95
	(-.26)		(-.37)		(-.21)		(-.55)		(.23)		(-.42)		(.10)	

	CON		IMG		CAT		MNG		FAM		NOA		PLS	
	M	SD	M	SD	M	SD	M	SD	M	SD	M	SD	M	SD
SLOWER	2.87	1.55	3.33	2.26	3.47	1.87	3.88	1.56	6.25	1.20	2.74	1.62	3.74	1.14
	(.18)		(.38)		(.71)		(.50)		(.33)		(−.21)		(−.09)	
SO	1.91	1.55	2.40	1.83	2.52	2.02	2.73	2.00	6.19	1.48	2.39	1.68	3.79	1.29
	(−.78)		(−.55)		(−.24)		(−.65)		(.27)		(−.56)		(−.04)	
SOLEMNITY	3.11	1.75	2.84	1.86	2.53	1.34	3.14	1.59	4.53	2.08	3.08	1.74	4.00	1.46
	(.42)		(−.11)		(−.23)		(−.24)		(−1.39)		(.13)		(.17)	
SOME	2.82	1.83	2.96	1.93	2.77	1.93	3.03	1.63	6.52	1.05	3.13	1.93	3.97	.93
	(.13)		(.01)		(.01)		(−.35)		(.60)		(.18)		(.14)	
SOON	2.57	1.92	2.72	1.93	2.47	1.77	3.07	1.57	6.21	1.36	2.73	1.78	4.45	1.47
	(−.12)		(−.23)		(−.29)		(−.31)		(.29)		(−.22)		(.62)	
SPAN	3.09	1.90	3.75	1.95	3.25	1.74	3.40	1.75	5.27	1.81	3.28	1.52	4.08	1.04
	(.40)		(.80)		(.49)		(.02)		(−.65)		(.33)		(.25)	
STAY	3.25	1.95	3.15	1.96	2.80	1.67	3.69	1.78	6.47	1.11	2.87	1.70	4.58	1.37F
	(.56)		(.20)		(.04)		(.31)		(.55)		(−.08)		(.75)	
STIFLE	2.88	1.89	3.75	1.88	2.63	1.45	3.71	1.78	5.27	1.83	3.38	1.58	2.69	1.34M
	(.19)		(.80)		(−.13)		(.33)		(−.65)		(.43)		(−1.14)	
SUCH	2.44	1.77	2.13	1.44	2.00	1.04	2.10	1.36	5.95	1.50	2.02	1.22	3.67	.87
	(−.25)		(−.82)		(−.76)		(−1.28)		(.03)		(−.93)		(−.16)	
SUFFIX	3.14	1.98	2.48	1.62	3.60	2.14	2.58	1.59	5.18	1.73	2.67	1.81	3.07	1.09
	(.45)		(−.47)		(.84)		(−.80)		(−.74)		(−.28)		(−.76)	
SUFFRAGE	2.79	1.84	3.09	2.07	3.20	1.85	3.71	1.99	4.92	2.08	3.59	2.05	2.96	1.75
	(.10)		(.14)		(.44)		(.33)		(−1.00)		(.64)		(−.87)	
SURE	2.77	2.15	2.79	1.94	2.55	1.56	3.78	1.67	6.26	1.17	3.36	1.85	4.66	1.44F
	(.08)		(−.16)		(−.21)		(.40)		(.34)		(.41)		(.83)	
TAKE	3.28	2.12	3.62	1.95	2.76	1.68	3.60	1.70	6.26	1.26	2.74	1.75	3.36	1.28
	(.59)		(.67)		(.00)		(.22)		(.34)		(−.21)		(−.47)	
THAN	1.84	1.56	2.07	1.68	1.92	1.43	2.69	2.11	6.19	1.69	2.27	1.72	3.67	1.16
	(−.85)		(−.88)		(−.84)		(−.69)		(.27)		(−.68)		(−.16)	
THAT	2.28	1.71	2.38	1.80	1.87	1.35	2.87	2.04	6.39	1.29	2.48	2.09	3.68	.84
	(−.41)		(−.57)		(−.89)		(−.51)		(.47)		(−.47)		(−.15)	
THE	2.33	2.08	1.87	1.35	2.07	1.74	2.12	1.67	6.66	1.12	2.41	2.17	3.25	1.28
	(−.36)		(−1.08)		(−.69)		(−1.26)		(.74)		(−.54)		(−.58)	
THEIR	2.53	1.83	2.51	1.81	2.80	1.75	3.10	1.74	6.56	.90	2.77	1.83	4.27	1.18
	(−.16)		(−.44)		(.04)		(−.28)		(.64)		(−.18)		(.44)	
THEM	3.40	2.25	3.62	2.22	2.75	1.81	3.89	1.93	6.16	1.59	3.56	1.98	3.69	1.27
	(.71)		(.67)		(−.01)		(.51)		(.24)		(.61)		(−.14)	
THEN	1.86	1.39	1.86	1.53	1.82	1.35	2.72	1.56	6.53	1.10	1.97	1.46	3.65	1.11
	(−.83)		(−1.09)		(−.94)		(−.66)		(.61)		(−.98)		(−.18)	
THEORETICAL	2.60	1.96	3.28	2.07	3.12	1.90	3.57	1.82	5.61	1.63	4.02	2.07	3.81	1.41
	(−.09)		(.33)		(.36)		(.19)		(−.31)		(1.07)		(−.02)	
THERE	2.12	1.64	3.02	1.89	2.67	1.77	2.77	1.79	6.23	1.41	2.79	1.57	3.87	1.03M
	(−.57)		(.07)		(−.09)		(−.61)		(.31)		(−.16)		(.04)	
THEREFORE	1.95	1.69	2.53	1.82	2.75	1.77	3.00	1.84	5.87	1.44	2.77	1.86	3.82	.97
	(−.74)		(−.42)		(−.01)		(−.38)		(−.05)		(−.18)		(−.01)	
THESE	2.56	1.92	2.61	2.00	2.27	1.65	3.08	1.80	6.21	1.54	2.77	1.84	3.56	1.20
	(−.13)		(−.34)		(−.49)		(−.30)		(.29)		(−.18)		(−.27)	
THEY	3.12	2.11	3.27	2.00	3.52	1.82	3.36	1.88	6.32	1.25	3.62	1.98	3.98	.98
	(.43)		(.32)		(.76)		(−.02)		(.40)		(.67)		(.15)	
THIS	2.36	1.90	3.09	2.03	2.69	1.80	3.03	1.97	6.26	1.41	3.13	1.96	3.66	1.01
	(−.33)		(.14)		(−.07)		(−.35)		(.34)		(.18)		(−.17)	
THOSE	2.50	1.73	2.41	1.63	2.62	1.74	2.98	1.89	6.44	1.09	2.64	1.76	3.67	.92
	(−.19)		(−.54)		(−.14)		(−.40)		(.52)		(−.31)		(−.16)	
THROUGH	2.70	1.77	3.14	2.04	2.57	1.52	3.90	1.68	6.61	.82	3.07	1.83	4.44	1.44
	(.01)		(.19)		(−.19)		(.52)		(.69)		(.12)		(.61)	

	CON	IMG	CAT	MNG	FAM	NOA	PLS
	M SD	M SD	M SD	M SD	M SD	M SD	M SD
THUS	1.93 1.60 (-.76)	2.61 2.24 (-.34)	2.53 1.57 (-.23)	2.75 1.80 (-.63)	5.81 1.47 (-.11)	2.48 1.59 (-.47)	4.09 1.12 (.26)
TO	1.95 1.46 (-.74)	2.13 1.65 (-.82)	2.10 1.43 (-.66)	2.45 1.71 (-.93)	6.58 1.00 (.66)	2.07 1.74 (-.88)	3.68 1.00 (-.15)
TOLD	3.14 1.81 (.45)	2.80 1.65 (-.15)	2.69 1.55 (-.07)	3.29 1.68 (-.09)	6.05 1.42 (.13)	2.49 1.64 (-.46)	3.58 1.27 (-.25)
TOO	2.04 1.58 (-.65)	2.55 2.01 (-.40)	2.59 1.88 (-.17)	2.97 1.83 (-.41)	6.69 .79 (.77)	2.59 2.01 (-.36)	3.92 1.23 (.09)
TRUISM	2.72 2.13 (.03)	2.86 1.99 (-.09)	2.66 1.67 (-.10)	3.10 1.65 (-.28)	4.72 1.96 (-1.20)	3.48 1.93 (.53)	4.29 1.59 (.46)
TURN	3.40 1.82 (.71)	3.64 2.01 (.69)	3.20 1.73 (.44)	3.47 1.62 (.09)	6.36 1.16 (.44)	3.08 1.41 (.13)	3.79 1.07 (-.04)
TYPICAL	2.64 1.79 (-.05)	2.93 1.92 (-.02)	2.63 1.53 (-.13)	4.03 1.75 (.65)	6.31 1.34 (.39)	2.75 1.58 (-.20)	3.18 1.40 (-.65)
UNREALITY	2.14 1.95 (-.55)	2.78 1.72 (-.17)	2.42 1.60 (-.34)	4.03 1.76 (.65)	5.42 1.65 (-.50)	4.16 2.03 (1.21)	3.75 1.68M (-.08)
UPON	3.07 2.11 (.38)	3.28 2.04 (.33)	2.90 1.90 (.14)	3.68 1.69 (.30)	6.49 .99 (.57)	2.89 1.75 (-.06)	4.33 1.54 (.50)
USED	3.11 1.98 (.42)	3.38 1.94 (.43)	2.85 1.84 (.09)	3.63 1.56 (.25)	6.41 .99 (.49)	3.03 1.75 (.08)	3.14 1.31 (-.69)
VAGUE	2.68 1.92 (-.01)	3.21 1.98 (.26)	2.83 1.57 (.07)	4.00 1.85 (.62)	5.80 1.46 (-.12)	3.10 2.05 (.15)	2.85 1.56 (-.98)
VARY	2.54 1.51 (-.06)	2.66 1.88 (-.29)	2.70 1.60 (-.06)	3.47 1.79 (.09)	5.59 1.52 (-.33)	3.33 1.90 (.38)	4.21 1.06 (.38)
VERY	2.19 1.89 (-.50)	2.45 1.73 (-.50)	2.47 1.69 (-.29)	3.07 1.88 (-.31)	6.47 1.16 (.55)	2.87 1.83 (-.08)	4.40 1.36 (.57)
WAIT	3.13 1.80 (.44)	3.55 2.10 (.60)	2.88 1.64 (.12)	3.80 1.83 (.42)	6.33 1.26 (.41)	3.06 1.56 (.11)	3.18 1.46 (-.65)
WAIVE	3.33 1.95 (.64)	3.44 2.08 (.49)	2.78 1.65 (.02)	3.31 1.74 (-.07)	5.34 1.71 (-.58)	2.84 1.42 (-.11)	4.15 .94 (.32)
WARN	3.11 1.59 (.42)	3.53 2.07 (.58)	3.22 1.90 (.46)	3.77 1.62 (.39)	5.65 1.53 (-.27)	3.41 1.54 (.46)	3.71 1.45 (-.12)
WARY	3.09 1.94 (.40)	3.09 1.80 (.14)	3.02 1.57 (.26)	3.73 1.75 (.35)	5.10 1.71 (-.82)	3.08 1.54 (.13)	3.37 1.26 (-.46)
WAS	1.90 1.55 (-.79)	2.68 1.99 (-.27)	2.45 1.71 (-.31)	2.72 1.95 (-.66)	6.41 1.26 (.49)	2.59 1.70 (-.36)	3.75 1.06 (-.08)
WAY	2.61 1.52 (-.08)	3.09 2.17 (.14)	2.88 1.77 (.12)	3.40 1.70 (.02)	6.41 1.19 (.49)	3.03 1.82 (.08)	4.29 1.09F (.46)
WEAR	3.56 1.93 (.87)	3.22 1.78 (.27)	3.00 1.69 (.24)	4.02 1.57 (.64)	6.10 1.40 (.18)	3.18 1.90 (.23)	4.16 1.12 (.33)
WENT	2.36 1.48 (-.33)	3.02 2.12 (.07)	2.87 1.65 (.11)	3.69 1.96 (.31)	6.68 .78 (.76)	2.85 1.58 (-.10)	3.90 1.26F (.07)
WERE	1.96 1.44 (-.73)	2.54 1.91 (-.41)	2.69 1.77 (-.07)	2.74 1.80 (-.64)	6.17 1.38 (.25)	2.52 1.58 (-.43)	3.63 1.07 (-.20)
WHAT	2.89 2.11 (.20)	2.69 2.09 (-.26)	2.88 1.94 (.12)	3.89 2.18 (.51)	6.49 1.10 (.57)	3.16 2.01 (-.20)	3.63 1.27F (-.20)
WHEN	2.15 1.74 (-.54)	2.29 1.83 (-.66)	2.33 2.07 (-.43)	3.05 1.94 (-.33)	6.57 1.08 (.65)	3.21 2.02 (.26)	3.70 1.09 (-.13)
WHERE	2.52 1.88 (-.17)	2.64 1.62 (-.31)	2.88 1.83 (.12)	3.60 1.99 (.22)	6.44 1.15 (.52)	3.10 1.87 (.15)	3.81 1.47 (-.02)
WHICH	2.11 1.63 (-.58)	2.51 1.99 (-.44)	2.42 1.53 (-.34)	2.90 1.76 (-.48)	6.29 1.30 (.37)	3.05 1.98 (.10)	3.40 1.15 (-.43)
WHILE	2.00 1.61 (-.69)	2.96 1.98 (.01)	2.80 1.84 (.04)	3.20 1.84 (-.18)	6.17 1.29 (.25)	2.64 1.47 (-.31)	3.94 .99 (.11)

	CON		IMG		CAT		MNG		FAM		NOA		PLS	
	M	SD	M	SD	M	SD	M	SD	M	SD	M	SD	M	SD
WHO	2.30	1.85	2.76	2.13	2.72	1.82	3.10	2.01	6.32	1.32	3.20	1.99	3.89	.93
	(-.39)		(-.19)		(-.04)		(-.28)		(.40)		(.25)		(.06)	
WHOM	2.39	1.77	2.95	2.15	3.00	1.99	3.82	2.04	5.75	1.77	3.28	2.07	3.79	1.42F
	(-.30)		(.00)		(.24)		(.44)		(-.17)		(.33)		(-.04)	
WHY	2.63	2.09	2.57	1.98	2.60	1.99	2.82	1.83	6.21	1.38	2.87	2.17	3.55	1.48F
	(-.06)		(-.38)		(-.16)		(-.56)		(.29)		(-.08)		(-.28)	
WIDER	3.31	2.00	3.72	1.93	3.17	1.81	3.75	1.41	5.84	1.49	3.38	1.65	3.84	1.19
	(.71)		(.59)		(.41)		(.37)		(.41)		(.42)		(.01)	
WILL	2.71	1.76	3.54	1.86	2.91	1.78	3.18	1.84	6.33	1.14	3.37	1.85	4.20	1.35
	(.02)		(.59)		(.15)		(-.20)		(.41)		(.42)		(.37)	
WITH	2.64	1.71	2.86	2.02	2.36	1.63	3.05	2.00	6.49	1.06	2.34	1.53	4.40	1.29F
	(-.05)		(-.09)		(-.40)		(-.33)		(.57)		(-.61)		(.57)	
WITHOUT	2.63	1.67	2.96	2.09	2.59	1.65	3.30	1.89	6.51	.90	2.44	1.65	3.08	1.22
	(-.06)		(.01)		(-.17)		(-.08)		(.59)		(-.51)		(-.75)	
WORTH	2.63	1.79	2.45	1.67	3.07	1.67	3.32	1.52	5.85	1.45	2.98	1.87	4.16	1.43
	(-.06)		(-.50)		(.31)		(-.06)		(-.07)		(.03)		(.33)	
WOULD	1.98	1.61	1.90	1.40	2.05	1.52	2.45	1.64	6.22	1.25	2.35	1.75	3.61	1.18F
	(-.71)		(-1.05)		(-.71)		(-.93)		(.30)		(-.60)		(-.22)	
YET	2.45	1.93	2.31	1.73	2.03	1.39	2.22	1.28	5.97	1.50	2.24	1.46	3.52	1.30
	(-.24)		(-.64)		(-.73)		(-1.16)		(.05)		(-.71)		(-.31)	
YOUR	2.52	1.88	2.83	1.89	2.62	1.90	3.80	2.08	6.55	1.11	3.13	1.79	4.39	1.16
	(-.17)		(-.12)		(-.14)		(.42)		(.63)		(.18)		(.56)	
ZEAL	3.00	1.93	3.41	1.73	2.48	1.59	3.63	1.99	4.62	1.85	3.49	1.63	4.74	1.45
	(.31)		(.46)		(-.28)		(.25)		(-1.30)		(.54)		(.91)	

	CON		IMG		CAT		MNG		FAM		NOA		PLS	
	M	SD	M	SD	M	SD	M	SD	M	SD	M	SD	M	SD
ABHOR	3.16	2.21	3.29	2.01	2.76	1.64	3.27	1.61	4.34	2.08	2.92	1.51	2.85	1.59M
	(-.95)		(-.65)		(-.90)		(.14)		(-.07)		(-.14)		(-.89)	
ABORIGINAL	3.31	2.08	3.83	2.19	3.46	2.23	2.90	1.80	3.69	1.92	3.30	1.72	3.38	1.44F
	(-.80)		(-.11)		(-.20)		(-.23)		(.24)		(.24)		(-.36)	
ABYSS	3.83	2.35	4.30	2.39	4.03	1.93	3.23	1.78	3.57	2.06	3.65	1.75	3.73	1.70M
	(-.28)		(.36)		(.37)		(.10)		(-.84)		(.59)		(-.01)	
ACCOMPLICE	3.91	1.94	3.85	1.99	3.98	1.86	3.45	1.52	5.20	1.77	3.17	1.53	3.20	1.48
	(-.20)		(-.09)		(.32)		(.32)		(.79)		(.11)		(-.54)	
AIL	3.81	2.05	3.85	2.16	2.67	1.78	3.02	1.51	4.44	2.25	3.21	1.78	3.16	1.46M
	(-.30)		(-.09)		(-.99)		(-.11)		(.03)		(.15)		(-.58)	
AIRY	3.30	1.81	3.62	1.93	3.18	1.55	3.53	1.58	4.97	1.97	3.23	1.56	4.64	1.71
	(-.81)		(-.32)		(-.48)		(.40)		(.56)		(.17)		(.90)	
ALBUMIN	4.11	2.40	3.46	2.44	3.53	2.08	2.05	1.56	2.91	2.13	2.75	1.84	3.84	1.40
	(.00)		(-.48)		(-.13)		(-1.08)		(-1.50)		(-.31)		(.10)	
APEX	4.04	2.13	3.69	2.26	3.32	2.10	2.70	1.87	3.95	2.05	2.59	1.59	4.00	1.40
	(-.07)		(-.25)		(-.34)		(-.43)		(-.46)		(-.47)		(.26)	
ARBOR	4.26	2.08	3.86	2.23	3.35	1.96	2.60	1.74	3.76	1.96	2.75	1.49	4.45	1.35
	(.15)		(-.08)		(-.31)		(-.53)		(-.65)		(-.31)		(.71)	
ARC	4.67	2.03	4.88	2.14	4.17	2.05	3.63	1.65	4.71	1.84	2.90	1.63	4.18	1.31
	(.56)		(.94)		(.51)		(.50)		(.30)		(-.16)		(.44)	
ARID	3.95	2.08	4.27	2.03	4.23	1.85	3.85	1.68	4.92	1.79	2.59	1.42	3.34	1.41
	(-.16)		(.33)		(.57)		(.72)		(.51)		(-.47)		(-.40)	
ASHEN	3.47	1.87	3.89	2.09	2.52	1.56	2.83	1.66	3.48	2.21	2.44	1.45	3.14	1.22
	(-.05)		(-.05)		(-1.14)		(-.30)		(-.93)		(-.62)		(-.60)	
AXIL	4.63	2.36	3.83	2.18	3.86	2.12	2.89	2.02	3.97	2.12	3.00	1.83	3.45	1.31
	(.52)		(-.11)		(.20)		(-.24)		(-.44)		(-.06)		(-.29)	
AXIOM	3.02	2.05	3.05	2.11	3.93	2.06	2.55	1.56	3.92	1.99	3.28	1.68	3.69	1.52
	(-1.09)		(-.89)		(.27)		(-.58)		(-.49)		(.22)		(-.05)	
BALE	4.58	2.16	4.67	2.11	3.69	1.88	2.78	1.52	4.60	2.18	2.68	1.41	3.59	1.34
	(.47)		(.73)		(.03)		(-.35)		(.19)		(-.38)		(-.15)	
BEECH	4.42	2.19	4.29	2.02	4.05	2.01	2.90	1.77	4.48	2.24	2.93	1.76	4.60	1.45
	(.31)		(.35)		(.39)		(-.23)		(.07)		(-.13)		(.86)	
BELLE	3.84	2.16	3.95	2.22	3.25	1.95	3.62	2.04	4.15	1.99	3.25	1.51	4.18	1.55
	(-.27)		(.01)		(-.41)		(.49)		(-.26)		(.19)		(.44)	
BERTH	4.21	2.25	3.96	2.17	3.72	2.10	2.87	1.59	4.53	1.93	3.11	1.71	4.08	1.15
	(.10)		(.02)		(.06)		(-.26)		(.12)		(.05)		(.34)	
BLAND	3.34	1.70	3.42	2.03	3.40	1.86	3.60	1.61	5.10	1.95	2.21	1.28	2.76	1.29
	(-.77)		(-.52)		(-.26)		(.47)		(.69)		(-.85)		(-.98)	
BORNE	3.20	1.74	3.40	1.93	3.23	1.80	2.72	1.72	4.54	2.14	2.79	1.54	4.53	1.41
	(-.91)		(-.54)		(-.43)		(-.41)		(.13)		(-.27)		(.79)	
BRAMBLE	3.74	2.31	3.81	2.12	3.00	1.86	2.98	1.90	3.69	2.08	2.61	1.57	3.66	1.38
	(-.37)		(-.13)		(-.66)		(-.15)		(-.72)		(-.45)		(-.08)	
BRED	3.04	1.60	3.81	1.91	3.62	1.76	3.87	1.71	4.97	1.92	3.21	1.55	4.10	1.18
	(-1.07)		(-.13)		(-.04)		(.74)		(.56)		(.15)		(.36)	
BRISKET	4.52	2.45	3.64	2.44	4.17	2.29	2.92	1.88	4.38	2.15	2.39	1.39	3.82	1.37
	(.41)		(-.30)		(.51)		(-.21)		(-.03)		(-.67)		(.08)	
BRUT	4.26	2.16	3.86	2.32	3.33	2.10	3.56	2.00	4.17	2.33	3.43	1.52	3.23	1.63
	(.15)		(-.08)		(-.33)		(.43)		(-.24)		(.37)		(-.51)	
BUFFOON	3.93	2.02	3.34	2.00	3.93	2.10	2.75	1.73	3.95	1.99	2.97	1.60	3.61	1.36
	(-.18)		(-.60)		(.27)		(-.38)		(-.46)		(-.09)		(-.13)	
BURROW	4.22	1.87	4.38	2.02	3.95	1.89	3.52	1.56	4.95	1.87	3.33	1.52	3.81	1.21F
	(.11)		(.44)		(.29)		(.39)		(.54)		(.27)		(.07)	
CARAT	4.84	2.07	3.39	2.09	4.37	2.14	3.13	1.49	4.57	2.10	2.82	1.67	4.14	1.47
	(.73)		(-.55)		(.71)		(.00)		(.16)		(-.24)		(.40)	

	CON		IMG		CAT		MNG		FAM		NOA		PLS	
	M	SD	M	SD	M	SD	M	SD	M	SD	M	SD	M	SD
CASTE	3.64	1.83	4.17	2.34	4.10	1.79	3.51	1.89	4.95	1.98	3.59	1.69	3.51	1.69M
	(-.47)		(.23)		(.44)		(.38)		(.54)		(.53)		(-.23)	
CAUCUS	3.98	2.12	3.58	2.00	3.32	1.87	3.11	1.77	4.50	2.08	3.49	1.55	3.18	1.34
	(-.13)		(-.36)		(-.34)		(-.02)		(.09)		(.43)		(-.56)	
CHAMOIS	4.84	2.13	4.58	2.23	3.47	2.31	2.30	1.65	3.50	2.27	2.46	1.26	4.50	1.28M
	(.73)		(.64)		(-.19)		(-.83)		(-.91)		(-.60)		(.76)	
CHARLATAN	3.29	2.12	3.18	2.11	3.44	1.64	3.08	1.95	3.17	2.03	3.41	1.82	4.02	1.48M
	(-.82)		(-.76)		(-.22)		(-.05)		(-1.24)		(.35)		(.28)	
CHORAL	4.56	2.18	4.84	1.79	4.43	1.97	3.37	1.75	4.85	2.03	3.52	1.81	4.14	1.40F
	(.45)		(.90)		(.77)		(.24)		(.44)		(.46)		(.40)	
CHUTE	4.92	2.09	4.61	2.02	3.95	2.01	3.17	1.52	5.11	1.92	2.95	1.34	3.95	1.06
	(.81)		(.67)		(.29)		(.04)		(.70)		(-.11)		(.21)	
CITE	3.33	1.91	3.25	2.22	3.50	1.75	2.80	1.47	4.40	2.10	2.56	1.47	3.69	1.10
	(-.78)		(-.69)		(-.16)		(-.33)		(-.01)		(-.50)		(-.05)	
CLAMOR	3.95	1.79	4.00	1.80	3.37	1.81	3.92	1.75	4.31	1.83	3.73	1.77	3.22	1.52
	(-.16)		(.06)		(-.29)		(.79)		(-.10)		(.67)		(-.52)	
CLEAT	5.42	1.92	4.75	2.04	4.35	2.05	3.03	1.83	4.07	2.18	2.80	1.44	3.41	1.40M
	(1.31)		(.81)		(.69)		(-.10)		(-.34)		(-.26)		(-.33)	
CLOVE	5.26	1.92	4.15	2.30	4.92	1.77	3.15	1.53	4.97	1.88	2.82	1.42	4.15	1.49F
	(1.15)		(.21)		(1.26)		(.02)		(.56)		(-.24)		(.41)	
COMMODE	4.78	2.21	4.41	2.26	4.15	2.04	3.76	2.08	4.28	1.85	3.46	1.56	3.92	1.53
	(.67)		(.47)		(.49)		(.63)		(-.13)		(.40)		(.18)	
CORNET	5.23	2.09	4.30	2.16	5.22	2.23	3.40	2.20	4.38	2.35	3.07	1.54	3.91	1.50
	(1.12)		(.36)		(1.56)		(.27)		(-.03)		(.01)		(.17)	
COWL	4.25	2.21	3.13	1.97	3.20	1.80	2.73	1.92	2.92	2.13	2.79	1.79	3.22	1.48
	(.14)		(-.81)		(-.46)		(-.40)		(-1.49)		(-.27)		(-.52)	
CURDS	5.19	2.02	4.57	2.11	3.83	1.74	2.56	1.60	4.31	2.05	3.17	1.75	2.97	1.58
	(1.08)		(.63)		(.17)		(-.57)		(-.10)		(.11)		(-.77)	
DETONATION	3.84	2.04	4.15	2.02	3.02	1.84	3.34	1.91	4.48	2.12	2.92	1.64	2.78	1.44M
	(-.27)		(.21)		(-.64)		(.21)		(.07)		(-.14)		(-.96)	
DOCILE	3.35	1.96	3.78	2.09	3.49	1.87	3.78	1.68	5.28	1.94	2.95	1.47	3.92	1.60F
	(-.76)		(-.16)		(-.17)		(.65)		(.87)		(-.11)		(.18)	
DOGMA	3.13	1.94	3.55	2.20	3.38	2.03	3.18	1.73	4.24	1.91	3.55	1.93	3.03	1.48M
	(-.98)		(-.39)		(-.28)		(.05)		(-.17)		(.49)		(-.71)	
DROPPER	4.88	1.99	4.27	2.14	4.17	1.87	3.43	1.66	5.41	1.70	2.93	1.62	3.47	1.08
	(.77)		(.33)		(.51)		(.30)		(1.00)		(-.13)		(-.27)	
EMERGENCE	3.42	1.98	3.81	1.99	3.40	1.67	3.50	1.61	5.33	1.62	3.67	1.81	3.96	1.50
	(-.69)		(-.13)		(-.26)		(.37)		(.92)		(.61)		(.22)	
ENTREE	4.14	2.23	4.07	1.86	4.24	1.85	3.67	1.65	5.15	2.00	3.43	1.56	4.63	1.49
	(.03)		(.13)		(.58)		(.54)		(.74)		(.37)		(.89)	
ENVOYS	3.80	2.02	3.50	2.05	2.88	1.86	2.66	1.65	3.63	1.97	3.43	1.72	3.79	1.25
	(-.31)		(-.44)		(-.78)		(-.47)		(-.78)		(.37)		(.05)	
EONS	3.02	2.19	3.52	2.22	3.70	2.16	3.00	1.83	4.14	1.94	3.45	1.94	4.24	1.54F
	(-1.09)		(-.42)		(.04)		(-.13)		(-.27)		(.39)		(.50)	
ETHER	4.87	2.10	3.82	2.21	5.10	1.90	2.93	1.58	4.97	2.00	3.19	1.85	3.29	1.66
	(.76)		(-.12)		(1.44)		(-.20)		(.56)		(.13)		(-.45)	
EWE	4.57	2.45	3.80	2.53	4.79	2.52	2.78	1.92	3.61	2.21	3.03	1.84	4.23	1.54F
	(.46)		(-.14)		(1.13)		(-.35)		(-.80)		(-.03)		(.49)	
FAZE	3.04	1.89	2.89	1.82	2.90	1.73	2.95	1.80	3.97	1.95	2.52	1.53	3.51	1.44
	(-1.07)		(-1.05)		(-.76)		(-.18)		(-.44)		(-.54)		(-.23)	
FETISH	2.84	1.67	4.11	1.87	3.45	1.62	3.17	1.80	4.54	2.18	3.97	1.83	3.11	1.57
	(-1.27)		(.17)		(-.21)		(.04)		(.13)		(.91)		(-.63)	
FIR	4.38	2.34	4.55	1.96	4.82	2.05	3.48	1.79	4.81	2.20	2.69	1.44	4.79	1.36
	(.27)		(.61)		(1.16)		(.35)		(.40)		(-.37)		(1.05)	

	CON M	CON SD	IMG M	IMG SD	CAT M	CAT SD	MNG M	MNG SD	FAM M	FAM SD	NOA M	NOA SD	PLS M	PLS SD
FLAX	4.91	2.27	3.83	2.13	3.85	1.99	3.28	1.78	4.15	2.07	2.57	1.54	4.08	1.15
	(.80)		(-.11)		(.19)		(.15)		(-.26)		(-.49)		(.34)	
FLICKER	4.11	1.95	5.00	1.76	3.42	1.72	3.65	1.66	5.44	1.76	2.87	1.79	4.34	1.35
	(.00)		(1.06)		(-.24)		(.52)		(1.03)		(-.19)		(.60)	
FOAL	4.16	2.32	4.42	2.19	4.17	2.24	3.53	2.05	4.12	2.27	2.92	1.79	4.05	1.52F
	(.05)		(.48)		(.51)		(.40)		(-.29)		(-.14)		(.31)	
FORMALDEHYDE	5.34	2.27	4.54	2.52	4.97	2.08	3.08	1.99	4.37	1.95	2.70	1.73	2.41	1.59
	(1.23)		(.60)		(1.31)		(-.05)		(-.04)		(-.36)		(-1.33)	
FRANC	4.75	2.32	4.20	2.14	4.54	2.18	3.39	1.94	4.62	2.10	2.57	1.48	4.22	1.45
	(.64)		(.26)		(.88)		(.26)		(.21)		(-.49)		(.48)	
FRANK	3.97	2.02	4.13	2.34	4.18	2.24	3.56	1.70	5.74	1.56	2.81	1.62	4.15	1.79
	(-.14)		(.19)		(.52)		(.43)		(1.33)		(-.25)		(.41)	
FRATERNAL	3.45	2.03	3.70	2.11	3.93	1.87	3.55	1.68	4.90	1.90	3.44	1.59	4.30	1.48
	(-.66)		(-.24)		(.27)		(.42)		(.49)		(.38)		(.56)	
FRAYS	3.89	2.17	3.65	1.79	2.82	1.67	2.95	1.38	3.66	2.06	2.93	1.65	3.42	1.45
	(-.22)		(-.29)		(-.84)		(-.18)		(-.75)		(-.13)		(-.32)	
FROCK	4.77	2.31	3.97	2.27	4.05	2.22	2.75	1.51	3.97	1.85	3.16	1.71	3.82	1.36F
	(.66)		(.03)		(.39)		(-.38)		(-.44)		(.10)		(.08)	
FRUGAL	3.00	1.67	3.61	2.11	3.00	1.96	3.33	1.65	3.88	1.97	3.23	1.54	3.48	1.32
	(-1.11)		(-.33)		(-.66)		(.20)		(-.53)		(.17)		(-.26)	
FUSELAGE	4.79	2.03	3.96	2.13	3.57	2.20	2.80	1.73	3.63	2.07	3.44	1.89	3.52	1.40M
	(.68)		(.02)		(-.09)		(-.33)		(-.78)		(.38)		(-.22)	
GABLE	4.45	2.30	4.18	2.25	4.17	2.06	3.05	2.03	4.29	2.23	3.16	1.82	4.18	1.25
	(.34)		(.24)		(.51)		(-.08)		(-.12)		(.10)		(.44)	
GAIT	3.77	2.12	3.71	2.16	3.45	2.11	3.28	1.75	4.43	2.02	3.44	1.62	4.00	1.19
	(-.34)		(-.23)		(-.21)		(.15)		(.02)		(.38)		(.26)	
GAUNTLET	4.93	2.16	3.46	2.22	3.20	1.92	2.57	1.77	2.98	2.05	2.98	1.62	3.49	1.38M
	(.82)		(-.48)		(-.46)		(-.56)		(-1.43)		(-.08)		(-.25)	
GENDER	4.39	2.10	4.11	2.29	3.97	2.06	4.05	1.98	5.22	1.71	3.30	1.86	4.31	1.19
	(.28)		(.17)		(.31)		(.92)		(.81)		(.24)		(.57)	
GILT	3.50	2.20	3.39	2.07	2.75	1.59	2.90	1.81	3.93	2.10	2.92	1.24	3.24	1.42
	(-.61)		(-.55)		(-.91)		(-.23)		(-.48)		(-.14)		(-.30)	
GNU	4.70	2.38	3.40	2.56	3.76	2.67	2.05	1.60	3.00	2.11	3.08	2.17	3.56	1.56F
	(.59)		(-.54)		(.10)		(-1.08)		(-1.41)		(.02)		(-.18)	
GRAFT	3.68	2.04	3.98	2.03	3.40	1.83	3.68	1.85	4.97	2.01	3.49	1.71	3.31	1.64
	(-.43)		(.04)		(-.26)		(.55)		(.56)		(.43)		(-.43)	
GRANULAR	4.46	2.07	4.98	1.91	4.10	1.67	3.13	1.69	4.97	1.89	3.30	1.61	3.90	.72
	(.35)		(1.04)		(.44)		(.00)		(.56)		(.24)		(.16)	
GRAPHED	3.13	1.89	4.09	2.26	3.73	1.77	2.98	1.52	4.76	2.17	3.07	1.45	3.71	1.21
	(-.98)		(.15)		(.07)		(-.15)		(.35)		(.01)		(-.03)	
GRATE	4.28	1.85	4.18	2.04	3.57	1.72	3.02	1.76	5.05	2.05	3.10	1.26	3.21	1.13
	(.17)		(.24)		(-.09)		(-.11)		(.64)		(.04)		(-.53)	
GRAYS	3.89	1.76	4.22	2.13	4.00	2.23	3.45	1.74	5.27	1.89	2.98	1.77	3.81	1.28
	(-.22)		(.28)		(.34)		(.32)		(.86)		(-.08)		(.07)	
GRAZE	4.05	2.00	4.64	2.14	3.85	1.81	3.70	1.36	5.27	1.71	3.21	1.46	4.47	1.41
	(-.06)		(.70)		(.19)		(.57)		(.86)		(.15)		(.73)	
GULLET	5.33	2.11	4.36	2.21	4.00	2.03	3.15	1.96	3.79	1.90	2.49	1.31	3.19	1.41
	(1.22)		(.42)		(.34)		(.02)		(-.62)		(-.57)		(-.55)	
HALE	3.27	2.12	3.70	2.19	2.60	1.59	2.67	1.66	4.44	2.07	2.68	1.40	3.73	1.27
	(-.84)		(-.24)		(-1.06)		(-.46)		(-.03)		(-.38)		(-.01)	
HALVE	3.67	2.02	4.19	2.15	4.07	1.91	3.66	1.82	5.33	2.10	2.62	1.39	3.77	1.02
	(-.44)		(.25)		(.41)		(.53)		(.92)		(-.44)		(.03)	
HENCHMAN	4.79	2.22	4.39	1.96	4.23	2.12	3.17	1.67	3.72	1.93	3.37	1.70	2.68	1.29
	(.68)		(.45)		(.57)		(.04)		(-.69)		(.31)		(-1.06)	

	CON		IMG		CAT		MNG		FAM		NOA		PLS	
	M	SD	M	SD	M	SD	M	SD	M	SD	M	SD	M	SD
HOARSE	3.78	2.15	3.97	1.91	3.28	1.58	3.21	1.53	5.25	1.78	2.76	1.43	2.75	1.12
	(-.33)		(.03)		(-.38)		(.08)		(.84)		(-.30)		(-.99)	
HYBRID	3.40	1.64	3.44	2.16	3.84	1.87	3.03	1.59	4.55	2.16	3.22	1.61	4.14	1.34
	(-.71)		(-.50)		(.18)		(-.10)		(.14)		(.16)		(.40)	
IMPOVERISHED	3.47	2.07	3.79	1.79	2.82	1.52	3.53	1.66	4.77	1.87	3.86	1.86	2.77	1.50M
	(-.64)		(-.15)		(-.84)		(.40)		(.36)		(.80)		(-.97)	
INCISE	3.35	1.83	3.65	1.97	3.09	1.79	2.80	1.70	4.19	1.98	3.05	1.54	3.42	1.23
	(-.76)		(-.29)		(-.57)		(-.33)		(-.22)		(-.01)		(-.32)	
JANGLE	3.69	2.01	3.86	1.82	3.15	1.34	2.90	1.50	4.52	1.87	2.28	1.21	3.91	1.45
	(-.42)		(-.08)		(-.51)		(-.23)		(.11)		(-.78)		(.17)	
JARGON	3.48	1.83	3.30	1.81	4.05	1.85	3.84	1.72	4.87	1.98	4.03	1.77	4.07	1.45
	(-.63)		(-.14)		(.39)		(.71)		(.46)		(.97)		(.33)	
KABOB	5.32	2.12	4.24	2.38	4.53	2.23	3.00	2.14	4.11	2.28	3.23	1.70	4.45	1.87
	(1.21)		(-.30)		(.87)		(-.13)		(-.30)		(.17)		(.71)	
KILOWATTS	4.32	2.24	3.51	2.30	4.62	2.12	3.21	2.02	4.90	2.13	2.70	1.78	3.41	1.53
	(.21)		(-.43)		(.96)		(.08)		(.49)		(-.36)		(-.33)	
KINDLE	3.82	1.77	4.09	1.87	3.36	1.88	3.38	1.56	5.31	1.58	3.23	1.42	4.53	1.39
	(-.29)		(.15)		(-.28)		(.25)		(.90)		(.17)		(.79)	
KNOLL	4.82	2.34	4.38	2.08	3.90	2.06	3.23	1.85	4.48	2.11	3.54	1.72	3.94	1.76
	(.71)		(.44)		(.24)		(.10)		(.07)		(.48)		(.20)	
LABYRINTH	4.86	2.11	4.16	2.32	3.58	2.22	3.18	1.94	4.31	2.01	3.56	2.13	3.70	1.70
	(.75)		(.22)		(-.08)		(.05)		(-.10)		(.50)		(-.04)	
LAIN	3.27	2.01	3.22	2.16	2.62	1.38	2.49	1.65	4.16	2.09	2.68	1.55	3.38	1.21
	(-.84)		(-.72)		(-1.04)		(-.64)		(-.25)		(-.38)		(-.36)	
LAIR	4.71	1.84	4.48	1.95	4.17	1.92	3.30	1.94	4.39	2.13	3.16	1.62	3.65	1.45
	(.60)		(.54)		(.51)		(.17)		(-.02)		(.10)		(-.09)	
LAMENT	3.16	2.01	3.47	1.87	2.76	1.43	3.27	1.76	4.64	1.96	2.81	1.41	3.53	1.48
	(-.95)		(-.47)		(-.90)		(.14)		(.23)		(-.25)		(-.21)	
LANCER	5.00	2.00	4.07	1.94	3.93	1.94	2.84	1.83	4.31	1.94	2.63	1.33	3.65	1.68
	(.89)		(.13)		(.27)		(-.29)		(-.10)		(-.43)		(-.09)	
LATHE	4.77	2.32	3.50	2.26	3.38	2.14	2.45	1.63	3.69	2.11	3.30	1.97	3.60	1.39M
	(.66)		(-.44)		(-.28)		(-.67)		(-.72)		(.24)		(-.14)	
LETTERHEAD	4.95	2.12	4.55	2.21	4.21	2.01	2.75	1.68	5.06	1.90	3.15	1.85	3.56	1.40
	(.84)		(.61)		(.55)		(-.38)		(.65)		(.09)		(-.18)	
LICHEN	5.43	2.02	3.99	2.18	4.56	2.18	2.92	1.72	4.39	1.94	3.93	1.92	4.00	1.50
	(1.32)		(.04)		(.90)		(-.21)		(-.02)		(.87)		(.26)	
LIKEN	3.18	2.20	3.16	1.93	3.22	1.99	3.00	1.78	4.59	2.07	2.97	1.67	3.94	1.72
	(-.93)		(-.78)		(-.44)		(-.13)		(.18)		(-.09)		(.20)	
LIMELIGHT	4.19	1.95	4.70	1.94	3.63	1.71	3.70	1.84	4.80	1.95	3.70	1.67	4.84	1.40
	(.08)		(.76)		(-.03)		(.57)		(.39)		(.64)		(1.10)	
LINKS	4.50	2.02	4.48	1.98	3.90	1.68	3.24	1.48	5.42	1.75	3.32	1.50	3.66	1.18
	(.39)		(.54)		(.24)		(.11)		(1.01)		(.26)		(-.08)	
LIRE	4.45	2.17	3.20	2.09	3.62	2.06	2.61	1.55	3.35	2.02	2.56	1.61	3.53	1.57
	(.34)		(-.74)		(-.04)		(-.52)		(-1.06)		(-.50)		(-.21)	
LITER	4.78	2.05	4.06	2.20	4.09	2.20	3.71	2.14	5.36	2.01	3.44	1.69	3.47	1.52
	(.67)		(.12)		(.43)		(.58)		(.95)		(.38)		(-.27)	
LODE	3.38	2.03	3.57	2.14	3.35	1.83	2.80	1.67	3.44	2.18	3.05	1.55	4.05	1.41
	(-.73)		(-.37)		(-.31)		(-.33)		(-.97)		(-.01)		(.31)	
LOON	4.77	2.00	3.42	2.44	3.30	2.11	2.75	1.74	3.77	2.01	3.08	1.69	3.80	1.72
	(.66)		(-.52)		(-.36)		(-.38)		(-.64)		(.02)		(.06)	
LORRY	4.16	2.43	3.16	2.21	3.28	2.24	2.36	1.68	2.89	2.09	2.85	1.71	3.64	1.36
	(.05)		(-.78)		(-.38)		(-.77)		(-1.52)		(-.21)		(-.10)	
LURE	4.18	2.05	3.83	1.97	3.41	1.64	3.58	1.49	5.25	1.76	3.14	1.59	4.01	1.57
	(.07)		(-.11)		(-.25)		(.45)		(.84)		(.08)		(.27)	

	CON M SD	IMG M SD	CAT M SD	MNG M SD	FAM M SD	NOA M SD	PLS M SD
LUTE	5.05 2.24 (.94)	4.23 2.28 (.29)	4.25 2.30 (.59)	3.16 1.95 (.03)	3.61 2.06 (-.80)	3.21 1.90 (.15)	4.76 1.40F (1.02)
LYE	5.11 2.19 (1.00)	3.66 2.24 (-.28)	4.23 2.21 (.57)	3.18 1.72 (.05)	4.88 1.93 (.47)	2.89 1.75 (-.17)	3.18 1.32 (-.56)
LYNX	5.33 2.14 (1.22)	4.22 2.35 (.28)	4.47 2.43 (.81)	2.93 1.80 (-.20)	3.74 2.31 (-.67)	3.42 1.78 (.36)	4.23 1.56 (.49)
LYRE	5.34 2.16 (1.23)	4.20 2.16 (.26)	4.18 2.17 (.52)	2.85 1.85 (-.28)	3.62 1.98 (-.79)	3.08 1.65 (.02)	4.34 1.54F (.60)
MAGNATE	4.09 1.96 (-.02)	3.54 2.36 (-.40)	3.70 2.07 (.04)	2.67 1.69 (-.46)	3.73 1.98 (-.68)	3.46 1.70 (.40)	3.83 1.39 (.09)
MAIZE	4.49 2.35 (.38)	4.14 2.24 (.20)	4.05 2.17 (.39)	2.74 1.78 (-.39)	4.08 2.15 (-.33)	2.72 1.69 (-.34)	4.35 1.45 (.61)
MAR	2.98 1.74 (-1.13)	4.47 2.06 (-.53)	2.95 1.62 (-.71)	3.12 1.67 (-.01)	4.27 2.23 (-.14)	2.90 1.49 (-.16)	2.98 1.25 (-.76)
MARTIAL	3.34 2.03 (-.77)	4.06 2.05 (.12)	3.81 1.93 (.15)	3.18 1.63 (.05)	5.34 1.82 (.93)	3.49 1.66 (.43)	3.51 1.62 (-.23)
MINCE	4.26 1.99 (.15)	4.13 1.97 (.19)	3.88 1.80 (.22)	3.17 1.37 (.04)	4.58 1.88 (.17)	2.80 1.50 (-.26)	3.68 1.25 (-.06)
MITE	4.59 2.13 (.48)	3.81 1.95 (-.13)	4.42 2.12 (.76)	2.89 1.78 (-.24)	3.65 2.13 (-.76)	2.84 1.44 (-.22)	3.26 1.39M (-.48)
MOAT	5.05 2.03 (.94)	4.91 2.07 (.97)	4.41 1.79 (.75)	3.12 1.61 (-.01)	5.17 1.85 (.76)	2.70 1.46 (-.36)	3.75 1.61 (.01)
MORTAR	5.00 2.17 (.89)	4.81 1.95 (.87)	4.31 1.59 (.75)	3.44 1.93 (.31)	4.70 1.95 (.29)	3.22 1.41 (.16)	3.25 1.53M (-.49)
MOSQUE	4.74 2.32 (.63)	4.55 2.22 (.61)	3.97 2.28 (.31)	3.61 2.13 (.48)	3.90 2.16 (-.51)	3.39 2.04 (.33)	4.13 1.29 (.39)
MOTE	3.93 2.37 (-.18)	4.32 2.25 (.38)	3.52 1.81 (-.14)	2.64 1.78 (-.49)	3.97 1.95 (-.44)	2.34 1.11 (-.72)	3.60 1.29 (-.14)
MOUSSE	4.88 2.20 (.77)	4.33 2.18 (.39)	4.23 2.37 (.57)	2.90 1.86 (-.23)	4.37 2.22 (-.04)	3.15 1.77 (.09)	4.22 1.63F (.48)
NEUTER	3.32 2.23 (-.79)	3.21 2.12 (-.73)	3.15 1.79 (-.51)	3.34 2.12 (.21)	4.42 2.03 (.01)	2.76 1.55 (-.30)	2.90 1.48 (-.84)
NOEL	3.59 2.12 (-.52)	4.57 2.21 (.63)	3.59 2.09 (-.07)	3.60 1.89 (.47)	4.83 2.02 (.42)	3.25 1.87 (.19)	4.98 1.68F (1.24)
ODE	3.77 1.96 (-.34)	3.38 1.87 (-.56)	3.73 2.22 (.07)	3.38 1.72 (.25)	4.34 1.84 (-.07)	3.21 1.74 (.15)	3.82 1.42 (.08)
OFFSHOOT	3.38 1.94 (-.73)	3.16 1.97 (-.78)	2.75 1.74 (-.91)	2.62 1.60 (-.51)	3.95 2.15 (-.46)	3.03 1.49 (-.03)	3.49 1.13 (-.25)
OHMS	3.53 2.27 (-.58)	3.11 2.21 (-.83)	3.92 2.32 (.26)	2.57 1.71 (-.56)	3.76 2.27 (-.65)	2.74 1.88 (-.32)	3.63 1.54F (-.11)
ORNATE	3.35 1.77 (-.76)	4.13 2.14 (.19)	3.75 1.68 (.09)	3.70 1.69 (.57)	4.75 1.88 (.34)	3.75 1.74 (.69)	4.06 1.39F (.32)
OUTFOX	3.14 1.99 (-.97)	3.71 2.20 (-.23)	3.27 1.86 (-.39)	4.13 1.86 (1.00)	4.68 1.89 (.27)	3.31 1.63 (.25)	4.24 1.61 (.50)
OXIDE	4.58 2.09 (.47)	3.26 2.18 (-.68)	5.43 1.81 (1.77)	3.64 2.03 (.51)	5.03 1.95 (.62)	3.41 1.95 (.35)	3.49 1.56 (-.25)
PANE	5.02 2.20 (.91)	4.04 2.23 (.10)	4.17 2.10 (.51)	3.46 1.91 (.33)	4.69 1.85 (.28)	2.53 1.27 (-.53)	4.02 1.24 (.28)
PARE	3.57 2.21 (-.54)	3.86 2.26 (-.08)	3.42 2.07 (-.24)	2.60 1.39 (-.53)	4.09 2.19 (-.32)	2.71 1.44 (-.35)	3.75 1.02 (.01)
PEAL	3.98 2.12 (-.13)	4.27 2.00 (.33)	3.48 1.90 (-.18)	3.81 1.73 (.68)	5.25 2.05 (.84)	2.69 1.40 (-.37)	3.71 1.29 (-.03)
PEEK	4.07 1.95 (-.04)	4.85 1.69 (.91)	3.38 1.58 (-.28)	3.62 1.65 (.49)	5.62 1.63 (1.21)	2.79 1.45 (-.27)	4.19 1.08 (.45)

	CON	IMG	CAT	MNG	FAM	NOA	PLS
	M SD	M SD	M SD	M SD	M SD	M SD	M SD
PEER	4.02 2.00 (-.09)	3.70 2.10 (-.24)	3.48 1.87 (-.18)	3.58 1.58 (.45)	5.34 1.71 (.93)	3.57 1.66 (.51)	4.13 1.21 (.39)
PEON	4.36 1.97 (.25)	4.49 2.38 (.55)	4.20 2.11 (.54)	3.90 1.78 (.77)	4.39 2.08 (-.02)	3.18 1.78 (.12)	2.66 1.59 (-1.08)
PERRY	3.46 2.24 (-.65)	3.50 2.42 (-.44)	2.85 1.96 (-.81)	2.48 1.84 (-.65)	4.00 2.25 (-.41)	2.41 1.63 (-.65)	3.84 1.31 (.10)
PESO	5.16 2.26 (1.05)	4.57 2.26 (.63)	4.70 2.40 (1.04)	3.42 1.90 (.29)	3.92 2.34 (-.49)	2.61 1.70 (-.45)	4.05 1.42 (.31)
PESTLE	4.61 2.30 (.50)	4.04 2.26 (.10)	3.37 1.99 (-.29)	2.41 1.51 (-.72)	3.54 2.31 (-.87)	2.67 1.62 (-.39)	3.34 1.51 (-.40)
PIDGIN	3.68 2.29 (-.43)	3.84 2.43 (-.10)	4.05 2.46 (.39)	2.34 1.72 (-.79)	3.48 2.25 (-.93)	3.14 1.47 (.08)	3.36 1.24 (-.38)
PLACARD	4.44 2.21 (.33)	3.76 2.09 (-.18)	3.21 1.87 (-.45)	2.65 1.74 (-.48)	3.74 2.12 (-.67)	2.95 1.66 (-.11)	3.75 1.17 (.01)
PLIABLE	3.73 1.77 (-.38)	3.58 1.85 (-.36)	3.02 1.67 (-.64)	3.35 1.64 (.22)	4.97 1.74 (.56)	3.56 1.51 (.50)	4.23 1.09 (.49)
PORE	4.88 2.11 (.77)	4.41 2.05 (.47)	3.73 1.98 (.12)	3.39 1.48 (.26)	5.11 1.88 (.70)	3.17 1.53 (.11)	2.99 1.49 (-.75)
PREFIX	3.66 2.11 (-.45)	3.61 2.29 (-.33)	3.77 2.02 (.11)	3.37 1.74 (.24)	4.98 1.94 (.57)	3.22 1.71 (.16)	3.49 1.06 (-.25)
PREPOSITION	3.49 2.02 (-.83)	3.11 2.07 (-.07)	3.73 2.04 (.11)	3.57 1.93 (.44)	4.93 1.71 (.52)	3.43 1.69 (.37)	3.67 1.33 (-.07)
PRIED	3.34 1.92 (-.77)	3.88 2.02 (-.06)	3.07 1.60 (-.59)	3.32 1.75 (.19)	4.95 1.89 (.54)	2.94 1.58 (-.12)	2.99 1.49 (-.75)
PROP	4.70 2.07 (.59)	4.44 2.01 (.50)	3.81 1.83 (.15)	2.93 1.53 (-.20)	5.18 1.80 (.77)	3.70 1.94 (.64)	4.01 1.12 (.27)
PROVINCIAL	3.25 2.11 (-.76)	3.16 1.92 (-.78)	3.41 1.82 (-.25)	3.12 1.72 (-.01)	4.95 1.86 (.54)	3.54 1.80 (.48)	3.81 1.44 (.07)
PROXY	3.47 2.13 (-.64)	2.44 2.07 (-.50)	3.30 2.00 (-.36)	3.27 1.80 (.14)	4.59 2.13 (.18)	2.87 1.66 (-.19)	3.72 .97 (-.02)
PSALM	4.05 2.17 (-.06)	4.21 2.15 (.27)	4.63 2.01 (.97)	3.48 2.03 (.35)	4.92 2.08 (.51)	3.35 1.79 (.29)	4.43 1.89 (.69)
PUMMEL	3.83 2.18 (-.28)	3.02 1.82 (-.92)	3.33 1.96 (-.33)	2.90 2.00 (-.23)	3.61 2.14 (-.80)	2.89 1.70 (-.17)	3.06 1.46 (-.68)
RACK	5.31 1.98 (1.20)	4.33 1.94 (.39)	3.97 1.88 (.31)	3.37 1.42 (.24)	5.60 1.50 (1.19)	3.21 1.42 (.15)	3.44 1.23 (-.30)
RAMROD	5.05 2.09 (.94)	4.50 2.12 (.56)	3.67 2.00 (.01)	2.87 1.67 (-.26)	3.68 2.12 (-.73)	2.56 1.48 (-.50)	3.47 1.58M (-.27)
REAP	3.69 1.82 (-.42)	4.02 1.88 (.08)	3.63 1.80 (-.03)	3.89 1.77 (.76)	5.15 2.01 (.74)	3.23 1.75 (.17)	4.38 1.59 (.64)
REAPER	4.51 2.05 (.40)	4.56 1.97 (.62)	3.78 1.85 (.12)	3.38 1.88 (.25)	4.75 1.90 (.34)	3.43 1.65 (.37)	3.56 1.26 (-.18)
REVERY	3.38 1.98 (-.73)	3.29 2.10 (-.65)	2.93 1.78 (-.73)	2.72 1.79 (-.41)	3.46 1.94 (-.95)	2.98 1.44 (-.08)	3.57 1.43 (-.17)
RHAPSODY	3.71 1.78 (-.40)	3.75 2.07 (-.19)	3.34 2.14 (.16)	3.29 1.62 (.16)	4.08 2.10 (-.33)	3.95 1.87 (.89)	4.90 1.54 (1.16)
RHOMBUS	4.15 2.20 (.04)	4.35 2.45 (.41)	4.13 2.33 (.41)	2.97 1.89 (-.16)	4.13 2.00 (-.28)	2.77 1.55 (-.29)	3.59 1.43 (-.15)
RITE	3.77 2.16 (-.34)	3.47 2.17 (-.47)	3.39 1.74 (-.28)	3.02 1.81 (-.11)	4.74 2.21 (.33)	3.34 1.89 (.28)	3.93 1.57 (.19)
ROE	3.93 2.21 (-.18)	3.43 2.16 (-.51)	2.85 1.89 (-.81)	2.65 1.93 (-.48)	3.07 1.90 (-1.34)	2.51 1.61 (-.55)	3.19 1.48 (-.55)
ROOMER	4.34 2.15 (.23)	4.09 2.19 (.15)	3.61 2.08 (-.05)	3.31 1.78 (.18)	5.13 1.95 (.72)	3.28 1.60 (.22)	3.60 1.35 (-.14)

	CON		IMG		CAT		MNG		FAM		NOA		PLS	
	M	SD	M	SD	M	SD	M	SD	M	SD	M	SD	M	SD
RUBBLE	4.40	2.06	4.43	1.95	3.81	1.86	3.63	1.51	5.11	1.83	3.59	1.57	3.11	1.32
	(.29)		(.49)		(.15)		(.50)		(.70)		(.53)		(-.63)	
RUFF	3.54	2.12	3.21	2.26	2.98	1.99	2.92	1.62	4.03	2.13	2.33	1.65	3.24	1.51
	(-.57)		(-.73)		(-.68)		(-.21)		(-.38)		(-.73)		(-.50)	
SABLE	5.09	2.23	4.13	2.36	4.03	2.22	3.25	1.57	4.25	2.18	3.16	1.76	4.41	1.54
	(.98)		(.19)		(.37)		(.12)		(-.16)		(.10)		(.67)	
SAGE	4.58	2.11	4.28	2.07	4.20	2.02	3.37	1.89	4.98	2.02	2.98	1.66	4.11	1.54
	(.47)		(.34)		(.54)		(.24)		(.57)		(-.08)		(.37)	
SALVE	4.30	2.40	3.85	2.33	3.62	2.12	2.84	2.02	4.03	2.25	3.25	1.78	3.74	1.47
	(.19)		(-.09)		(-.04)		(-.29)		(-.38)		(.19)		(.00)	
SANCTITY	2.89	2.05	3.24	1.83	3.00	1.67	2.77	1.75	4.12	2.15	3.41	1.78	4.21	1.50
	(-1.22)		(-.70)		(-.66)		(-.36)		(-.29)		(.35)		(.47)	
SANDER	4.52	2.14	4.11	2.25	4.28	2.12	2.25	1.48	4.45	2.11	2.81	1.68	3.94	1.09
	(.41)		(.17)		(.62)		(-.88)		(.04)		(-.25)		(.20)	
SASH	5.36	2.01	4.82	1.86	4.18	1.88	3.34	1.62	4.59	1.94	2.80	1.30	4.21	1.32
	(1.25)		(.88)		(.52)		(.21)		(.18)		(-.26)		(.47)	
SEALING	3.53	2.03	3.66	2.07	3.75	1.84	3.17	1.67	5.22	1.71	3.08	1.50	3.67	1.12
	(-.58)		(-.28)		(.09)		(.04)		(.81)		(.02)		(-.07)	
SEAR	2.88	2.07	2.93	2.07	2.92	1.85	2.59	1.94	3.90	2.09	2.73	1.53	3.48	1.37
	(-1.23)		(-1.01)		(-.74)		(-.54)		(-.51)		(-.33)		(-.26)	
SEEL	4.13	2.27	3.35	2.08	3.57	1.99	3.00	1.83	3.75	2.40	2.92	1.73	4.00	1.12
	(.02)		(-.59)		(-.09)		(-.13)		(-.66)		(-.14)		(.26)	
SEER	3.19	2.15	3.12	1.99	3.49	1.95	2.90	1.85	3.33	2.21	2.83	1.68	3.89	1.51M
	(-.92)		(-.82)		(-.17)		(-.23)		(-1.08)		(-.23)		(.15)	
SEINE	3.47	2.32	3.61	2.37	2.98	2.16	2.80	1.93	3.20	2.15	3.02	1.68	4.21	1.51F
	(-.64)		(-.33)		(-.68)		(-.33)		(-1.21)		(-.04)		(.47)	
SEQUEL	3.59	2.03	3.40	2.17	3.34	1.81	2.93	1.47	4.41	1.89	3.38	1.39	4.03	1.12
	(-.52)		(-.54)		(-.32)		(-.20)		(.00)		(.32)		(.29)	
SERF	4.79	2.23	4.58	1.96	4.47	1.86	3.61	1.59	5.07	1.89	3.25	1.67	3.18	1.49
	(.68)		(.64)		(.81)		(.48)		(.66)		(.19)		(-.56)	
SERIAL	3.61	2.13	3.34	2.06	3.22	1.85	3.10	1.65	5.14	1.73	2.93	1.44	3.74	1.12
	(-.50)		(-.60)		(-.44)		(-.03)		(.73)		(-.13)		(.00)	
SHALE	4.54	2.24	3.95	2.18	4.90	2.12	2.95	1.52	4.33	1.96	3.30	1.44	3.70	1.32F
	(.43)		(.01)		(1.24)		(-.18)		(-.08)		(.24)		(-.04)	
SHIEK	4.19	2.15	4.98	1.90	4.17	1.95	3.75	1.97	4.73	2.12	3.33	1.81	4.37	1.63F
	(.08)		(1.04)		(.51)		(.62)		(.32)		(.27)		(.63)	
SILOS	5.00	2.36	4.69	2.36	4.07	2.11	2.93	2.01	3.85	2.31	3.48	1.76	4.15	1.46M
	(.89)		(.75)		(.41)		(-.20)		(-.56)		(.42)		(.41)	
SINE	3.15	1.86	3.71	2.42	3.17	2.20	2.15	1.66	4.27	2.28	2.55	1.73	3.42	1.47
	(-.96)		(-.23)		(-.49)		(-.98)		(-.14)		(-.51)		(-.32)	
SLAG	4.22	2.23	3.67	2.24	2.75	1.56	2.51	1.63	3.84	1.99	2.83	1.59	2.70	1.07
	(.11)		(-.27)		(-.91)		(-.62)		(-.57)		(-.23)		(-1.04)	
SLEAVE	4.17	2.47	3.75	2.23	2.98	2.10	2.22	1.70	3.82	2.37	2.52	1.35	3.56	1.00
	(.06)		(-.19)		(-.68)		(-.91)		(-.59)		(-.54)		(-.18)	
SLOVENLY	3.07	1.77	3.98	2.14	2.40	1.67	3.38	1.91	3.71	2.08	2.95	1.53	2.87	1.44
	(-1.04)		(.04)		(-1.26)		(.25)		(-.70)		(-.11)		(-.87)	
SMELT	4.71	1.91	4.67	2.21	4.50	1.85	3.36	1.44	5.18	1.74	3.45	1.81	3.32	1.31
	(.60)		(.73)		(.84)		(.23)		(.77)		(.39)		(-.42)	
SONATA	4.67	2.02	4.16	2.21	4.55	2.13	3.49	1.71	4.34	1.96	3.88	1.94	4.76	1.68
	(.56)		(.22)		(.89)		(.36)		(-.07)		(.82)		(1.02)	
SPANGLE	3.67	1.82	3.50	2.11	2.58	1.57	2.62	1.33	4.18	1.76	2.74	1.49	4.16	1.41F
	(-.44)		(-.44)		(-1.08)		(-.51)		(-.23)		(-.32)		(.42)	
SPAYED	3.63	2.06	3.55	1.77	3.64	1.75	3.10	1.63	4.89	2.20	3.05	1.76	3.09	1.48
	(-.48)		(-.39)		(-.02)		(-.03)		(.48)		(-.01)		(-.65)	

	CON M	CON SD	IMG M	IMG SD	CAT M	CAT SD	MNG M	MNG SD	FAM M	FAM SD	NOA M	NOA SD	PLS M	PLS SD
SPOUT	4.64	2.34 (.53)	4.60	1.83 (.66)	3.97	1.81 (.31)	2.95	1.49 (-.18)	5.07	1.80 (.66)	3.16	1.60 (.10)	3.90	1.23 (.16)
SPUTTERING	3.75	1.96 (-.36)	4.52	2.21 (.58)	3.30	1.34 (-.36)	3.38	1.54 (.25)	4.89	1.93 (.48)	3.51	1.96 (.45)	2.70	1.21 (-1.04)
SQUIB	3.98	2.48 (-.13)	3.84	2.28 (-.10)	3.10	1.95 (-.56)	2.34	1.63 (-.79)	3.57	2.08 (-.84)	2.57	1.56 (-.49)	2.99	1.38 (-.75)
STALK	4.11	2.03 (.00)	3.91	1.97 (-.03)	3.75	1.83 (.09)	3.88	1.50 (.75)	4.95	1.79 (.54)	3.36	1.39 (.30)	3.53	1.28M (-.21)
STEPPE	4.75	2.06 (.64)	4.21	2.59 (.27)	3.68	2.27 (.02)	2.52	1.48 (-.43)	3.98	2.01 (-.43)	3.02	1.73 (-.04)	4.00	1.36F (.26)
STILE	3.67	2.41 (-.44)	3.18	2.15 (-.76)	2.98	1.81 (-.68)	2.36	1.64 (-.77)	3.40	2.02 (-1.01)	2.49	1.46 (-.57)	3.81	1.38M (.07)
SURTAX	3.77	2.41 (-.34)	3.38	2.12 (-.56)	3.73	2.07 (.07)	2.25	1.42 (-.88)	3.64	1.89 (-.77)	3.05	1.68 (-.01)	3.06	1.31 (-.68)
TANG	4.74	2.26 (.63)	5.12	2.05 (1.18)	3.84	2.30 (.18)	3.56	1.88 (.43)	5.10	1.86 (.69)	2.75	1.40 (-.31)	4.71	1.70 (.97)
TAPER	3.58	1.92 (-.53)	3.66	2.27 (-.28)	3.17	1.60 (-.49)	2.92	1.74 (-.21)	4.58	2.04 (.17)	2.31	1.18 (-.75)	3.92	1.51 (.18)
TEEM	3.36	2.28 (-.75)	3.40	2.29 (-.54)	2.95	2.13 (-.71)	2.45	1.75 (-.68)	3.97	2.32 (-.44)	2.54	1.65 (-.52)	4.19	1.40 (.45)
TEMPEST	4.11	2.27 (.00)	4.75	1.83 (.81)	3.62	1.82 (-.04)	3.90	1.91 (.77)	4.55	1.80 (.14)	3.56	1.61 (.50)	4.07	1.36M (.33)
TENURE	3.41	1.91 (-.70)	3.20	2.11 (-.74)	3.12	1.80 (-.54)	2.89	1.78 (-.24)	4.70	1.92 (.29)	3.05	1.44 (-.01)	3.78	1.64 (.04)
THRONG	3.96	2.07 (-.15)	4.46	2.07 (.52)	3.17	1.79 (-.49)	3.60	1.94 (.47)	4.51	1.76 (.10)	3.52	1.59 (.46)	3.55	1.17 (-.19)
THUD	4.19	1.94 (.08)	4.47	1.84 (.53)	4.03	1.99 (.37)	3.52	1.71 (.39)	5.30	1.61 (.89)	2.47	1.57 (-.59)	3.26	1.11 (-.48)
THWART	3.36	1.78 (-.75)	3.18	1.96 (-.76)	2.85	1.79 (-.81)	3.32	1.70 (.19)	4.35	1.80 (-.06)	2.89	1.42 (-.17)	3.41	1.37 (-.33)
THYME	5.44	1.95 (1.33)	4.37	2.30 (.43)	4.90	2.24 (1.24)	3.46	1.85 (.33)	4.08	1.92 (-.33)	2.77	1.46 (-.29)	4.47	1.75F (.73)
TILL	3.61	2.51 (-.50)	3.58	2.21 (-.36)	3.15	1.89 (-.51)	3.53	2.14 (.40)	5.16	2.03 (.75)	3.23	1.72 (.17)	3.65	1.42 (-.09)
TOW	4.05	1.83 (-.06)	4.00	1.97 (.06)	3.49	1.83 (-.17)	3.40	1.51 (.27)	5.42	1.87 (1.01)	2.75	1.25 (-.31)	3.32	1.35 (-.42)
TRANCE	3.64	2.04 (-.47)	4.20	1.99 (.26)	3.52	1.77 (-.14)	3.59	1.50 (.46)	5.05	1.80 (.64)	3.31	1.60 (.25)	3.70	1.11 (-.04)
TRAWL	4.41	2.13 (.30)	3.46	2.28 (-.48)	2.93	1.77 (-.73)	2.75	1.95 (-.38)	3.95	2.25 (-.46)	3.06	1.70 (.00)	3.82	1.46 (.08)
TROUPE	4.75	1.87 (.64)	3.98	2.40 (.04)	3.58	1.82 (-.08)	3.38	1.64 (.25)	4.37	2.03 (-.04)	3.72	1.62 (.66)	3.72	1.46 (-.02)
TUFF	3.48	2.13 (-.63)	3.60	2.27 (-.34)	3.34	1.96 (-.32)	3.15	2.06 (.02)	4.15	2.14 (-.26)	2.52	1.64 (-.54)	3.72	1.56 (-.02)
TWANG	3.67	2.05 (-.44)	3.81	2.07 (-.13)	3.02	1.75 (-.44)	2.88	1.40 (-.25)	4.45	2.14 (.04)	2.51	1.28 (-.55)	3.38	1.32M (-.36)
URN	4.92	2.34 (.81)	4.61	2.15 (.67)	4.30	2.10 (.64)	3.50	1.84 (.37)	4.50	2.04 (.09)	3.10	1.61 (.04)	3.75	1.30M (.01)
VALE	4.25	2.25 (.14)	3.53	2.27 (-.41)	3.50	2.07 (-.16)	3.02	1.87 (-.11)	3.82	2.02 (-.59)	3.02	1.56 (-.04)	4.28	1.55M (.54)
VANE	3.96	2.30 (-.15)	3.71	2.16 (-.23)	3.17	1.81 (-.49)	3.10	1.69 (-.03)	4.85	2.00 (.44)	3.31	1.60 (.25)	3.25	1.50 (-.49)
VESTMENT	4.00	2.22 (-.11)	3.59	1.98 (-.35)	3.37	1.67 (-.29)	3.18	1.87 (.05)	3.92	1.94 (-.49)	3.41	1.58 (.35)	3.77	1.30 (.03)

	CON		IMG		CAT		MNG		FAM		NOA		PLS	
	M	SD	M	SD	M	SD	M	SD	M	SD	M	SD	M	SD
VIAL	4.81	2.25	4.18	2.09	3.75	2.02	3.30	1.64	4.45	2.30	3.38	1.71	3.43	1.43
	(.70)		(.24)		(.09)		(.17)		(.04)		(.32)		(-.31)	
VISE	3.98	2.36	4.26	2.29	3.43	1.75	2.95	1.89	4.42	2.14	3.76	1.71	3.51	1.38M
	(-.13)		(.32)		(-.23)		(-.18)		(.01)		(.70)		(-.23)	
VOLT	4.85	2.11	4.09	2.15	4.98	1.80	3.62	1.75	5.09	1.97	3.22	1.73	3.33	1.48
	(.74)		(.15)		(1.32)		(.49)		(.68)		(.16)		(-.41)	
WAMPUM	4.36	2.18	4.14	2.13	3.86	2.31	3.12	2.16	3.84	2.16	3.14	1.83	4.41	1.56M
	(.25)		(.20)		(.20)		(-.01)		(-.57)		(.08)		(.67)	
WARE	3.64	1.90	3.93	1.91	3.20	1.72	3.47	1.67	4.68	2.04	3.51	1.75	3.55	1.05
	(-.47)		(-.01)		(-.46)		(.34)		(.27)		(.45)		(-.19)	
WHALEBONE	5.43	2.04	4.44	2.25	4.82	2.04	2.74	1.85	4.32	2.16	2.83	1.76	4.00	1.55M
	(1.32)		(.50)		(1.16)		(-.39)		(-.09)		(-.23)		(.26)	
WHIFF	4.09	2.13	4.55	2.03	3.02	1.58	3.82	1.66	5.00	1.92	3.15	1.59	3.84	1.19
	(-.02)		(.61)		(-.64)		(.69)		(.59)		(.09)		(.10)	
WICKET	5.12	2.15	4.67	2.16	3.53	1.94	2.98	1.71	4.24	2.08	2.64	1.33	3.40	1.30
	(1.01)		(.73)		(-.13)		(-.15)		(-.17)		(-.42)		(-.34)	
WRACK	3.50	2.01	4.18	2.19	3.40	2.09	3.03	1.78	3.83	2.34	2.72	1.62	3.19	1.30M
	(-.61)		(.24)		(-.26)		(-.10)		(-.58)		(-.34)		(-.55)	
WREST	3.33	2.06	3.07	2.09	2.95	1.90	2.07	1.41	3.93	2.36	2.37	1.42	3.57	1.30M
	(-.78)		(-.87)		(-.71)		(-1.06)		(-.48)		(-.69)		(-.17)	
WRUNG	3.57	1.88	3.46	1.94	2.88	1.76	3.15	1.49	4.57	2.07	2.56	1.57	3.30	1.32
	(-.54)		(-.48)		(-.78)		(.02)		(.16)		(-.50)		(-.44)	
YONDER	3.25	1.87	3.54	2.08	2.84	1.65	2.97	1.43	4.61	2.00	2.87	1.58	4.46	1.43
	(-.86)		(-.40)		(-.82)		(-.16)		(.20)		(-.19)		(.72)	
ZENITH	4.26	2.24	4.43	2.26	3.62	2.09	3.17	1.90	4.90	1.81	3.77	1.98	4.91	1.61
	(.15)		(.49)		(-.04)		(.04)		(.49)		(.71)		(1.17)	

CLUSTER 4

	CON		IMG		CAT		MNG		FAM		NOA		PLS	
	M	SD	M	SD	M	SD	M	SD	M	SD	M	SD	M	SD
ABDUCTION	3.07	1.88 (-.51)	4.27	2.11 (.10)	3.90	1.66 (.14)	3.90	1.62 (-.40)	5.07	1.81 (-.77)	3.77	1.92 (.33)	3.00	1.47 (-.02)
ABRUPT	2.62	1.63 (-.96)	3.63	1.86 (-.54)	3.92	1.83 (.16)	4.39	1.74 (.09)	5.51	1.65 (-.33)	2.74	1.47 (-.70)	3.10	1.20 (.08)
ACCOUNT	3.61	2.04 (.03)	3.55	1.93 (-.62)	4.05	1.80 (.29)	3.92	1.92 (-.38)	5.97	1.40 (.13)	3.59	1.44 (.15)	3.95	1.27 (.93)
ACHE	4.39	2.07 (.81)	4.37	2.23 (.20)	3.65	1.87 (-.11)	4.84	1.56 (.54)	5.97	1.67 (.13)	3.41	1.77 (-.03)	2.16	1.51 (-.86)
ADDING	3.81	2.06 (.23)	3.46	2.06 (-.71)	4.26	2.03 (.50)	3.69	1.70 (-.61)	6.25	1.28 (.41)	3.21	1.78 (-.23)	4.00	1.26 (.98)
ADJECTIVE	3.12	1.84 (-.46)	3.88	2.18 (-.29)	5.37	1.78 (1.61)	3.92	1.99 (-.38)	5.89	1.68 (.05)	3.72	1.98 (.28)	3.51	1.42F (.49)
ADVERB	3.48	2.04 (-.10)	3.09	1.97 (-1.08)	5.09	1.81 (1.33)	3.22	1.96 (-1.08)	5.47	1.81 (-.37)	3.29	2.01 (-.15)	3.35	1.26 (.33)
AFRAID	3.32	2.21 (-.26)	4.42	1.99 (.25)	3.60	1.75 (-.16)	5.07	1.83 (.77)	6.24	1.34 (.40)	3.77	1.97 (.33)	2.63	1.35 (-.39)
AGONY	3.60	2.10 (.02)	4.42	1.90 (.25)	3.42	1.81 (-.34)	4.85	1.74 (.55)	5.81	1.42 (-.03)	3.61	1.67 (.17)	2.28	1.45M (-.74)
ALIEN	3.95	2.12 (.37)	4.64	1.82 (.47)	4.20	1.83 (.44)	4.22	1.76 (-.08)	5.53	1.69 (-.31)	4.21	1.98 (.77)	3.24	1.42 (.22)
ALONE	3.86	2.16 (.28)	4.64	1.84 (.47)	3.53	2.00 (-.23)	4.60	1.72 (.30)	6.36	1.17 (.52)	3.23	1.68 (-.21)	3.51	1.96 (.49)
ANGER	3.80	2.20 (.22)	4.82	2.01 (.65)	4.07	1.88 (.31)	4.89	1.87 (.59)	6.19	1.32 (.35)	4.20	1.95 (.76)	2.45	1.52 (-.57)
APART	3.00	1.94 (-.58)	3.58	2.17 (-.59)	3.37	1.87 (-.39)	3.98	1.50 (-.32)	6.29	1.15 (.45)	3.08	1.72 (-.36)	2.98	1.40 (-.04)
APATHY	3.60	2.23 (.02)	3.70	2.10 (-.47)	3.03	1.98 (-.73)	3.77	1.64 (-.53)	5.46	1.49 (-.38)	3.64	1.88 (.20)	2.85	1.51 (-.17)
ARTIFICIAL	3.46	1.87 (-.12)	3.80	2.24 (-.37)	4.02	1.82 (.26)	4.28	1.58 (-.02)	5.88	1.26 (.04)	4.18	1.94 (.74)	3.18	1.56M (.16)
ASHAMED	3.21	2.17 (-.37)	3.91	1.90 (-.26)	3.22	1.91 (-.54)	4.31	1.77 (.01)	5.90	1.60 (.06)	3.43	1.71 (-.01)	2.21	1.53 (-.81)
ATTACK	4.07	1.91 (.49)	4.95	1.87 (.78)	4.10	1.63 (.34)	4.76	1.55 (.46)	6.16	1.20 (.32)	3.97	1.87 (.53)	2.71	1.68M (-.31)
AUDITION	3.66	2.07 (.08)	3.89	2.03 (-.28)	4.03	1.97 (.27)	3.97	1.60 (-.33)	5.53	1.54 (-.31)	3.82	1.53 (.38)	3.81	1.26 (.79)
AWKWARD	3.25	1.78 (-.33)	4.55	1.73 (.38)	3.13	1.79 (-.63)	4.76	1.75 (.46)	5.92	1.43 (.08)	3.77	1.93 (.33)	2.93	1.46 (-.09)
BAD	3.04	1.92 (-.54)	4.13	2.01 (-.04)	4.38	1.97 (.62)	5.31	1.88 (1.01)	6.32	1.24 (.48)	4.36	1.99 (.92)	2.19	1.05M (-.83)
BANG	4.31	2.06 (.73)	4.64	2.11 (.47)	4.02	1.67 (.26)	3.91	1.79 (-.39)	5.77	1.66 (-.07)	2.88	1.66 (-.56)	3.18	1.20 (.16)
BANNED	2.96	1.93 (-.62)	3.47	1.81 (-.70)	2.97	1.55 (-.79)	4.05	1.74 (-.25)	5.48	1.68 (-.36)	3.70	1.74 (.26)	2.74	1.33M (-.28)
BAWL	3.80	1.91 (.22)	4.11	1.97 (-.06)	3.50	1.75 (-.26)	3.70	1.69 (-.60)	5.03	1.82 (-.81)	2.98	1.61 (-.46)	2.78	1.68M (-.24)
BEAT	3.57	2.03 (-.01)	4.00	1.90 (-.17)	3.83	1.64 (.07)	4.71	1.99 (.41)	6.10	1.20 (.26)	3.71	1.68 (.26)	3.23	1.74M (.21)
BEG	2.96	1.81 (-.62)	4.25	1.87 (.08)	3.30	1.54 (-.46)	4.21	1.77 (-.09)	6.03	1.41 (.19)	3.23	1.60 (-.21)	2.42	1.33 (-.60)
BILLED	3.73	1.98 (.15)	3.49	1.93 (-.68)	3.23	1.83 (-.53)	2.98	1.48 (-1.32)	5.71	1.64 (-.13)	3.17	1.54 (-.27)	2.73	1.29 (-.29)
BIT	3.88	2.14 (.30)	4.26	1.91 (.09)	3.43	1.92 (-.33)	3.92	1.81 (-.38)	5.34	1.73 (-.50)	2.97	1.29 (-.47)	3.32	1.33 (.30)

	CON		IMG		CAT		MNG		FAM		NOA		PLS	
	M	SD	M	SD	M	SD	M	SD	M	SD	M	SD	M	SD
BITTER	4.05	2.06	4.74	2.13	4.55	1.85	4.32	1.85	6.16	1.28	3.33	1.59	2.31	1.45
	(.47)		(.57)		(.79)		(.02)		(.32)		(-.11)		(-.71)	
BLEAK	3.03	1.86	4.29	2.07	3.02	1.62	4.15	1.50	5.40	1.68	3.25	1.71	2.60	1.33
	(-.55)		(.12)		(-.74)		(-.15)		(-.44)		(-.19)		(-.42)	
BLEW	3.63	1.85	3.98	2.06	3.32	1.81	4.15	1.83	6.07	1.39	2.59	1.36	3.94	1.52M
	(.05)		(-.19)		(-.44)		(-.15)		(.23)		(-.85)		(.92)	
BLIND	4.39	2.28	4.79	2.00	4.52	1.88	4.17	1.85	6.05	1.44	3.60	1.71	2.47	1.49
	(.81)		(.62)		(.76)		(-.13)		(.21)		(.16)		(-.55)	
BLOW	3.93	1.82	4.52	2.06	3.59	1.88	4.02	1.64	6.02	1.41	3.52	1.62	3.97	1.69
	(.35)		(.35)		(-.17)		(-.28)		(.18)		(.08)		(.95)	
BLUNDER	3.18	1.69	4.26	1.85	3.53	1.65	4.08	1.54	5.49	1.68	3.13	1.77	2.76	1.20
	(-.40)		(.09)		(-.23)		(-.22)		(-.35)		(-.31)		(-.26)	
BORE	3.40	2.00	3.98	2.35	3.45	2.01	4.30	1.48	6.17	1.33	3.11	1.44	2.45	1.35
	(-.18)		(-.19)		(-.31)		(.00)		(.33)		(-.33)		(-.57)	
BORED	3.18	1.95	4.39	1.98	4.05	1.84	4.59	1.87	6.24	1.37	3.08	1.79	2.30	1.37
	(-.40)		(.22)		(.29)		(.29)		(.40)		(-.36)		(-.72)	
BREAK	3.56	1.73	4.10	2.02	3.71	1.99	3.90	1.48	6.13	1.27	3.11	1.70	3.05	1.21
	(-.02)		(-.07)		(-.05)		(-.40)		(.29)		(-.33)		(.03)	
BRIBE	3.63	1.97	4.19	2.18	4.02	1.76	4.36	1.71	6.05	1.40	3.54	1.57	2.91	1.76M
	(.05)		(.02)		(.26)		(.06)		(.21)		(.10)		(-.11)	
BRIEF	3.57	2.05	3.38	1.96	3.42	1.93	4.08	1.77	5.97	1.36	2.89	1.34	3.68	1.23
	(-.01)		(-.79)		(-.34)		(-.22)		(.13)		(-.55)		(.66)	
BROAD	3.95	2.13	4.57	2.09	4.03	1.96	4.72	1.75	5.97	1.44	3.63	2.01	3.60	1.57M
	(.37)		(.40)		(.27)		(.42)		(.13)		(.19)		(.58)	
BROADER	3.22	1.61	3.67	1.58	3.13	1.58	4.48	1.58	5.51	1.76	3.21	1.62	3.79	1.52M
	(-.36)		(-.50)		(-.63)		(.18)		(-.33)		(-.23)		(.77)	
BROKE	3.90	1.80	4.79	1.91	4.08	1.72	4.32	1.50	6.02	1.33	3.44	1.59	2.60	1.30
	(.32)		(.62)		(.32)		(.02)		(.18)		(.00)		(-.42)	
BROKEN	3.79	1.98	4.61	1.92	3.77	1.57	4.90	1.82	6.37	1.18	3.63	1.72	2.85	1.39M
	(.21)		(.44)		(.01)		(.60)		(.53)		(.19)		(-.17)	
BRUTAL	3.98	2.00	4.36	1.76	4.17	1.74	4.67	1.60	5.48	1.78	3.66	1.91	2.46	1.64
	(.40)		(.19)		(.41)		(.37)		(-.36)		(.22)		(-.56)	
BRUTE	4.28	1.57	4.46	2.12	4.40	1.66	4.22	1.45	5.44	1.68	3.49	1.71	2.77	1.55
	(.70)		(.29)		(.64)		(-.08)		(-.40)		(.05)		(-.25)	
BURY	3.68	2.00	3.95	2.04	3.43	1.70	3.80	1.69	5.53	1.71	3.21	1.60	2.74	1.48M
	(.10)		(-.22)		(-.33)		(-.50)		(-.31)		(-.23)		(-.28)	
CARRY	3.60	1.91	4.02	1.91	3.80	1.80	4.36	1.73	6.07	1.48	3.43	1.61	3.77	1.03
	(.02)		(-.15)		(.04)		(.06)		(.23)		(-.01)		(.75)	
CAUGHT	3.36	1.85	3.95	2.04	3.30	1.65	4.44	1.73	6.24	1.24	3.11	1.56	2.88	1.59
	(-.22)		(-.22)		(-.46)		(.14)		(.40)		(-.33)		(-.14)	
CHAOTIC	3.09	1.99	4.28	2.02	2.90	1.71	4.48	1.80	5.13	1.77	4.43	1.87	3.34	1.70M
	(-.49)		(.11)		(-.86)		(.18)		(-.71)		(.99)		(.32)	
CHEAT	3.25	1.83	4.51	2.04	3.93	1.60	4.46	1.74	6.23	1.32	3.63	1.76	2.29	1.40
	(-.33)		(.34)		(.17)		(.16)		(.39)		(.19)		(-.73)	
CHILLY	3.75	1.82	4.54	1.96	4.13	1.94	4.75	1.65	6.10	1.30	2.89	1.56	3.13	1.53
	(.17)		(.37)		(.37)		(.45)		(.26)		(-.55)		(.11)	
CLAMMY	3.89	1.85	4.60	1.97	3.52	1.58	4.15	1.63	5.33	1.79	2.98	1.50	2.60	1.51
	(.31)		(.43)		(-.24)		(-.15)		(-.51)		(-.46)		(-.42)	
CLANG	4.19	2.16	4.39	1.96	4.16	1.84	4.22	1.87	5.05	1.88	2.79	1.71	3.14	1.44M
	(.61)		(.22)		(.40)		(-.08)		(-.79)		(-.65)		(.12)	
CLINCH	3.65	2.07	4.17	2.21	3.43	1.63	3.81	1.74	5.48	1.72	2.90	1.31	3.66	1.66M
	(.07)		(.00)		(-.33)		(-.49)		(-.36)		(-.54)		(.64)	
CLUMSY	3.82	2.06	4.25	1.73	3.73	1.72	4.30	1.38	5.79	1.58	3.03	1.39	2.89	1.36
	(.24)		(.08)		(-.03)		(.00)		(-.05)		(-.41)		(-.13)	

	CON	IMG	CAT	MNG	FAM	NOA	PLS
	M SD	M SD	M SD	M SD	M SD	M SD	M SD
COLDER	3.56 1.98 (-.02)	4.15 1.90 (-.02)	3.87 1.74 (.11)	4.39 1.64 (.09)	6.24 1.27 (.40)	2.95 1.54 (-.49)	3.13 1.45 (.11)
COMBINE	3.98 1.97 (.40)	3.53 1.90 (-.64)	3.90 1.79 (.14)	3.64 1.37 (-.17)	5.67 1.67 (.19)	3.63 1.78	3.97 1.36 (.95)
COMMAND	3.73 1.94 (.15)	3.86 1.85 (-.31)	3.67 1.73 (-.09)	4.08 1.61 (-.22)	5.92 1.46 (.08)	3.22 1.88 (-.22)	3.10 1.59 (.08)
CONDEMN	3.10 1.88 (-.48)	3.43 2.22 (-.74)	3.08 1.59 (-.68)	4.20 1.62 (-.10)	5.74 1.58 (-.10)	3.36 1.66 (-.08)	2.66 1.62M (-.36)
CONFISCATE	3.19 1.91 (-.39)	3.87 1.97 (-.30)	3.38 1.70 (-.38)	4.07 1.54 (-.23)	5.30 1.73 (-.54)	3.23 1.81 (-.21)	2.66 1.43M (-.36)
CONSPIRATORS	4.07 1.99 (.49)	4.20 1.90 (.03)	4.09 1.76 (.33)	4.02 1.55 (-.28)	5.36 1.77 (-.48)	3.81 1.82 (.37)	2.91 1.43M (-.11)
CORPS	4.34 2.03 (.76)	4.02 2.33 (-.15)	4.17 1.89 (.41)	3.90 1.66 (-.40)	5.07 1.79 (-.77)	3.90 1.64 (.46)	3.34 1.40 (.32)
COST	3.33 1.82 (-.25)	4.09 1.99 (-.08)	4.25 2.04 (.49)	4.37 1.65 (.07)	6.37 1.26 (.53)	4.15 1.72 (.71)	3.32 1.25 (.30)
COUNT	3.47 1.98 (-.11)	4.53 2.13 (.36)	3.50 1.70 (-.26)	4.16 1.97 (-.14)	6.48 1.28 (.64)	3.77 2.04 (.33)	3.56 1.31 (.54)
COWARDICE	2.59 1.77 (-.99)	3.38 1.73 (-.79)	3.00 1.63 (-.76)	3.79 1.81 (-.51)	5.05 1.89 (-.79)	3.56 1.79 (.12)	2.43 1.19 (-.59)
COWARDLY	2.41 1.75 (-1.17)	3.56 1.88 (-.61)	3.30 1.72 (-.46)	4.32 1.79 (.02)	5.87 1.62 (.03)	3.60 1.86 (.16)	2.40 1.33M (-.62)
CRIME	4.13 1.96 (.55)	4.93 1.76 (.76)	4.70 1.74 (.94)	4.82 1.42 (.52)	6.05 1.53 (.21)	4.70 1.99 (1.26)	2.10 1.33 (-.92)
CRITICISM	3.58 2.14 (.00)	3.23 1.99 (-.94)	2.93 1.58 (-.83)	4.32 1.61 (.02)	5.93 1.40 (.09)	3.66 2.05 (.22)	3.09 1.26 (.07)
CROAK	3.91 2.29 (.33)	4.39 2.02 (.22)	4.00 1.70 (.24)	3.85 1.79 (-.45)	5.20 1.96 (-.64)	3.13 1.47 (-.31)	2.97 1.62M (-.05)
CROOKED	3.83 1.88 (.25)	4.81 1.83 (.64)	4.05 1.78 (.29)	4.20 1.50 (-.10)	5.61 1.82 (-.23)	3.25 1.53 (-.19)	2.94 1.16 (-.08)
CRUEL	3.63 1.85 (.05)	4.16 1.90 (-.01)	3.58 1.83 (-.18)	4.87 1.47 (.57)	5.95 1.47 (.11)	3.80 1.60 (.36)	2.06 1.39M (-.96)
CRY	4.32 2.07 (.74)	4.53 2.06 (.36)	4.17 1.70 (.41)	4.44 1.68 (.14)	6.25 1.12 (.41)	3.90 1.93 (.46)	2.76 1.43 (-.26)
CURFEW	4.22 2.25 (.64)	4.71 2.03 (.54)	4.23 1.81 (.47)	4.25 1.66 (-.05)	5.53 1.65 (-.31)	3.44 1.86 (.00)	2.94 1.51 (-.08)
CURSE	4.07 2.14 (.49)	4.14 2.08 (-.03)	4.22 2.01 (.46)	4.48 1.72 (.18)	6.05 1.48 (.21)	3.69 1.62 (.25)	2.93 1.44 (-.09)
CUT	4.26 2.29 (.68)	4.54 1.95 (.37)	3.93 1.90 (.17)	4.31 1.89 (.01)	6.55 1.06 (.48)	2.94 1.67 (-.50)	2.66 1.32 (-.36)
DANGER	3.68 1.79 (.10)	4.85 1.89 (.68)	3.62 1.97 (-.14)	4.98 1.60 (.68)	6.32 1.16 (.48)	4.36 1.78 (.92)	2.94 1.51 (-.08)
DARE	2.87 1.80 (-.71)	4.25 1.88 (.08)	3.34 1.45 (-.42)	3.95 1.48 (-.35)	5.87 1.43 (.03)	3.31 1.59 (-.13)	3.99 1.66M (.97)
DEAD	4.25 2.36 (.67)	4.98 1.87 (.81)	4.00 2.22 (.24)	4.97 1.66 (.67)	6.21 1.51 (.37)	3.93 2.32 (.49)	2.22 1.45 (-.80)
DEATH	3.96 2.35 (.38)	4.93 2.16 (.76)	4.50 2.19 (.74)	5.10 1.64 (.80)	6.32 1.18 (.48)	4.93 2.06 (1.49)	2.27 1.58 (-.75)
DEBT	4.12 2.13 (.54)	3.78 2.26 (-.39)	4.17 1.85 (.41)	4.37 1.44 (.07)	5.68 1.68 (-.16)	3.52 1.49 (.08)	2.41 1.60 (-.61)
DECAY	3.66 1.99 (.08)	4.44 2.09 (.27)	3.68 1.82 (-.08)	4.69 1.76 (.39)	5.87 1.58 (.03)	3.62 1.77 (.18)	2.33 1.47M (-.69)
DECAYED	3.71 1.77 (.13)	4.37 1.74 (.20)	3.60 1.92 (-.16)	4.35 1.78 (.05)	5.56 1.73 (-.28)	3.56 1.46 (.12)	2.46 1.57 (-.56)

	CON		IMG		CAT		MNG		FAM		NOA		PLS	
	M	SD	M	SD	M	SD	M	SD	M	SD	M	SD	M	SD
DEFACE	3.93	1.97	4.19	1.80	3.52	1.84	4.40	1.65	5.64	1.72	3.33	1.62	2.10	1.25
	(.35)		(.02)		(-.24)		(.10)		(-.20)		(-.11)		(-.92)	
DEFEAT	3.59	1.88	3.96	2.10	3.64	1.85	4.73	1.58	5.93	1.50	3.46	1.68	2.79	1.55
	(.01)		(-.21)		(-.12)		(.43)		(.09)		(.02)		(-.23)	
DEFEATED	3.91	2.14	4.22	2.23	3.65	1.78	4.73	1.57	6.05	1.43	3.51	1.71	2.37	1.47
	(.33)		(.05)		(-.11)		(.43)		(.21)		(.07)		(-.65)	
DEFICIENT	3.25	1.75	3.52	2.01	3.42	1.73	4.31	1.70	5.39	1.71	3.55	1.81	2.49	1.35
	(-.33)		(-.65)		(-.34)		(.01)		(-.45)		(.11)		(-.53)	
DEGRADED	2.58	1.73	3.19	1.55	3.37	1.84	4.24	1.74	5.70	1.66	3.51	1.78	2.29	1.23M
	(-1.00)		(-.98)		(-.39)		(-.06)		(-.14)		(.07)		(-.73)	
DEMOLISH	3.66	1.79	4.91	2.03	3.67	1.68	4.62	1.67	5.75	1.47	3.77	1.87	2.57	1.67
	(.08)		(.74)		(-.09)		(.32)		(-.09)		(.33)		(-.45)	
DENSE	3.49	1.69	4.55	2.08	3.93	1.64	4.25	1.64	5.98	1.47	3.65	1.78	3.84	1.64F
	(-.09)		(.38)		(.17)		(-.05)		(.14)		(.21)		(.82)	
DESOLATE	3.21	2.15	4.29	1.91	3.33	1.50	4.37	1.79	5.33	1.68	3.44	1.74	3.03	1.49M
	(-.37)		(.12)		(-.43)		(.07)		(-.51)		(.00)		(.01)	
DESPAIR	2.88	1.92	3.67	1.90	2.98	1.48	4.10	1.63	5.78	1.46	3.56	1.74	2.43	1.24
	(-.70)		(-.50)		(-.78)		(-.20)		(-.06)		(.12)		(-.59)	
DESPISE	3.10	1.88	4.44	2.13	3.83	1.81	4.84	1.76	5.43	1.72	3.39	1.74	2.34	1.34
	(-.48)		(.27)		(.07)		(.54)		(-.41)		(-.05)		(-.68)	
DESTROY	3.63	2.24	4.38	2.04	3.50	1.93	5.16	1.82	6.25	1.29	4.11	1.87	2.43	1.62
	(.05)		(.21)		(-.26)		(.86)		(.41)		(.67)		(-.59)	
DIE	3.54	2.25	4.93	1.93	4.42	2.17	5.74	1.63	6.43	1.21	4.16	2.02	2.20	1.46
	(-.04)		(.76)		(.66)		(1.44)		(.59)		(.72)		(-.82)	
DIM	3.98	2.05	4.44	2.10	3.62	1.76	3.67	1.46	5.69	1.58	2.73	1.38	3.53	1.20
	(.40)		(.27)		(-.14)		(-.63)		(-.15)		(-.71)		(.51)	
DISAPPOINT	3.27	1.95	3.45	2.13	3.47	1.74	4.21	1.57	6.11	1.22	3.08	1.65	2.10	1.24
	(-.31)		(-.72)		(-.29)		(-.09)		(.27)		(-.36)		(-.92)	
DISAPPOINTED	2.86	1.94	3.78	1.89	3.18	1.74	4.66	1.91	6.21	1.18	3.85	2.05	2.23	1.32
	(-.72)		(-.39)		(-.58)		(.36)		(.37)		(.41)		(-.79)	
DISCOLOR	3.94	1.82	4.22	1.99	3.21	1.82	3.38	1.52	5.34	1.72	2.98	1.44	3.02	1.23M
	(.36)		(.05)		(-.55)		(-.92)		(-.50)		(-.46)		(.00)	
DISCONNECTION	3.13	1.94	3.51	1.95	3.00	1.87	4.05	1.66	5.43	1.79	3.13	1.79	2.54	1.13
	(-.45)		(-.66)		(-.76)		(-.25)		(-.41)		(-.31)		(-.48)	
DISCORD	2.71	1.78	3.89	1.97	3.07	1.73	3.76	1.77	4.97	1.69	3.84	1.80	3.08	1.49M
	(-.87)		(-.28)		(-.69)		(-.54)		(-.87)		(.40)		(.06)	
DISOBEDIENT	3.44	1.90	3.95	2.05	3.42	1.80	4.00	1.46	5.64	1.52	3.56	1.43	2.92	1.29
	(-.14)		(-.22)		(-.34)		(-.30)		(-.12)		(.12)		(-.10)	
DISRUPTIVE	3.14	1.74	3.61	1.96	3.53	1.94	4.33	1.57	5.27	1.70	3.62	1.59	2.56	1.36
	(-.44)		(-.56)		(-.23)		(.03)		(-.57)		(.18)		(-.46)	
DISTORTION	3.61	2.15	4.22	2.01	3.30	1.77	4.15	1.67	5.36	1.80	4.03	1.91	2.67	1.51
	(.03)		(.05)		(-.46)		(-.15)		(-.48)		(.59)		(-.35)	
DIVISION	3.46	2.01	4.37	2.13	3.75	1.58	4.03	1.65	5.82	1.48	3.72	1.79	3.57	1.43
	(-.12)		(.20)		(-.01)		(-.27)		(-.02)		(.28)		(.55)	
DOWN	3.35	2.08	4.53	2.12	4.30	1.98	4.44	1.82	6.20	1.28	2.97	1.45	3.93	1.34
	(-.23)		(.36)		(.54)		(.14)		(.36)		(-.47)		(.91)	
DREARY	3.20	1.88	4.57	2.10	3.62	1.62	4.52	1.63	5.80	1.50	3.11	1.77	2.69	1.43
	(-.38)		(.40)		(-.14)		(.22)		(-.04)		(-.33)		(-.33)	
DROP	3.16	1.69	4.11	2.22	2.95	1.70	4.00	1.83	6.51	1.03	2.49	1.37	2.74	1.47
	(-.42)		(-.06)		(-.81)		(-.30)		(.67)		(-.95)		(-.28)	
DUAL	3.40	1.96	4.20	2.09	4.10	1.87	3.85	1.64	5.37	1.75	3.03	1.46	3.52	1.32M
	(-.18)		(.03)		(.34)		(-.45)		(-.47)		(-.41)		(.50)	
DUMB	3.36	1.75	3.93	2.04	3.92	1.93	5.27	1.68	6.20	1.30	3.30	1.77	2.62	1.49
	(-.22)		(-.24)		(.16)		(.97)		(.36)		(-.14)		(-.40)	

	CON		IMG		CAT		MNG		FAM		NOA		PLS	
	M	SD	M	SD	M	SD	M	SD	M	SD	M	SD	M	SD
DYNASTY	4.02	2.01	3.76	1.93	3.95	1.68	4.29	1.78	5.31	1.74	4.31	1.93	3.76	1.56M
	(.44)		(-.41)		(.19)		(-.01)		(-.53)		(.87)		(.74)	
EDGE	4.34	2.22	5.11	1.76	3.30	1.92	4.02	2.02	6.21	1.31	2.66	1.36	3.03	1.27
	(.76)		(.94)		(-.46)		(-.28)		(.37)		(-.78)		(.01)	
EERIE	2.91	1.88	4.17	1.87	3.27	1.75	4.60	1.78	5.41	1.66	3.48	1.86	3.31	1.61
	(-.67)		(.00)		(-.49)		(.30)		(-.43)		(.04)		(.29)	
EMBARRASSED	3.41	2.06	4.58	2.14	3.62	1.75	4.50	1.67	5.95	1.48	3.85	1.82	2.77	1.48
	(-.17)		(.41)		(-.14)		(.20)		(.11)		(.41)		(-.25)	
EMISSION	3.93	2.13	4.10	2.16	3.25	1.68	3.81	1.79	5.20	1.74	3.26	1.83	3.37	1.60F
	(.35)		(-.07)		(-.51)		(-.49)		(-.64)		(-.18)		(.35)	
EMPTY	3.70	2.25	5.02	1.92	4.53	1.92	4.80	1.67	6.00	1.43	3.15	1.68	2.85	1.29
	(.12)		(.85)		(.77)		(.50)		(.16)		(-.29)		(-.17)	
END	3.16	2.06	4.56	2.21	3.75	2.10	4.98	1.78	6.66	.99	3.75	2.18	3.23	1.73
	(-.42)		(.39)		(-.01)		(.68)		(.82)		(.31)		(.21)	
EVALUATE	3.84	2.01	3.34	2.08	3.17	1.68	3.72	1.53	5.76	1.47	3.44	1.61	3.62	1.29
	(.26)		(-.83)		(-.59)		(-.58)		(-.08)		(.00)		(.60)	
EXPULSION	3.55	1.97	3.57	2.21	3.57	1.74	3.73	1.76	4.77	1.90	3.97	1.67	2.69	1.57
	(-.03)		(-.60)		(-.19)		(-.57)		(-1.07)		(.53)		(-.33)	
FAIL	3.23	2.01	3.70	1.99	3.50	1.83	4.40	1.56	6.03	1.41	3.61	1.86	2.19	1.38
	(-.35)		(-.47)		(-.26)		(.10)		(.19)		(.17)		(-.83)	
FAILING	2.93	1.86	4.13	2.11	3.73	1.58	4.70	1.81	5.85	1.61	3.70	1.84	2.15	1.42
	(-.65)		(-.04)		(-.03)		(.40)		(.01)		(.26)		(-.87)	
FAINT	4.58	2.00	4.60	1.92	4.03	1.87	3.58	1.61	5.90	1.55	3.19	1.72	3.00	1.21
	(1.00)		(.43)		(.27)		(-.72)		(.06)		(-.25)		(-.02)	
FAR	2.98	1.94	4.29	1.95	3.63	1.80	4.63	1.88	6.46	1.16	3.10	1.81	3.66	1.50
	(-.60)		(.12)		(-.13)		(.33)		(.62)		(-.34)		(.64)	
FARE	4.09	2.01	3.78	2.18	4.05	1.81	3.61	1.63	5.56	1.66	3.43	1.48	3.60	1.27M
	(.51)		(-.39)		(.29)		(-.69)		(-.28)		(-.01)		(.58)	
FARTHER	3.22	1.78	3.84	2.00	3.55	1.93	3.68	1.80	5.85	1.56	2.90	1.67	3.78	1.26
	(-.36)		(-.33)		(-.21)		(-.62)		(.01)		(-.54)		(.76)	
FATE	2.75	1.76	3.87	1.96	3.47	1.72	4.72	1.75	5.85	1.52	4.59	1.93	3.47	1.51
	(-.83)		(-.29)		(-.29)		(.42)		(.01)		(1.15)		(.45)	
FATTER	3.75	2.04	4.44	1.94	3.66	1.93	4.43	1.84	6.02	1.43	3.44	1.85	2.60	1.65M
	(.17)		(.27)		(-.10)		(.13)		(.18)		(.00)		(-.42)	
FEAR	3.22	2.14	3.88	2.01	3.87	1.84	5.38	1.64	6.43	1.05	4.10	2.01	2.84	1.47M
	(-.36)		(-.29)		(.11)		(1.08)		(.59)		(.66)		(-.18)	
FELL	4.03	1.98	4.25	1.86	3.35	1.70	4.03	1.51	6.20	1.24	2.82	1.49	2.65	1.09
	(.45)		(.08)		(-.41)		(-.27)		(.36)		(-.62)		(-.37)	
FEUDALISM	3.32	1.97	4.05	2.17	4.40	1.91	3.69	1.92	5.08	1.88	3.94	2.13	3.19	1.46M
	(-.26)		(-.12)		(.64)		(-.61)		(-.76)		(.50)		(.17)	
FILTH	4.63	1.74	5.11	1.86	4.50	1.64	4.77	1.65	5.66	1.50	3.49	1.79	2.53	1.63
	(1.05)		(.94)		(.74)		(.47)		(-.18)		(.05)		(-.49)	
FINITE	3.33	2.36	3.59	2.10	3.90	2.25	4.16	2.07	5.44	1.63	3.08	2.10	3.84	1.67
	(-.25)		(-.58)		(.14)		(-.14)		(-.40)		(-.36)		(.82)	
FLEE	3.96	2.03	4.25	1.94	4.03	2.09	3.76	1.48	5.60	1.60	3.23	1.71	3.14	1.41
	(.38)		(.08)		(.27)		(-.54)		(-.24)		(-.21)		(.12)	
FLUTTERING	3.45	1.91	4.20	1.89	3.02	1.51	3.75	1.60	5.16	1.76	3.61	1.68	3.69	1.39
	(-.13)		(.03)		(-.74)		(-.55)		(-.68)		(.17)		(.67)	
FOOL	3.50	1.84	4.30	2.14	4.09	1.76	4.68	1.67	6.25	1.06	3.33	1.72	3.35	1.63
	(-.08)		(.13)		(.33)		(.38)		(.41)		(-.11)		(.33)	
FOOLISH	2.40	1.86	3.07	1.50	3.18	1.73	4.71	1.79	6.18	1.21	3.57	1.71	2.79	1.28M
	(-1.18)		(-1.10)		(-.58)		(.41)		(.34)		(.13)		(-.23)	
FORBID	3.44	2.06	3.61	2.06	3.22	1.88	4.54	1.85	5.79	1.55	2.69	1.59	2.77	1.63
	(-.14)		(-.56)		(-.54)		(.24)		(-.05)		(-.75)		(-.25)	

	CON		IMG		CAT		MNG		FAM		NOA		PLS	
	M	SD	M	SD	M	SD	M	SD	M	SD	M	SD	M	SD
FORM	3.86	2.00	4.19	2.15	3.83	1.81	3.89	1.60	6.06	1.34	3.92	1.92	3.91	1.39
	(.28)		(.02)		(.07)		(-.41)		(.22)		(.48)		(.89)	
FOUL	3.47	2.00	4.61	1.94	4.28	1.66	4.07	1.90	5.57	1.60	3.25	1.72	2.55	1.59
	(-.11)		(.44)		(.52)		(-.23)		(-.27)		(-.19)		(-.47)	
FOURTH	3.03	1.78	3.78	1.95	4.32	2.00	3.74	1.77	6.23	1.37	2.76	1.47	3.69	1.01
	(-.55)		(-.39)		(.56)		(-.56)		(.39)		(-.68)		(.67)	
FRAIL	3.79	1.93	4.24	1.96	3.83	1.73	4.11	1.63	5.33	1.70	3.00	1.63	3.30	1.36
	(.21)		(.07)		(.07)		(-.19)		(-.51)		(-.44)		(.28)	
FRAUD	2.72	1.78	3.91	1.98	3.90	1.67	4.10	1.79	5.53	1.79	3.98	1.64	2.23	1.21
	(-.86)		(-.26)		(.14)		(-.20)		(-.31)		(.54)		(-.79)	
FRIGID	4.07	1.94	4.55	2.11	4.00	1.67	4.45	1.72	5.62	1.70	3.73	1.80	2.31	1.60M
	(.49)		(.38)		(.24)		(.15)		(-.22)		(.29)		(-.71)	
FRUSTRATE	3.18	1.99	3.75	1.92	3.52	1.74	4.23	1.70	6.03	1.25	3.73	1.75	2.53	1.39M
	(-.40)		(-.42)		(-.24)		(-.07)		(.19)		(.29)		(-.49)	
GLOOM	3.95	2.04	4.45	2.03	3.67	1.71	4.50	1.63	5.78	1.33	3.38	1.78	2.58	1.55
	(.37)		(.28)		(-.09)		(.20)		(-.06)		(-.06)		(-.44)	
GLUTTON	4.78	2.02	5.32	1.82	4.07	1.96	4.79	1.71	5.64	1.46	3.28	1.59	2.50	1.62
	(1.20)		(1.15)		(.31)		(.49)		(-.20)		(-.16)		(-.52)	
GOOF	3.44	1.96	3.54	1.88	3.40	1.76	4.66	1.88	5.87	1.48	3.26	1.71	3.31	1.57
	(-.14)		(-.63)		(-.36)		(.36)		(.03)		(-.18)		(.29)	
GREEDY	3.56	2.12	4.35	1.98	4.27	1.83	4.61	1.58	5.94	1.33	3.44	1.82	1.88	1.28
	(-.02)		(.18)		(.51)		(.31)		(.10)		(.00)		(-1.14)	
GRIEF	3.35	2.13	4.60	1.95	4.05	1.86	4.89	1.72	6.05	1.41	3.92	2.08	2.73	1.78
	(-.23)		(.43)		(.29)		(.59)		(.21)		(.48)		(-.29)	
GRIND	4.37	1.78	4.79	1.83	4.55	1.85	4.00	1.57	5.60	1.65	3.38	1.68	3.00	1.55
	(.79)		(.62)		(.79)		(-.30)		(-.24)		(-.06)		(-.02)	
GRISLY	3.42	1.91	4.31	2.09	3.45	1.86	3.69	1.85	4.69	2.06	3.66	1.75	2.87	1.56
	(-.16)		(.14)		(-.31)		(-.61)		(-1.15)		(.22)		(-.15)	
GROAN	4.07	1.95	4.85	1.85	3.68	1.60	4.39	1.65	6.08	1.39	3.03	1.58	2.85	1.50
	(.49)		(.68)		(-.08)		(.09)		(.24)		(-.41)		(-.17)	
GRUDGE	3.09	1.90	3.67	2.08	3.42	1.96	4.56	1.76	5.84	1.39	3.52	1.82	2.54	1.37
	(-.49)		(-.50)		(-.34)		(.26)		(.00)		(.08)		(-.48)	
GUILT	2.95	1.98	3.75	1.98	3.47	1.88	4.21	1.66	6.33	1.11	3.81	1.80	2.43	1.33M
	(-.63)		(-.42)		(-.29)		(-.09)		(.49)		(.37)		(-.59)	
HALF	3.71	2.03	4.42	2.01	4.32	1.99	4.08	1.95	6.62	.87	3.22	1.80	3.68	.91
	(.13)		(.25)		(.56)		(-.22)		(.78)		(-.22)		(.66)	
HALT	3.41	2.05	4.11	2.03	3.60	1.68	4.31	1.80	5.39	1.94	2.59	1.51	3.15	1.40
	(-.17)		(-.06)		(-.16)		(.01)		(-.45)		(-.85)		(.13)	
HANG	3.93	1.81	5.31	1.81	4.08	1.82	4.28	1.68	5.88	1.46	3.51	1.69	2.77	1.54M
	(.35)		(1.14)		(.32)		(-.02)		(.04)		(.07)		(-.25)	
HARSH	3.55	1.92	3.73	1.87	3.34	1.61	4.07	1.41	5.83	1.43	3.06	1.55	2.52	1.31
	(-.03)		(-.44)		(-.42)		(-.23)		(-.01)		(-.38)		(-.50)	
HASTY	2.86	1.90	3.86	1.84	3.48	1.53	4.46	1.48	5.69	1.59	3.16	1.56	2.96	1.12
	(-.72)		(-.31)		(-.28)		(.16)		(-.15)		(-.28)		(-.06)	
HATE	3.91	1.97	4.38	2.14	4.05	1.96	5.17	1.75	6.29	1.38	4.31	1.88	2.06	1.32M
	(.33)		(.21)		(.29)		(.87)		(.45)		(.87)		(-.96)	
HAUL	3.54	1.76	4.07	1.85	3.50	1.71	4.23	1.71	5.81	1.63	3.27	1.65	3.34	1.38
	(-.04)		(-.10)		(-.26)		(-.07)		(-.03)		(-.17)		(.32)	
HAZARD	3.38	1.93	3.88	1.90	3.10	1.70	5.13	1.65	5.80	1.51	3.66	1.97	2.33	1.38
	(-.20)		(-.29)		(-.66)		(.83)		(-.04)		(.22)		(-.69)	
HEARTLESS	3.00	1.69	3.67	2.01	3.55	1.86	4.74	1.85	6.03	1.57	3.34	1.72	2.38	1.68
	(-.58)		(-.50)		(-.21)		(.44)		(.19)		(-.10)		(-.64)	
HELL	3.62	2.39	4.33	2.24	3.85	2.07	4.87	2.09	6.38	1.20	4.80	2.09	2.40	1.55
	(.04)		(.16)		(.09)		(.57)		(.54)		(1.36)		(-.62)	

	CON		IMG		CAT		MNG		FAM		NOA		PLS	
	M	SD	M	SD	M	SD	M	SD	M	SD	M	SD	M	SD
HIDE	3.95	1.88	4.22	2.02	3.95	1.90	3.88	1.49	6.22	1.28	3.57	1.61	3.62	1.38F
	(.37)		(.05)		(.19)		(-.42)		(.38)		(.13)		(.60)	
HIERARCHY	3.39	1.97	3.76	2.05	4.42	2.12	4.38	1.98	5.56	1.46	3.87	1.99	3.21	1.76M
	(-.19)		(-.41)		(.66)		(.08)		(-.28)		(.43)		(.19)	
HOTTER	4.29	2.12	4.00	2.01	3.95	2.03	3.83	1.72	5.79	1.58	3.22	1.61	3.78	1.33
	(.71)		(-.17)		(.19)		(-.47)		(-.05)		(-.22)		(.76)	
HUMILIATION	3.34	1.97	3.46	1.89	3.53	1.71	4.20	1.61	5.75	1.50	3.76	2.04	2.68	1.57M
	(-.24)		(-.71)		(-.23)		(-.10)		(-.09)		(.32)		(-.34)	
HUNGER	4.16	2.13	4.81	1.93	4.27	1.97	5.06	1.85	6.48	1.16	4.19	1.96	2.75	1.40
	(.58)		(.64)		(.51)		(.76)		(.64)		(.75)		(-.27)	
HURT	3.66	1.98	4.82	1.92	3.73	1.83	5.30	1.57	6.56	.99	4.03	1.91	2.38	1.55
	(.08)		(.65)		(-.03)		(1.00)		(.72)		(.59)		(-.64)	
IDLE	3.14	2.05	4.38	2.08	3.65	1.79	4.12	1.60	5.71	1.72	3.32	1.74	3.46	1.70
	(-.44)		(.21)		(-.11)		(-.18)		(-.13)		(-.12)		(.44)	
IGNORE	3.16	1.75	3.94	2.04	3.83	1.74	4.00	1.69	5.88	1.45	3.11	1.68	2.34	1.25
	(-.42)		(-.23)		(.07)		(-.30)		(.04)		(-.33)		(-.68)	
IMITATE	3.44	2.20	4.30	1.90	3.62	1.65	4.48	1.56	5.78	1.55	4.02	1.88	3.85	1.43
	(-.14)		(.13)		(-.14)		(.18)		(-.06)		(.58)		(.83)	
IMPOTENCY	3.46	1.96	4.26	2.10	3.87	1.96	4.20	1.75	5.20	1.97	3.41	1.71	2.34	1.47M
	(-.12)		(.09)		(.11)		(-.10)		(-.64)		(-.03)		(-.68)	
INADEQUATE	2.70	1.89	3.50	1.97	3.38	1.77	4.37	1.69	5.71	1.69	3.30	1.81	2.43	1.41
	(-.88)		(-.67)		(-.38)		(.07)		(-.13)		(-.14)		(-.59)	
INANIMATE	3.34	2.09	3.42	2.27	3.40	1.81	4.00	1.70	4.85	2.01	3.55	1.83	3.43	1.27
	(-.24)		(-.75)		(-.36)		(-.30)		(-.99)		(.11)		(.41)	
INCAPABLE	3.13	2.05	3.31	2.01	3.00	1.66	4.24	1.44	5.59	1.62	3.11	1.86	2.89	1.45
	(-.45)		(-.86)		(-.76)		(-.06)		(-.25)		(-.33)		(-.13)	
INFERIOR	3.07	1.82	3.73	2.16	3.75	1.78	4.87	1.67	6.21	1.23	3.64	1.98	2.76	1.75
	(-.51)		(-.44)		(-.01)		(.57)		(.37)		(.20)		(-.26)	
INSOLENT	3.07	1.97	3.59	2.06	3.03	1.78	3.67	1.56	4.74	1.78	3.30	1.72	2.68	1.44
	(-.51)		(-.58)		(-.73)		(-.63)		(-1.10)		(-.14)		(-.34)	
INSULT	3.71	1.81	4.71	1.89	4.28	1.63	4.90	1.47	6.26	1.19	4.00	1.93	2.38	1.58
	(.13)		(.54)		(.52)		(.60)		(.42)		(.56)		(-.64)	
ITCH	4.84	2.01	4.80	1.97	4.32	1.91	4.42	1.59	6.00	1.44	3.07	1.33	2.66	1.41
	(1.26)		(.63)		(.56)		(.12)		(.16)		(-.37)		(-.36)	
ITEM	3.98	2.26	3.50	2.07	3.68	2.08	3.98	1.90	6.13	1.37	3.61	2.12	3.70	1.04
	(.40)		(-.67)		(-.08)		(-.32)		(.29)		(.17)		(.68)	
JERK	4.60	2.11	4.68	1.94	4.18	1.87	4.68	1.79	5.66	1.58	3.39	1.52	2.86	1.26
	(1.02)		(.51)		(.42)		(.38)		(-.18)		(-.05)		(-.16)	
KILL	3.82	2.17	4.75	1.99	4.31	1.88	5.37	1.30	6.23	1.38	4.05	2.07	1.95	1.58M
	(.24)		(.58)		(.55)		(1.07)		(.39)		(.61)		(-1.07)	
LAST	2.95	1.92	4.07	2.23	3.88	2.02	4.70	1.82	6.38	1.40	3.38	1.95	3.21	1.53F
	(-.63)		(-.10)		(.12)		(.40)		(.54)		(-.06)		(.19)	
LATE	2.58	1.61	3.85	1.92	3.87	1.71	4.23	1.89	6.09	1.44	2.97	1.44	2.98	1.29
	(-1.00)		(-.32)		(.11)		(-.07)		(.25)		(-.47)		(-.04)	
LAZY	3.50	1.74	4.81	2.10	4.50	1.59	4.39	1.76	6.05	1.51	3.05	1.59	3.45	1.73M
	(-.08)		(.64)		(.74)		(.09)		(.21)		(-.39)		(.43)	
LEASE	3.67	2.19	4.20	1.69	3.88	1.73	3.77	1.62	5.78	1.43	3.69	1.72	3.69	1.36
	(.09)		(.03)		(.12)		(-.53)		(-.06)		(.25)		(.67)	
LED	3.66	2.09	3.88	2.13	3.53	1.87	3.56	1.83	6.00	1.51	2.95	1.44	3.85	.98
	(.08)		(-.29)		(-.23)		(-.74)		(.16)		(-.49)		(.83)	
LEGALITY	3.27	1.84	3.41	1.96	3.15	1.89	4.21	2.09	5.85	1.44	4.03	1.95	3.57	1.50
	(-.31)		(-.76)		(-.61)		(-.09)		(.01)		(.59)		(.55)	
LEVEL	4.18	1.96	3.79	1.80	3.82	1.84	4.03	1.55	5.78	1.44	3.46	1.63	3.90	.84
	(.60)		(-.38)		(.06)		(-.27)		(-.06)		(.02)		(.88)	

	CON		IMG		CAT		MNG		FAM		NOA		PLS	
	M	SD	M	SD	M	SD	M	SD	M	SD	M	SD	M	SD
LIAR	3.89	1.97	4.15	2.05	4.33	1.88	4.28	1.82	6.19	1.22	3.65	2.10	2.30	1.80
	(.31)		(-.02)		(.57)		(-.02)		(.35)		(.21)		(-.72)	
LIE	4.04	2.10	3.75	2.28	3.83	1.99	4.47	1.58	6.07	1.59	3.97	1.70	2.48	1.50
	(.46)		(-.42)		(.07)		(.17)		(.23)		(.53)		(-.54)	
LIFT	3.75	1.94	4.55	1.85	3.77	1.80	4.15	1.75	5.95	1.49	3.20	1.44	4.16	1.24
	(.17)		(.38)		(.01)		(-.15)		(.11)		(-.24)		(1.14)	
LIGHTER	3.96	1.98	4.52	2.17	3.46	1.76	4.00	1.46	6.20	1.19	2.82	1.44	4.21	1.33F
	(.38)		(.35)		(-.30)		(-.30)		(.36)		(-.62)		(1.19)	
LIMP	4.77	1.94	5.06	1.70	4.00	1.84	4.00	1.72	5.68	1.57	3.07	1.34	2.75	1.32M
	(1.19)		(.89)		(.24)		(-.30)		(-.16)		(-.37)		(-.27)	
LOAFER	4.13	2.07	4.50	1.89	4.07	2.00	4.23	1.53	5.53	1.54	3.36	1.33	3.06	1.34
	(.55)		(.33)		(.31)		(-.07)		(-.31)		(-.08)		(.04)	
LOAN	3.74	2.07	4.65	1.92	4.02	1.73	3.95	1.83	5.92	1.47	3.64	1.59	3.40	1.48
	(.16)		(.48)		(.26)		(-.35)		(.08)		(.20)		(.38)	
LONE	3.21	1.92	4.51	2.02	3.63	1.67	3.77	1.80	5.38	1.80	3.20	1.61	3.47	1.68
	(-.37)		(.34)		(-.13)		(-.53)		(-.46)		(-.24)		(.45)	
LOSE	2.95	1.88	3.67	2.01	2.88	1.74	3.90	1.91	6.08	1.59	3.15	1.92	2.62	1.24
	(-.63)		(-.50)		(-.88)		(-.40)		(.24)		(-.29)		(-.40)	
LOSS	3.34	1.93	3.95	2.12	3.60	2.03	4.63	1.88	6.52	.89	3.73	2.05	2.83	1.46
	(-.24)		(-.22)		(-.16)		(.33)		(.68)		(.29)		(-.19)	
LOW	3.18	1.95	3.63	2.03	3.65	2.07	4.27	1.96	6.53	1.19	3.06	1.86	2.93	1.22
	(-.40)		(-.54)		(-.11)		(-.03)		(.69)		(-.38)		(-.09)	
MAD	3.04	1.95	4.86	1.98	3.58	2.01	5.69	1.46	6.59	.92	3.95	1.90	2.82	1.68
	(-.54)		(.69)		(-.18)		(1.39)		(.75)		(.51)		(-.20)	
MARK	4.60	1.94	4.28	1.94	3.83	2.01	3.76	2.01	6.07	1.38	3.03	1.79	3.70	1.28
	(1.02)		(.11)		(.07)		(-.54)		(.23)		(-.41)		(.68)	
MASH	4.14	1.95	4.66	1.96	3.40	1.78	3.82	1.78	5.55	1.65	3.60	1.68	3.54	1.62
	(.56)		(.49)		(-.36)		(-.48)		(-.29)		(.16)		(.52)	
MATHEMATICAL	3.24	2.05	4.24	1.99	4.17	1.98	4.69	1.95	6.15	1.51	4.31	2.05	3.65	1.83
	(-.34)		(.07)		(.41)		(.39)		(.31)		(.87)		(.63)	
MEAN	3.09	1.89	4.13	2.04	3.38	1.88	5.65	1.56	6.13	1.27	3.77	1.90	2.87	1.75M
	(-.49)		(-.04)		(-.38)		(1.35)		(.29)		(.33)		(-.15)	
MEEK	2.95	1.83	3.86	2.17	3.87	1.63	4.70	1.62	5.44	1.67	3.34	1.64	3.09	1.31
	(-.63)		(-.31)		(.11)		(.40)		(-.40)		(-.10)		(.07)	
MELANCHOLY	3.25	1.94	3.64	1.99	3.30	1.99	4.21	1.80	5.05	1.70	3.59	1.88	3.44	1.59
	(-.33)		(-.53)		(-.46)		(-.09)		(-.79)		(.15)		(.42)	
MELT	4.09	1.77	4.55	1.98	3.67	1.71	3.97	1.72	5.95	1.54	3.13	1.53	3.80	1.26
	(.51)		(.38)		(-.09)		(-.33)		(.11)		(-.31)		(.78)	
MIMIC	3.25	1.86	3.84	1.76	3.53	1.56	3.78	1.61	5.38	1.67	3.61	1.96	3.68	1.47
	(-.33)		(-.33)		(-.23)		(-.52)		(-.46)		(.17)		(.66)	
MINOR	3.49	2.05	4.33	1.95	3.97	1.89	4.58	1.88	6.42	1.00	3.65	1.87	3.58	1.18
	(-.09)		(.16)		(.21)		(.28)		(.58)		(.21)		(.56)	
MISERY	3.24	1.99	4.54	2.10	3.75	1.65	4.97	1.55	5.89	1.54	3.51	1.99	2.04	1.40
	(-.34)		(.37)		(-.01)		(.67)		(.05)		(.07)		(-.98)	
MISTER	3.45	1.92	3.59	1.94	4.00	1.84	3.48	1.65	6.03	1.58	2.67	1.45	3.80	1.34F
	(-.13)		(-.58)		(.24)		(-.82)		(.19)		(-.77)		(.78)	
MISUSE	3.14	1.81	3.61	1.96	3.13	1.49	4.25	1.67	5.31	1.86	3.54	1.78	2.53	1.38
	(-.44)		(-.56)		(-.63)		(-.05)		(-.53)		(.10)		(-.49)	
MORBID	3.54	2.10	4.14	1.99	3.27	1.80	4.30	1.62	5.39	1.64	3.25	1.61	2.19	1.53F
	(-.04)		(-.03)		(-.49)		(.00)		(-.45)		(-.19)		(-.83)	
MORTGAGE	4.18	1.94	3.52	1.85	4.17	1.85	4.13	1.95	5.80	1.55	3.43	1.52	2.64	1.20M
	(.60)		(-.65)		(.41)		(-.17)		(-.04)		(-.01)		(-.38)	
MULTIPLYING	3.55	2.03	4.05	1.99	4.85	1.92	4.32	1.93	5.87	1.66	3.44	1.70	3.74	1.53
	(-.03)		(-.12)		(1.09)		(.02)		(.03)		(.00)		(.72)	

	CON		IMG		CAT		MNG		FAM		NOA		PLS	
	M	SD	M	SD	M	SD	M	SD	M	SD	M	SD	M	SD
MUTINY	3.63	1.99	4.41	2.05	4.32	1.71	3.85	1.77	5.02	1.77	3.77	1.80	3.00	1.46
	(.05)		(.24)		(.56)		(-.45)		(-.82)		(.33)		(-.02)	
NAG	3.88	1.93	5.02	2.22	3.70	1.79	4.56	1.52	5.66	1.76	3.10	1.64	2.16	1.35
	(.30)		(.85)		(-.06)		(.26)		(-.18)		(-.34)		(-.86)	
NARROW	3.68	1.95	5.02	1.69	3.93	1.61	4.51	1.62	6.11	1.29	3.22	1.67	3.40	1.59M
	(.10)		(.85)		(.17)		(.21)		(.27)		(-.22)		(.38)	
NERVOUS	3.34	2.16	4.75	2.02	3.78	1.86	4.90	1.60	6.39	1.15	3.40	1.89	2.16	1.29
	(-.24)		(.58)		(.02)		(.60)		(.55)		(-.04)		(-.86)	
NO	3.14	2.35	3.55	2.35	3.43	2.29	4.52	2.36	6.79	.76	2.74	2.21	2.48	1.45
	(-.44)		(-.62)		(-.33)		(.22)		(.95)		(-.70)		(-.54)	
NONE	2.84	2.04	4.19	2.42	3.35	2.17	4.22	2.04	6.43	1.02	2.52	1.92	2.47	1.53
	(-.74)		(.02)		(-.41)		(-.08)		(.59)		(-.92)		(-.55)	
NUMB	3.75	2.20	4.71	1.98	3.95	1.71	3.69	1.74	5.61	1.55	2.75	1.43	3.11	1.55
	(.17)		(.54)		(.19)		(-.61)		(-.23)		(-.69)		(.09)	
OFFEND	3.17	1.91	3.66	2.00	3.53	1.51	4.54	1.69	5.72	1.50	3.40	1.81	2.43	1.37
	(-.41)		(-.51)		(-.23)		(.24)		(-.12)		(-.04)		(-.59)	
OLDER	3.44	1.74	4.73	1.84	4.02	1.95	4.58	1.53	6.22	1.28	4.07	1.67	3.62	1.44
	(-.14)		(.56)		(.26)		(.28)		(.38)		(.63)		(.60)	
OMEN	3.38	2.02	4.38	2.01	4.07	1.68	4.02	1.69	5.35	1.56	3.82	1.68	3.80	1.73
	(-.20)		(.21)		(.31)		(-.28)		(-.49)		(.38)		(.78)	
ONE	3.75	2.41	4.45	2.21	4.83	2.46	4.46	2.25	6.62	1.14	2.49	1.93	3.64	1.59
	(.17)		(.28)		(1.07)		(.16)		(.78)		(-.95)		(.62)	
OPPONENT	4.36	1.96	4.02	1.86	4.28	1.88	4.32	1.40	5.69	1.43	3.70	1.85	3.52	1.48
	(.78)		(-.15)		(.52)		(.02)		(-.15)		(.26)		(.50)	
ORDER	3.41	1.76	3.66	1.98	3.60	1.73	3.97	1.61	6.24	1.28	3.63	1.71	3.56	1.46
	(-.17)		(-.51)		(-.16)		(-.33)		(.40)		(.19)		(.54)	
ORDERLY	3.84	2.19	3.88	1.95	3.72	1.81	4.51	1.56	5.88	1.54	3.33	1.72	3.91	1.70
	(.26)		(-.29)		(-.04)		(.21)		(.04)		(-.11)		(.89)	
PAIN	4.22	2.17	4.96	2.14	4.17	2.04	5.57	1.58	6.43	1.15	4.40	2.28	2.46	1.83F
	(.64)		(.79)		(.41)		(1.27)		(.59)		(.96)		(-.56)	
PALE	3.81	2.14	5.26	1.62	4.50	1.75	4.23	1.80	5.73	1.56	3.28	1.57	3.10	1.47M
	(.23)		(1.09)		(.74)		(-.07)		(-.11)		(-.16)		(.08)	
PANIC	3.66	2.33	4.72	1.84	3.88	2.01	4.94	1.74	6.43	1.11	4.17	1.92	2.49	1.43M
	(.08)		(.55)		(.12)		(.64)		(.59)		(.73)		(-.53)	
PAT	3.96	1.79	3.80	2.15	3.40	1.69	3.95	1.65	5.66	1.60	2.86	1.58	3.97	1.32
	(.38)		(-.37)		(-.36)		(-.35)		(-.18)		(-.58)		(.95)	
PATHETIC	2.52	1.72	3.91	1.95	3.23	1.57	4.22	1.70	5.34	1.82	3.39	1.72	2.58	1.54M
	(-1.06)		(-.26)		(-.53)		(-.08)		(-.50)		(-.05)		(-.44)	
PEEL	4.28	1.95	4.30	1.93	3.65	1.78	3.87	1.43	5.81	1.51	3.10	1.22	4.00	1.15
	(.70)		(.13)		(-.11)		(-.43)		(-.03)		(-.34)		(.98)	
PERISH	3.25	1.83	3.98	1.97	3.60	1.85	4.34	1.73	5.57	1.62	3.71	1.75	2.31	1.31M
	(-.33)		(-.19)		(-.16)		(.04)		(-.27)		(.27)		(-.71)	
PERJURY	3.30	1.90	3.30	2.00	3.52	1.74	3.67	1.57	5.13	1.75	3.51	1.77	2.22	1.40
	(-.28)		(-.87)		(-.24)		(-.63)		(-.71)		(.07)		(-.80)	
PERMANENT	3.32	2.12	3.84	2.15	4.00	1.91	4.47	1.61	6.00	1.31	3.11	1.85	3.82	1.92
	(-.26)		(-.33)		(.24)		(.17)		(.16)		(-.33)		(.80)	
PERMIT	4.00	2.17	3.60	1.96	3.67	1.63	4.35	1.76	6.15	1.40	3.75	1.41	3.89	1.38F
	(.42)		(-.57)		(-.09)		(.05)		(.31)		(.31)		(.80)	
PIECE	3.80	2.21	3.89	1.81	3.09	1.70	3.87	1.82	5.85	1.60	3.77	1.88	3.95	1.53M
	(.22)		(-.28)		(-.67)		(-.43)		(.01)		(.33)		(.93)	
PIOUS	2.84	1.85	3.72	2.06	3.28	1.96	4.03	1.93	4.85	1.90	3.61	1.71	3.55	1.63
	(-.74)		(-.45)		(-.48)		(-.27)		(-.99)		(.17)		(.53)	
PITY	3.34	1.98	3.71	1.98	3.33	1.87	4.20	1.65	5.61	1.59	3.64	1.73	3.24	1.44
	(-.24)		(-.46)		(-.43)		(-.10)		(-.23)		(.20)		(.22)	

	CON		IMG		CAT		MNG		FAM		NOA		PLS	
	M	SD	M	SD	M	SD	M	SD	M	SD	M	SD	M	SD
PLAIN	3.77	1.97	4.34	1.72	3.80	1.80	4.77	1.51	6.34	1.30	2.95	1.60	3.43	1.33
	(.19)		(.17)		(.04)		(.47)		(.50)		(-.49)		(.41)	
PLEA	3.04	1.89	3.41	1.71	3.03	1.65	4.16	1.54	5.52	1.70	3.23	1.73	3.05	1.24
	(-.54)		(-.76)		(-.73)		(-.14)		(-.32)		(-.21)		(.03)	
PLEDGE	3.88	2.07	4.20	1.94	3.79	1.76	3.75	1.48	5.82	1.57	3.52	1.72	4.12	1.40
	(.30)		(.03)		(.03)		(-.55)		(-.02)		(.08)		(1.10)	
POOR	3.07	1.87	4.25	1.97	3.77	1.75	5.31	1.56	6.20	1.55	4.07	2.01	2.13	1.38
	(-.51)		(.08)		(.01)		(1.01)		(.36)		(.63)		(-.89)	
POUR	3.52	1.77	4.89	1.82	3.73	1.64	3.93	1.78	6.19	1.27	2.92	1.58	3.94	1.39
	(-.06)		(.72)		(-.03)		(-.37)		(.35)		(-.52)		(.92)	
PRAY	3.68	2.04	4.38	1.93	3.71	1.76	4.03	1.95	6.02	1.44	3.59	1.75	3.88	1.76
	(.10)		(.21)		(-.05)		(-.27)		(.18)		(.15)		(.86)	
PREJUDICE	3.36	1.92	4.13	2.06	4.02	1.76	4.62	1.76	5.82	1.49	4.23	1.87	2.23	1.17
	(-.22)		(-.04)		(.26)		(.32)		(-.02)		(.79)		(-.79)	
PROBLEM	3.64	2.05	4.45	2.03	3.93	1.78	4.82	1.75	6.39	1.15	4.68	1.79	2.88	1.61
	(.06)		(.28)		(.17)		(.52)		(.55)		(1.24)		(-.14)	
PROHIBIT	2.97	1.79	3.67	2.03	3.37	1.73	4.72	1.70	5.90	1.36	3.24	1.85	2.81	1.47
	(-.61)		(-.50)		(-.39)		(.42)		(.06)		(-.20)		(-.21)	
PRONOUN	3.42	2.15	3.96	2.19	4.83	2.09	3.49	1.80	5.54	1.65	3.72	1.96	3.73	1.23
	(-.16)		(-.21)		(1.07)		(-.81)		(-.30)		(.28)		(.71)	
PULL	3.56	1.77	4.40	1.86	3.68	1.65	4.10	1.71	6.39	1.24	3.09	1.72	3.66	1.25
	(-.02)		(.23)		(-.08)		(-.20)		(.55)		(-.35)		(.64)	
PUNISH	3.40	1.74	4.68	2.05	3.87	1.61	5.19	1.44	6.10	1.48	3.79	1.60	2.44	1.40
	(-.18)		(.51)		(.11)		(.89)		(.26)		(.35)		(-.58)	
PUNY	3.23	1.91	3.89	2.09	3.53	1.81	4.27	1.89	5.00	1.82	2.89	1.46	3.03	1.27
	(-.35)		(-.28)		(-.23)		(-.03)		(-.84)		(-.55)		(.01)	
QUACK	4.55	1.72	4.40	2.09	4.47	1.90	4.23	1.75	5.41	1.74	3.30	1.74	3.13	1.71
	(.97)		(.23)		(.71)		(-.07)		(-.43)		(-.14)		(.11)	
QUAKE	4.36	2.00	4.57	2.08	3.88	1.97	3.97	1.78	5.48	1.66	3.62	1.68	3.19	1.45
	(.78)		(.40)		(.12)		(-.33)		(-.36)		(.18)		(.17)	
QUARREL	3.75	2.02	4.73	1.84	3.92	2.04	5.15	1.61	5.37	1.83	4.02	1.52	2.67	1.59
	(.17)		(.56)		(.16)		(.85)		(-.47)		(.58)		(-.35)	
RAID	4.24	1.83	4.82	1.90	4.03	1.55	4.20	1.82	5.64	1.55	3.77	1.48	2.71	1.44
	(.66)		(.65)		(.27)		(-.10)		(-.20)		(.33)		(-.31)	
RANCID	3.38	2.16	3.63	2.34	3.38	1.77	3.98	1.90	4.49	2.00	2.92	1.59	1.82	1.31
	(-.20)		(-.54)		(-.38)		(-.32)		(-1.35)		(-.52)		(-1.20)	
RAP	4.00	1.84	3.82	2.01	3.50	1.69	3.86	1.63	5.75	1.58	3.34	1.69	3.46	1.55
	(.42)		(-.35)		(-.26)		(-.44)		(-.09)		(-.10)		(.44)	
RATE	3.16	2.08	3.46	1.99	3.40	1.77	4.16	1.68	5.92	1.61	2.98	1.53	3.51	1.36
	(-.42)		(-.71)		(-.36)		(-.14)		(.08)		(-.46)		(.49)	
RATION	3.86	1.94	3.86	2.02	3.59	1.65	3.77	1.56	5.47	1.56	3.43	1.42	3.31	1.33
	(.28)		(-.31)		(-.17)		(-.53)		(-.37)		(-.01)		(.29)	
RAW	3.95	1.91	4.64	1.91	4.38	1.56	4.13	1.63	5.83	1.50	3.03	1.61	3.34	1.31
	(.37)		(.47)		(.62)		(-.17)		(-.01)		(-.41)		(.32)	
REAR	3.98	1.98	4.49	2.02	3.93	1.82	5.00	1.61	6.21	1.23	3.18	1.69	3.75	1.64M
	(.40)		(.32)		(.17)		(.70)		(.37)		(-.26)		(.73)	
RECRUIT	3.89	2.00	4.06	2.07	3.57	1.83	3.90	1.59	5.45	1.71	3.56	1.77	3.00	1.55
	(.31)		(-.11)		(-.19)		(-.40)		(-.39)		(.12)		(-.02)	
REFRAIN	3.21	1.99	3.64	1.99	3.58	1.92	4.18	1.47	5.97	1.43	3.00	1.63	3.66	1.54
	(-.37)		(-.53)		(-.18)		(-.12)		(.13)		(-.44)		(.64)	
REFUSE	3.46	2.08	4.00	2.03	3.37	1.78	4.37	1.70	5.73	1.53	3.21	1.56	2.94	1.30F
	(-.12)		(-.17)		(-.39)		(.07)		(-.11)		(-.23)		(-.08)	
REGULATION	3.59	1.83	3.39	1.89	3.95	1.82	4.57	1.61	5.78	1.60	3.89	1.68	3.25	1.46
	(.01)		(-.78)		(.19)		(.27)		(-.06)		(.45)		(.23)	

	CON		IMG		CAT		MNG		FAM		NOA		PLS	
	M	SD	M	SD	M	SD	M	SD	M	SD	M	SD	M	SD
REJECTED	2.82	1.82	3.42	1.81	2.87	1.79	4.57	1.77	5.97	1.46	3.26	1.58	2.21	1.13
	(-.76)		(-.75)		(-.89)		(.27)		(.13)		(-.18)		(-.81)	
RELUCTANT	2.59	1.53	4.25	2.02	3.37	1.81	4.15	1.63	5.46	1.52	3.20	1.40	3.18	1.08
	(-.99)		(.08)		(-.39)		(-.15)		(-.38)		(-.24)		(.16)	
RENT	4.13	2.05	4.24	2.05	4.58	1.85	4.62	1.92	6.20	1.50	3.36	1.73	2.75	1.42
	(.55)		(.07)		(.82)		(.32)		(.36)		(-.08)		(-.27)	
REPLACEMENT	3.52	1.85	3.41	1.89	3.56	1.63	4.16	1.65	6.22	1.14	3.50	1.78	3.51	1.25
	(-.06)		(-.76)		(-.20)		(-.14)		(.38)		(.06)		(.49)	
REPRESS	3.41	1.79	3.59	2.07	3.19	1.79	3.68	1.51	4.93	1.63	3.48	1.71	2.76	1.36
	(-.17)		(-.58)		(-.57)		(-.62)		(-.91)		(.04)		(-.26)	
REPULSIVE	3.32	1.94	4.20	2.35	3.58	1.92	4.62	1.54	5.48	1.71	3.69	1.68	2.52	1.47
	(-.26)		(.03)		(-.18)		(.32)		(-.36)		(.25)		(-.50)	
RETARD	3.41	1.79	4.75	2.00	4.10	1.91	4.33	1.63	5.79	1.62	3.71	1.58	2.41	1.32
	(-.17)		(.58)		(.34)		(.03)		(-.05)		(.27)		(-.61)	
RETREAT	3.50	1.76	3.89	1.99	3.75	1.77	3.90	1.56	5.83	1.42	3.74	1.64	3.62	1.51F
	(-.08)		(-.28)		(-.01)		(-.40)		(-.01)		(.30)		(.60)	
RIDICULE	3.06	1.72	3.84	2.09	3.02	1.48	4.88	1.64	5.84	1.50	3.08	1.58	2.49	1.70
	(-.52)		(-.33)		(-.74)		(.58)		(.00)		(-.36)		(-.53)	
RIGID	4.07	1.91	4.82	1.84	3.98	1.90	4.25	1.43	5.77	1.41	3.42	1.52	3.00	1.38
	(.49)		(.65)		(.22)		(-.05)		(-.07)		(-.02)		(-.02)	
RODE	3.49	1.92	4.45	1.78	3.46	1.51	3.79	1.87	5.70	1.62	3.08	1.41	4.03	1.12
	(-.09)		(.28)		(-.30)		(-.51)		(-.14)		(-.36)		(1.01)	
ROLE	3.31	1.91	3.79	2.22	3.55	1.59	4.38	1.75	5.98	1.49	4.00	1.99	3.58	1.35
	(-.27)		(-.38)		(-.21)		(.08)		(.14)		(.56)		(.56)	
RULE	2.82	1.50	4.09	2.12	4.22	1.73	4.42	1.52	6.08	1.43	4.11	1.63	2.87	1.24
	(-.76)		(-.08)		(.46)		(.12)		(.24)		(.67)		(-.15)	
RUMBLE	4.03	2.20	4.88	1.84	3.72	1.72	4.15	1.74	5.50	1.60	3.75	1.43	3.19	1.56M
	(.45)		(.71)		(-.04)		(-.15)		(-.34)		(.31)		(.17)	
RURAL	3.54	1.93	3.96	1.95	3.86	1.68	3.70	1.58	5.39	1.69	3.44	1.76	4.12	1.57
	(-.04)		(-.21)		(.10)		(-.60)		(-.45)		(.00)		(1.10)	
RUSH	3.46	1.92	3.98	1.93	3.38	1.71	4.57	1.75	6.20	1.29	3.35	1.50	3.87	1.58M
	(-.12)		(-.19)		(-.38)		(.27)		(.36)		(-.09)		(.85)	
SAD	3.56	2.04	3.98	2.11	4.31	2.00	5.00	1.73	6.44	1.04	3.52	2.03	2.55	1.50
	(-.02)		(-.19)		(.55)		(.70)		(.60)		(.08)		(-.47)	
SCARCE	2.93	1.71	3.74	2.00	3.47	1.78	4.66	1.50	5.82	1.62	2.97	1.67	3.36	1.47
	(-.65)		(-.43)		(-.29)		(.36)		(-.02)		(-.47)		(.34)	
SCARE	4.12	1.87	4.84	2.00	3.65	1.53	5.03	1.45	6.11	1.31	3.56	1.75	2.91	1.42
	(.54)		(.67)		(-.11)		(.73)		(.27)		(.12)		(-.11)	
SCORCHING	4.72	1.66	5.19	1.70	4.03	1.66	4.69	1.66	5.48	1.58	3.25	1.64	2.38	1.56
	(1.14)		(1.02)		(.27)		(.39)		(-.36)		(-.19)		(-.64)	
SCOWL	3.82	1.89	4.50	1.97	3.85	1.76	4.05	1.95	5.38	1.79	3.11	1.61	2.66	1.25M
	(.24)		(.33)		(.09)		(-.25)		(-.46)		(-.33)		(-.36)	
SECOND	3.61	2.26	3.58	2.16	4.78	1.98	3.97	1.99	6.37	1.22	2.72	1.57	3.72	1.28
	(.03)		(-.59)		(1.02)		(-.33)		(.53)		(-.72)		(.70)	
SELL	3.38	2.01	4.05	1.82	3.43	1.57	4.95	1.74	6.53	1.03	3.94	1.82	3.46	1.42M
	(-.20)		(-.12)		(-.33)		(.65)		(.69)		(.50)		(.44)	
SELLER	4.05	2.16	4.11	1.89	4.47	1.70	3.69	1.58	5.31	1.77	3.75	1.66	3.52	1.37
	(.47)		(-.06)		(.71)		(-.61)		(-.53)		(.31)		(.50)	
SELLING	3.66	1.88	3.70	1.76	3.42	1.65	3.90	1.56	5.88	1.34	3.56	1.64	3.62	1.28
	(.08)		(-.47)		(-.34)		(-.40)		(.04)		(.12)		(.60)	
SELLOUT	3.21	1.88	4.09	1.97	3.90	1.98	3.94	1.74	5.47	1.76	3.75	1.96	3.71	1.75M
	(-.37)		(-.08)		(.14)		(-.36)		(-.37)		(.31)		(.69)	
SEVER	4.00	1.78	4.33	2.11	3.48	1.67	3.98	1.73	5.03	1.92	3.39	1.66	2.50	1.40
	(.42)		(.16)		(-.28)		(-.32)		(-.81)		(-.05)		(-.52)	

	CON	IMG	CAT	MNG	FAM	NOA	PLS
	M SD	M SD	M SD	M SD	M SD	M SD	M SD
SEVERE	2.82 1.93 (-.76)	3.46 1.84 (-.71)	3.27 1.73 (-.49)	4.84 1.69 (.54)	6.00 1.44 (.16)	3.56 1.89 (.12)	2.66 1.39M (-.36)
SHALLOW	3.26 1.84 (-.32)	4.59 2.15 (.42)	3.93 1.90 (.17)	4.15 1.89 (-.15)	6.08 1.30 (.24)	2.88 1.29 (-.56)	3.26 1.65 (.24)
SHAME	3.40 2.14 (-.18)	3.95 2.16 (-.22)	3.42 1.83 (-.34)	4.57 1.69 (.27)	6.15 1.35 (.31)	3.18 1.77 (-.26)	2.64 1.59 (-.38)
SHOOT	4.41 1.97 (.83)	4.88 1.87 (.71)	4.03 1.82 (.27)	4.57 1.63 (.27)	6.10 1.40 (.26)	3.59 1.62 (.15)	2.66 1.74M (-.36)
SHORT	3.47 2.00 (-.11)	4.40 2.02 (.23)	4.38 1.83 (.62)	4.84 1.59 (.54)	6.34 1.28 (.50)	2.87 1.66 (-.57)	3.28 1.50M (.26)
SICK	4.00 2.05 (.42)	4.50 2.05 (.33)	4.33 1.88 (.57)	5.00 1.63 (.70)	6.45 1.10 (.61)	4.37 1.81 (.93)	2.08 1.26 (-.94)
SICKNESS	4.45 1.87 (.52)	4.69 1.80	4.75 1.70 (.99)	4.73 1.64 (.43)	5.93 1.45 (.09)	4.51 1.90 (1.07)	2.29 1.44 (-.73)
SIDE	3.90 1.86 (-.32)	3.80 2.06 (-.37)	3.72 1.64 (-.04)	3.80 1.81 (-.50)	6.40 1.19 (.56)	3.28 1.60 (-.16)	3.65 1.02 (.63)
SIN	2.63 1.93 (-.95)	4.24 2.15 (.07)	3.75 1.94 (-.01)	4.15 2.02 (-.15)	5.81 1.62 (-.03)	4.33 2.07 (.89)	2.71 1.68 (-.31)
SIZE	3.50 1.81 (-.08)	4.09 2.05 (-.08)	3.98 1.88 (.22)	4.66 1.72 (.36)	6.40 1.19 (.56)	3.85 2.17 (.41)	3.80 1.33 (.78)
SLAVERY	3.89 1.95 (.31)	5.11 1.95 (.94)	5.00 1.68 (1.24)	4.75 1.77 (.45)	5.86 1.49 (.02)	4.34 1.85 (.90)	1.87 1.37 (-1.15)
SLAY	4.07 1.82 (.49)	4.48 1.84 (.31)	3.67 1.88 (-.09)	4.66 1.71 (.36)	5.55 1.64 (-.29)	3.40 1.96 (-.04)	2.03 1.37 (-.99)
SLOW	2.89 1.78 (-.69)	3.55 2.04 (-.62)	3.57 1.84 (-.19)	4.25 1.67 (-.05)	6.71 .79 (.87)	2.79 1.70 (-.65)	3.25 1.22 (.23)
SLUGGISH	3.39 1.83 (-.19)	3.76 2.01 (-.41)	3.33 1.65 (-.43)	3.85 1.54 (-.45)	5.55 1.65 (-.29)	2.51 1.28 (-.93)	2.63 1.27M (-.39)
SMEAR	3.51 1.60 (-.07)	4.09 1.83 (-.08)	3.36 1.63 (-.40)	3.62 1.53 (-.68)	5.54 1.65 (-.30)	2.97 1.60 (-.47)	3.26 1.39 (.24)
SMOTHER	3.73 2.00 (.15)	4.07 1.92 (-.10)	3.57 1.66 (-.19)	3.67 1.48 (-.63)	5.51 1.78 (-.33)	2.92 1.47 (-.52)	2.78 1.43 (-.24)
SNAP	4.16 2.33 (.58)	4.04 2.11 (-.13)	3.61 1.91 (-.15)	3.73 1.69 (-.57)	6.00 1.40 (.16)	2.49 1.47 (-.95)	3.65 1.24 (.63)
SNORED	4.05 2.16 (.47)	4.41 2.05 (.24)	3.66 1.96 (-.10)	3.53 1.61 (-.77)	5.73 1.65 (-.11)	2.84 1.58 (-.60)	2.81 1.47 (-.21)
SOB	4.21 2.15 (.63)	4.77 1.94 (.60)	3.67 2.07 (-.09)	4.90 1.85 (.60)	5.90 1.54 (.06)	2.56 1.45 (-.88)	2.66 1.38M (-.36)
SOLD	3.21 1.96 (-.37)	4.18 2.12 (.01)	3.66 1.65 (-.10)	4.23 1.83 (-.07)	5.95 1.48 (.11)	3.16 1.57 (-.28)	3.64 1.25 (.62)
SOLEMN	3.18 1.89 (-.40)	4.24 2.25 (.07)	3.90 1.70 (.14)	4.46 1.66 (.16)	5.52 1.55 (-.32)	3.48 1.65 (.04)	3.80 1.45 (.78)
SOLIDIFY	3.59 2.00 (.01)	4.39 2.09 (.22)	3.72 1.76 (-.04)	4.07 1.65 (-.23)	5.48 1.61 (-.36)	3.29 1.75 (-.15)	3.94 1.40 (.92)
SPANK	4.75 1.86 (1.17)	5.16 1.92 (.99)	4.05 1.81 (.29)	4.50 1.63 (.20)	6.10 1.37 (.26)	2.64 1.33 (-.80)	2.80 1.51 (-.22)
SPOOK	4.13 2.12 (.55)	4.43 1.92 (.26)	4.10 1.97 (.34)	4.32 1.57 (.02)	5.49 1.75 (-.35)	3.06 1.42 (-.38)	3.55 1.57F (.53)
SQUEAK	4.57 2.11 (.99)	4.86 1.87 (.69)	4.43 1.79 (.67)	4.38 1.74 (.08)	5.80 1.45 (-.04)	3.25 1.69 (-.19)	2.76 1.17 (-.26)
SQUINT	4.52 1.82 (.94)	5.09 1.84 (.92)	4.07 1.96 (.31)	4.13 2.01 (-.17)	6.02 1.41 (.18)	2.63 1.31 (-.81)	2.79 1.44 (-.23)
STALE	3.89 2.02 (.31)	4.06 2.01 (-.11)	3.65 1.74 (-.11)	3.44 1.49 (-.86)	5.83 1.50 (-.01)	2.76 1.47 (-.68)	2.78 1.28 (-.24)

	CON		IMG		CAT		MNG		FAM		NOA		PLS	
	M	SD	M	SD	M	SD	M	SD	M	SD	M	SD	M	SD
STARE	3.61	1.97	4.14	2.09	3.15	1.66	4.05	1.47	5.82	1.56	3.00	1.38	3.73	1.30
	(.03)		(-.03)		(-.61)		(-.25)		(-.02)		(-.44)		(.71)	
STEAL	3.59	2.00	4.40	1.88	4.03	1.74	4.89	1.74	6.23	1.26	3.62	1.78	2.50	1.47M
	(.01)		(.23)		(.27)		(.59)		(.39)		(.18)		(-.52)	
STEALING	3.47	1.98	4.14	1.77	3.95	1.66	4.68	1.85	6.13	1.38	3.86	1.97	2.46	1.38M
	(-.11)		(-.03)		(.19)		(.38)		(.29)		(.42)		(-.56)	
STERN	3.45	2.03	4.16	2.17	3.78	2.04	4.35	1.68	5.47	1.70	3.38	1.75	3.26	1.44M
	(-.13)		(-.01)		(.02)		(.05)		(-.37)		(-.06)		(.24)	
STINGY	2.95	1.49	4.00	1.95	3.92	1.49	4.30	1.71	5.41	1.85	3.13	1.28	2.50	1.31
	(-.63)		(-.17)		(.16)		(.00)		(-.43)		(-.31)		(-.52)	
STOLE	3.38	2.09	4.35	1.89	3.95	1.85	4.59	1.73	6.23	1.42	3.71	1.56	2.89	1.47M
	(-.20)		(.18)		(.19)		(.29)		(.39)		(.27)		(-.13)	
STOP	3.04	1.92	4.46	2.09	4.05	2.20	4.85	1.71	6.37	1.24	2.66	1.68	3.27	1.49
	(-.54)		(.29)		(.29)		(.55)		(.53)		(-.78)		(.25)	
STRAND	4.38	1.92	4.25	2.04	3.42	1.73	4.19	1.67	5.74	1.65	3.30	1.60	3.55	1.32
	(.80)		(.08)		(-.34)		(-.11)		(-.10)		(-.14)		(.53)	
STUMBLE	4.29	1.84	4.79	1.79	3.55	1.47	4.98	1.63	6.10	1.23	2.98	1.26	2.76	1.29
	(.71)		(.62)		(-.21)		(.68)		(.26)		(-.46)		(-.26)	
STUPID	3.47	1.96	3.75	2.04	3.86	1.92	4.87	1.67	6.24	1.38	3.57	1.64	2.65	1.51M
	(-.11)		(-.42)		(.10)		(.57)		(.40)		(.13)		(-.37)	
SUBTRACTING	3.08	1.89	3.78	1.95	4.58	1.92	4.21	2.05	6.10	1.64	2.81	1.62	3.69	1.25M
	(-.50)		(-.39)		(.82)		(-.09)		(.26)		(-.63)		(.67)	
SUBTRACTION	2.89	1.92	4.16	2.21	4.93	1.80	4.00	1.64	5.88	1.57	3.13	1.75	3.68	1.39
	(-.69)		(-.01)		(1.17)		(-.30)		(.04)		(-.31)		(.66)	
SUCKER	4.00	1.95	4.13	2.04	3.97	1.92	4.37	1.50	5.66	1.75	3.15	1.45	2.73	1.71M
	(-.04)		(-.04)		(.21)		(.07)		(-.18)		(-.29)		(-.29)	
SUFFOCATE	3.87	2.12	4.80	1.95	3.67	2.00	3.87	1.77	5.48	1.76	2.84	1.66	1.81	1.40
	(.29)		(.63)		(-.09)		(-.43)		(-.36)		(-.60)		(-1.21)	
SWARM	4.02	1.87	4.82	1.73	3.82	1.84	4.25	1.80	5.37	1.74	3.66	1.50	3.17	1.51M
	(.44)		(.65)		(.06)		(-.05)		(-.47)		(.22)		(.15)	
SWAYED	3.24	2.00	3.98	2.01	3.17	1.73	3.89	1.75	5.67	1.60	2.98	1.55	3.37	1.32M
	(-.34)		(-.19)		(-.59)		(-.41)		(-.17)		(-.46)		(.35)	
TAME	3.31	1.60	4.41	1.72	3.55	1.78	4.02	1.71	5.75	1.53	3.11	1.54	3.81	1.56
	(-.27)		(.24)		(-.21)		(-.28)		(-.09)		(-.33)		(.79)	
TARNISH	4.39	2.12	4.50	1.87	3.68	1.65	3.83	1.65	5.29	1.84	3.07	1.42	3.47	1.40
	(.81)		(.33)		(-.08)		(-.47)		(-.55)		(-.37)		(.45)	
TEAR	4.69	2.13	5.02	1.88	3.47	1.74	4.98	1.60	6.18	1.30	3.15	1.48	3.01	1.51
	(1.11)		(.85)		(-.29)		(.68)		(.34)		(-.29)		(-.01)	
TEMPT	2.79	1.69	4.31	2.32	3.27	1.66	4.43	1.83	5.69	1.52	3.39	1.42	3.72	1.58
	(-.79)		(.14)		(-.49)		(.13)		(-.15)		(-.05)		(.70)	
TENSE	3.61	2.05	4.50	1.93	3.77	1.49	4.30	1.50	6.15	1.20	3.38	1.65	2.60	1.63
	(.03)		(.33)		(.01)		(.00)		(.31)		(-.06)		(-.42)	
TERM	3.63	2.02	3.46	1.92	3.93	1.72	4.50	1.66	6.35	1.20	3.84	1.62	3.43	1.07
	(.05)		(-.71)		(.17)		(.20)		(.51)		(.40)		(.41)	
TESTIMONY	3.77	2.01	3.71	1.74	3.68	1.83	3.90	1.84	5.82	1.56	3.92	1.63	3.57	1.43M
	(.19)		(-.46)		(-.08)		(-.40)		(-.02)		(.48)		(.55)	
THAW	3.40	1.98	4.07	2.08	3.50	1.78	4.16	1.52	5.74	1.61	2.59	1.30	3.71	1.23
	(-.18)		(-.10)		(-.26)		(-.14)		(-.10)		(-.85)		(.69)	
THEFT	3.62	1.93	4.18	1.79	3.90	1.89	4.84	1.77	6.15	1.23	3.54	1.60	2.59	1.23
	(.04)		(.01)		(.14)		(.54)		(.31)		(.10)		(-.43)	
THEME	3.32	1.91	3.89	2.24	3.65	1.74	4.34	1.59	5.98	1.48	3.70	1.96	3.75	1.35M
	(-.26)		(-.28)		(-.11)		(.04)		(.14)		(.26)		(.73)	
THICK	3.82	1.71	4.57	2.03	3.85	1.81	4.28	1.62	6.41	1.02	3.30	1.81	3.92	1.30
	(.24)		(.40)		(.09)		(-.02)		(.57)		(-.14)		(.90)	

	CON		IMG		CAT		MNG		FAM		NOA		PLS	
	M	SD	M	SD	M	SD	M	SD	M	SD	M	SD	M	SD
THREAT	3.22	1.86	3.75	2.15	3.25	1.32	3.80	1.57	6.07	1.23	3.84	1.74	2.60	1.21
	(-.36)		(-.42)		(-.51)		(-.50)		(.23)		(.40)		(-.42)	
THREW	3.29	1.86	4.36	1.95	3.47	1.77	4.03	1.79	6.23	1.27	3.27	1.80	3.87	1.12
	(-.29)		(.19)		(-.29)		(-.27)		(.39)		(-.17)		(.85)	
TIED	3.70	2.02	4.04	2.11	3.12	1.73	3.67	1.46	6.28	1.10	2.97	1.61	3.22	1.21
	(.12)		(-.13)		(-.64)		(-.63)		(.44)		(-.47)		(.20)	
TOIL	3.82	1.81	3.87	1.85	3.69	1.77	4.05	1.68	5.42	1.66	3.13	1.55	3.53	1.43
	(.24)		(-.30)		(-.07)		(-.25)		(-.42)		(-.31)		(.51)	
TOLL	4.20	2.26	4.13	1.88	3.48	1.92	3.71	1.72	5.59	1.75	2.82	1.47	2.82	1.23
	(.62)		(-.04)		(-.28)		(-.59)		(-.25)		(-.62)		(-.20)	
TRACE	3.67	1.99	3.78	1.88	3.50	1.81	3.71	1.44	6.05	1.47	3.00	1.47	4.01	1.28
	(.09)		(-.39)		(-.26)		(-.59)		(.21)		(-.44)		(.99)	
TRAGEDY	3.53	1.99	4.75	1.88	4.12	1.83	4.77	1.65	5.86	1.48	4.70	1.89	2.30	1.45
	(-.05)		(.58)		(.36)		(.47)		(.02)		(1.26)		(-.72)	
TRAITOR	4.63	1.92	4.37	1.96	4.70	1.67	4.02	1.76	5.36	1.88	3.67	1.84	2.40	1.37M
	(1.05)		(.20)		(.94)		(-.28)		(-.48)		(.23)		(-.62)	
TREND	3.24	1.83	3.67	1.86	3.56	1.80	3.68	1.57	5.77	1.38	3.45	1.82	3.85	1.18
	(-.34)		(-.50)		(-.20)		(-.62)		(-.07)		(.01)		(.83)	
TROUBLE	3.23	1.69	3.91	1.94	3.15	1.55	4.75	1.73	6.57	.99	3.82	1.76	2.37	1.38
	(-.35)		(-.26)		(-.61)		(.45)		(.73)		(.38)		(-.65)	
TUMBLE	4.56	2.04	4.64	1.93	3.78	1.53	4.59	1.81	6.10	1.26	3.11	1.52	3.49	1.82
	(.98)		(.47)		(.02)		(.29)		(.26)		(-.33)		(.47)	
TYRANNY	2.98	1.97	3.80	1.94	3.56	1.83	3.98	1.75	4.93	1.91	4.02	1.81	2.56	1.27M
	(-.60)		(-.37)		(-.20)		(-.32)		(-.91)		(.58)		(-.46)	
UGLY	3.73	2.00	4.73	2.05	4.02	1.94	4.90	1.55	6.16	1.44	4.20	2.01	2.27	1.19
	(.15)		(.56)		(.26)		(.60)		(.32)		(.76)		(-.75)	
UNDER	3.15	1.87	4.20	2.21	3.20	1.59	4.05	1.85	6.18	1.35	3.45	2.01	3.46	1.29
	(-.43)		(.03)		(-.56)		(-.25)		(.34)		(.01)		(.44)	
UNJUST	2.40	1.56	3.60	2.05	3.28	1.70	4.34	1.74	5.78	1.52	3.52	1.64	2.28	1.39
	(-1.18)		(-.57)		(-.48)		(.04)		(-.06)		(.08)		(-.74)	
UNREST	3.54	2.13	3.82	2.13	3.26	1.60	3.92	1.82	5.51	1.58	3.09	1.70	3.31	1.59M
	(-.04)		(-.35)		(-.50)		(-.38)		(-.33)		(-.35)		(.29)	
UNSUCCESSFUL	3.35	2.25	2.87	1.79	2.98	1.81	4.12	1.70	5.81	1.64	3.46	1.87	2.33	1.33
	(-.23)		(-1.30)		(-.78)		(-.18)		(-.03)		(.02)		(-.69)	
UTTER	3.61	1.84	3.64	1.94	3.32	1.95	4.21	1.63	5.54	1.71	3.00	1.68	3.44	1.38
	(.03)		(-.53)		(-.44)		(-.09)		(-.30)		(-.44)		(.42)	
VACANT	3.14	2.03	4.69	2.07	3.83	1.76	4.95	1.82	6.08	1.44	2.92	1.64	3.05	1.32
	(-.44)		(.52)		(.07)		(.65)		(.24)		(-.52)		(.03)	
VACATE	3.47	1.90	3.77	1.97	3.28	1.66	3.97	1.58	5.05	1.87	3.20	1.44	3.05	1.21
	(-.11)		(-.40)		(-.48)		(-.33)		(-.79)		(-.24)		(.03)	
VAIN	3.11	2.07	3.54	2.09	3.66	1.63	3.83	1.49	5.83	1.44	3.63	1.64	2.89	1.46
	(-.47)		(-.63)		(-.10)		(-.47)		(-.01)		(.19)		(-.13)	
VALIDATION	3.63	1.94	3.55	2.04	3.40	1.98	3.84	1.87	5.43	1.85	3.24	1.63	3.66	1.55
	(.05)		(-.62)		(-.36)		(-.46)		(-.41)		(-.20)		(.64)	
VERB	3.36	2.07	3.86	2.24	5.55	1.56	4.31	1.87	6.23	1.31	3.64	1.95	3.35	1.45
	(-.22)		(-.31)		(1.79)		(.01)		(.39)		(.20)		(.33)	
VERTICAL	3.96	2.05	4.48	1.99	4.21	1.81	3.14	1.55	6.12	1.28	2.68	1.76	3.98	1.12
	(.38)		(.31)		(.45)		(-1.16)		(.28)		(-.76)		(.96)	
VICE	4.09	2.14	3.91	1.99	4.13	1.81	4.22	1.83	5.47	1.64	3.80	1.81	3.41	1.34
	(.51)		(-.26)		(.37)		(-.08)		(-.37)		(.36)		(.39)	
VILE	3.75	2.01	4.38	1.95	3.93	1.90	3.93	1.84	4.78	2.09	3.72	1.92	2.45	1.51M
	(.17)		(.21)		(.17)		(-.37)		(-1.06)		(.28)		(-.57)	
VULGAR	3.55	1.99	4.27	2.07	3.68	1.76	5.05	1.64	5.87	1.47	3.39	1.80	2.43	1.57F
	(-.03)		(.10)		(-.08)		(.75)		(.03)		(-.05)		(-.59)	

	CON		IMG		CAT		MNG		FAM		NOA		PLS	
	M	SD	M	SD	M	SD	M	SD	M	SD	M	SD	M	SD
WAIL	4.35	2.07	4.46	1.91	4.45	2.04	4.26	1.87	5.00	1.97	2.95	1.44	2.98	1.43M
	(.77)		(.29)		(.69)		(-.04)		(-.84)		(-.49)		(-.04)	
WASTE	4.00	2.06	4.71	2.06	4.15	1.77	4.89	1.61	6.31	1.30	4.05	1.85	2.51	1.53
	(.42)		(.54)		(.39)		(.59)		(.47)		(.61)		(-.51)	
WEAK	3.47	2.19	4.32	2.02	4.42	1.68	4.66	1.82	6.21	1.31	3.16	1.64	2.39	1.22
	(.22)		(.15)		(.66)		(.36)		(.37)		(-.28)		(-.63)	
WEEP	4.32	2.21	5.04	1.97	4.15	1.91	4.76	1.51	5.37	1.91	3.59	1.53	2.81	1.55
	(.74)		(.87)		(.39)		(.46)		(.15)		(.15)		(-.21)	
WEIGH	3.59	1.72	4.05	1.89	3.98	1.91	4.00	1.57	6.10	1.36	3.84	1.79	3.58	1.12M
	(.01)		(-.12)		(.22)		(-.30)		(.26)		(.40)		(.56)	
WEIRD	2.49	1.61	4.60	2.13	3.77	1.92	4.77	1.82	6.13	1.10	4.25	1.86	3.40	1.41M
	(-1.09)		(.43)		(.01)		(.47)		(.29)		(.81)		(.38)	
WELFARE	3.25	1.95	3.63	2.14	3.82	1.89	4.57	1.76	5.76	1.60	4.18	1.54	2.85	1.32
	(-.33)		(-.54)		(.06)		(.27)		(-.08)		(.74)		(-.17)	
WITHER	3.80	1.90	4.32	1.93	2.95	1.52	3.82	1.56	5.19	1.67	3.31	1.48	2.87	1.22
	(.22)		(.15)		(-.81)		(-.48)		(-.65)		(-.13)		(-.15)	
WORN	3.53	1.97	4.51	1.74	3.25	1.55	4.21	1.55	6.11	1.28	2.85	1.50	3.24	1.27
	(-.05)		(.34)		(-.51)		(-.09)		(.27)		(-.59)		(.22)	
WORSE	2.75	1.99	3.33	1.97	3.50	1.91	3.90	1.86	6.03	1.29	3.03	1.67	2.60	1.48
	(-.83)		(-.84)		(-.26)		(-.40)		(.19)		(-.41)		(-.42)	
WRATH	3.00	1.91	3.71	1.76	3.39	1.70	4.56	1.51	5.40	1.76	3.62	1.61	3.19	1.65
	(-.58)		(-.46)		(-.37)		(.26)		(-.44)		(.18)		(.17)	
ZERO	3.37	2.26	4.77	2.28	5.30	2.26	4.11	1.98	6.43	1.25	2.45	1.82	2.75	1.69M
	(-.21)		(.60)		(1.54)		(-.19)		(.59)		(-.99)		(-.27)	
	.00	.00	.00	.00	.00	.00	.00	.00	.00	.00	.00	.00	.00	.00
	(-3.58)		(-4.17)		(-3.76)		(-4.30)		(-5.84)		(-3.44)		(-3.02)	

CLUSTER 5

	CON		IMG		CAT		MNG		FAM		NOA		PLS	
	M	SD	M	SD	M	SD	M	SD	M	SD	M	SD	M	SD
ABUNDANT	3.47	1.88	4.37	1.91	3.62	1.81	4.95	1.69	5.98	1.28	4.00	1.89	5.32	1.26
	(.12)		(.33)		(-.06)		(.43)		(-.14)		(.06)		(.43)	
ACT	3.73	1.67	4.31	1.99	3.63	1.79	4.31	1.77	6.35	1.15	4.37	2.02	4.46	1.55M
	(.38)		(.27)		(-.05)		(-.21)		(.23)		(.43)		(-.43)	
ADDITION	3.42	2.00	3.53	1.98	4.57	1.99	4.05	1.81	5.93	1.48	3.27	1.70	4.21	1.20
	(.07)		(-.51)		(.89)		(-.47)		(-.19)		(-.67)		(-.68)	
ADMIRE	2.92	1.89	3.84	2.10	3.60	1.67	4.57	1.44	6.05	1.38	3.71	1.83	5.16	1.48
	(-.43)		(-.20)		(-.08)		(.05)		(-.07)		(-.23)		(.27)	
AGILE	3.52	1.84	4.91	1.57	4.02	1.73	4.36	1.87	5.44	1.66	3.28	1.72	5.21	1.48F
	(.17)		(.87)		(.34)		(-.16)		(-.68)		(-.66)		(.32)	
AID	3.68	2.08	4.07	1.83	3.87	2.01	4.33	1.48	6.10	1.28	3.84	1.61	4.86	1.51
	(.33)		(.03)		(.19)		(-.19)		(-.02)		(-.10)		(-.03)	
ALERT	3.96	1.99	4.28	1.93	3.76	1.58	4.30	1.60	6.15	1.26	3.52	1.79	4.99	1.28
	(.61)		(.24)		(.08)		(-.22)		(.03)		(-.42)		(.10)	
ALL	2.63	1.77	3.26	2.27	2.90	2.03	5.13	2.00	6.56	1.26	4.75	2.43	4.94	1.77
	(-.72)		(-.78)		(-.78)		(.61)		(.44)		(.81)		(.05)	
AMBITION	3.25	2.16	2.94	1.82	3.07	1.55	4.17	1.77	5.89	1.44	4.37	1.97	5.09	1.39
	(-.10)		(-1.10)		(-.61)		(-.35)		(-.23)		(.43)		(.20)	
AMUSE	3.17	1.94	4.49	1.89	3.73	1.61	4.16	1.66	5.60	1.49	4.25	1.69	5.55	1.11F
	(-.18)		(.45)		(.05)		(-.36)		(-.52)		(.31)		(.66)	
ANSWER	3.85	2.07	4.09	2.06	3.83	1.77	4.66	1.67	6.52	.95	4.03	1.93	4.24	1.46
	(.50)		(.05)		(.15)		(.14)		(.40)		(.09)		(-.65)	
AREA	3.68	1.75	3.87	1.81	3.68	1.73	3.98	1.80	6.29	1.18	4.34	1.83	3.99	1.24
	(.33)		(-.17)		(.00)		(-.54)		(.17)		(.40)		(-.90)	
ASSIST	3.38	1.90	3.62	1.85	3.19	1.61	4.25	1.51	5.90	1.44	3.57	1.89	4.50	1.37
	(.03)		(-.42)		(-.49)		(-.27)		(-.22)		(-.37)		(-.39)	
ATE	3.81	2.24	3.58	2.03	3.69	1.85	4.03	1.75	6.36	1.27	2.81	1.62	4.35	1.40
	(.46)		(-.46)		(.01)		(-.49)		(.24)		(-1.13)		(-.54)	
ATTEND	3.20	1.95	3.80	1.92	3.18	1.47	4.10	1.65	6.19	1.40	3.14	1.70	4.28	1.30
	(-.15)		(-.24)		(-.50)		(-.42)		(.07)		(-.80)		(-.61)	
AUTHENTIC	2.72	1.75	4.22	2.02	4.50	1.97	4.70	1.71	5.51	1.55	3.46	1.66	5.08	1.52F
	(-.63)		(.18)		(.82)		(.18)		(-.61)		(-.48)		(.19)	
AWARENESS	2.61	1.66	3.22	1.93	2.95	1.74	4.42	1.79	6.23	1.27	3.89	2.00	5.28	1.56F
	(-.74)		(-.82)		(-.73)		(-.10)		(.11)		(-.05)		(.39)	
BARE	3.95	2.16	4.81	2.01	3.57	1.63	4.53	1.69	5.95	1.41	3.44	1.93	4.66	1.59
	(.60)		(.77)		(-.11)		(.01)		(-.17)		(-.50)		(-.23)	
BEAUTY	3.34	2.20	5.21	1.64	3.87	2.04	5.98	1.30	6.52	1.11	5.33	1.87	6.07	1.20
	(-.01)		(1.17)		(.19)		(1.46)		(.40)		(1.39)		(1.18)	
BELIEF	2.96	1.99	3.04	2.10	3.60	1.80	4.18	1.72	6.46	.95	4.56	1.88	4.56	1.34
	(-.39)		(-1.00)		(-.08)		(-.34)		(.34)		(.62)		(-.33)	
BENEFICIAL	2.47	1.54	3.56	2.04	3.13	1.58	4.23	1.81	5.70	1.53	3.30	1.71	5.21	1.62
	(-.88)		(-.48)		(-.55)		(-.29)		(-.42)		(-.64)		(.32)	
BENEFIT	3.72	2.06	4.39	2.00	3.67	1.84	4.15	1.77	5.55	1.56	3.75	1.60	5.02	1.48
	(.37)		(.35)		(-.01)		(-.37)		(-.57)		(-.19)		(.13)	
BEST	2.78	1.95	3.36	2.22	3.53	2.00	4.84	1.71	6.39	1.27	3.61	2.04	5.09	1.64
	(-.57)		(-.68)		(-.15)		(.32)		(.27)		(-.33)		(.20)	
BORN	3.32	1.97	4.24	1.84	3.87	1.92	4.84	1.83	6.33	1.26	3.98	1.85	5.48	1.41
	(-.03)		(.20)		(.19)		(.32)		(.21)		(.04)		(.59)	
BRAVE	2.79	1.83	4.19	1.86	3.48	1.75	5.11	1.76	6.53	.83	4.25	1.93	5.27	1.23
	(-.56)		(.15)		(-.20)		(.59)		(.41)		(.31)		(.38)	
BRILLIANT	3.46	1.98	4.89	2.13	4.43	1.86	4.90	1.81	5.73	1.52	4.10	1.61	5.47	1.34
	(.11)		(.85)		(.75)		(.38)		(-.39)		(.16)		(.58)	
BUILD	3.98	1.89	3.93	1.85	3.90	1.62	4.34	1.38	6.28	1.17	4.05	1.90	4.46	1.29
	(.63)		(-.11)		(.22)		(-.18)		(.16)		(.11)		(-.43)	

	CON		IMG		CAT		MNG		FAM		NOA		PLS	
	M	SD	M	SD	M	SD	M	SD	M	SD	M	SD	M	SD
BUSY	3.25	1.63	3.96	1.78	3.51	1.56	3.85	1.64	6.47	.90	3.74	1.72	4.24	1.29F
	(-.10)		(-.08)		(-.17)		(-.67)		(.35)		(-.20)		(-.65)	
BUY	3.66	2.22	3.91	1.83	4.00	1.88	4.50	1.64	6.49	1.18	3.67	2.06	4.76	1.49
	(.31)		(-.13)		(.32)		(-.02)		(.37)		(-.27)		(-.13)	
BUYING	3.35	1.77	3.93	2.01	3.42	1.76	4.50	1.88	6.61	.95	3.11	1.67	4.91	1.48F
	(.00)		(-.11)		(-.26)		(-.02)		(.49)		(-.83)		(.02)	
CALL	3.80	1.93	4.44	2.03	3.88	1.74	4.30	1.59	6.43	1.19	3.67	1.87	4.26	1.24
	(.45)		(.40)		(.20)		(-.22)		(.31)		(-.27)		(-.63)	
CALM	3.56	2.01	4.60	2.09	4.28	1.90	4.69	1.63	6.00	1.39	3.28	1.55	5.55	1.18
	(.21)		(.56)		(.60)		(.17)		(-.12)		(-.66)		(.66)	
CARE	3.38	1.67	3.77	2.08	3.40	1.75	4.55	1.40	6.37	1.17	4.07	1.91	5.19	1.26
	(.03)		(-.27)		(-.28)		(.03)		(.25)		(.13)		(.30)	
CARES	3.07	1.75	3.63	1.83	3.20	1.59	4.56	1.71	6.28	1.33	3.75	1.80	5.06	1.61F
	(-.28)		(-.41)		(-.49)		(.04)		(.16)		(-.19)		(.17)	
CENTENNIAL	3.37	2.17	4.09	1.89	4.30	2.05	3.84	1.68	5.23	1.67	3.52	1.89	4.82	1.40
	(.02)		(.05)		(.62)		(-.68)		(-.89)		(-.42)		(-.07)	
CHANCE	2.71	1.82	3.93	1.88	3.29	1.66	3.98	1.82	6.05	1.37	3.84	1.86	4.65	1.33F
	(-.64)		(-.06)		(-.40)		(-.54)		(-.07)		(-.10)		(-.24)	
CHARM	4.20	2.29	4.33	2.04	3.57	1.68	4.75	1.67	6.05	1.36	3.89	1.78	4.81	1.59
	(.85)		(.29)		(-.11)		(.23)		(-.07)		(-.05)		(-.08)	
CHARMING	3.82	2.02	4.55	1.93	3.97	1.88	4.70	1.59	5.88	1.49	4.08	1.86	5.17	1.62F
	(.47)		(.51)		(.29)		(.18)		(-.24)		(.14)		(.28)	
CHEERFUL	3.59	2.00	4.93	2.06	4.27	1.88	5.00	1.69	6.15	1.34	3.85	2.10	5.90	1.29
	(.23)		(.89)		(.59)		(.48)		(.03)		(-.09)		(1.01)	
CLEAN	3.88	1.91	4.34	1.98	4.05	1.76	4.93	1.49	6.48	1.00	4.15	1.67	5.14	1.44F
	(.53)		(.30)		(.37)		(.41)		(.36)		(.21)		(.25)	
CLEAR	3.55	1.86	4.55	1.99	3.85	1.84	4.55	1.62	6.47	.95	3.25	1.63	5.41	1.48F
	(.20)		(.51)		(.17)		(.03)		(.35)		(-.69)		(.52)	
CLEVER	3.55	2.00	3.32	1.91	3.76	1.84	4.02	1.63	5.41	1.66	3.52	1.85	4.72	1.49
	(.20)		(-.72)		(.08)		(-.50)		(-.71)		(-.42)		(-.17)	
CLOSER	3.19	1.86	4.27	1.94	3.77	1.74	3.95	1.84	6.00	1.35	3.31	1.76	4.84	1.38F
	(-.16)		(.23)		(.09)		(-.57)		(-.12)		(-.63)		(-.05)	
CLUE	3.76	2.03	3.69	2.03	3.75	1.75	4.44	1.53	6.07	1.33	3.79	1.85	4.25	1.37
	(.41)		(-.35)		(.07)		(-.08)		(-.05)		(-.15)		(-.64)	
COME	3.51	2.20	3.30	2.06	3.25	1.95	4.08	1.79	6.59	.89	3.16	1.76	4.79	1.47F
	(.16)		(-.74)		(-.43)		(-.44)		(.47)		(-.78)		(-.10)	
COMFORT	3.98	2.03	4.67	1.95	3.87	1.62	4.56	1.73	6.25	1.20	4.03	1.75	5.65	1.38
	(.63)		(.63)		(.19)		(.04)		(.13)		(.09)		(.76)	
COMPLIMENT	3.29	2.13	4.35	2.02	3.98	1.75	4.45	1.56	6.19	1.14	4.22	1.78	5.37	1.48
	(-.06)		(.31)		(.30)		(-.07)		(.07)		(.28)		(.48)	
COMPOSURE	3.20	1.52	3.55	2.11	3.34	1.69	3.82	1.68	5.32	1.44	3.77	1.59	4.71	1.42
	(-.15)		(-.49)		(-.34)		(-.70)		(-.80)		(-.17)		(-.18)	
CONSIDERABLE	2.98	2.12	3.21	1.95	2.92	1.71	4.27	1.82	6.12	1.15	3.94	1.77	4.58	1.30M
	(-.37)		(-.83)		(-.76)		(-.25)		(.00)		(.00)		(-.31)	
COOL	3.60	1.88	4.00	1.95	4.21	1.65	4.27	1.65	6.18	1.22	3.27	1.87	4.84	1.46
	(.25)		(-.04)		(.53)		(-.25)		(.06)		(-.67)		(-.05)	
COPE	3.43	2.03	3.38	2.14	3.46	1.70	4.23	1.62	5.90	1.36	3.74	1.83	4.40	1.49
	(.08)		(-.66)		(-.22)		(-.29)		(-.22)		(-.20)		(-.49)	
COURSE	3.85	1.70	3.85	1.98	4.10	1.74	4.29	1.87	6.38	1.04	4.13	1.63	3.97	1.20
	(.50)		(-.19)		(.42)		(-.24)		(.26)		(.19)		(-.92)	
COURTEOUS	3.60	2.07	3.83	1.96	3.27	1.70	4.67	1.56	5.83	1.49	3.77	1.71	5.03	1.49
	(.25)		(-.16)		(-.41)		(.15)		(-.29)		(-.17)		(.14)	
CULTURE	3.47	2.02	3.33	1.93	3.60	2.04	4.37	1.75	5.97	1.16	5.30	1.63	4.41	1.13
	(.12)		(-.71)		(-.08)		(-.15)		(-.15)		(1.36)		(-.48)	

	CON		IMG		CAT		MNG		FAM		NOA		PLS	
	M	SD	M	SD	M	SD	M	SD	M	SD	M	SD	M	SD
CURE	3.59	2.01	3.86	1.88	3.73	1.92	4.77	1.67	6.03	1.37	3.75	1.84	5.18	1.59
	(.24)		(-.18)		(.05)		(.25)		(-.09)		(-.19)		(.29)	
CUSTOM	3.10	1.81	3.47	2.13	3.72	1.70	4.38	1.43	6.05	1.33	4.37	1.76	3.90	1.28F
	(-.25)		(-.57)		(.04)		(-.14)		(-.07)		(.43)		(-.99)	
DEAL	3.21	1.82	4.27	1.93	3.47	1.86	4.32	1.48	5.93	1.49	3.81	1.83	4.05	1.15
	(-.14)		(.23)		(-.20)		(-.20)		(-.14)		(-.13)		(-.84)	
DEAR	3.22	1.95	3.68	2.17	3.35	1.91	4.38	1.97	6.10	1.54	3.75	2.08	5.25	1.53
	(-.13)		(-.36)		(-.33)		(-.14)		(-.02)		(-.19)		(.36)	
DELIVER	3.89	2.06	3.82	1.83	3.71	1.79	3.95	1.49	6.03	1.38	3.70	1.81	4.32	1.17
	(.54)		(-.22)		(.03)		(-.57)		(-.09)		(-.24)		(-.57)	
DEMOCRACY	3.39	2.03	4.21	2.06	4.80	1.97	5.02	1.74	6.53	.94	5.44	1.88	4.70	1.56
	(.04)		(.17)		(1.12)		(.50)		(.41)		(1.50)		(-.19)	
DIVERSITY	2.64	1.63	2.95	1.61	3.02	1.67	4.23	1.91	5.75	1.47	3.95	2.09	4.88	1.39
	(-.71)		(-1.08)		(-.66)		(-.29)		(-.37)		(-.01)		(-.01)	
DONOR	4.05	2.17	4.00	2.12	4.20	1.88	3.93	1.82	5.53	1.61	3.56	1.69	4.42	1.54
	(.70)		(-.04)		(.52)		(-.59)		(-.59)		(-.38)		(-.47)	
DUTY	3.52	1.84	3.31	2.15	4.47	1.77	4.13	1.59	6.25	1.15	4.21	1.84	4.08	1.21
	(.17)		(-.73)		(.79)		(-.39)		(.13)		(.27)		(-.81)	
EAGER	2.98	1.93	4.13	1.99	3.58	1.87	4.57	1.70	5.79	1.59	3.49	1.67	5.03	1.44
	(-.37)		(.09)		(-.10)		(.05)		(-.33)		(-.45)		(.14)	
EARN	3.45	2.12	4.31	2.04	3.85	1.69	4.92	1.39	6.31	1.22	3.82	1.78	4.97	1.59
	(.10)		(.27)		(.17)		(.40)		(.19)		(-.12)		(.08)	
EASIER	2.71	1.63	3.68	1.87	3.30	1.66	3.81	1.75	6.09	1.44	3.25	1.67	4.98	1.32
	(-.64)		(-.36)		(-.38)		(-.71)		(-.03)		(-.69)		(.09)	
EASY	2.84	1.53	3.30	1.81	3.25	1.70	4.45	1.69	6.53	1.04	3.20	1.80	4.84	1.45
	(-.51)		(-.74)		(-.43)		(-.07)		(.41)		(-.74)		(-.05)	
ELEGANT	3.05	1.91	4.02	2.11	2.90	1.69	4.42	1.64	5.58	1.60	3.86	1.89	5.17	1.54F
	(-.30)		(-.02)		(-.78)		(-.10)		(-.54)		(-.08)		(.28)	
EMANCIPATION	3.24	1.98	3.63	1.83	3.05	1.95	4.44	1.87	5.43	1.73	4.15	1.98	4.85	1.68F
	(-.11)		(-.41)		(-.63)		(-.08)		(-.69)		(.21)		(-.04)	
ENTERTAIN	3.98	1.92	4.29	1.94	4.05	1.57	4.73	1.60	6.11	1.25	4.76	1.77	5.18	1.20
	(.63)		(.25)		(.37)		(.21)		(-.01)		(.82)		(.29)	
EQUALITY	3.38	2.42	3.40	2.11	3.34	1.82	4.43	1.87	6.02	1.35	4.39	2.25	5.32	1.58F
	(.03)		(-.64)		(-.34)		(-.09)		(-.10)		(.45)		(.43)	
ETERNAL	2.10	1.69	3.97	2.40	3.28	1.91	4.55	2.00	5.74	1.61	4.00	2.20	5.31	1.60
	(-1.25)		(-.07)		(-.40)		(.03)		(-.38)		(.06)		(.42)	
ETERNITY	2.98	2.26	3.23	2.32	3.68	2.11	4.74	1.85	5.87	1.41	5.23	2.12	5.04	1.94
	(-.37)		(-.11)		(.00)		(.22)		(-.25)		(1.29)		(.15)	
EVOLUTION	3.00	1.73	3.26	1.97	4.12	2.11	4.51	1.87	5.97	1.54	4.87	1.99	4.75	1.37M
	(-.35)		(-.08)		(.44)		(-.01)		(-.15)		(.93)		(-.14)	
EXPANSION	3.21	1.83	4.11	1.96	3.57	1.67	4.44	1.71	5.89	1.40	3.95	1.75	4.15	1.59
	(-.14)		(.07)		(-.11)		(-.08)		(-.23)		(.01)		(-.74)	
EXPOSURE	3.35	2.10	4.25	2.01	3.41	1.55	4.05	1.78	6.12	1.30	3.97	1.62	3.90	1.23M
	(.00)		(.21)		(-.27)		(-.47)		(.00)		(.03)		(-.99)	
EXTRAVAGANT	3.39	2.06	4.17	2.14	3.24	1.73	4.56	1.58	5.69	1.43	3.81	2.17	4.78	1.49M
	(.04)		(.13)		(-.44)		(.04)		(-.43)		(-.13)		(-.11)	
FACT	3.08	2.10	3.18	1.96	3.92	1.86	4.63	1.81	6.50	1.02	3.86	1.97	4.20	1.42
	(-.27)		(-.86)		(.24)		(.11)		(.38)		(-.08)		(-.69)	
FANTASY	3.17	2.10	5.07	1.89	3.87	2.00	5.21	1.60	6.37	1.13	5.52	1.65	5.82	1.30
	(-.18)		(1.03)		(.19)		(.69)		(.25)		(1.58)		(.93)	
FASHION	3.75	2.17	4.64	1.91	4.08	1.71	5.05	1.53	6.18	1.35	4.29	1.99	4.78	1.45F
	(.40)		(.60)		(.40)		(.53)		(.06)		(.35)		(-.11)	
FAST	3.00	2.00	4.04	1.79	3.95	1.72	5.23	1.67	6.58	.93	3.38	2.00	4.78	1.28M
	(-.35)		(.00)		(.27)		(.71)		(.46)		(-.56)		(-.11)	

	CON		IMG		CAT		MNG		FAM		NOA		PLS	
	M	SD	M	SD	M	SD	M	SD	M	SD	M	SD	M	SD
FASTER	3.40	1.74	3.65	1.93	3.57	1.73	4.42	1.74	6.34	1.17	3.05	1.73	4.51	1.12
	(.05)		(-.39)		(-.11)		(-.10)		(.22)		(-.89)		(-.38)	
FEAT	3.41	2.04	3.59	1.85	3.33	1.59	3.77	1.75	5.23	1.86	3.51	1.55	4.34	1.30
	(.06)		(-.45)		(-.35)		(-.75)		(-.89)		(-.43)		(-.55)	
FEEL	3.20	2.11	3.57	1.97	3.27	1.87	5.02	1.79	6.62	.94	4.54	1.99	5.52	1.25
	(-.15)		(-.47)		(-.41)		(.50)		(.50)		(.60)		(.63)	
FILL	3.68	1.92	4.09	2.00	3.55	1.74	3.72	1.80	5.95	1.49	3.21	1.66	4.35	1.27
	(.33)		(.05)		(-.13)		(-.80)		(-.17)		(-.73)		(-.54)	
FIND	3.47	1.83	4.21	1.99	3.87	1.74	3.84	1.66	6.17	1.26	3.38	1.56	5.06	1.56
	(.12)		(.17)		(.19)		(-.68)		(.05)		(-.56)		(.17)	
FINE	3.24	2.04	3.86	2.29	3.28	1.91	4.95	1.68	6.34	1.26	3.48	1.75	5.04	1.59M
	(-.11)		(-.40)		(-.40)		(.43)		(.22)		(-.46)		(.15)	
FIRM	3.96	2.25	3.98	2.06	3.85	1.64	4.65	1.74	6.41	1.07	3.74	1.87	4.22	1.77M
	(.61)		(-.06)		(.17)		(.13)		(.29)		(-.20)		(-.67)	
FIRST	3.07	1.95	4.32	2.21	4.83	2.20	4.29	2.15	6.24	1.44	3.41	2.23	4.90	1.36
	(-.28)		(.28)		(1.15)		(-.23)		(.12)		(-.53)		(.01)	
FLAIR	3.31	1.87	4.19	1.83	3.12	1.88	3.82	1.66	5.63	1.47	3.41	1.58	4.78	1.28
	(-.04)		(.15)		(-.56)		(-.70)		(-.49)		(-.53)		(-.11)	
FLEXIBILITY	3.56	1.90	3.64	1.98	3.27	1.70	4.25	1.70	5.59	1.59	4.05	1.66	4.67	1.38
	(.21)		(-.40)		(-.41)		(-.27)		(-.53)		(.11)		(-.22)	
FLOW	3.07	1.69	4.11	1.96	3.15	1.55	4.19	1.71	5.92	1.66	3.16	1.74	4.35	1.52
	(-.28)		(.07)		(-.53)		(-.33)		(-.20)		(-.78)		(-.54)	
FORECAST	3.04	1.78	4.29	1.86	4.50	1.52	4.44	1.54	5.98	1.33	4.34	1.76	4.44	1.02
	(-.31)		(.25)		(.82)		(-.08)		(-.14)		(.40)		(-.45)	
FREE	3.24	2.15	3.93	2.13	3.63	1.98	5.28	1.73	6.54	1.07	4.33	2.29	5.90	1.52
	(-.11)		(-.11)		(-.05)		(.76)		(.42)		(.39)		(1.01)	
FREEDOM	3.03	2.11	4.48	2.14	3.62	1.95	5.15	1.94	6.40	1.06	4.73	2.03	6.30	1.10
	(-.32)		(.28)		(-.06)		(.63)		(.28)		(.79)		(1.41)	
FULL	3.74	1.92	4.16	1.99	3.55	1.85	4.48	1.58	6.62	.85	3.52	2.02	4.51	1.31
	(.39)		(.12)		(-.13)		(-.04)		(.50)		(-.42)		(-.38)	
GALLANT	2.36	1.34	4.41	1.93	3.57	1.77	4.18	1.79	5.03	2.04	3.13	1.59	5.00	1.44F
	(-.99)		(.37)		(-.11)		(-.34)		(-1.09)		(-.81)		(.11)	
GENEROUS	2.56	1.76	3.42	1.92	3.18	1.66	4.67	1.95	6.12	1.35	4.11	1.61	5.90	1.14
	(-.79)		(-.62)		(-.50)		(.15)		(.00)		(.17)		(1.01)	
GENTLE	3.18	1.81	4.20	1.98	3.70	1.76	5.18	1.72	6.36	1.17	3.70	1.94	5.76	1.55F
	(-.17)		(.16)		(.02)		(.66)		(.24)		(-.24)		(.87)	
GENUINE	2.91	1.95	3.72	2.07	3.47	1.89	4.85	1.67	5.77	1.55	3.52	1.90	5.26	1.71
	(-.44)		(-.32)		(-.21)		(.33)		(-.35)		(-.42)		(.37)	
GEOGRAPHICAL	3.51	1.94	3.94	2.13	4.56	1.71	4.21	1.63	5.75	1.58	4.50	1.81	4.09	1.38
	(.16)		(-.10)		(.88)		(-.31)		(-.37)		(.56)		(-.80)	
GIVE	3.22	2.01	3.88	2.17	2.95	1.70	4.65	1.86	6.39	1.19	3.33	1.61	5.00	1.88F
	(-.13)		(-.16)		(-.73)		(.13)		(.27)		(-.61)		(.11)	
GLAD	3.14	1.87	4.49	2.08	3.80	1.69	5.16	1.59	6.34	1.40	3.98	2.02	5.65	1.53F
	(-.21)		(.45)		(.12)		(.64)		(.22)		(.04)		(.76)	
GLORY	3.53	2.20	3.43	1.95	3.31	1.62	4.15	1.85	5.80	1.39	3.68	2.01	4.85	1.72
	(.18)		(-.61)		(-.37)		(-.37)		(-.32)		(-.04)		(-.04)	
GO	3.33	2.06	3.61	2.28	3.35	1.95	4.30	1.78	6.71	.72	3.21	2.02	4.65	1.26
	(-.02)		(-.43)		(-.33)		(-.22)		(.59)		(-.73)		(-.24)	
GOD	3.61	2.64	4.55	2.33	4.82	2.45	5.47	1.75	6.41	1.36	5.21	2.15	4.92	1.73
	(.26)		(.51)		(1.14)		(.95)		(.29)		(1.27)		(.03)	
GOOD	2.93	1.96	3.89	2.12	3.78	1.99	5.55	1.71	6.66	.95	4.41	2.04	5.35	1.38
	(-.42)		(-.15)		(.10)		(1.03)		(.54)		(.47)		(.46)	
GRACE	3.10	1.75	4.35	2.17	3.62	2.02	3.89	1.74	5.52	1.64	3.35	1.57	4.74	1.55
	(-.25)		(.31)		(-.06)		(-.63)		(-.60)		(-.59)		(-.15)	

	CON		IMG		CAT		MNG		FAM		NOA		PLS	
	M	SD	M	SD	M	SD	M	SD	M	SD	M	SD	M	SD
GRACEFUL	3.17	1.76	4.77	1.94	3.93	1.80	4.62	1.56	5.87	1.45	3.92	1.75	5.32	1.50
	(-.18)		(.73)		(.25)		(.10)		(-.25)		(-.02)		(.43)	
GREAT	3.07	1.85	3.79	2.06	3.45	1.84	4.87	1.82	6.31	1.40	4.08	1.84	5.19	1.57
	(-.28)		(-.25)		(-.23)		(.35)		(.19)		(.14)		(.30)	
GROW	4.05	1.87	3.65	1.88	4.21	1.86	5.05	1.68	6.36	1.20	4.33	2.00	5.21	1.39
	(.70)		(-.39)		(.53)		(.53)		(.24)		(.14)		(.32)	
HAPPY	3.51	2.03	5.41	1.86	4.43	2.04	5.68	1.54	6.84	.55	4.67	2.18	6.10	1.49
	(.16)		(1.37)		(.75)		(1.16)		(.72)		(.73)		(1.21)	
HARDER	2.70	1.76	3.77	2.04	2.92	1.83	4.35	1.79	6.47	1.07	3.68	1.90	4.13	1.31
	(-.65)		(-.27)		(-.76)		(-.17)		(.35)		(-.26)		(-.76)	
HARMONY	3.68	2.14	4.17	1.97	4.17	1.77	4.49	1.55	6.08	1.50	3.66	1.67	5.39	1.67F
	(.33)		(.13)		(.49)		(-.03)		(-.04)		(-.28)		(.50)	
HEAL	4.13	2.16	4.32	1.92	4.45	1.76	4.65	1.90	6.10	1.43	3.60	1.76	5.28	1.36
	(.78)		(.28)		(.77)		(.13)		(-.02)		(-.34)		(.39)	
HEALTH	3.67	2.02	4.09	1.84	4.15	1.69	5.03	1.66	6.23	1.35	4.81	1.93	5.43	1.33
	(.32)		(.05)		(.47)		(.51)		(.11)		(.87)		(.54)	
HEIR	3.80	2.00	3.88	2.08	4.13	1.67	3.72	1.72	5.27	1.76	3.65	1.71	4.80	1.58
	(.45)		(-.16)		(.45)		(-.80)		(-.85)		(-.29)		(-.09)	
HELP	2.86	1.66	4.33	1.95	3.52	1.88	5.03	1.69	6.61	.97	4.38	1.99	4.36	1.48
	(-.49)		(.29)		(-.16)		(.51)		(.49)		(.44)		(-.53)	
HER	4.15	2.24	4.58	2.16	4.00	1.90	5.07	2.01	6.43	1.30	3.39	2.06	5.30	1.61M
	(.80)		(.54)		(.32)		(.55)		(.31)		(-.55)		(.41)	
HIGH	3.67	2.02	4.88	2.05	3.83	1.91	5.21	1.67	6.64	1.00	3.92	1.92	5.26	1.51
	(.32)		(.84)		(.15)		(.69)		(.52)		(-.02)		(.37)	
HIGHER	3.20	1.71	4.58	1.74	3.62	1.80	5.18	1.65	6.48	1.01	3.57	2.00	4.94	1.68M
	(-.15)		(.54)		(-.06)		(.66)		(.36)		(-.37)		(.05)	
HIM	3.64	2.14	3.79	2.24	3.19	1.83	3.88	1.93	6.66	.78	3.16	2.10	4.65	1.39F
	(.29)		(-.25)		(-.49)		(-.64)		(.54)		(-.78)		(-.24)	
HOLD	4.08	1.92	4.66	1.86	3.63	1.56	4.72	1.64	6.50	1.14	3.54	1.70	5.06	1.44
	(.73)		(.62)		(-.05)		(.20)		(.38)		(-.40)		(.17)	
HONESTY	2.74	2.00	3.80	2.23	3.87	1.64	4.90	1.75	6.52	.95	4.48	1.85	5.95	1.12
	(-.61)		(-.24)		(.19)		(.38)		(.40)		(.54)		(1.06)	
HOPE	3.05	1.95	4.29	2.27	3.58	2.04	4.93	1.96	6.34	1.31	4.25	2.01	5.46	1.57
	(-.30)		(.25)		(-.10)		(.41)		(.22)		(.31)		(.57)	
HUE	3.66	2.07	3.93	2.00	3.93	2.03	4.02	1.64	5.08	1.86	4.13	2.03	4.93	1.46
	(.31)		(-.11)		(.25)		(-.50)		(-1.04)		(.19)		(.04)	
HUMANE	3.28	2.13	3.77	2.04	3.47	1.71	4.52	1.65	5.82	1.41	4.52	1.88	5.00	1.61
	(-.07)		(-.27)		(-.21)		(.00)		(-.30)		(.58)		(.11)	
HUMANITY	3.77	1.99	4.36	2.01	3.90	1.86	4.98	1.87	6.00	1.21	5.39	1.77	5.03	1.51F
	(.42)		(.32)		(.22)		(.46)		(-.12)		(1.45)		(.14)	
HUMBLE	2.27	1.52	3.71	1.95	3.08	1.69	4.52	1.68	5.93	1.35	3.31	1.95	4.38	1.63
	(-1.08)		(-.33)		(-.60)		(.00)		(-.19)		(-.63)		(-.51)	
HUMOR	3.52	1.79	4.26	2.12	4.02	1.84	5.35	1.77	6.31	1.18	4.33	1.80	5.40	1.73
	(.17)		(.22)		(.34)		(.83)		(.19)		(.39)		(.51)	
IDEA	2.87	1.88	3.53	2.24	3.47	1.95	4.95	1.87	6.33	1.27	4.87	1.96	5.16	1.40
	(-.48)		(-.51)		(-.21)		(.43)		(.21)		(.93)		(.27)	
IDEAL	2.57	1.96	3.12	2.09	2.98	1.75	4.12	1.72	5.77	1.36	3.92	2.07	5.06	1.39F
	(-.78)		(-.92)		(-.70)		(-.40)		(-.35)		(-.02)		(.17)	
IMAGINATION	3.00	2.04	4.35	2.20	3.50	1.69	4.80	1.74	6.26	1.17	5.08	1.89	5.54	1.47F
	(-.35)		(.31)		(-.18)		(.28)		(.14)		(1.14)		(.65)	
IMPORT	3.16	2.11	3.55	2.04	3.37	1.95	4.02	2.00	5.85	1.53	3.39	2.12	4.29	1.83F
	(-.19)		(-.49)		(-.31)		(-.50)		(-.27)		(-.55)		(-.60)	
INFINITE	2.63	2.06	3.95	2.27	3.17	2.17	4.66	1.78	5.88	1.51	5.13	2.09	4.40	1.48
	(-.72)		(-.09)		(-.51)		(.14)		(-.24)		(1.19)		(-.49)	

	CON		IMG		CAT		MNG		FAM		NOA		PLS	
	M	SD	M	SD	M	SD	M	SD	M	SD	M	SD	M	SD
INHALE	4.13	1.93	4.55	1.86	3.49	1.74	4.02	1.68	5.90	1.31	3.31	1.54	4.51	1.34
	(.78)		(.51)		(-.19)		(-.50)		(-.22)		(-.63)		(-.38)	
INTEGRITY	2.43	1.43	3.73	1.90	3.68	1.73	4.21	1.70	5.55	1.52	3.92	1.83	5.15	1.61F
	(-.92)		(-.31)		(.00)		(-.31)		(-.57)		(-.02)		(.26)	
INTENSE	3.57	1.86	3.34	1.91	2.77	1.49	4.32	1.37	5.64	1.63	3.48	1.60	4.25	1.41
	(.22)		(-.70)		(-.91)		(-.20)		(-.48)		(-.46)		(-.64)	
INTEREST	3.20	1.82	3.56	2.04	3.43	1.89	4.27	1.66	6.31	1.04	4.39	1.84	5.21	1.22
	(-.15)		(-.48)		(-.25)		(-.20)		(.19)		(.45)		(.32)	
INTIMATE	2.90	2.00	4.86	1.83	3.25	1.95	4.74	1.85	5.90	1.53	4.29	1.95	5.57	1.54M
	(-.45)		(.82)		(-.43)		(.22)		(-.22)		(.35)		(.68)	
JOIN	2.88	1.72	3.47	1.71	2.85	1.73	4.64	1.62	6.30	1.12	3.31	1.42	4.26	1.26F
	(-.47)		(-.57)		(-.83)		(.12)		(.18)		(-.63)		(-.63)	
JOKE	3.48	1.96	4.85	1.94	4.40	1.86	4.84	1.72	6.17	1.37	4.11	1.55	5.29	1.32
	(.13)		(.81)		(.72)		(.32)		(.05)		(.17)		(.40)	
JOY	3.59	2.05	5.25	1.83	4.45	1.82	5.67	1.49	6.27	1.30	4.84	1.95	6.00	1.37F
	(.24)		(.77)		(.77)		(1.15)		(.15)		(.90)		(1.11)	
JUBILANT	3.41	1.91	4.64	1.91	4.05	1.86	4.81	1.63	5.02	1.77	3.72	1.85	5.44	1.58
	(.06)		(.60)		(.37)		(.29)		(-1.10)		(-.22)		(.55)	
JUSTICE	3.69	2.17	3.27	1.97	4.00	1.96	4.60	1.80	5.97	1.22	4.85	1.70	4.90	1.50
	(.34)		(-.77)		(.32)		(.08)		(-.15)		(.91)		(.01)	
KIND	3.19	1.81	3.75	2.07	3.40	1.65	4.61	1.75	6.26	1.26	3.90	1.98	5.34	1.60F
	(-.16)		(-.29)		(-.28)		(.09)		(.14)		(-.04)		(.45)	
KNOW	2.70	1.97	2.98	2.13	2.70	1.80	4.39	1.95	6.40	1.26	3.94	2.02	5.05	1.36
	(-.65)		(-1.06)		(-.98)		(-.13)		(.28)		(.00)		(.16)	
KNOWLEDGE	2.98	2.06	3.46	2.01	3.62	1.82	5.08	1.79	6.53	.96	5.23	2.01	5.62	1.37
	(-.37)		(-.58)		(-.06)		(.56)		(.41)		(1.29)		(.73)	
LAID	3.46	1.79	4.87	2.09	3.37	1.74	4.27	1.84	5.81	1.50	3.64	1.78	4.43	1.59M
	(.11)		(.83)		(-.31)		(-.25)		(-.31)		(-.30)		(-.46)	
LEARN	3.65	2.05	3.55	1.92	3.65	1.72	4.33	1.68	6.26	1.25	4.27	2.10	5.09	1.38
	(.31)		(-.49)		(-.02)		(-.19)		(.14)		(.33)		(.20)	
LEGENDARY	2.68	1.72	4.07	2.02	3.83	1.66	4.02	1.57	5.40	1.72	4.33	1.74	4.81	1.16
	(-.67)		(.03)		(.15)		(-.50)		(-.72)		(.39)		(-.08)	
LEGITIMATE	2.61	1.75	3.15	2.01	3.70	1.92	4.20	1.62	5.61	1.56	3.69	1.94	4.73	1.59F
	(-.74)		(-.89)		(.02)		(-.32)		(-.51)		(-.25)		(-.16)	
LENIENT	2.81	1.54	3.69	1.99	3.72	1.75	4.07	1.72	5.47	1.71	3.02	1.43	4.92	1.51
	(-.54)		(-.35)		(.04)		(-.45)		(-.65)		(-.92)		(.03)	
LIBERTY	3.57	2.28	3.76	2.24	3.90	1.83	4.57	1.77	5.72	1.47	4.68	2.00	5.41	1.49
	(.22)		(-.28)		(.22)		(.05)		(-.40)		(.74)		(.52)	
LIKE	2.82	1.77	3.77	2.15	3.68	2.14	5.16	1.69	6.52	1.07	4.08	2.07	5.06	1.72
	(-.53)		(-.27)		(.00)		(.40)		(.40)		(.14)		(.17)	
LISTEN	4.04	2.05	3.72	1.95	3.66	1.86	4.33	1.75	6.17	1.35	3.49	2.02	4.94	1.45F
	(.69)		(-.32)		(-.02)		(-.19)		(.05)		(-.45)		(.05)	
LIVE	4.32	2.16	4.56	2.02	3.18	1.81	5.22	1.62	6.59	.94	5.34	1.88	5.77	1.52F
	(.97)		(.52)		(-.50)		(.70)		(.47)		(1.40)		(.88)	
LOCK	3.74	1.97	4.39	1.94	3.63	1.84	4.32	1.43	6.24	1.43	4.08	1.83	4.46	1.22
	(.39)		(.35)		(-.05)		(-.20)		(.12)		(.14)		(-.43)	
LOVELY	3.14	1.82	4.85	1.91	4.35	1.64	5.05	1.78	5.97	1.41	4.30	2.03	5.62	1.64
	(-.21)		(.81)		(.67)		(.53)		(-.15)		(.36)		(.73)	
LUST	3.20	2.11	4.38	1.90	3.65	1.89	4.68	1.72	5.46	1.79	4.05	1.94	4.12	1.93M
	(-.15)		(.34)		(-.03)		(.16)		(-.65)		(.11)		(-.77)	
MAKE	2.95	1.83	3.32	2.03	2.97	1.81	4.74	1.74	5.68	.68	3.62	2.04	4.73	1.38
	(-.40)		(-.72)		(-.71)		(.22)		(.56)		(-.32)		(-.16)	
MANY	2.72	1.71	4.31	2.12	3.15	1.64	4.59	1.99	6.53	1.10	3.57	1.87	4.32	1.43
	(-.63)		(.27)		(-.53)		(.07)		(.41)		(-.37)		(-.57)	

	CON M	SD	IMG M	SD	CAT M	SD	MNG M	SD	FAM M	SD	NOA M	SD	PLS M	SD
MAY	3.28	2.11	3.64	2.21	4.50	2.10	4.05	1.87	6.50	.98	3.44	2.01	5.17	1.46F
	(-.07)		(-.40)		(.82)		(-.47)		(.38)		(-.50)		(.28)	
MEET	3.37	1.81	4.32	2.12	3.48	1.52	4.62	1.69	6.49	1.18	3.83	1.80	4.82	1.21
	(.02)		(.28)		(-.20)		(.10)		(.37)		(-.11)		(-.07)	
MEETING	3.41	1.63	3.93	1.83	3.53	1.56	4.31	1.61	6.37	1.33	3.63	1.67	4.15	1.30
	(.06)		(-.11)		(-.15)		(-.21)		(.25)		(-.31)		(-.74)	
MEMORY	3.12	1.96	4.26	2.18	3.62	1.63	4.30	1.61	6.27	1.44	4.72	1.80	5.07	1.21
	(-.23)		(.22)		(-.06)		(-.22)		(.15)		(.78)		(.18)	
MERRY	3.66	1.94	5.13	1.90	3.92	1.68	5.13	1.58	6.00	1.40	3.97	1.79	5.75	1.42
	(.31)		(1.09)		(.24)		(.61)		(-.12)		(.03)		(.86)	
METHOD	3.07	1.51	3.20	1.78	3.73	1.77	4.02	1.42	6.17	1.16	4.10	1.78	4.00	1.19
	(-.28)		(-.84)		(.05)		(-.50)		(.05)		(.16)		(-.89)	
MIGHT	2.40	1.53	4.15	1.89	3.57	1.74	3.80	1.87	5.86	1.41	3.85	1.74	4.19	1.37
	(-.95)		(.11)		(-.11)		(-.72)		(-.26)		(-.09)		(-.70)	
MILD	3.26	1.85	3.72	1.76	3.57	1.67	4.37	1.71	6.35	1.09	3.51	1.65	5.15	1.24
	(-.09)		(-.32)		(-.11)		(-.15)		(.23)		(-.43)		(.26)	
MIND	3.57	2.02	3.96	2.08	4.05	2.17	4.37	1.96	6.45	.99	5.16	2.23	4.80	1.61F
	(.22)		(-.08)		(.37)		(-.15)		(.33)		(1.22)		(-.09)	
MISCHIEVOUS	2.88	1.83	4.61	2.00	3.77	1.61	4.34	1.54	5.71	1.52	3.62	1.84	4.18	1.58
	(-.47)		(.57)		(.09)		(-.18)		(-.41)		(-.32)		(-.71)	
MISS	3.68	2.03	4.59	2.06	3.87	1.85	4.52	1.80	6.37	1.18	2.94	1.65	4.19	1.63M
	(.33)		(.55)		(.19)		(.00)		(.25)		(-1.00)		(-.70)	
MOMENT	2.75	1.81	3.78	2.11	3.58	1.82	4.02	1.58	5.88	1.43	3.70	1.85	4.72	1.11F
	(-.60)		(-.26)		(-.10)		(-.50)		(-.24)		(-.24)		(-.17)	
MOTION	3.63	2.16	4.10	1.95	3.80	1.70	4.54	1.88	6.15	1.22	4.14	1.97	4.56	1.05
	(.28)		(.06)		(.12)		(.02)		(.03)		(.20)		(-.33)	
MYSTIC	3.41	1.92	4.89	1.90	3.88	1.56	4.42	1.58	5.29	1.79	4.10	1.86	4.66	1.41
	(.06)		(.85)		(.20)		(-.10)		(-.83)		(.16)		(-.23)	
MYTH	3.30	2.02	3.53	1.91	4.63	1.84	4.20	1.64	5.88	1.43	4.87	1.86	4.70	1.38F
	(-.05)		(-.51)		(.95)		(-.32)		(-.24)		(.93)		(-.19)	
NEAR	3.33	1.91	4.37	2.02	3.56	1.88	4.65	1.74	6.39	1.19	3.35	1.95	5.10	1.46
	(-.02)		(.33)		(-.12)		(.13)		(.27)		(-.59)		(.21)	
NEAT	3.10	2.01	4.89	1.81	3.95	1.90	4.93	1.66	6.02	1.33	3.70	1.85	4.81	1.56
	(-.25)		(.85)		(.27)		(.41)		(-.10)		(-.24)		(-.08)	
NEED	3.10	2.07	3.21	1.81	3.10	1.97	4.73	2.03	6.63	.94	4.13	1.82	4.20	1.62F
	(-.25)		(-.83)		(-.58)		(.21)		(.51)		(.19)		(-.69)	
NEW	3.44	1.90	4.50	2.15	3.83	1.88	5.25	1.79	6.59	1.10	3.67	2.05	5.66	1.35
	(.09)		(.46)		(.15)		(.73)		(.47)		(-.27)		(.77)	
NICE	2.75	1.65	4.20	1.89	4.15	1.89	5.25	1.64	6.31	1.22	3.74	1.91	5.50	1.43
	(-.60)		(.16)		(.47)		(.73)		(.19)		(-.20)		(.61)	
OPEN	3.77	1.87	4.36	1.99	3.65	1.88	4.02	1.87	6.63	.87	3.74	1.75	4.95	1.21
	(.42)		(.32)		(-.03)		(-.50)		(.51)		(-.20)		(.06)	
OVER	2.83	1.76	3.72	2.23	3.13	1.85	4.23	1.82	6.54	1.06	3.28	1.92	4.21	1.38
	(-.52)		(-.32)		(-.55)		(-.29)		(.42)		(-.66)		(-.68)	
OWN	3.13	2.16	3.31	2.01	3.48	2.07	4.85	2.01	6.72	.74	3.90	1.94	4.85	1.44F
	(-.22)		(-.73)		(-.20)		(.33)		(.60)		(-.04)		(-.04)	
PAID	3.82	2.13	4.23	2.09	3.98	2.04	4.87	1.75	6.51	.94	3.52	1.88	5.16	1.80
	(.47)		(.19)		(.30)		(.35)		(.39)		(-.42)		(.27)	
PAIR	3.73	1.86	4.74	1.94	4.08	2.04	5.10	1.71	6.18	1.53	3.33	1.87	4.57	1.56
	(.38)		(.70)		(.40)		(.58)		(.06)		(-.61)		(-.32)	
PANORAMA	3.81	2.04	4.65	1.94	3.62	1.77	4.00	1.88	5.12	1.66	4.80	1.75	5.24	1.36
	(.46)		(.61)		(-.02)		(-.52)		(-1.00)		(.86)		(.35)	
PARDON	2.98	1.83	3.60	1.96	3.08	1.58	4.13	1.86	5.95	1.47	3.80	1.64	4.46	1.26F
	(-.37)		(-.44)		(-.60)		(-.39)		(-.17)		(-.14)		(-.43)	

	CON		IMG		CAT		MNG		FAM		NOA		PLS	
	M	SD	M	SD	M	SD	M	SD	M	SD	M	SD	M	SD
PASS	3.81 (.46)	2.00	4.73 (.69)	1.81	4.15 (.47)	1.69	4.40 (-.12)	1.61	6.09 (-.03)	1.44	3.38 (-.56)	1.69	4.82 (-.07)	1.34
PASSION	3.53 (.18)	2.05	4.07 (.03)	2.11	4.33 (.65)	1.85	4.87 (.35)	1.80	5.71 (-.41)	1.67	4.08 (.14)	1.77	5.85 (.96)	1.33
PAST	2.89 (-.46)	1.72	4.40 (.36)	2.08	3.75 (.07)	1.91	4.37 (-.15)	1.90	6.19 (.07)	1.32	4.46 (.52)	2.03	4.23 (-.66)	1.60F
PATIENCE	2.47 (-.88)	1.89	3.17 (-.87)	1.77	2.80 (-.88)	1.57	4.29 (-.23)	1.72	6.05 (-.07)	1.33	3.95 (.01)	2.01	4.84 (-.05)	1.21
PEACE	3.05 (-.30)	2.00	4.40 (.36)	2.25	4.38 (.70)	1.80	5.03 (.51)	1.66	6.45 (.33)	1.00	4.97 (1.03)	2.08	6.00 (1.11)	1.23F
PEACEFUL	3.56 (.21)	2.10	4.20 (.16)	1.91	3.70 (.02)	1.80	5.27 (.75)	1.53	6.34 (.22)	.90	4.13 (.19)	1.79	5.79 (.90)	1.43F
PEACEMAKER	3.98 (.63)	2.21	4.03 (-.01)	2.07	4.35 (.67)	2.07	4.74 (.22)	1.85	5.98 (-.14)	1.47	4.40 (.46)	1.69	5.77 (.88)	1.22
PERSONAL	3.07 (-.28)	1.85	4.02 (-.02)	2.23	3.13 (-.55)	1.81	4.53 (.01)	1.71	6.33 (.21)	1.27	4.20 (.26)	1.84	4.91 (.02)	1.24
PHILOSOPHY	2.67 (-.68)	1.81	3.85 (-.19)	2.14	4.77 (1.09)	2.05	4.38 (-.14)	1.91	5.69 (-.43)	1.56	5.34 (1.40)	1.90	4.44 (-.45)	1.50F
PHRASE	3.17 (-.18)	1.98	3.36 (-.68)	2.04	3.82 (.14)	1.72	3.77 (-.75)	1.73	5.95 (-.17)	1.48	3.76 (-.18)	1.61	4.28 (-.61)	1.21
PLACE	3.98 (.63)	2.18	3.76 (-.28)	1.93	3.63 (-.05)	1.78	4.56 (.04)	1.71	6.57 (.45)	1.13	3.70 (-.24)	2.08	4.48 (-.41)	1.34
PLAN	3.53 (.18)	1.96	3.75 (-.29)	2.46	3.35 (-.33)	1.64	4.31 (-.21)	1.89	6.47 (.35)	1.05	4.05 (.11)	1.92	4.24 (-.65)	1.42
PLAY	4.22 (.87)	1.89	4.49 (.45)	1.77	3.75 (.07)	1.74	4.97 (.45)	1.80	6.53 (.41)	.96	4.36 (.42)	1.92	5.35 (.46)	1.35
PLAYING	3.75 (.40)	1.97	4.88 (.84)	1.80	3.98 (.30)	1.46	5.26 (.74)	1.49	6.32 (.20)	1.26	4.94 (1.00)	1.78	5.60 (.71)	1.36
PLENTIFUL	3.13 (-.22)	1.77	4.02 (-.02)	1.90	3.47 (-.21)	1.35	4.57 (.05)	1.64	5.92 (-.20)	1.50	3.86 (-.08)	1.88	5.34 (.45)	1.49
POLITE	3.38 (.03)	2.02	3.51 (-.53)	1.95	3.22 (-.46)	1.35	4.38 (-.14)	1.67	5.90 (-.22)	1.52	3.27 (-.67)	1.69	4.75 (-.14)	1.32M
POWER	3.32 (-.03)	2.11	4.38 (.34)	1.81	3.60 (-.08)	1.67	5.05 (.53)	1.73	6.48 (.36)	.98	4.69 (.75)	1.72	4.27 (-.62)	1.59
PRAISE	3.50 (.15)	1.98	4.61 (.57)	1.86	3.47 (-.21)	1.57	4.68 (.16)	1.83	5.76 (-.36)	1.43	4.13 (.19)	1.88	5.63 (.74)	1.22
PREDICT	2.84 (-.51)	1.84	3.66 (-.38)	2.29	3.20 (-.48)	1.55	4.00 (-.52)	1.39	5.89 (-.23)	1.46	3.56 (-.38)	1.74	4.46 (-.43)	1.50
PRESENCE	3.37 (.02)	2.00	3.50 (-.54)	1.85	3.30 (-.38)	1.67	4.02 (-.50)	1.81	6.02 (-.10)	1.36	3.70 (-.24)	1.80	4.82 (-.07)	1.06
PRETTY	3.37 (.02)	1.90	5.52 (1.48)	1.76	4.87 (1.19)	1.72	5.48 (.96)	1.58	6.25 (.13)	1.22	4.49 (.55)	2.13	5.73 (.84)	1.24
PREVIEW	3.51 (.16)	1.83	4.00 (-.04)	1.91	3.82 (.14)	1.71	3.69 (-.83)	1.70	5.68 (-.44)	1.66	3.54 (-.40)	1.63	4.35 (-.54)	1.36
PRIDE	3.04 (-.31)	2.00	4.05 (.01)	2.18	3.88 (.20)	1.98	4.69 (.17)	1.86	6.36 (.24)	1.07	3.77 (-.17)	1.99	5.34 (.45)	1.59
PRIME	3.56 (.21)	1.93	3.80 (-.24)	2.00	3.23 (-.45)	1.69	4.75 (.23)	1.68	5.66 (-.46)	1.78	3.59 (-.35)	1.89	4.61 (-.28)	1.59M
PRIVATE	3.46 (.11)	2.10	4.77 (.73)	2.16	3.68 (.00)	1.78	4.48 (-.04)	1.80	6.48 (.36)	1.04	3.73 (-.21)	1.78	4.90 (.01)	1.44
PRODUCTIVE	3.05 (-.30)	1.85	3.32 (-.72)	1.74	3.22 (-.46)	1.40	4.18 (-.34)	1.78	6.17 (.05)	1.20	3.84 (-.10)	1.65	5.02 (.13)	1.52
PROFIT	3.60 (.25)	2.00	4.91 (.87)	1.83	4.73 (1.05)	1.89	4.68 (.16)	1.71	6.26 (.14)	1.16	4.37 (.43)	1.81	5.16 (.27)	1.47

	CON		IMG		CAT		MNG		FAM		NOA		PLS	
	M	SD	M	SD	M	SD	M	SD	M	SD	M	SD	M	SD
PROOF	3.51	2.04	3.78	1.85	3.55	1.82	4.13	1.71	6.38	1.04	3.38	1.86	4.13	1.33
	(.16)		(-.26)		(-.13)		(-.39)		(.26)		(-.56)		(-.76)	
PROSPER	3.52	1.87	3.86	1.89	3.26	1.35	4.19	1.50	5.77	1.60	3.87	1.95	4.95	1.39
	(.17)		(-.18)		(-.42)		(-.33)		(-.35)		(-.07)		(.06)	
PROUD	3.23	2.03	4.18	2.10	3.67	1.94	4.46	1.89	6.38	1.03	3.77	1.97	5.31	1.52
	(-.12)		(.14)		(-.01)		(-.06)		(.26)		(-.17)		(.42)	
QUESTION	3.91	2.05	3.96	2.13	4.10	2.03	4.23	1.69	6.64	.74	4.26	1.99	4.22	1.26
	(.56)		(-.08)		(.42)		(-.29)		(.52)		(.32)		(-.67)	
QUICK	3.39	1.82	3.52	1.86	3.67	1.70	4.53	1.56	6.30	1.09	2.75	1.51	4.52	1.46
	(.04)		(-.52)		(-.01)		(.01)		(.18)		(-1.19)		(-.37)	
QUICKLY	2.88	1.83	3.86	1.91	3.33	1.87	4.73	1.74	6.48	1.05	3.22	1.68	4.26	1.30
	(-.47)		(-.18)		(-.35)		(.21)		(.36)		(-.72)		(-.63)	
QUIET	3.85	1.91	4.46	1.92	3.66	1.77	4.51	1.72	6.23	1.23	3.07	1.81	4.71	1.49
	(.50)		(.42)		(-.02)		(-.01)		(.11)		(-.87)		(-.18)	
QUIETLY	2.96	1.82	3.61	1.97	3.28	1.89	4.56	1.63	6.40	1.01	2.95	1.58	5.20	1.33
	(-.39)		(-.43)		(-.40)		(.04)		(.28)		(-.99)		(.31)	
RAISE	3.36	1.69	4.12	2.05	3.20	1.67	4.31	1.67	6.08	1.37	3.20	1.38	4.15	1.24
	(.01)		(.08)		(-.48)		(-.21)		(-.04)		(-.74)		(-.74)	
RAPID	4.11	2.02	3.81	1.93	3.93	1.67	4.73	1.49	5.98	1.41	3.30	1.65	4.20	1.28
	(.76)		(-.23)		(.25)		(.21)		(-.14)		(-.64)		(-.69)	
RARE	3.23	1.96	4.33	2.07	3.53	1.86	4.82	1.55	6.33	1.17	3.80	1.98	5.21	1.59
	(-.12)		(.29)		(-.15)		(.30)		(.21)		(-.14)		(.32)	
REACH	3.64	1.94	3.85	1.97	3.13	1.76	3.95	1.61	6.51	.90	3.34	1.58	4.71	1.21F
	(.29)		(-.19)		(-.55)		(-.57)		(.39)		(-.60)		(-.18)	
READING	3.73	1.80	4.30	1.92	3.88	1.80	4.61	1.72	6.55	1.15	4.29	1.75	4.51	1.41F
	(.38)		(.26)		(.09)		(.09)		(.43)		(.35)		(-.38)	
REAL	2.81	1.94	3.19	2.12	3.17	1.99	4.64	1.98	6.57	1.24	4.87	2.07	5.16	1.56
	(-.54)		(-.85)		(-.51)		(.12)		(.45)		(.93)		(.27)	
REALITY	3.36	2.30	3.11	2.12	2.90	1.67	4.35	1.75	6.32	1.02	4.90	2.05	4.92	1.29
	(.01)		(-.93)		(-.78)		(-.17)		(.20)		(.96)		(.03)	
REASON	3.48	1.92	3.11	1.86	3.33	1.89	3.93	1.60	6.38	1.12	3.98	1.74	4.11	1.20F
	(.13)		(-.93)		(-.35)		(-.59)		(.26)		(.04)		(-.78)	
RECALL	3.15	1.92	4.18	2.13	3.32	1.55	4.25	1.55	6.00	1.37	3.75	1.78	4.34	1.55
	(-.20)		(.14)		(-.36)		(-.27)		(-.12)		(-.19)		(-.55)	
REFRESH	3.58	1.93	3.48	1.75	3.12	1.35	3.85	1.65	5.88	1.39	3.56	1.78	5.42	1.25
	(.23)		(-.56)		(-.56)		(-.67)		(-.24)		(-.38)		(.53)	
REIGN	3.02	1.83	3.86	1.90	4.00	1.84	3.89	1.68	5.17	1.94	3.82	1.70	4.13	1.54
	(-.33)		(-.18)		(.32)		(-.63)		(-.95)		(-.12)		(-.76)	
REJOICE	3.25	1.82	4.26	1.87	3.55	1.66	4.68	1.70	6.03	1.47	3.41	1.74	5.64	1.54
	(-.10)		(.22)		(-.13)		(.16)		(-.09)		(-.53)		(.75)	
RELAXED	3.76	2.01	3.87	1.96	3.26	1.60	4.52	1.44	6.16	1.29	3.65	1.80	5.48	1.45
	(.41)		(-.17)		(-.42)		(.00)		(.04)		(-.29)		(.59)	
RESPONSIVE	3.02	2.06	3.41	2.10	3.05	1.43	4.07	1.77	5.89	1.31	3.92	1.93	5.03	1.44
	(-.33)		(-.63)		(-.63)		(-.45)		(-.23)		(-.02)		(.14)	
REST	3.48	1.81	3.63	1.81	3.48	1.59	4.08	1.52	6.24	1.09	2.98	1.48	4.83	1.49
	(.13)		(-.41)		(-.20)		(-.44)		(.12)		(-.96)		(-.06)	
RICH	3.73	1.98	4.68	1.87	4.22	1.86	5.03	1.54	6.24	1.16	4.49	1.83	4.79	1.59F
	(.38)		(.64)		(.54)		(.51)		(.12)		(.55)		(-.10)	
RIGHT	3.57	2.16	3.76	2.16	3.93	1.98	4.13	1.83	6.41	1.10	3.63	2.00	4.42	1.50
	(.22)		(-.28)		(.25)		(-.39)		(.29)		(-.31)		(-.47)	
RIPE	3.56	1.72	4.84	1.70	3.87	1.66	3.92	1.74	6.08	1.58	3.59	1.56	4.90	1.37
	(.21)		(.80)		(.19)		(-.60)		(-.04)		(-.35)		(.01)	
RISE	3.64	2.02	4.45	1.86	3.72	2.02	4.73	1.74	6.20	1.46	3.25	1.65	4.75	1.37
	(.29)		(.41)		(.04)		(.21)		(.08)		(-.69)		(-.14)	

	CON		IMG		CAT		MNG		FAM		NOA		PLS	
	M	SD	M	SD	M	SD	M	SD	M	SD	M	SD	M	SD
ROBUSTNESS	3.27	1.78	3.86	1.95	3.32	1.85	4.32	1.74	4.77	1.83	3.72	1.86	4.83	1.66
	(-.08)		(-.18)		(-.36)		(-.20)		(-1.35)		(-.22)		(-.06)	
RUGGED	3.80	1.77	4.92	1.67	3.72	1.81	4.71	1.52	5.66	1.80	3.70	1.78	4.74	1.55
	(.45)		(.78)		(.04)		(.19)		(-.46)		(-.24)		(-.15)	
SAFE	3.72	2.10	4.68	2.12	3.88	1.91	4.74	1.71	6.05	1.48	3.41	1.55	5.21	1.47
	(.37)		(.64)		(.20)		(.22)		(-.07)		(-.53)		(.32)	
SAFETY	3.51	1.85	3.63	2.15	4.08	1.78	4.05	1.56	6.08	1.30	4.33	1.82	4.75	1.65
	(.16)		(-.41)		(.40)		(-.47)		(-.04)		(.39)		(-.14)	
SALE	3.60	1.92	4.16	2.01	3.93	1.82	4.34	1.68	6.29	1.41	3.77	1.77	4.30	1.54
	(.25)		(.12)		(.25)		(-.18)		(.17)		(-.17)		(-.59)	
SANE	2.86	2.01	3.58	2.27	3.35	1.74	4.28	1.66	5.82	1.45	3.79	1.78	4.56	1.24
	(-.49)		(-.46)		(-.33)		(-.24)		(-.30)		(-.15)		(-.33)	
SAVE	3.10	1.93	4.25	2.04	3.58	1.64	4.38	1.70	6.37	1.26	3.60	1.81	4.69	1.83
	(-.25)		(.21)		(-.10)		(-.14)		(.25)		(-.34)		(-.20)	
SAVORY	3.69	1.93	4.40	1.81	3.67	1.92	3.83	1.76	4.80	2.06	3.49	1.89	5.10	1.49M
	(.34)		(.36)		(-.01)		(-.69)		(-1.32)		(-.45)		(.21)	
SCENE	4.05	1.83	4.55	2.10	3.80	1.67	5.16	1.69	6.14	1.33	4.64	1.70	4.59	1.43
	(.70)		(.51)		(.12)		(.64)		(.02)		(.70)		(-.30)	
SEE	3.48	2.22	3.97	1.83	3.57	1.95	5.25	1.77	6.83	.53	4.23	2.08	5.28	1.58F
	(.13)		(-.07)		(-.11)		(.73)		(.71)		(.29)		(.39)	
SEEK	3.71	1.87	3.29	1.76	3.03	1.69	4.12	1.72	5.80	1.41	3.57	1.84	4.72	1.14
	(.36)		(-.75)		(-.65)		(-.40)		(-.32)		(-.37)		(-.17)	
SEND	3.20	1.75	4.17	2.13	3.38	1.66	3.84	1.69	6.03	1.52	3.08	1.35	4.31	1.12
	(-.15)		(.13)		(-.30)		(-.68)		(-.09)		(-.86)		(-.58)	
SENSE	3.02	2.12	3.58	2.01	3.78	1.85	4.84	1.69	6.20	1.19	4.30	1.74	4.98	1.41
	(-.33)		(-.46)		(.10)		(.32)		(.08)		(.36)		(.09)	
SHE	4.02	2.32	4.68	2.25	4.03	2.15	4.87	1.88	6.73	.87	3.40	2.00	4.84	1.53M
	(.67)		(.64)		(.35)		(.35)		(.61)		(-.54)		(-.05)	
SHEER	3.93	1.86	4.34	2.06	3.95	1.85	4.10	1.83	5.42	1.55	3.40	1.42	4.52	1.29M
	(.58)		(.30)		(.27)		(-.42)		(-.70)		(-.54)		(-.37)	
SHOW	3.98	2.23	4.18	1.97	3.55	1.81	4.58	1.64	6.33	1.23	3.95	2.09	4.34	1.61
	(.63)		(.14)		(-.13)		(.06)		(.21)		(.01)		(-.55)	
SIGHT	3.89	2.13	4.00	2.20	4.38	1.89	4.90	1.80	6.33	1.09	4.45	2.05	5.33	1.61
	(.54)		(.17)		(.70)		(.38)		(.21)		(.52)		(.44)	
SIMPLE	3.02	1.75	3.45	2.14	3.56	1.50	4.60	1.68	6.44	.97	3.00	1.49	4.66	1.48F
	(-.33)		(-.59)		(-.12)		(.08)		(.32)		(-.94)		(-.23)	
SITE	4.04	2.09	4.00	1.92	3.93	1.85	4.15	1.45	5.81	1.45	3.86	1.81	4.23	1.24
	(.69)		(-.04)		(.25)		(-.37)		(-.31)		(-.08)		(-.66)	
SLEPT	3.79	1.86	3.97	2.07	3.12	1.71	3.77	1.77	6.36	1.26	2.94	1.56	5.06	1.47
	(.44)		(-.17)		(-.56)		(-.75)		(.24)		(-1.00)		(.17)	
SLOWLY	3.45	1.95	3.96	1.89	4.02	1.82	4.12	1.81	6.33	1.24	2.98	1.59	4.18	1.25
	(.10)		(-.08)		(.34)		(-.40)		(.21)		(-.96)		(-.71)	
SMART	3.00	2.08	3.96	1.94	3.95	1.97	5.15	1.68	6.58	.87	4.05	1.80	5.03	1.61
	(-.35)		(-.08)		(.27)		(.63)		(.46)		(.11)		(.14)	
SMOOTH	4.02	1.85	4.84	2.03	3.98	1.97	4.78	1.74	6.20	1.11	3.18	1.78	5.19	1.59
	(.67)		(.80)		(.30)		(.26)		(.08)		(-.76)		(.30)	
SOAR	3.62	1.89	4.30	2.00	3.48	1.78	4.70	1.65	5.70	1.57	3.64	1.82	4.94	1.89
	(.27)		(.26)		(-.20)		(.18)		(-.42)		(-.30)		(.05)	
SOARED	3.39	1.86	4.64	1.83	3.64	1.83	4.20	1.71	5.56	1.67	3.69	1.49	5.34	1.48F
	(.04)		(.60)		(-.04)		(-.56)		(-.32)		(-.25)		(.45)	
SOCIAL	2.38	1.58	3.80	2.03	3.67	1.72	4.37	1.82	5.71	1.63	4.44	1.78	4.39	1.36
	(-.97)		(-.24)		(-.01)		(-.15)		(-.41)		(.50)		(-.50)	
SOFT	4.10	2.06	4.64	1.84	3.98	1.70	4.76	1.71	6.60	1.01	3.68	1.95	5.69	1.27
	(.75)		(.60)		(.30)		(.24)		(.48)		(-.26)		(.80)	

	CON M	CON SD	IMG M	IMG SD	CAT M	CAT SD	MNG M	MNG SD	FAM M	FAM SD	NOA M	NOA SD	PLS M	PLS SD
SOFTLY	3.59	2.05	4.50	2.06	4.37	1.80	4.77	1.63	5.98	1.42	3.57	1.87	6.00	1.13
	(.24)		(.46)		(.69)		(.25)		(-.14)		(-.37)		(1.11)	
SOUL	3.17	2.10	4.52	2.25	3.53	1.90	4.28	2.00	6.16	1.30	4.53	2.13	5.15	1.64
	(-.18)		(.48)		(-.15)		(-.24)		(.04)		(.59)		(.26)	
SPACE	3.64	2.24	5.45	1.85	4.42	2.22	5.36	1.71	6.53	.95	5.17	2.06	5.47	1.47
	(.29)		(1.41)		(.74)		(.84)		(.41)		(1.23)		(.58)	
STILL	3.50	2.18	3.39	2.21	3.37	1.92	3.97	2.06	6.31	1.22	2.95	1.71	4.67	1.22F
	(.15)		(-.65)		(-.31)		(-.55)		(.19)		(-.99)		(-.22)	
STYLE	3.75	2.07	4.14	1.94	3.83	1.90	5.10	1.58	6.35	1.04	4.68	2.01	4.80	1.14
	(.40)		(.10)		(.15)		(.58)		(.23)		(.74)		(-.09)	
SUCCEED	3.00	1.95	4.10	1.93	3.43	1.76	4.95	1.71	6.65	.71	4.06	1.90	5.41	1.44
	(-.35)		(.06)		(-.25)		(.43)		(.53)		(.12)		(.52)	
SWIFT	3.34	1.92	4.78	1.87	4.00	1.71	4.93	1.71	5.95	1.48	3.49	1.77	4.97	1.46F
	(-.01)		(.74)		(.32)		(.41)		(-.17)		(-.45)		(.08)	
SYMBOL	3.98	2.32	4.41	2.04	3.77	1.94	4.90	1.84	6.10	1.30	4.97	1.86	4.44	1.26
	(.63)		(.37)		(.09)		(.38)		(-.02)		(1.03)		(-.45)	
SYMBOLISM	2.69	1.98	4.32	2.25	3.45	1.69	4.36	1.84	6.03	1.25	4.80	1.98	4.46	1.55
	(-.66)		(.28)		(-.23)		(-.16)		(-.09)		(.86)		(-.43)	
SYMPATHETIC	3.16	2.21	3.95	1.98	3.41	1.79	4.60	1.88	6.03	1.51	3.79	1.66	4.54	1.67
	(-.19)		(-.09)		(-.27)		(.08)		(-.09)		(-.15)		(-.35)	
TALE	3.48	1.88	3.39	1.97	4.12	1.77	4.02	1.39	5.79	1.56	4.00	1.87	4.20	1.31
	(.13)		(-.65)		(.44)		(-.50)		(-.33)		(.06)		(-.69)	
TEACH	3.49	1.88	4.23	1.82	4.48	1.61	4.55	1.69	6.26	1.18	4.55	2.07	4.84	1.30
	(.14)		(.19)		(.80)		(.03)		(.14)		(.61)		(-.05)	
TELL	3.02	1.84	3.83	2.11	2.87	1.61	4.65	1.74	6.49	1.15	3.33	1.78	4.04	1.42
	(-.33)		(-.21)		(-.81)		(.13)		(.37)		(-.61)		(-.85)	
THEORY	3.24	2.12	3.36	2.20	4.10	1.89	4.08	1.66	5.85	1.47	4.57	1.86	3.97	1.34
	(-.11)		(-.68)		(.42)		(-.44)		(-.27)		(.63)		(-.92)	
THING	3.46	2.17	3.52	2.07	2.62	1.91	4.79	2.18	6.61	1.00	4.62	2.31	3.84	1.41
	(.11)		(-.52)		(-1.06)		(.27)		(.49)		(.68)		(-1.05)	
THINK	3.42	2.18	4.52	2.16	3.78	1.79	5.00	1.77	6.68	.95	5.03	2.07	5.36	1.64
	(.07)		(.48)		(.10)		(.48)		(.56)		(1.09)		(.47)	
THINNER	3.05	1.76	4.93	2.01	3.95	2.00	4.26	1.72	5.98	1.37	3.52	1.65	4.61	1.57F
	(-.30)		(.89)		(.27)		(-.26)		(-.14)		(-.42)		(-.28)	
THOUGHT	3.24	2.15	3.42	2.02	3.43	1.86	4.95	2.15	6.53	1.03	5.30	1.77	5.46	1.39
	(-.11)		(-.62)		(-.27)		(.43)		(.41)		(1.36)		(.57)	
THOUGHTFUL	3.09	2.15	4.20	1.98	3.73	1.81	4.74	1.77	6.21	1.18	3.98	1.69	5.47	1.52
	(-.26)		(.16)		(.05)		(.22)		(.09)		(.04)		(.58)	
THRIFTY	2.93	1.64	3.79	1.91	3.42	1.42	4.02	1.45	5.55	1.65	3.46	1.64	4.22	1.48
	(-.42)		(-.25)		(-.26)		(-.50)		(-.57)		(-.48)		(-.67)	
TIDY	3.07	1.71	4.72	1.95	4.28	1.72	4.72	1.93	5.64	1.66	3.41	1.65	4.45	1.56F
	(-.28)		(.68)		(.60)		(.20)		(-.48)		(-.53)		(-.44)	
TIME	3.84	2.32	3.91	2.32	4.03	2.14	4.53	2.06	6.39	1.16	4.58	2.17	4.15	1.49
	(.49)		(-.13)		(.35)		(.01)		(.27)		(.64)		(-.74)	
TOLERANT	2.61	1.81	3.32	1.72	2.98	1.48	4.02	1.58	5.93	1.34	4.00	1.49	4.49	1.59
	(-.74)		(-.72)		(-.70)		(-.50)		(-.19)		(.06)		(-.40)	
TRADITION	3.13	1.91	3.32	2.08	3.75	1.73	4.45	1.88	6.13	1.31	4.38	1.90	4.25	1.63
	(-.22)		(-.72)		(.07)		(-.07)		(.01)		(.44)		(-.64)	
TRANQUIL	3.30	2.05	5.02	1.81	4.00	1.88	4.62	1.86	5.53	1.61	3.56	1.94	5.77	1.48
	(-.05)		(.98)		(.32)		(.10)		(-.59)		(-.38)		(.88)	
TRAVEL	3.98	1.93	5.00	1.88	4.35	1.81	5.20	1.62	6.24	1.19	5.10	1.78	5.73	1.34F
	(.63)		(.96)		(.32)		(.68)		(.12)		(1.16)		(.84)	
TREAT	3.95	2.17	3.54	1.93	3.43	1.77	4.42	1.66	6.08	1.39	3.54	1.58	4.54	1.41
	(.60)		(-.50)		(-.25)		(-.10)		(-.04)		(-.40)		(-.35)	

	CON		IMG		CAT		MNG		FAM		NOA		PLS	
	M	SD	M	SD	M	SD	M	SD	M	SD	M	SD	M	SD
TRIUMPH	3.41	2.04	4.29	2.05	3.52	1.85	4.92	1.72	5.97	1.41	3.90	1.81	5.30	1.58
	(.06)		(.25)		(-.16)		(.40)		(-.15)		(-.04)		(.41)	
TRUE	2.65	1.94	3.84	2.08	3.47	1.92	4.75	1.83	6.51	1.07	3.93	1.94	5.45	1.27
	(-.70)		(-.20)		(-.21)		(.23)		(.39)		(-.01)		(.56)	
TRUST	3.35	1.95	3.54	2.23	3.85	1.90	4.60	1.60	6.32	1.17	4.56	1.82	5.52	1.43F
	(.00)		(-.50)		(.17)		(.08)		(.20)		(.62)		(.63)	
TRUTH	2.72	2.13	4.22	2.17	3.80	2.01	4.52	1.91	6.31	1.25	4.28	2.29	5.66	1.47
	(-.63)		(.18)		(.12)		(.00)		(.19)		(.34)		(.77)	
UNIQUE	2.96	2.07	3.73	2.18	3.58	2.04	4.73	1.89	6.08	1.44	4.18	2.18	5.22	1.50F
	(-.39)		(-.31)		(-.10)		(.21)		(-.04)		(.24)		(.33)	
UNITE	3.05	1.72	4.68	1.91	3.75	1.95	4.43	1.67	5.68	1.55	3.87	1.66	5.27	1.34
	(-.30)		(.64)		(.07)		(-.09)		(-.44)		(-.07)		(.38)	
UNIVERSAL	3.35	2.07	3.50	2.16	4.02	2.01	4.87	1.98	6.34	1.11	5.15	1.93	5.06	1.21F
	(.0C)		(-.54)		(.34)		(.35)		(.22)		(1.21)		(.17)	
UNLIMITED	2.59	1.88	3.84	2.14	3.48	1.89	4.90	1.74	6.06	1.25	4.38	2.18	5.00	1.55
	(-.76)		(-.20)		(-.20)		(.38)		(-.06)		(.44)		(.11)	
UP	3.96	2.22	3.82	1.97	4.02	2.09	3.59	2.04	6.47	1.14	3.08	2.04	4.85	1.58
	(.61)		(-.22)		(.34)		(-.93)		(.35)		(-.86)		(-.04)	
US	3.93	2.17	4.39	2.17	2.83	1.62	4.10	2.11	6.74	.76	3.51	2.07	4.92	1.70F
	(.58)		(.35)		(-.85)		(-.42)		(.62)		(-.43)		(.03)	
VALOR	3.08	2.04	3.65	2.21	3.12	1.68	3.87	1.78	5.06	1.82	3.51	1.68	4.93	1.55
	(-.27)		(-.39)		(-.56)		(-.65)		(-1.06)		(-.43)		(.04)	
VICTORY	4.30	2.06	4.07	1.99	3.71	1.99	4.76	1.72	5.79	1.60	4.05	2.09	5.08	1.58
	(.95)		(.03)		(.03)		(.24)		(-.33)		(.11)		(.19)	
VIEW	3.75	1.96	4.24	1.98	3.10	1.68	4.17	1.56	5.97	1.38	4.10	2.02	5.00	1.68
	(.40)		(.20)		(-.58)		(-.35)		(-.15)		(.16)		(.11)	
VISION	4.27	1.99	4.15	1.92	4.47	1.86	4.40	1.66	6.02	1.26	4.68	2.13	5.45	1.32
	(.11)		(.21)		(.79)		(-.12)		(-.10)		(.74)		(.56)	
VOLUNTARY	3.05	1.76	3.21	1.82	3.33	1.72	4.27	1.83	6.32	1.14	3.81	1.66	4.82	1.35
	(-.30)		(-.83)		(-.35)		(-.25)		(.20)		(-.13)		(-.07)	
VOW	3.18	1.82	3.53	1.81	3.67	1.73	4.55	1.62	5.63	1.88	3.45	1.48	4.46	1.39F
	(-.17)		(-.51)		(-.01)		(.03)		(-.49)		(-.49)		(-.43)	
WANDER	3.16	1.73	4.00	1.75	3.27	1.57	4.34	1.57	6.13	1.26	3.66	1.53	5.00	1.39
	(-.19)		(-.04)		(-.41)		(-.18)		(.01)		(-.28)		(.11)	
WANT	2.98	1.88	3.81	2.26	2.97	1.90	4.72	1.95	6.48	1.15	3.74	1.91	3.90	1.54
	(-.37)		(-.23)		(-.71)		(.20)		(.36)		(-.20)		(-.99)	
WE	2.66	1.93	3.81	2.02	3.05	2.05	4.27	2.15	6.60	1.17	3.87	2.20	5.16	1.54F
	(-.69)		(-.23)		(-.63)		(-.25)		(.48)		(-.07)		(.27)	
WEALTH	3.66	1.96	4.94	1.78	4.45	1.92	5.28	1.52	6.31	1.09	4.81	1.81	5.14	1.43
	(.31)		(.90)		(.77)		(.76)		(.19)		(.87)		(.25)	
WHOLE	3.63	2.02	3.95	2.21	3.32	1.71	4.62	1.70	6.48	.84	3.54	2.06	4.71	1.49
	(.28)		(-.09)		(-.36)		(.10)		(.36)		(-.40)		(-.18)	
WILD	3.77	2.03	4.87	1.81	3.81	1.69	5.37	1.43	6.25	1.23	4.30	1.81	4.94	1.40
	(.42)		(.83)		(.13)		(.85)		(.13)		(.36)		(.05)	
WISDOM	3.13	2.05	3.78	2.20	3.28	1.92	5.18	1.77	6.34	1.30	5.13	1.99	6.03	1.15
	(-.22)		(-.26)		(-.40)		(.66)		(.22)		(1.19)		(1.14)	
WISE	2.64	1.69	4.40	1.95	4.27	1.97	5.15	1.71	5.98	1.47	4.36	1.80	5.58	1.31F
	(-.71)		(.36)		(.59)		(.63)		(-.14)		(.42)		(.69)	
WISH	2.66	1.74	4.16	1.92	3.85	1.76	4.23	1.71	6.12	1.40	4.25	2.00	5.37	1.28F
	(-.69)		(.12)		(.17)		(-.29)		(.00)		(-.31)		(.48)	
WON	3.20	1.97	4.10	2.22	3.18	1.85	4.41	2.09	6.21	1.48	3.05	1.51	4.96	1.97M
	(-.15)		(.06)		(-.50)		(-.11)		(.09)		(-.89)		(.07)	
WORKING	3.79	1.94	4.60	2.03	3.73	1.72	5.34	1.79	6.70	.87	4.21	1.77	4.42	1.63M
	(.44)		(.56)		(.05)		(.82)		(.58)		(.27)		(-.47)	

	CON		IMG		CAT		MNG		FAM		NOA		PLS	
	M	SD	M	SD	M	SD	M	SD	M	SD	M	SD	M	SD
WORTHWHILE	3.04	1.75	3.23	1.97	3.08	1.57	4.08	1.79	6.17	1.08	3.82	1.92	5.17	1.55F
	(-.31)		(-.81)		(-.60)		(-.44)		(.05)		(-.12)		(.28)	
WROTE	3.81	1.87	4.63	1.93	3.95	1.55	4.38	1.62	6.48	1.18	3.83	1.92	4.40	1.52F
	(.46)		(.59)		(.27)		(-.14)		(.36)		(-.11)		(-.49)	
YEARS	3.78	2.21	3.59	1.87	4.83	2.04	4.79	1.85	6.70	.74	3.76	1.88	4.13	1.44
	(.43)		(-.45)		(1.15)		(.27)		(.58)		(-.18)		(-.76)	
YOU	3.66	2.25	4.28	2.30	3.48	2.27	4.32	2.40	6.82	.65	4.69	2.15	4.96	1.57
	(.31)		(.24)		(-.20)		(-.20)		(.70)		(.75)		(.07)	
YOUNGER	3.18	1.81	3.89	1.93	3.85	1.81	4.61	1.82	6.31	1.22	3.21	1.82	4.62	1.59
	(-.17)		(-.15)		(.17)		(.09)		(.19)		(-.73)		(-.27)	
ZOOLOGY	3.52	2.04	3.58	1.83	5.40	1.81	4.16	1.94	5.22	1.92	4.11	2.12	4.80	1.33
	(.17)		(-.46)		(1.72)		(-.36)		(-.90)		(.17)		(-.09)	

	CON (M SD)	IMG (M SD)	CAT (M SD)	MNG (M SD)	FAM (M SD)	NOA (M SD)	PLS (M SD)
ABODE	4.70 2.05 (.15)	4.37 2.06 (-.50)	4.27 1.96 (-.30)	4.19 1.91 (-.22)	4.53 2.09 (-1.47)	4.07 2.03 (.17)	4.54 1.60F (.43)
ACADEMY	4.95 2.02 (.40)	4.98 1.91 (.11)	4.52 1.83 (-.05)	4.21 1.57 (-.20)	5.83 1.44 (-.17)	3.74 1.59 (-.16)	3.75 1.74 (-.36)
AGE	4.19 2.00 (-.36)	4.38 2.17 (-.49)	4.67 2.04 (.10)	4.28 1.76 (-.13)	6.17 1.36 (.17)	4.33 2.03 (.43)	4.06 1.30 (-.05)
AIR	5.25 2.03 (.70)	4.62 2.02 (-.10)	4.47 1.98 (-.10)	4.97 1.91 (.56)	6.53 .93 (.53)	4.03 1.97 (.13)	5.50 1.19 (1.39)
AISLE	5.05 1.99 (.50)	5.22 1.75 (.35)	4.00 2.07 (-.57)	4.00 1.75 (-.41)	5.77 1.74 (-.23)	2.89 1.54 (-1.01)	3.64 1.46 (-.47)
ALTER	4.26 2.23 (-.29)	4.07 2.09 (-.80)	4.62 2.04 (.05)	4.47 1.69 (.06)	5.77 1.62 (-.23)	3.75 1.68 (-.15)	4.06 1.27F (-.05)
ANGLE	4.54 2.08 (-.01)	4.64 1.98 (-.23)	4.70 1.87 (.13)	3.90 1.79 (-.51)	5.98 1.34 (-.02)	2.95 1.48 (-.95)	4.19 1.28 (.08)
ANTIQUE	4.78 2.20 (.23)	5.36 1.73 (.49)	4.88 1.80 (.31)	4.05 1.77 (-.36)	5.72 1.69 (-.28)	4.37 1.60 (.47)	5.16 1.57F (1.05)
ARCH	4.85 2.04 (.30)	5.37 1.61 (.50)	4.12 1.83 (-.45)	3.71 1.83 (-.70)	5.80 1.48 (-.20)	3.41 1.38 (-.49)	4.56 1.04M (.45)
ART	4.36 2.01 (-.19)	4.87 1.93 (.00)	5.12 1.99 (.55)	5.65 1.53 (1.24)	6.03 1.47 (.03)	5.57 1.70 (1.67)	5.09 1.70F (.98)
ATOM	4.77 2.35 (.22)	4.93 2.10 (.06)	5.48 1.95 (.91)	4.26 1.92 (-.15)	5.87 1.66 (-.13)	3.85 2.29 (-.05)	3.74 1.77M (-.37)
AUTHOR	4.75 2.08 (.20)	4.61 1.97 (-.26)	5.10 1.80 (.53)	5.02 1.72 (.43)	6.43 1.09 (.53)	3.85 1.79 (-.05)	4.12 1.19 (.01)
BACK	4.96 2.11 (.41)	4.87 2.01 (.00)	5.28 1.75 (.71)	4.18 1.81 (-.23)	6.33 1.19 (.33)	3.83 1.91 (-.07)	4.14 1.34 (.03)
BAIL	4.37 2.01 (-.18)	4.74 1.95 (-.13)	4.30 1.83 (-.27)	3.84 1.63 (-.57)	5.59 1.84 (-.41)	3.31 1.70 (-.59)	3.37 1.54 (-.74)
BASE	4.34 2.03 (-.21)	4.34 2.22 (-.53)	4.30 1.89 (-.27)	3.98 1.71 (-.43)	5.62 1.63 (-.38)	3.52 1.76 (-.38)	3.79 1.16 (-.32)
BEAM	4.98 2.17 (.43)	5.02 2.00 (.15)	4.28 1.86 (-.29)	3.86 1.62 (-.55)	5.67 1.65 (-.33)	3.51 1.67 (-.39)	4.41 1.38 (.30)
BIOLOGY	3.96 1.93 (-.59)	4.35 1.91 (-.52)	5.52 1.57 (.95)	4.69 1.94 (.28)	6.00 1.63 (.00)	4.77 2.03 (.87)	4.36 1.59 (.25)
BIRTH	4.73 2.10 (.18)	5.17 1.94 (.30)	4.32 1.99 (-.25)	5.05 1.96 (.64)	6.24 1.30 (.24)	4.64 1.96 (.74)	5.09 1.47 (.98)
BLUSH	4.59 1.78 (.04)	5.59 1.71 (.72)	4.40 1.93 (-.17)	4.82 1.66 (.41)	6.08 1.53 (.08)	3.43 1.66 (-.47)	4.28 1.41 (.17)
BLUSHING	3.96 2.02 (-.59)	4.57 1.80 (-.30)	4.03 1.72 (-.54)	3.90 1.53 (-.51)	5.78 1.47 (-.22)	3.33 1.41 (-.57)	4.14 1.51 (.03)
BOIL	4.63 2.01 (.08)	5.27 1.80 (.40)	4.58 1.70 (.01)	4.39 1.58 (-.02)	6.07 1.48 (.07)	3.11 1.68 (-.79)	3.44 1.47 (-.67)
BOTANY	4.40 2.10 (-.15)	4.04 1.90 (-.83)	5.33 1.75 (.76)	4.35 2.03 (-.06)	5.33 1.62 (-.67)	4.56 2.05 (.66)	4.03 1.62F (-.08)
BRAT	4.97 1.95 (.42)	5.30 1.86 (.43)	4.52 1.91 (-.05)	4.69 1.74 (.28)	5.81 1.56 (-.19)	3.68 1.61 (-.22)	2.82 1.86 (-1.29)
BRAWL	4.76 1.84 (.21)	5.10 1.78 (.23)	3.88 1.65 (-.69)	4.46 1.79 (.05)	5.20 1.78 (-.80)	3.88 1.65 (-.02)	3.05 1.60M (-1.06)
BREATH	4.91 1.85 (.36)	5.00 1.89 (.13)	4.52 1.89 (-.05)	4.45 1.88 (.04)	6.25 1.34 (.25)	3.21 1.76 (-.69)	5.00 1.77M (.89)
BRIGHT	4.69 1.99 (.14)	4.98 1.95 (.11)	4.41 1.77 (-.16)	4.32 1.57 (-.09)	6.37 1.23 (.37)	4.15 1.81 (.25)	4.95 1.33F (.84)
BROIL	4.44 2.06 (-.11)	5.09 1.86 (.22)	4.68 1.73 (.11)	4.07 1.83 (-.34)	5.76 1.72 (-.24)	3.30 1.71 (-.60)	4.29 1.40 (.18)

	CON M SD	IMG M SD	CAT M SD	MNG M SD	FAM M SD	NOA M SD	PLS M SD
BUD	5.05 2.01 (.50)	4.48 2.08 (-.39)	4.70 2.00 (.13)	3.75 1.46 (-.66)	5.55 1.72 (-.45)	3.69 1.61 (-.21)	4.78 1.50F (.67)
BUMP	5.21 1.90 (.66)	4.70 2.07 (-.17)	3.83 1.78 (-.74)	4.21 1.76 (-.20)	6.15 1.35 (.15)	3.57 1.57 (-.33)	3.18 1.07 (-.93)
BUNCH	4.05 1.84 (-.50)	4.67 1.93 (-.20)	4.03 1.74 (-.54)	4.48 1.69 (.07)	5.73 1.59 (-.27)	4.26 1.56 (.36)	3.77 1.11 (-.34)
BUNGALOW	5.38 1.99 (.83)	4.95 1.95 (.08)	5.08 2.10 (.51)	4.25 1.83 (-.16)	5.07 1.72 (-.93)	4.56 1.88 (.66)	4.90 1.67F (.79)
BURN	4.81 1.72 (.26)	4.95 1.82 (.08)	4.17 1.86 (-.40)	4.00 1.73 (-.41)	6.21 1.20 (.21)	3.59 1.67 (-.31)	2.88 1.66M (-1.23)
BURNER	4.96 1.99 (.41)	4.82 1.60 (-.05)	4.62 1.67 (.05)	3.77 1.47 (-.64)	5.92 1.37 (-.08)	3.72 1.48 (-.18)	3.53 1.35 (-.58)
BUSINESS	4.05 1.89 (-.50)	4.88 1.92 (.01)	4.80 1.68 (.23)	4.61 1.87 (.20)	6.09 1.29 (.09)	5.07 1.76 (1.17)	3.95 1.52 (-.16)
CAPITAL	4.95 1.89	5.54 1.96 (.67)	5.08 1.71 (.51)	4.36 1.64 (-.05)	6.03 1.37 (.03)	4.06 1.88 (.16)	4.39 1.33 (.28)
CASE	5.12 1.96 (.57)	4.95 2.11 (.08)	3.93 1.91 (-.64)	4.08 1.67 (-.33)	6.18 1.22 (.18)	4.02 1.50 (.12)	3.80 1.15 (-.31)
CAST	4.98 2.03 (.43)	4.77 2.00 (-.10)	4.67 1.76 (.10)	3.85 1.54 (-.56)	5.69 1.41 (-.31)	3.85 1.61 (-.05)	3.34 1.25 (-.77)
CENTER	3.67 2.06 (-.88)	4.78 1.82 (-.09)	4.57 1.79 (.00)	4.52 1.68 (.11)	6.00 1.40 (.00)	3.49 1.87 (-.41)	4.19 1.05 (.08)
CENTURY	3.80 2.15 (-.75)	3.82 2.06 (-1.05)	5.00 2.03 (.43)	4.00 1.76 (-.41)	5.97 1.28 (-.03)	4.26 1.99 (.36)	4.41 1.14 (.30)
CEREMONY	4.26 1.98 (-.29)	5.22 1.63 (.35)	4.20 1.73 (-.37)	5.05 1.52 (.64)	6.10 1.28 (.10)	5.03 1.63 (1.13)	4.61 1.57F (.50)
CHART	5.28 1.91 (.73)	5.25 1.92 (.38)	4.49 1.81 (-.08)	4.03 1.49 (-.38)	6.07 1.40 (.07)	3.84 1.86 (-.06)	3.84 1.00 (-.27)
CHEMISTRY	3.70 2.16 (-.85)	4.52 2.01 (-.35)	6.09 1.22 (1.52)	4.35 1.81 (-.06)	6.07 1.33 (.07)	5.30 1.90 (1.40)	3.34 1.85 (-.77)
CHEW	4.38 2.12 (-.17)	5.21 1.82 (.34)	4.57 1.90 (.00)	4.74 1.78 (.33)	6.44 1.22 (.44)	3.00 1.53 (-.90)	4.21 1.51 (.10)
CHIC	4.50 2.17 (-.05)	4.31 2.33 (-.56)	3.69 1.90 (-.88)	3.97 1.86 (-.44)	5.14 2.00 (-.86)	3.85 1.61 (-.05)	4.56 1.65 (.45)
CHIEF	4.82 1.98 (.27)	5.03 1.87 (.16)	5.40 1.47 (.83)	4.55 1.78 (.14)	5.82 1.37 (-.18)	4.37 1.64 (.47)	4.21 1.40 (.10)
CHUCKLE	4.25 2.08 (-.30)	4.91 1.69 (.04)	4.72 1.66 (.15)	5.28 1.50 (.87)	5.79 1.60 (-.21)	3.72 1.62 (-.18)	5.31 1.43 (1.20)
CIRCULAR	4.00 1.99 (-.55)	5.37 1.76 (.50)	5.03 1.88 (.46)	4.51 1.75 (.10)	5.61 1.71 (-.39)	3.10 1.74 (-.80)	4.65 1.42 (.54)
CITIZEN	4.51 2.04 (-.04)	4.30 1.85 (-.57)	4.66 1.86 (-.09)	4.73 1.68 (.32)	5.90 1.47 (-.10)	4.70 1.94 (.80)	4.31 1.27 (.20)
CLUB	5.05 1.94 (.50)	5.16 1.74 (.29)	4.73 1.74 (.16)	4.57 1.74 (.16)	6.07 1.46 (.07)	4.03 1.63 (.13)	3.77 1.40M (-.34)
COACH	5.06 1.70 (.51)	5.20 1.79 (.33)	4.90 1.72 (.33)	4.10 1.61 (-.31)	5.86 1.57 (-.14)	4.18 1.80 (.28)	4.09 1.48M (-.02)
COARSE	4.41 1.78 (-.14)	4.88 2.09 (.01)	4.52 1.78 (-.05)	4.63 1.52 (.22)	5.80 1.46 (-.20)	3.89 1.71 (-.01)	3.10 1.34F (-1.01)
COIL	4.86 1.89 (.31)	4.86 1.88 (-.21)	4.36 1.69 (-.01)	3.47 1.47 (-.94)	5.72 1.53 (-.28)	3.10 1.69 (-.80)	3.43 1.06 (-.68)
COLD	4.73 2.33 (.18)	5.42 1.74 (.55)	5.63 1.71 (1.06)	5.39 1.50 (.98)	6.51 1.07 (.51)	3.74 1.91 (-.16)	3.63 1.59 (-.48)
COLONY	4.98 2.13 (.43)	4.50 1.93 (-.37)	5.35 1.84 (.78)	4.62 1.57 (.21)	5.47 1.61 (-.53)	5.16 1.71 (1.26)	4.38 1.07 (.27)

	CON	IMG	CAT	MNG	FAM	NOA	PLS
	M SD	M SD	M SD	M SD	M SD	M SD	M SD
COMMERCIAL	4.76 2.15	5.31 1.85	4.79 1.93	4.89 1.90	6.33 1.25	4.51 1.83	3.19 1.53
	(.21)	(.44)	(.22)	(.48)	(.33)	(.61)	(-.92)
COMPACT	4.37 1.88	4.56 1.96	3.60 1.87	4.52 1.55	5.92 1.33	3.55 1.77	4.28 1.13
	(-.18)	(-.31)	(-.97)	(.11)	(-.08)	(-.35)	(.17)
CONFERENCE	3.95 2.15	4.49 2.00	4.17 1.88	4.49 1.55	5.86 1.56	4.52 1.60	3.81 1.35
	(-.60)	(-.38)	(-.40)	(.08)	(-.14)	(.62)	(-.30)
CONSTITUTION	4.18 2.13	5.09 1.83	4.40 1.96	4.33 2.05	5.67 1.62	4.75 2.08	4.18 1.61M
	(-.37)	(.22)	(-.17)	(-.08)	(-.33)	(.85)	(.07)
CONTACT	4.52 2.17	4.43 2.26	4.27 1.85	4.08 1.73	6.17 1.20	4.38 1.45	4.68 1.45F
	(-.03)	(-.44)	(-.30)	(-.33)	(.17)	(.48)	(.57)
CONTRACT	4.50 2.16	4.50 1.81	4.38 1.95	4.10 1.58	5.79 1.43	4.00 2.06	3.78 1.28
	(-.05)	(-.37)	(-.19)	(-.31)	(-.21)	(.10)	(-.33)
COOK	4.98 1.91	4.98 1.83	5.18 1.71	4.43 1.59	6.42 1.15	4.54 1.89	4.75 1.60
	(.43)	(.11)	(.61)	(.02)	(.42)	(.64)	(.64)
COURT	5.05 1.99	5.46 1.77	4.72 1.72	4.52 1.85	6.23 1.21	4.40 1.72	3.67 1.61
	(.50)	(.59)	(.15)	(.11)	(.23)	(.50)	(-.44)
CRANK	4.44 2.16	5.18 1.70	4.05 1.67	4.02 1.68	5.49 1.81	3.79 1.60	3.34 1.19
	(-.11)	(-.52)	(-.52)	(-.39)	(-.51)	(-.11)	(-.77)
CRAWL	4.04 2.11	4.82 1.97	4.37 1.85	4.25 1.72	5.93 1.52	3.34 1.52	3.89 1.26
	(-.51)	(-.05)	(-.20)	(-.16)	(-.07)	(-.56)	(-.22)
CROSS	5.10 2.00	5.00 2.25	4.35 2.00	4.32 1.69	5.85 1.66	3.41 1.72	4.13 1.51
	(.55)	(.13)	(-.22)	(-.09)	(-.15)	(-.49)	(.02)
CURVE	4.40 2.03	4.55 1.73	4.00 2.03	3.67 1.75	5.92 1.36	3.11 1.74	4.38 1.36M
	(-.15)	(-.32)	(-.57)	(-.74)	(-.08)	(-.79)	(.27)
CURVED	4.23 2.04	5.22 1.82	4.23 1.84	4.52 1.59	6.20 1.38	3.44 1.81	4.33 1.62
	(-.32)	(.35)	(-.34)	(.11)	(.20)	(-.46)	(.22)
DARK	4.93 1.80	6.19 1.37	4.40 2.01	5.48 1.58	6.52 1.09	3.25 1.87	4.40 1.35
	(.38)	(1.32)	(-.17)	(1.07)	(.52)	(-.65)	(.29)
DECK	5.38 2.12	5.05 2.22	4.45 1.93	4.45 1.60	6.12 1.42	3.90 1.73	4.17 1.51M
	(.83)	(.18)	(-.12)	(.04)	(.12)	(.00)	(.06)
DECORATE	4.19 1.91	5.02 1.79	4.28 1.60	4.00 1.54	5.63 1.65	4.02 1.71	5.08 1.50F
	(-.36)	(.15)	(-.29)	(-.41)	(-.37)	(.12)	(.97)
DECOY	4.82 1.93	4.67 2.04	3.95 1.74	3.92 1.57	5.72 1.60	3.89 1.86	3.58 1.26M
	(.27)	(-.20)	(-.62)	(-.49)	(-.28)	(-.01)	(-.53)
DEEP	3.96 2.12	5.17 1.93	4.43 1.70	4.64 1.76	6.27 1.18	4.03 1.70	4.49 1.57F
	(-.59)	(.30)	(-.14)	(.23)	(.27)	(.13)	(.38)
DERBY	4.91 2.21	4.89 1.89	4.37 1.91	3.87 1.88	5.30 1.84	3.63 1.54	4.02 1.48
	(.36)	(.02)	(-.20)	(-.54)	(-.70)	(-.27)	(-.09)
DEVICE	4.47 2.20	4.17 1.94	3.62 1.90	4.19 1.59	5.84 1.40	4.08 1.88	3.75 1.31
	(-.08)	(-.70)	(-.95)	(-.22)	(-.16)	(.18)	(-.36)
DIRT	5.51 1.84	5.05 1.87	4.88 1.72	4.82 1.46	6.41 .99	4.07 1.69	3.46 1.41M
	(.96)	(.18)	(.31)	(.41)	(.41)	(.17)	(-.65)
DRAMA	3.71 1.98	4.68 1.90	4.83 1.67	4.92 1.74	6.07 1.35	4.13 1.81	4.30 1.48F
	(-.84)	(-.26)	(.26)	(.51)	(.07)	(.23)	(.19)
DRAW	4.38 1.85	4.29 2.23	4.03 1.81	4.23 1.78	6.25 1.28	4.38 1.92	4.49 1.45F
	(-.17)	(-.58)	(-.54)	(-.18)	(.25)	(.48)	(.38)
DREAM	4.34 2.11	4.98 1.98	4.36 2.01	4.77 1.79	6.25 1.18	5.19 1.97	5.60 1.43F
	(-.21)	(.11)	(-.21)	(.36)	(.25)	(1.29)	(1.49)
DRINK	5.09 1.57	5.49 1.60	4.88 1.79	4.88 1.90	6.40 1.11	4.06 1.91	4.69 1.52
	(.54)	(.62)	(.31)	(.47)	(.40)	(.16)	(.58)
DUEL	4.70 1.92	4.60 1.93	4.28 1.82	3.56 1.47	5.67 1.64	3.30 1.65	3.71 1.51M
	(.15)	(-.27)	(-.29)	(-.85)	(-.33)	(-.60)	(-.40)
DUMP	4.67 1.97	5.18 1.74	4.17 1.81	4.33 1.68	5.82 1.58	3.75 1.96	2.99 1.37
	(.12)	(.31)	(-.40)	(-.08)	(-.18)	(-.15)	(-1.12)

	CON		IMG		CAT		MNG		FAM		NOA		PLS	
	M	SD	M	SD	M	SD	M	SD	M	SD	M	SD	M	SD
DUSK	4.97	1.88	5.68	1.61	4.58	1.61	4.56	1.74	5.63	1.48	3.26	1.72	5.02	1.60
	(.42)		(.81)		(.01)		(.15)		(-.37)		(-.64)		(.91)	
DUSTY	4.48	1.83	5.00	1.97	4.12	1.39	4.44	1.67	6.11	1.46	3.20	1.67	3.13	1.47
	(-.07)		(.13)		(-.45)		(.03)		(.11)		(-.70)		(-.98)	
EAST	3.59	1.94	4.91	1.88	5.68	1.89	4.39	2.07	6.48	1.07	3.41	2.04	4.65	1.54F
	(-.96)		(.04)		(1.11)		(-.02)		(.48)		(-.49)		(.54)	
EIGHT	3.74	2.20	4.67	2.15	5.70	1.96	3.65	2.24	6.65	1.05	3.20	1.95	4.16	1.25
	(-.81)		(-.20)		(1.13)		(-.76)		(.65)		(-.70)		(.05)	
EMPIRE	4.25	2.22	4.64	1.87	4.17	1.93	3.97	1.83	5.53	1.77	4.59	1.66	3.90	1.49
	(-.30)		(-.23)		(-.40)		(-.44)		(-.47)		(.69)		(-.21)	
ENAMEL	5.29	2.01	4.45	2.00	4.02	1.85	3.23	1.79	5.50	1.73	3.41	1.50	3.97	1.25
	(.74)		(-.42)		(-.55)		(-1.18)		(-.50)		(-.49)		(-.14)	
ENGINEER	5.33	1.75	4.66	2.13	5.59	1.62	4.30	1.78	6.08	1.18	5.00	1.86	3.82	1.45
	(.78)		(-.21)		(1.02)		(-.11)		(.08)		(1.10)		(-.29)	
ENTRANCE	4.92	2.13	5.37	1.76	4.33	1.92	4.67	1.60	6.27	1.07	3.87	1.81	4.45	1.40
	(.37)		(.50)		(-.24)		(.26)		(.27)		(-.03)		(.34)	
FABLE	4.55	1.98	4.71	2.16	4.97	1.75	4.43	1.60	5.51	1.71	3.83	1.68	4.69	1.48F
	(.00)		(-.16)		(.02)		(.02)		(-.49)		(-.07)		(.58)	
FAIR	4.09	2.32	4.64	2.34	4.05	1.80	4.74	1.56	6.28	1.24	4.08	1.93	4.67	1.66F
	(-.46)		(-.23)		(-.52)		(.33)		(.28)		(.18)		(.56)	
FAIRY	4.55	2.29	5.02	1.87	4.80	1.71	3.93	1.92	5.82	1.60	3.78	1.79	4.31	1.72F
	(.00)		(.15)		(.23)		(-.48)		(-.18)		(-.12)		(.20)	
FALL	4.05	1.70	5.41	1.78	4.27	1.98	4.67	1.85	6.46	1.13	3.64	1.69	3.31	1.63
	(-.50)		(.54)		(-.30)		(.26)		(.46)		(-.26)		(-.80)	
FELT	4.33	2.07	4.77	2.06	3.90	1.79	3.87	1.75	5.78	1.49	3.62	1.73	4.73	1.18
	(-.22)		(-.10)		(-.67)		(-.54)		(-.22)		(-.28)		(.62)	
FERTILE	4.26	1.92	4.40	1.92	4.17	1.83	4.42	1.59	5.76	1.44	4.23	1.50	5.02	1.52
	(-.29)		(-.47)		(-.40)		(.01)		(-.24)		(.33)		(.91)	
FIGURE	4.68	1.91	5.04	2.06	4.26	1.78	5.13	1.49	6.35	1.04	4.45	1.86	4.48	1.40
	(.13)		(.17)		(-.31)		(.72)		(.35)		(.55)		(.37)	
FILE	4.76	2.01	4.36	2.23	4.32	1.94	3.78	1.64	5.78	1.49	3.13	1.55	3.51	1.19
	(.21)		(-.51)		(-.25)		(-.63)		(-.22)		(-.77)		(-.60)	
FIVE	3.61	2.26	5.23	2.10	5.73	1.90	3.92	2.28	6.27	1.33	3.15	1.86	4.16	.91
	(-.94)		(.36)		(1.16)		(-.49)		(.27)		(-.75)		(.05)	
FLARE	4.63	2.26	5.03	1.81	4.25	1.85	3.89	1.71	5.82	1.50	3.57	1.56	4.72	1.33
	(.08)		(.16)		(-.32)		(-.52)		(-.18)		(-.33)		(.61)	
FLASH	4.82	1.84	5.37	1.91	3.76	1.65	4.69	1.52	5.88	1.46	3.28	1.58	4.57	1.36
	(.27)		(.50)		(-.81)		(.28)		(-.12)		(-.62)		(.46)	
FLEECE	5.25	2.00	5.31	1.59	4.33	1.98	3.87	1.75	4.85	1.63	3.56	1.62	4.84	1.58
	(.70)		(.44)		(-.24)		(-.54)		(-1.15)		(-.34)		(.73)	
FLEET	5.16	1.89	5.04	1.89	4.76	1.82	3.87	1.66	5.39	1.73	4.61	1.74	4.56	1.34
	(.61)		(.17)		(.19)		(-.54)		(-.61)		(.71)		(.45)	
FLOAT	4.47	2.10	5.19	1.83	4.58	1.82	4.45	1.97	6.27	1.30	3.62	1.36	5.08	1.61
	(-.08)		(.32)		(.01)		(.04)		(.27)		(-.28)		(.97)	
FLUSH	4.43	1.91	5.24	1.89	3.98	1.71	3.82	1.78	5.81	1.41	3.21	1.51	3.40	1.54
	(-.12)		(.37)		(-.59)		(-.59)		(-.19)		(-.69)		(-.71)	
FOIL	5.05	1.99	4.89	2.08	4.48	1.89	3.98	1.71	5.90	1.50	3.67	1.65	3.44	1.42
	(.50)		(.02)		(-.09)		(-.43)		(-.10)		(-.23)		(-.67)	
FOUR	3.61	2.33	4.85	2.23	5.40	2.02	4.02	2.05	6.27	1.35	2.87	1.64	4.25	.98
	(-.94)		(-.02)		(.83)		(-.39)		(.27)		(-1.03)		(.14)	
FOWL	4.93	1.94	4.84	2.18	4.80	2.03	4.59	1.88	5.53	1.69	3.75	1.57	3.56	1.64
	(.38)		(-.03)		(.23)		(.18)		(-.47)		(-.15)		(-.55)	
FRATERNITY	4.25	2.00	5.02	2.12	4.79	1.96	4.07	1.93	5.84	1.65	4.25	2.14	2.98	1.76
	(-.30)		(.15)		(.22)		(-.34)		(-.16)		(.35)		(-1.13)	

	CON		IMG		CAT		MNG		FAM		NOA		PLS	
	M	SD	M	SD	M	SD	M	SD	M	SD	M	SD	M	SD
FREEZE	4.76	1.80	5.15	1.82	4.49	2.05	3.93	1.96	6.37	1.09	3.32	1.83	3.89	1.47
	(.21)		(.28)		(-.08)		(-.48)		(.37)		(-.58)		(-.22)	
FRONT	4.20	2.18	4.29	2.07	4.07	2.08	4.05	1.77	6.18	1.26	3.38	1.94	4.07	1.15
	(-.35)		(-.58)		(-.50)		(-.36)		(.18)		(-.52)		(-.04)	
FUSE	4.96	1.99	4.73	2.21	4.68	1.85	3.90	1.70	5.23	1.79	3.51	1.40	3.72	.97
	(.41)		(-.14)		(.11)		(-.51)		(-.77)		(-.39)		(-.39)	
FUZZY	4.46	2.04	5.13	1.79	4.55	1.95	4.38	1.65	5.56	1.51	3.52	1.51	4.49	1.58
	(-.09)		(.26)		(-.02)		(-.03)		(-.44)		(-.38)		(.38)	
GARMENT	5.30	1.80	4.82	1.99	5.42	1.63	5.03	1.57	5.60	1.69	4.47	2.10	4.08	1.24F
	(.75)		(-.05)		(.85)		(.62)		(-.40)		(.57)		(-.03)	
GENERAL	4.04	2.54	4.85	2.20	3.55	2.02	4.80	1.85	6.42	1.00	3.87	1.88	3.80	1.15
	(-.51)		(-.02)		(-1.02)		(.39)		(.42)		(-.03)		(-.31)	
GENES	5.14	2.10	4.42	1.98	5.28	1.74	4.28	1.83	5.90	1.33	4.31	2.31	4.40	1.55
	(.59)		(-.45)		(.71)		(-.13)		(-.10)		(.41)		(.29)	
GENTLEMAN	4.53	2.27	5.33	1.69	5.40	1.52	4.70	1.75	6.07	1.35	4.59	1.93	4.94	1.63F
	(-.02)		(.46)		(.83)		(.29)		(.07)		(.69)		(.83)	
GERM	4.83	2.09	4.15	1.99	4.89	1.86	4.85	1.51	6.14	1.42	4.80	1.85	2.59	1.43
	(.28)		(-.72)		(.32)		(.44)		(.14)		(.90)		(-1.52)	
GHOST	4.25	2.21	5.72	1.60	4.98	1.91	4.36	1.91	6.17	1.49	3.73	1.82	3.62	1.58M
	(-.30)		(.85)		(.41)		(-.05)		(.17)		(-.17)		(-.49)	
GLITTER	4.16	2.03	4.80	1.77	3.97	1.62	4.22	1.71	5.41	1.69	3.20	1.54	4.52	1.54
	(-.39)		(-.07)		(-.60)		(-.19)		(-.59)		(-.70)		(.41)	
GRAMMAR	3.98	2.05	3.86	2.15	4.78	1.92	4.62	1.61	6.05	1.21	4.62	1.80	3.49	1.48
	(-.57)		(-1.01)		(.21)		(.21)		(.05)		(.72)		(-.62)	
GRIZZLY	4.39	1.93	5.17	1.85	4.93	1.89	3.89	1.81	5.45	1.72	3.83	1.76	3.75	1.69M
	(-.16)		(.30)		(.36)		(-.52)		(-.55)		(-.07)		(-.36)	
GROUND	5.44	2.06	4.93	2.00	4.48	1.77	4.42	1.89	6.38	1.21	3.84	1.90	4.39	1.43
	(.89)		(.06)		(-.09)		(.01)		(.38)		(-.06)		(.28)	
GROUP	4.47	2.00	4.61	1.82	4.26	1.81	4.74	1.64	6.27	1.16	4.40	2.06	4.11	1.31
	(-.08)		(-.26)		(-.31)		(.33)		(.27)		(.50)		(.00)	
GUARD	5.05	2.12	5.24	1.74	4.59	1.84	4.85	1.71	5.86	1.47	4.15	1.50	3.53	1.28
	(.50)		(.37)		(.02)		(.44)		(-.14)		(.25)		(-.58)	
GUEST	5.15	1.73	4.91	1.81	4.58	1.69	5.02	1.41	6.34	1.19	4.40	1.61	4.97	1.30
	(.60)		(.04)		(.01)		(.61)		(.34)		(.50)		(.86)	
GUIDE	4.35	1.93	4.53	1.94	4.35	1.82	4.54	1.60	5.98	1.47	4.39	1.52	4.48	1.26
	(-.20)		(-.34)		(-.22)		(.13)		(-.02)		(.49)		(.37)	
HAIL	4.26	2.11	4.57	2.05	4.15	2.00	3.61	1.50	5.41	1.71	3.33	1.49	3.84	1.48
	(-.29)		(-.30)		(-.42)		(-.80)		(-.59)		(-.57)		(-.27)	
HARD	4.21	2.20	4.67	2.17	4.68	1.93	4.97	1.67	6.38	1.24	3.77	1.88	3.73	1.30M
	(-.34)		(-.20)		(.11)		(.56)		(.38)		(-.13)		(-.38)	
HAREM	5.14	2.13	5.09	1.93	4.31	1.81	4.13	1.91	4.90	1.96	3.93	1.98	4.09	2.05M
	(.59)		(.22)		(-.26)		(-.28)		(-1.10)		(.03)		(-.02)	
HE	3.95	2.17	4.37	2.23	4.42	2.26	4.48	2.22	6.31	1.43	3.75	2.22	4.60	1.42F
	(-.60)		(-.50)		(-.15)		(.07)		(.31)		(-.15)		(.49)	
HEAR	3.90	1.84	4.60	2.03	4.47	1.64	4.61	1.92	6.63	1.00	4.08	1.91	4.74	1.50
	(-.65)		(-.27)		(-.10)		(.20)		(.63)		(.18)		(.63)	
HEAT	4.84	1.78	4.67	1.81	4.48	1.64	4.68	1.60	6.26	1.24	4.03	1.76	4.20	1.39
	(.29)		(-.20)		(-.09)		(.27)		(.26)		(.13)		(.09)	
HEAVY	4.09	2.05	4.93	1.92	5.00	2.03	4.72	1.76	6.34	1.11	4.43	1.88	3.50	1.40
	(-.46)		(.06)		(.43)		(.31)		(.34)		(.53)		(-.61)	
HERO	4.22	2.17	4.55	2.10	4.38	1.90	4.77	1.82	6.20	1.38	4.51	1.78	4.97	1.65
	(-.33)		(-.32)		(-.19)		(.36)		(.20)		(.61)		(.86)	
HOLE	4.81	2.09	5.21	1.73	4.20	1.83	4.52	1.55	6.19	1.37	3.43	1.51	3.67	1.24
	(.26)		(.34)		(-.37)		(.11)		(.19)		(-.47)		(-.44)	

	CON		IMG		CAT		MNG		FAM		NOA		PLS	
	M	SD	M	SD	M	SD	M	SD	M	SD	M	SD	M	SD
HORIZONTAL	4.00	2.11	5.15	1.96	4.83	1.79	4.03	1.96	6.02	1.43	2.34	1.69	4.29	1.44
	(−.55)		(.28)		(.26)		(−.38)		(.02)		(−1.56)		(.18)	
HOT	5.03	1.87	5.53	1.84	5.23	1.84	5.26	1.67	6.66	.96	3.95	2.00	3.18	1.64
	(.48)		(.66)		(.66)		(.85)		(.66)		(.05)		(−.93)	
HOUR	4.19	2.07	4.21	2.36	5.37	1.74	4.92	1.74	6.57	1.02	3.23	1.83	3.56	1.47
	(−.36)		(−.66)		(.80)		(.51)		(.57)		(−.67)		(−.55)	
HUMP	4.93	2.07	5.18	1.74	4.00	1.88	4.33	1.62	5.44	1.89	3.38	1.53	3.98	1.35M
	(.38)		(.31)		(−.57)		(−.08)		(−.56)		(−.52)		(−.13)	
HUNGRY	4.35	2.11	4.98	2.20	4.58	1.61	4.90	1.68	6.50	1.24	3.80	1.91	3.00	1.80
	(−.20)		(.11)		(.01)		(.49)		(.50)		(−.10)		(−1.11)	
HUNT	4.12	1.89	5.21	1.80	4.32	1.61	4.57	1.71	5.97	1.43	4.08	1.56	3.37	1.76M
	(−.43)		(.34)		(−.25)		(.16)		(−.03)		(.18)		(−.74)	
HYMN	4.98	2.00	4.25	2.08	5.27	1.65	4.00	1.68	5.08	2.02	3.59	1.90	4.05	1.57
	(.43)		(−.62)		(.70)		(−.41)		(−.92)		(−.31)		(−.06)	
I	4.79	2.43	5.07	2.38	4.05	2.44	5.06	2.15	6.82	.67	4.66	2.55	5.11	1.87
	(.24)		(.20)		(−.52)		(.65)		(.82)		(.76)		(1.00)	
IGNITION	4.66	2.17	4.90	1.80	4.53	1.89	3.82	1.72	6.08	1.43	3.52	1.50	4.03	1.14M
	(.11)		(.03)		(−.04)		(−.59)		(.08)		(−.38)		(−.08)	
INCH	4.47	2.18	4.91	1.99	5.25	2.10	4.44	1.90	6.57	.95	2.75	1.54	3.51	.98
	(−.08)		(.04)		(.68)		(.03)		(.57)		(−1.15)		(−.60)	
INSTITUTE	4.76	2.12	4.98	1.77	4.78	1.67	4.45	1.72	5.91	1.53	5.07	1.88	3.37	1.56
	(.21)		(.11)		(.21)		(.04)		(−.09)		(1.17)		(−.74)	
INSTITUTION	4.74	2.18	4.56	2.12	4.95	1.83	5.20	1.58	5.78	1.33	5.20	1.64	3.02	1.40
	(.19)		(−.31)		(.38)		(.79)		(−.22)		(1.30)		(−1.09)	
INSTRUMENT	5.36	1.85	4.87	1.95	5.10	2.07	5.28	1.70	6.25	1.12	4.54	1.98	4.41	1.54
	(.81)		(.00)		(.53)		(.87)		(.25)		(.64)		(.30)	
ISLANDER	5.00	1.81	4.58	1.79	4.42	1.83	4.13	1.81	5.48	1.79	3.77	1.89	4.10	1.66
	(.45)		(−.29)		(−.15)		(−.28)		(−.52)		(−.13)		(−.01)	
ISLE	5.26	1.81	5.14	1.98	4.67	1.84	3.95	1.58	5.45	1.66	3.75	1.86	4.86	1.58
	(.71)		(.27)		(.10)		(−.46)		(−.55)		(−.15)		(.75)	
JAGGED	4.40	1.98	5.06	1.77	3.57	1.82	4.28	1.79	5.44	1.60	3.77	1.48	3.56	1.36
	(−.15)		(.19)		(−1.00)		(−.13)		(−.56)		(−.13)		(−.55)	
JOB	4.28	1.87	4.64	1.90	4.66	1.89	5.03	1.72	6.52	1.08	4.92	1.92	4.57	1.62
	(−.27)		(−.23)		(.09)		(.62)		(.52)		(1.02)		(.46)	
JOG	4.60	1.95	4.98	1.79	4.67	1.85	4.32	1.59	6.05	1.36	3.21	1.64	4.53	1.33
	(.05)		(.11)		(.10)		(−.09)		(.05)		(−.69)		(.42)	
JOURNAL	5.58	1.68	4.94	1.99	5.05	1.72	4.23	1.71	5.60	1.60	4.54	1.74	4.47	1.43
	(1.03)		(.07)		(.48)		(−.18)		(−.40)		(.64)		(.36)	
JUDGE	4.63	2.34	5.14	1.93	4.75	1.75	4.60	1.60	6.32	1.17	4.45	1.69	3.76	1.34
	(.08)		(.27)		(.18)		(.19)		(.32)		(.55)		(−.35)	
JUMP	4.44	2.04	5.32	1.73	4.90	1.97	4.66	1.75	6.25	1.41	3.66	1.77	4.05	1.17
	(−.11)		(.45)		(.33)		(.25)		(.25)		(−.24)		(−.06)	
JUNCTION	4.73	2.01	4.96	1.89	4.34	1.92	4.19	1.79	5.63	1.58	3.56	1.65	4.10	1.16
	(.18)		(.09)		(−.23)		(−.22)		(−.37)		(−.34)		(−.01)	
KINGDOM	3.88	1.91	4.88	1.91	4.55	1.82	4.72	1.61	5.87	1.49	4.89	1.89	4.68	1.39
	(−.67)		(.01)		(−.02)		(.31)		(−.13)		(.99)		(.57)	
LABOR	4.49	1.89	4.59	2.00	4.93	1.61	4.62	1.72	5.86	1.58	4.26	1.74	3.42	1.35
	(−.06)		(−.28)		(.36)		(.21)		(−.14)		(.36)		(−.69)	
LACE	5.41	1.81	5.00	1.79	4.67	1.79	4.02	1.58	5.42	1.77	3.52	1.65	4.75	1.37F
	(.86)		(.13)		(.10)		(−.39)		(−.58)		(−.38)		(.64)	
LAD	5.04	2.18	4.87	2.00	4.80	2.09	4.27	1.83	5.39	1.93	3.56	1.71	4.36	1.45F
	(.49)		(.00)		(.23)		(−.14)		(−.61)		(−.34)		(.25)	
LANE	5.15	1.96	5.12	1.92	4.27	1.82	4.16	1.75	6.11	1.36	3.03	1.45	4.25	1.44
	(.60)		(.25)		(−.30)		(−.25)		(.11)		(−.87)		(.14)	

	CON M SD	IMG M SD	CAT M SD	MNG M SD	FAM M SD	NOA M SD	PLS M SD
LAUGH	4.29 2.12 (-.26)	5.22 1.81 (.35)	4.73 1.76 (.16)	5.28 1.47 (.87)	6.68 .87 (.68)	4.03 1.79 (.13)	6.00 1.33 (1.89)
LAW	3.54 2.06 (-1.01)	3.96 2.06 (-.91)	4.88 2.10 (.31)	4.55 1.72 (.14)	6.15 1.23 (.15)	4.82 2.08 (.92)	4.17 1.34 (.06)
LEAD	5.13 2.04 (.58)	4.40 2.01 (-.47)	4.93 2.11 (.36)	4.00 1.71 (-.41)	6.03 1.34 (.03)	3.34 1.58 (-.56)	3.62 1.35 (-.49)
LEAN	3.91 2.06 (-.64)	4.66 1.73 (-.21)	4.02 1.75 (-.55)	4.77 1.54 (.36)	6.23 1.32 (.23)	3.10 1.56 (-.80)	4.21 1.50 (.10)
LEAP	3.85 2.08 (-.70)	4.88 1.84 (.01)	4.03 1.75 (-.54)	5.10 1.63 (.69)	6.13 1.27 (.13)	3.11 1.74 (-.79)	4.15 1.61 (.04)
LESSON	4.19 1.86 (-.36)	4.47 2.22 (-.40)	3.89 1.78 (-.69)	4.89 1.59 (.48)	6.34 1.05 (.34)	4.48 1.64 (.58)	3.97 1.39F (-.14)
LINE	4.82 2.35 (.27)	4.86 2.19 (-.01)	4.72 2.09 (.15)	4.63 1.83 (.22)	6.47 1.23 (.47)	3.27 1.99 (-.63)	3.68 1.17 (-.43)
LITERATURE	4.40 1.89 (-.15)	4.63 2.04 (-.24)	5.20 1.88 (.63)	5.20 1.63 (.79)	6.12 1.30 (.12)	5.61 1.74 (1.71)	4.86 1.33 (.75)
LITTLE	3.74 1.89 (-.81)	5.51 1.85 (.64)	4.75 1.91 (.18)	5.46 1.62 (1.05)	6.46 1.16 (.46)	3.70 2.16 (-.20)	3.79 1.32 (-.32)
LOAD	4.35 1.89 (-.20)	4.55 1.88 (-.32)	4.58 1.74 (.01)	4.52 1.26 (.11)	6.36 .97 (.36)	3.70 1.67 (-.20)	3.84 1.19 (-.27)
LONG	3.77 1.94 (-.78)	5.09 1.70 (.22)	5.07 1.60 (.50)	4.92 1.66 (.51)	6.07 1.45 (.07)	3.46 1.80 (-.44)	4.13 1.15 (.02)
LOOP	4.86 2.05 (.31)	4.86 1.98 (-.01)	3.95 1.71 (-.62)	3.97 1.76 (-.44)	5.68 1.58 (-.32)	3.28 1.62 (-.62)	3.82 1.30 (-.29)
LORD	3.71 2.44 (-.84)	4.86 1.96 (-.01)	4.93 2.16 (.36)	5.25 1.78 (.84)	6.30 1.41 (.30)	4.75 2.17 (.85)	5.18 1.69 (1.07)
LOTION	5.30 1.83 (.75)	4.89 2.04 (.02)	4.78 1.60 (.21)	3.88 1.53 (-.53)	5.83 1.44 (-.17)	3.31 1.52 (-.59)	4.47 1.34 (.36)
LOUD	4.09 2.06 (-.46)	4.51 2.15 (-.36)	4.92 1.74 (.35)	4.79 1.77 (.38)	6.37 1.30 (.37)	3.66 1.67 (-.24)	3.18 1.48 (-.93)
MAIL	5.04 2.10 (.49)	5.42 1.91 (.55)	4.74 1.83 (.17)	4.30 1.95 (-.11)	6.28 1.31 (.28)	4.32 1.80 (.42)	5.06 1.52 (.95)
MANOR	4.79 1.99 (.24)	4.65 1.96 (-.22)	4.27 1.76 (-.30)	3.61 1.70 (-.80)	5.17 1.88 (-.83)	3.69 1.42 (-.21)	4.24 1.10 (.13)
MARCH	4.26 2.12 (-.29)	4.80 1.99 (-.07)	5.15 1.83 (.58)	4.36 1.87 (-.05)	6.20 1.49 (.20)	3.46 1.59 (-.44)	4.41 1.46 (.30)
MARRY	3.58 2.17 (-.97)	5.17 2.23 (.30)	3.98 1.95 (-.59)	4.61 2.31 (.20)	6.31 1.26 (.31)	3.67 2.02 (-.23)	4.42 1.75 (.31)
MASS	4.09 2.08 (-.46)	4.89 1.96 (.02)	4.42 2.11 (-.15)	4.44 1.68 (.03)	5.62 1.61 (-.38)	4.11 1.80 (.21)	4.27 1.48 (.16)
MATCH	5.31 1.84 (.76)	4.84 2.04 (-.03)	4.63 2.02 (.06)	4.61 1.39 (.20)	6.32 1.06 (.32)	3.57 1.72 (-.33)	3.97 1.11 (-.14)
MATE	5.03 2.13 (.48)	5.00 1.69 (.13)	4.70 1.82 (.13)	5.02 1.78 (.61)	6.27 1.19 (.27)	4.49 1.72 (.59)	5.57 1.36 (1.46)
MATH	3.82 2.14 (-.73)	4.81 2.10 (-.06)	5.17 1.80 (.60)	4.25 1.83 (-.16)	6.22 1.25 (.22)	4.62 1.95 (.72)	3.86 1.63F (-.25)
MATHEMATICS	4.02 2.18 (-.53)	4.95 1.97 (.08)	5.32 1.92 (.75)	4.64 2.01 (.23)	6.28 1.39 (.28)	4.61 1.93 (.71)	3.82 1.61M (-.29)
ME	5.07 2.41 (.52)	5.07 2.26 (.20)	3.75 2.30 (-.62)	5.21 1.98 (.80)	6.60 1.26 (.60)	3.62 2.59 (-.28)	5.40 1.39 (1.29)
MECHANICAL	3.81 1.99 (-.74)	4.76 1.86 (-.11)	4.12 1.62 (-.45)	4.70 1.72 (.29)	6.07 1.21 (.07)	4.38 1.83 (.48)	3.90 1.46M (-.21)
MESSAGE	4.55 1.89 (.00)	4.32 2.15 (-.55)	3.87 1.85 (-.70)	4.82 1.47 (.41)	6.31 1.29 (.31)	3.93 1.79 (.03)	4.51 1.62F (.40)

	CON		IMG		CAT		MNG		FAM		NOA		PLS	
	M	SD	M	SD	M	SD	M	SD	M	SD	M	SD	M	SD
MINE	4.48	2.29	5.16	1.83	3.97	1.95	4.35	1.92	6.31	1.33	3.95	2.03	4.17	1.61
	(-.07)		(.29)		(-.60)		(-.06)		(.31)		(.05)		(.06)	
MINSTREL	5.26	1.89	5.25	1.86	4.45	1.85	3.67	1.68	4.87	1.79	3.98	1.75	4.57	1.73
	(.71)		(.38)		(-.12)		(-.74)		(-1.13)		(.08)		(.46)	
MINUTE	3.74	2.00	4.78	2.32	5.88	1.42	4.87	1.76	6.46	1.18	3.00	1.57	3.81	1.45
	(-.81)		(-.09)		(1.31)		(.46)		(.46)		(-.90)		(-.30)	
MIRAGE	3.86	2.27	4.76	2.17	3.87	1.94	3.90	1.79	5.66	1.73	3.64	1.94	4.09	1.55F
	(-.69)		(-.11)		(-.70)		(-.51)		(-.34)		(-.26)		(-.02)	
MOLD	4.82	1.97	4.48	1.86	4.19	1.90	3.93	1.65	5.77	1.59	3.47	1.43	3.29	1.28
	(.27)		(-.39)		(-.38)		(-.48)		(-.23)		(-.43)		(-.82)	
MOLECULE	4.14	2.20	4.80	1.98	5.33	1.72	4.11	1.92	5.53	1.70	4.51	2.09	4.18	1.44
	(-.41)		(-.07)		(.76)		(-.30)		(-.47)		(.61)		(.07)	
MOVE	3.86	1.94	4.63	1.97	4.19	1.77	4.28	1.89	6.12	1.47	4.02	1.78	4.26	1.15
	(-.69)		(-.24)		(-.38)		(-.13)		(.12)		(.12)		(.15)	
MURAL	5.11	2.04	5.09	1.87	4.30	1.79	3.72	1.94	5.25	1.76	3.89	1.94	4.39	1.49
	(.56)		(.22)		(-.27)		(-.69)		(-.75)		(-.01)		(.28)	
NAME	4.01	2.08	4.69	2.20	4.68	1.89	4.74	1.88	6.47	1.18	4.34	2.26	4.65	1.42F
	(-.54)		(-.18)		(.11)		(.33)		(.47)		(.44)		(.54)	
NATION	4.17	1.89	4.33	2.11	5.05	1.59	4.57	1.74	5.93	1.53	4.97	1.81	4.09	1.23
	(-.38)		(-.54)		(.48)		(.16)		(-.07)		(1.07)		(-.02)	
NATIVE	4.67	2.22	5.09	1.79	4.57	1.93	4.47	1.72	6.10	1.36	4.17	1.65	4.33	1.17
	(.12)		(.22)		(.00)		(.06)		(.10)		(.27)		(.22)	
NERVE	4.81	2.18	4.67	1.94	5.27	1.68	4.39	1.73	6.31	1.22	4.42	1.79	3.84	1.61
	(.26)		(-.20)		(.70)		(-.02)		(.31)		(.52)		(-.27)	
NEWS	4.33	2.04	4.78	1.89	4.63	1.78	5.07	1.74	6.34	1.20	5.14	2.12	4.43	1.53
	(-.22)		(-.09)		(.06)		(.66)		(.34)		(1.24)		(.32)	
NINE	4.48	2.21	4.88	1.64	5.93	1.64	4.24	2.31	6.45	1.08	3.15	2.03	4.08	1.19
	(-.07)		(.01)		(1.36)		(-.17)		(.45)		(-.75)		(-.03)	
NOTE	4.86	2.09	4.95	1.98	4.55	1.75	4.38	1.51	6.47	1.17	4.00	1.61	3.99	1.33F
	(.31)		(.08)		(-.02)		(-.03)		(.47)		(.10)		(-.12)	
NOUN	3.93	2.36	3.98	2.28	5.33	1.92	4.36	2.01	6.11	1.50	3.64	2.18	3.28	1.28
	(-.62)		(-.89)		(.76)		(-.05)		(.11)		(-.26)		(-.83)	
NUMBER	3.76	2.23	4.73	2.01	5.05	2.09	4.73	1.99	6.22	1.36	4.63	2.04	3.97	1.23
	(-.79)		(-.14)		(.48)		(.32)		(.22)		(.73)		(-.14)	
NURSERY	4.93	1.88	4.95	1.89	5.00	1.76	4.22	1.44	5.46	1.73	4.33	1.79	4.54	1.62F
	(.38)		(.08)		(.43)		(-.19)		(-.54)		(.43)		(.43)	
OLD	3.45	2.06	4.91	1.98	4.27	2.17	5.68	1.69	6.72	.78	4.11	1.84	3.72	1.46
	(-1.10)		(.04)		(-.30)		(1.27)		(.72)		(.21)		(-.39)	
OUNCE	4.98	2.06	4.51	2.12	5.63	1.78	4.59	1.96	6.39	1.05	3.00	1.75	4.09	1.52M
	(.43)		(-.36)		(1.06)		(.18)		(.39)		(-.90)		(-.02)	
OWNER	4.09	1.91	4.06	1.87	4.05	2.03	4.59	1.74	6.26	1.24	3.51	1.79	4.07	1.64M
	(-.46)		(-.81)		(-.52)		(.18)		(.26)		(-.39)		(-.04)	
OXYGEN	4.73	2.10	4.13	2.26	5.54	1.66	3.88	1.68	6.12	1.19	3.02	1.95	4.52	1.60
	(.18)		(-.74)		(.97)		(-.53)		(.12)		(-.88)		(.41)	
PACKS	4.89	2.04	5.09	2.03	4.15	1.93	3.77	1.48	5.69	1.73	3.56	1.46	4.15	1.33
	(.34)		(.22)		(-.42)		(-.64)		(-.31)		(-.34)		(.04)	
PARAGRAPH	4.89	1.99	4.76	1.93	4.98	2.00	4.19	1.94	6.33	1.26	4.11	1.91	3.41	1.33
	(.34)		(-.11)		(.41)		(-.22)		(.33)		(-.21)		(-.70)	
PARCEL	5.21	2.15	5.03	1.83	4.55	1.76	4.18	1.72	5.77	1.47	3.98	1.52	4.69	1.30F
	(.66)		(.16)		(-.02)		(-.23)		(-.23)		(.08)		(.58)	
PARISH	4.30	2.15	4.77	1.67	4.33	1.85	4.11	1.90	5.08	1.84	4.00	1.97	3.65	1.53
	(-.25)		(-.10)		(-.24)		(-.30)		(-.92)		(.10)		(-.46)	
PATH	5.00	1.85	5.31	1.63	4.31	1.64	4.47	1.56	6.05	1.25	4.13	1.77	4.56	1.49F
	(.45)		(.44)		(-.26)		(.06)		(.05)		(.23)		(.45)	

	CON		IMG		CAT		MNG		FAM		NOA		PLS	
	M	SD	M	SD	M	SD	M	SD	M	SD	M	SD	M	SD
PATIENTS	5.18	2.02	5.07	1.95	4.59	1.92	4.22	1.74	6.00	1.45	4.73	2.01	3.70	1.48
	(.63)		(.20)		(.02)		(-.19)		(.00)		(.83)		(-.41)	
PAWN	4.76	2.14	4.73	2.04	4.47	2.03	3.76	1.76	5.51	1.66	3.51	1.74	3.34	1.31M
	(.21)		(-.14)		(-.10)		(-.65)		(-.49)		(-.39)		(-.77)	
PEDDLE	4.78	2.04	5.02	1.95	4.38	1.83	3.77	1.63	5.75	1.67	3.57	1.61	4.02	1.09
	(.23)		(.15)		(-.19)		(-.64)		(-.25)		(-.33)		(-.09)	
PHANTOM	4.24	1.97	4.92	2.08	4.37	1.97	4.23	1.96	5.39	1.74	3.74	1.70	3.87	1.87M
	(-.31)		(.05)		(-.20)		(-.18)		(-.61)		(-.16)		(-.24)	
PHYSICS	4.02	2.34	4.19	2.19	5.75	1.74	3.80	1.91	5.57	1.65	4.84	1.85	3.04	1.92
	(-.53)		(-.68)		(1.18)		(-.61)		(-.43)		(.94)		(-1.07)	
PICK	4.98	2.00	5.07	1.93	4.25	1.76	4.30	1.66	5.98	1.37	3.22	1.53	3.63	1.07
	(.43)		(.20)		(-.32)		(-.11)		(-.02)		(-.68)		(-.48)	
PILE	5.00	1.92	5.07	1.70	4.17	1.85	4.21	1.97	5.95	1.47	4.06	1.64	3.59	1.30M
	(.45)		(.20)		(-.40)		(-.20)		(-.05)		(.16)		(-.52)	
PLOT	4.16	1.94	4.39	2.24	4.10	1.69	4.12	1.57	5.97	1.47	4.33	1.93	3.49	1.56
	(-.39)		(-.48)		(-.47)		(-.29)		(-.03)		(.43)		(-.62)	
PLUMB	4.55	2.32	4.95	2.14	5.07	2.15	3.51	1.89	5.35	1.81	3.47	1.72	4.39	1.43
	(.00)		(.08)		(.50)		(-.90)		(-.65)		(-.43)		(.28)	
POINT	4.60	1.89	4.75	1.84	3.84	1.97	3.76	1.61	6.12	1.42	3.24	1.92	3.94	1.25
	(.05)		(-.12)		(-.73)		(-.65)		(.12)		(-.66)		(-.17)	
POLL	4.25	2.20	4.82	1.89	4.17	1.92	3.87	1.66	5.27	1.77	3.41	1.55	3.80	1.22
	(-.30)		(-.05)		(-.40)		(-.54)		(-.73)		(-.49)		(-.31)	
POLLUTION	5.15	1.82	5.44	1.71	4.45	2.01	5.08	1.59	6.30	1.23	5.13	1.96	2.17	1.43
	(.60)		(.57)		(-.12)		(.67)		(.30)		(1.23)		(-1.94)	
PORT	4.96	1.86	5.19	1.84	4.80	1.65	4.05	1.71	5.68	1.60	4.17	1.78	4.40	1.44
	(.41)		(.32)		(.23)		(-.36)		(-.32)		(.27)		(.29)	
POST	5.27	1.92	5.25	1.90	3.85	1.79	3.98	1.65	6.24	1.22	3.60	1.61	3.84	1.20F
	(.72)		(.38)		(-.72)		(-.43)		(.24)		(-.30)		(-.27)	
POUND	4.82	2.04	5.35	1.67	5.47	1.83	4.75	1.77	6.44	1.23	3.65	1.81	3.62	1.63M
	(.27)		(.48)		(.90)		(.34)		(.44)		(-.25)		(-.49)	
POWDER	5.09	2.05	5.18	1.76	4.74	1.81	3.77	1.43	5.95	1.31	3.87	1.71	4.15	1.66
	(.54)		(.31)		(.17)		(-.64)		(-.05)		(-.03)		(.04)	
PRAYER	3.88	2.21	4.89	2.20	4.77	1.94	4.41	1.83	6.05	1.44	4.08	1.91	4.66	1.89
	(-.67)		(.02)		(.20)		(.00)		(.05)		(.18)		(.55)	
PREY	4.69	1.88	5.11	1.71	4.82	1.85	4.36	1.69	5.40	1.66	4.10	1.46	3.34	1.48M
	(.14)		(.24)		(.25)		(-.05)		(-.60)		(.20)		(-.77)	
PRIZE	4.70	2.01	5.11	1.74	4.70	1.67	4.41	1.66	5.82	1.58	4.12	1.93	5.31	1.37
	(.15)		(.24)		(.13)		(.00)		(-.18)		(.22)		(1.20)	
PRODUCE	4.31	1.99	4.19	2.27	4.14	1.70	4.18	1.72	5.85	1.39	4.03	1.93	4.25	1.38
	(-.24)		(-.68)		(-.43)		(-.23)		(-.15)		(.13)		(.14)	
PROPERTY	4.23	2.02	4.69	1.79	3.93	1.72	4.61	1.62	6.32	1.31	4.28	1.69	4.37	1.18
	(-.32)		(-.18)		(-.64)		(.20)		(.32)		(.38)		(.26)	
PROPHET	4.46	2.11	4.61	2.02	4.65	1.86	3.90	1.72	5.77	1.61	4.40	1.99	4.46	1.43
	(-.09)		(-.26)		(.08)		(-.51)		(-.23)		(.50)		(.35)	
PSYCHOLOGY	3.46	2.18	3.47	2.28	5.45	1.98	4.75	1.87	6.23	1.26	4.97	2.01	3.58	1.67
	(-1.09)		(-1.40)		(.88)		(.34)		(-.23)		(1.07)		(-.53)	
PUNCH	5.48	1.62	4.96	2.04	4.20	2.02	4.85	1.72	5.58	1.76	3.38	1.40	3.27	1.47M
	(.93)		(.09)		(-.37)		(.44)		(-.42)		(-.52)		(-.84)	
RACE	4.59	1.75	4.51	2.01	4.72	1.76	4.41	1.58	6.17	1.20	4.49	1.97	4.38	1.36
	(.04)		(-.36)		(.15)		(.00)		(.17)		(.59)		(.27)	
RACES	5.05	1.67	5.40	1.95	4.25	1.87	4.56	1.68	5.97	1.40	4.51	1.58	4.33	1.36
	(.50)		(.53)		(-.32)		(.15)		(-.03)		(.61)		(.22)	
READ	4.16	2.18	4.93	2.15	4.52	1.84	4.67	1.97	6.42	1.13	4.48	1.95	5.11	1.34F
	(-.39)		(.06)		(-.05)		(.26)		(.42)		(.58)		(1.00)	

	CON		IMG		CAT		MNG		FAM		NOA		PLS	
	M	SD	M	SD	M	SD	M	SD	M	SD	M	SD.	M	SD
RECEIVER	4.16	2.13	4.98	2.14	4.55	1.96	4.68	1.86	6.15	1.40	4.13	1.76	4.22	1.71
	(-.39)		(.11)		(-.02)		(.27)		(.15)		(.23)		(.11)	
REEL	4.98	2.05	4.81	1.81	3.83	1.87	3.69	1.75	5.30	1.79	3.11	1.64	4.15	1.25
	(.43)		(-.06)		(-.74)		(-.72)		(-.70)		(-.79)		(.04)	
REGION	4.37	1.86	4.53	1.88	5.17	1.67	4.69	1.63	5.85	1.60	4.28	1.65	4.18	1.15
	(-.18)		(-.34)		(.60)		(.28)		(-.15)		(.38)		(.07)	
RELIC	5.24	1.91	5.20	2.04	4.75	1.96	4.03	1.70	5.44	1.63	4.02	1.82	4.54	1.49
	(.69)		(.33)		(.18)		(-.38)		(-.56)		(.12)		(.43)	
RELIGION	3.71	2.44	4.49	2.02	4.82	2.22	5.34	1.62	6.27	1.46	5.60	1.70	4.38	1.52
	(-.84)		(-.38)		(.25)		(.93)		(.27)		(1.70)		(.27)	
RESEARCH	3.82	1.97	4.55	1.87	4.35	1.84	4.89	1.78	6.23	1.17	5.30	1.65	4.40	1.45
	(-.73)		(-.32)		(-.22)		(.48)		(.23)		(1.40)		(.29)	
RESORT	4.95	1.91	5.17	2.01	4.28	1.85	4.69	1.80	5.97	1.52	4.78	1.63	4.72	1.64M
	(.40)		(.30)		(-.29)		(.28)		(-.03)		(.88)		(.61)	
RIDDLE	4.00	1.94	4.49	2.03	4.68	1.84	4.05	1.63	5.63	1.67	4.20	1.40	4.74	1.40
	(-.55)		(-.38)		(-.11)		(-.36)		(-.37)		(.30)		(.63)	
RIDE	4.20	1.92	4.70	2.01	4.09	1.74	4.57	1.87	6.26	1.29	3.97	1.65	4.87	1.51
	(-.35)		(-.17)		(-.48)		(.16)		(.26)		(.07)		(.76)	
RIM	5.07	2.13	5.03	1.96	4.25	1.71	3.94	1.77	5.75	1.57	3.11	1.43	4.10	1.21M
	(.52)		(.16)		(-.32)		(-.47)		(-.25)		(-.79)		(-.01)	
ROBBERY	4.28	2.09	4.64	1.75	5.08	1.71	4.80	1.25	6.02	1.44	4.20	1.65	2.50	1.38
	(-.27)		(-.23)		(.51)		(.39)		(.02)		(.30)		(-1.61)	
ROLL	4.53	1.83	4.90	2.08	4.18	1.82	4.21	1.75	6.21	1.25	3.67	1.90	3.97	1.26
	(-.02)		(.03)		(-.39)		(-.20)		(.21)		(-.23)		(-.14)	
ROUGH	4.48	1.92	4.96	2.08	4.38	1.91	4.89	1.69	6.30	1.12	3.63	1.80	3.41	1.34
	(-.07)		(.09)		(-.19)		(.48)		(.30)		(-.27)		(-.70)	
ROUND	4.34	1.97	5.82	1.66	4.97	1.77	4.89	1.70	6.23	1.46	3.44	1.67	4.49	1.28
	(-.21)		(.95)		(.40)		(.48)		(.23)		(-.46)		(.38)	
ROUTE	4.42	2.00	4.50	1.77	4.20	1.59	4.82	1.67	5.93	1.39	4.07	1.70	4.28	1.41
	(-.13)		(-.37)		(-.37)		(.41)		(-.07)		(.17)		(.17)	
ROWS	4.91	1.78	4.34	1.85	3.97	1.93	3.27	1.66	5.87	1.62	3.23	1.63	3.75	1.05
	(.36)		(-.53)		(-.60)		(-1.14)		(-.13)		(-.67)		(-.36)	
RUNNING	4.40	2.06	5.21	1.86	4.72	1.96	4.73	1.76	6.61	.81	3.67	1.62	4.56	1.40F
	(-.15)		(.34)		(.15)		(.32)		(.61)		(-.23)		(.45)	
SAINT	4.54	2.09	3.88	2.13	4.82	1.93	3.78	1.69	5.37	1.82	4.23	2.01	4.31	1.59F
	(-.01)		(-.99)		(.25)		(-.63)		(-.63)		(.33)		(.20)	
SALTY	4.86	1.85	5.43	1.92	4.58	1.83	4.15	1.70	6.05	1.45	3.27	1.62	3.84	1.55
	(.31)		(.56)		(.01)		(-.26)		(.05)		(-.63)		(-.27)	
SALUTE	4.75	2.03	5.13	1.82	3.92	1.92	3.89	1.79	5.84	1.58	2.74	1.46	3.52	1.51
	(.20)		(.26)		(-.52)		(-.52)		(-.16)		(-1.16)		(-.59)	
SANCTUARY	4.82	2.00	4.75	1.88	4.35	1.94	4.13	2.00	5.23	1.86	3.89	1.71	4.34	1.64M
	(.27)		(-.12)		(-.22)		(-.28)		(-.77)		(-.01)		(.23)	
SANDY	4.95	2.06	5.48	1.64	4.49	1.72	3.90	1.73	6.02	1.30	3.54	1.47	5.13	1.48
	(.40)		(.61)		(-.08)		(-.51)		(.02)		(-.36)		(1.02)	
SAVAGE	4.25	2.09	5.50	1.74	4.60	1.68	4.58	1.48	5.66	1.68	3.86	1.54	3.38	1.81F
	(-.30)		(.63)		(.03)		(.17)		(-.34)		(-.04)		(-.73)	
SAW	4.64	2.16	4.76	2.14	4.59	2.13	3.90	1.52	6.31	1.30	3.30	1.50	3.80	1.13
	(.09)		(-.11)		(.02)		(-.51)		(.31)		(-.60)		(-.31)	
SCALE	4.82	2.20	4.60	2.28	4.32	1.69	4.05	1.48	5.82	1.62	3.84	1.61	3.56	1.19
	(.27)		(-.27)		(-.25)		(-.36)		(-.18)		(-.06)		(-.55)	
SCAVENGER	4.82	1.74	4.95	1.76	4.68	1.72	4.23	1.73	5.48	1.74	3.97	1.72	3.10	1.69
	(.27)		(.08)		(.11)		(-.18)		(-.52)		(.07)		(-1.01)	
SCENT	4.58	2.26	4.15	1.81	4.05	1.62	4.30	1.79	5.75	1.61	4.28	1.79	4.92	1.35
	(.03)		(-.72)		(-.52)		(-.11)		(-.25)		(.38)		(.81)	

	CON		IMG		CAT		MNG		FAM		NOA		PLS	
	M	SD	M	SD	M	SD	M	SD	M	SD	M	SD	M	SD
SCHOLAR	4.46	1.79	4.45	2.00	4.90	1.72	4.45	1.55	5.63	1.78	5.11	1.72	4.57	1.55F
	(-.09)		(-.42)		(.33)		(.04)		(-.37)		(1.21)		(.46)	
SCIENCE	4.14	2.25	3.96	2.23	5.12	1.94	5.12	1.82	6.42	.89	5.90	1.73	4.18	1.47
	(-.41)		(-.91)		(.55)		(.71)		(.42)		(2.00)		(.07)	
SHADY	4.04	2.02	4.81	2.09	3.98	1.97	4.60	1.63	6.07	1.40	3.43	1.66	4.35	1.63
	(-.51)		(-.06)		(-.59)		(.19)		(.07)		(-.47)		(.24)	
SHAPE	4.44	1.95	4.85	2.06	4.55	1.75	4.89	1.66	6.30	1.22	4.47	1.93	4.13	1.58M
	(-.11)		(-.02)		(-.02)		(.48)		(.30)		(.57)		(.02)	
SHEAR	4.52	1.85	4.78	1.93	4.30	1.84	3.67	1.83	5.02	1.91	3.48	1.48	3.74	1.34
	(-.03)		(-.09)		(-.27)		(-.74)		(-.98)		(-.42)		(-.37)	
SHINY	4.07	1.88	5.31	1.74	3.86	1.79	4.18	1.83	6.15	1.22	3.41	1.79	5.05	1.42
	(-.48)		(.44)		(-.71)		(-.23)		(.15)		(-.49)		(.94)	
SHOP	5.00	2.20	5.46	1.75	4.65	1.90	5.18	1.58	6.47	1.26	4.16	1.62	4.43	1.24
	(.45)		(.59)		(.08)		(.77)		(.47)		(.26)		(.32)	
SHOPPER	4.93	2.06	5.13	1.91	4.67	1.71	4.23	1.72	6.02	1.37	4.28	1.65	3.69	1.43
	(.38)		(.10)		(.10)		(-.18)		(.02)		(.38)		(-.42)	
SHOUT	4.67	2.04	4.94	2.09	4.37	1.77	5.25	1.61	5.90	1.47	3.30	1.60	3.38	1.60
	(.12)		(.07)		(-.20)		(.84)		(-.10)		(-.60)		(-.73)	
SHRIEK	4.89	1.82	4.62	2.29	4.33	1.91	4.53	1.61	5.56	1.59	3.47	2.12	3.01	1.39
	(.34)		(-.25)		(-.24)		(.12)		(-.44)		(-.43)		(-1.10)	
SIGN	5.16	2.08	5.28	1.80	4.57	1.96	4.33	1.48	6.17	1.22	3.75	1.72	3.81	.88
	(.61)		(.41)		(.00)		(-.08)		(.17)		(-.15)		(-.30)	
SING	4.17	2.09	5.21	1.75	4.40	2.01	4.72	1.91	6.50	1.10	3.87	1.57	5.59	1.20
	(-.38)		(.34)		(-.17)		(.31)		(.50)		(-.03)		(1.48)	
SIT	4.33	2.13	5.05	1.84	4.42	1.99	4.41	1.72	6.27	1.38	3.18	1.48	4.29	1.08
	(-.22)		(.18)		(-.15)		(.00)		(.27)		(-.72)		(.18)	
SLANG	3.91	2.04	4.10	1.95	4.18	1.77	4.36	1.74	6.07	1.41	3.93	1.80	4.03	1.30
	(-.64)		(-.77)		(-.39)		(-.05)		(.07)		(.03)		(-.08)	
SLAP	5.07	1.85	5.36	1.95	3.98	1.56	4.75	1.52	5.95	1.54	3.58	1.80	2.81	1.61
	(.52)		(.49)		(-.59)		(.34)		(-.05)		(-.32)		(-1.30)	
SLEEP	4.80	1.87	5.30	1.84	4.85	1.85	4.75	1.58	6.53	.92	3.92	1.64	5.41	1.55
	(.25)		(.43)		(.28)		(.34)		(.53)		(.02)		(1.30)	
SLICE	4.23	1.59	4.64	2.01	4.30	1.82	4.38	1.73	5.80	1.65	3.67	1.64	4.02	1.49
	(-.32)		(-.23)		(-.27)		(-.03)		(-.20)		(-.23)		(-.09)	
SLIDE	5.00	1.60	4.84	1.81	4.10	1.89	3.54	1.32	6.03	1.46	3.48	1.67	4.14	1.16
	(.45)		(-.03)		(-.47)		(-.87)		(.03)		(-.42)		(.03)	
SLIP	4.44	1.87	4.95	1.98	3.95	1.69	4.07	1.56	6.03	1.38	3.43	1.45	3.47	1.14
	(-.11)		(.08)		(-.62)		(-.34)		(.03)		(-.47)		(-.64)	
SMACK	4.47	1.96	5.95	1.43	3.80	1.77	4.81	1.66	5.85	1.63	3.46	1.70	3.39	1.80
	(-.08)		(1.08)		(-.77)		(.40)		(-.15)		(-.44)		(-.72)	
SMALL	3.98	2.13	4.78	1.99	5.32	1.82	5.63	1.46	6.80	.63	3.49	2.07	4.08	1.31F
	(-.57)		(-.09)		(.75)		(1.22)		(.80)		(-.41)		(-.03)	
SMELL	4.46	2.13	4.71	2.00	4.95	2.01	4.98	1.81	6.56	.94	4.26	1.87	3.88	1.74
	(-.09)		(-.16)		(.38)		(.57)		(.56)		(.36)		(-.23)	
SMOKE	5.23	2.08	5.88	1.51	4.53	1.85	5.34	1.72	6.51	1.29	3.90	1.59	3.13	1.95
	(.68)		(1.01)		(-.04)		(.93)		(.51)		(.00)		(-.98)	
SOLE	4.80	2.13	4.56	1.89	4.38	1.82	3.93	1.58	5.47	1.84	3.41	1.62	3.68	1.23
	(.25)		(-.31)		(-.19)		(-.48)		(-.53)		(-.49)		(-.43)	
SORE	4.98	1.98	4.80	1.80	4.17	1.68	4.31	1.69	6.18	1.38	3.71	1.61	2.74	1.40M
	(.43)		(-.07)		(-.40)		(-.10)		(.18)		(-.19)		(-1.37)	
SOUND	5.44	1.81	5.09	2.05	4.86	1.79	4.38	1.87	6.41	1.19	4.75	2.10	4.54	1.46
	(.89)		(.22)		(.29)		(-.03)		(.41)		(.85)		(.43)	
SOUR	4.54	1.98	5.13	1.98	4.93	1.76	4.33	1.75	6.11	1.32	3.41	1.72	3.07	1.49F
	(-.01)		(.26)		(.36)		(-.08)		(.11)		(-.49)		(-1.04)	

	CON		IMG		CAT		MNG		FAM		NOA		PLS	
	M	SD	M	SD	M	SD	M	SD	M	SD	M	SD	M	SD
SOUTH	3.43 1.95 (-1.12)		4.70 2.18 (-.17)		5.33 1.77 (.76)		4.34 1.78 (-.07)		6.14 1.48 (.14)		3.49 2.13 (-.41)		4.02 1.14 (-.09)	
SPARK	5.22 1.86 (.67)		5.33 1.64 (.46)		3.88 1.60 (-.69)		4.49 1.51 (.08)		5.79 1.51 (-.21)		3.57 1.61 (-.33)		4.39 1.45 (.28)	
SPEAK	4.15 2.02 (-.40)		4.81 1.93 (-.06)		4.02 1.87 (-.55)		5.08 1.73 (.67)		6.52 1.07 (.52)		3.95 1.94 (.05)		4.65 1.47 (.54)	
SPECIMEN	4.77 1.97 (.22)		4.11 1.96 (-.76)		5.03 1.78 (.46)		4.05 1.59 (-.36)		5.86 1.33 (-.14)		4.07 1.73 (.17)		3.46 1.37 (-.65)	
SPECK	4.65 2.13 (.10)		4.89 1.81 (.02)		4.05 1.86 (-.52)		3.81 1.69 (-.60)		5.79 1.55 (-.21)		3.08 1.85 (-.82)		3.43 1.35 (-.68)	
SPICY	4.74 1.90 (.19)		4.88 1.89 (.01)		4.42 1.49 (-.15)		4.50 1.35 (.09)		5.83 1.51 (-.17)		4.23 1.64 (.33)		4.60 1.28F (.49)	
SPOKE	4.70 2.03 (.15)		4.09 1.99 (-.78)		4.03 1.96 (-.54)		4.13 1.51 (-.28)		6.24 1.21 (.24)		3.39 1.62 (-.51)		4.00 1.15 (-.11)	
SPOT	4.77 1.98 (.22)		4.57 2.00 (-.30)		4.30 1.78 (-.27)		4.42 1.49 (.01)		6.08 1.50 (.08)		3.07 1.64 (-.83)		3.41 1.43 (-.70)	
SPRAY	4.81 1.84 (.26)		5.24 1.86 (.37)		4.12 1.90 (-.45)		4.15 1.79 (-.26)		6.05 1.51 (.05)		3.28 1.50 (-.62)		4.00 1.40 (-.11)	
SQUIRT	4.49 2.18 (-.06)		4.90 1.93 (.03)		3.92 1.79 (-.65)		3.92 1.95 (-.49)		5.66 1.61 (-.34)		2.90 1.45 (-1.00)		4.03 1.67 (-.08)	
STABLE	5.20 2.13 (.65)		4.86 2.12 (-.01)		4.28 1.80 (-.29)		4.90 1.67 (.49)		6.02 1.40 (.02)		3.70 1.52 (-.20)		4.48 1.48F (.37)	
STAND	4.46 1.95 (-.09)		5.04 2.05 (.17)		4.37 1.78 (-.20)		4.17 1.83 (-.24)		5.92 1.67 (-.08)		3.48 1.71 (-.42)		4.11 1.24 (.00)	
STATE	4.36 2.03 (-.19)		5.05 1.92 (.18)		5.10 1.72 (.53)		4.66 1.76 (.25)		6.34 1.25 (.34)		4.45 2.00 (.55)		4.00 1.37 (-.11)	
STATES	4.51 2.08 (-.04)		4.75 1.93 (-.12)		5.17 1.77 (.60)		4.90 1.65 (.49)		5.81 1.51 (-.19)		5.08 1.86 (1.18)		4.16 1.15 (.05)	
STEP	4.91 1.97 (.36)		4.34 1.98 (-.53)		4.08 1.86 (-.49)		4.13 1.63 (-.28)		6.22 1.16 (.22)		3.21 1.57 (-.69)		3.70 .91 (-.41)	
STORE	5.44 1.90 (.89)		5.00 1.98 (.13)		4.77 2.09 (.20)		4.73 1.75 (.32)		6.36 1.13 (.36)		5.05 1.86 (1.15)		4.48 1.14 (.37)	
STORM	4.92 2.00 (.37)		5.59 1.87 (.72)		5.05 1.89 (.48)		5.24 1.58 (.83)		6.40 1.15 (.40)		4.38 1.60 (.48)		4.25 1.66 (.14)	
STORY	4.23 1.96 (-.32)		5.04 2.06 (.17)		4.92 1.63 (.35)		5.18 1.45 (.77)		6.15 1.41 (.15)		5.39 1.59 (1.49)		5.08 1.30F (.97)	
STOUT	4.09 1.93 (-.46)		5.15 1.75 (.28)		4.28 1.84 (-.29)		4.92 1.60 (.51)		5.85 1.68 (-.15)		3.30 1.64 (-.60)		3.85 1.81M (-.26)	
STRAIGHT	4.00 2.15 (-.55)		4.41 1.91 (-.46)		4.12 1.79 (-.26)		4.15 2.01 (-.26)		6.33 1.01 (.33)		3.29 1.83 (-.61)		4.13 1.32 (.02)	
STREAMER	5.14 2.05 (.59)		4.98 1.91 (.11)		4.31 2.02 (-.26)		3.15 1.72 (-1.26)		5.49 1.61 (-.51)		3.28 1.67 (-.62)		4.35 1.36 (.24)	
STROKE	4.59 1.70 (.04)		4.75 1.91 (-.12)		4.42 1.93 (-.15)		4.41 1.70 (.00)		5.85 1.50 (-.15)		3.76 1.75 (-.14)		3.10 1.85F (-1.01)	
STUDYING	3.75 1.99 (-.80)		5.26 1.96 (.39)		4.03 1.72 (-.54)		4.64 1.69 (.23)		6.53 .99 (.53)		4.29 1.69 (.39)		3.60 1.52F (-.51)	
STUMP	5.14 2.05 (.59)		4.74 2.23 (-.13)		4.63 1.71 (.06)		4.11 1.86 (-.30)		5.60 1.65 (-.40)		3.65 1.42 (-.25)		3.20 1.42M (-.91)	
STUNT	3.89 1.88 (-.66)		4.23 1.85 (-.64)		4.09 1.69 (-.48)		3.78 1.60 (-.63)		5.64 1.62 (-.36)		3.73 1.68 (-.17)		4.25 1.19M (.14)	
SUE	4.28 2.19 (-.27)		4.43 2.41 (-.44)		4.52 2.23 (-.05)		3.95 1.76 (-.46)		6.02 1.55 (.02)		3.77 2.02 (-.13)		3.72 1.91M (-.39)	
SUM	3.50 2.03 (-1.05)		4.67 1.77 (-.20)		4.68 1.74 (.11)		4.29 1.69 (-.12)		6.07 1.46 (.07)		3.75 1.90 (-.15)		4.33 1.19 (.22)	

	CON		IMG		CAT		MNG		FAM		NOA		PLS	
	M	SD	M	SD	M	SD	M	SD	M	SD	M	SD	M	SD
SWALLOW	5.02	2.14	5.29	1.69	4.73	1.70	4.39	1.66	6.36	1.29	3.05	1.51	4.12	1.43F
	(.47)		(.42)		(.16)		(-.02)		(.36)		(-.85)		(.01)	
SWEEP	4.82	1.83	5.06	1.95	4.35	1.75	4.15	1.56	5.83	1.44	3.38	1.37	3.97	1.24
	(.27)		(.19)		(-.22)		(-.26)		(-.17)		(-.52)		(-.14)	
SWEET	4.59	2.03	5.04	1.68	4.82	1.64	4.95	1.54	6.15	1.51	3.80	1.81	5.55	1.34
	(.04)		(.17)		(.25)		(.54)		(.15)		(-.10)		(1.44)	
TALES	4.41	2.16	4.60	1.99	4.47	1.94	5.03	1.59	6.03	1.47	4.25	1.82	4.22	1.42
	(-.14)		(-.27)		(-.10)		(.62)		(.03)		(.35)		(.11)	
TALK	4.18	2.10	5.02	2.00	4.58	1.98	5.66	1.59	6.75	.70	4.88	1.98	4.90	1.62F
	(-.37)		(.15)		(.01)		(1.25)		(.75)		(.98)		(.79)	
TALL	4.35	1.87	5.53	1.56	5.15	1.70	5.25	1.80	6.41	1.28	3.64	1.70	4.75	1.34
	(-.20)		(.66)		(.58)		(.84)		(.41)		(-.26)		(.64)	
TAP	4.95	1.74	5.30	1.97	4.18	1.79	4.10	1.87	5.86	1.54	3.43	1.77	4.48	.95
	(.40)		(.43)		(-.39)		(-.31)		(-.14)		(-.47)		(.37)	
TASTE	4.60	2.04	4.42	2.08	4.27	2.02	4.31	1.68	6.22	1.19	4.34	1.91	5.24	1.21F
	(.05)		(-.45)		(-.30)		(-.10)		(.22)		(.44)		(1.13)	
TAX	4.34	2.13	4.27	2.00	4.93	1.75	3.98	1.63	6.00	1.55	4.59	1.83	2.81	1.40
	(-.21)		(-.60)		(.36)		(-.43)		(.00)		(.69)		(-1.30)	
TEMPERATURE	4.68	1.78	4.54	2.15	4.60	1.90	4.15	1.96	6.21	1.34	4.45	1.91	3.94	1.14
	(.13)		(-.33)		(.03)		(-.26)		(.21)		(.55)		(-.17)	
TEMPLE	5.52	1.95	5.02	1.96	4.90	1.95	4.27	1.49	5.34	1.83	4.61	1.94	4.29	1.37
	(.97)		(.15)		(.33)		(-.14)		(-.66)		(.71)		(.18)	
TEST	5.16	2.12	5.22	1.94	4.87	1.93	4.87	1.84	6.40	1.15	5.13	1.88	2.82	1.41
	(.61)		(.35)		(.30)		(.46)		(.40)		(1.23)		(-1.29)	
THIN	3.88	2.14	5.22	1.84	5.02	1.84	4.74	1.70	6.25	1.41	3.43	1.71	4.69	1.58F
	(-.67)		(.35)		(.45)		(.33)		(.25)		(-.47)		(.58)	
THIRSTY	4.47	2.09	4.93	2.09	4.58	1.73	4.43	1.62	6.63	1.00	3.65	1.78	3.24	1.58
	(-.08)		(.06)		(.01)		(.02)		(.63)		(-.25)		(-.87)	
THROW	4.11	1.66	4.80	1.98	3.79	1.86	4.18	1.50	6.08	1.51	3.48	1.87	4.05	1.28
	(-.44)		(-.07)		(-.78)		(-.23)		(.08)		(-.42)		(-.06)	
TICKLE	4.69	2.19	4.86	2.04	4.07	1.85	3.71	1.86	5.98	1.33	3.34	1.83	5.08	1.34
	(.14)		(-.01)		(-.50)		(-.70)		(-.02)		(-.56)		(.97)	
TIDE	5.20	1.84	4.98	1.99	4.90	1.71	4.08	1.74	5.92	1.38	4.00	1.73	5.00	1.60F
	(.65)		(.11)		(.33)		(-.33)		(-.08)		(.10)		(.89)	
TIGHT	4.21	1.89	4.89	1.89	3.80	1.77	4.57	1.90	6.29	1.28	3.63	1.91	3.57	1.72
	(-.34)		(.02)		(-.77)		(.16)		(.29)		(-.27)		(-.54)	
TIP	4.55	1.93	4.85	1.82	4.08	1.81	3.74	1.71	5.58	1.70	3.10	1.67	4.45	1.30
	(.00)		(-.02)		(-.49)		(-.67)		(-.42)		(-.80)		(.34)	
TOP	4.31	2.15	5.12	1.66	4.77	1.92	4.77	1.78	6.05	1.42	3.49	1.89	4.40	1.26
	(-.24)		(.25)		(.20)		(.36)		(.05)		(-.41)		(.29)	
TOUGH	4.00	1.89	4.80	1.87	4.22	1.77	4.56	1.71	6.08	1.36	3.87	1.43	3.52	1.36
	(-.55)		(-.07)		(-.35)		(.15)		(.08)		(-.03)		(-.59)	
TOURIST	5.29	2.12	5.71	1.64	4.98	1.93	4.98	1.62	6.10	1.47	4.44	1.81	3.72	1.71
	(.74)		(.84)		(.41)		(.57)		(.10)		(.54)		(-.39)	
TRAIL	5.30	1.93	5.65	1.58	4.42	1.76	4.66	1.52	6.20	1.35	3.90	1.76	4.49	1.81
	(.75)		(.78)		(-.15)		(.25)		(.20)		(.00)		(.38)	
TRANSPORTATION	4.30	2.18	4.48	1.93	4.48	1.87	5.70	1.39	6.30	1.12	5.80	1.71	4.33	1.40
	(-.25)		(-.39)		(-.09)		(1.29)		(.30)		(1.90)		(.22)	
TRIAL	4.92	1.84	5.27	1.79	4.13	1.79	4.33	1.63	6.10	1.36	4.30	1.50	3.07	1.30
	(.37)		(.40)		(-.44)		(-.08)		(.10)		(.40)		(-1.04)	
TRIBE	5.00	1.79	5.09	1.68	5.19	1.65	4.12	1.62	5.77	1.36	4.62	1.76	4.21	1.35
	(.45)		(.22)		(.62)		(-.29)		(-.23)		(.72)		(.10)	
TROOP	5.20	1.83	5.20	1.58	4.62	1.76	4.56	1.65	5.84	1.52	4.33	1.87	3.31	1.49
	(.65)		(.33)		(.05)		(.15)		(-.16)		(.43)		(-.80)	

	CON M	SD	IMG M	SD	CAT M	SD	MNG M	SD	FAM M	SD	NOA M	SD	PLS M	SD
TUNE	4.60	1.94	4.57	1.98	4.80	1.87	4.87	1.47	6.19	1.35	5.13	1.72	5.34	1.39F
	(.05)		(-.30)		(.23)		(.46)		(.19)		(1.23)		(1.23)	
TWIST	4.19	1.90	5.23	1.56	4.36	1.88	4.27	1.71	5.84	1.39	3.26	1.35	3.87	1.55
	(-.36)		(.36)		(-.21)		(-.14)		(-.16)		(-.64)		(-.24)	
TWO	3.79	2.17	4.39	2.22	5.48	2.09	3.89	2.34	6.70	.94	2.56	1.82	4.64	1.65F
	(-.76)		(-.48)		(.91)		(-.52)		(.70)		(-1.34)		(.53)	
TYPE	4.40	1.88	4.31	2.03	3.92	1.83	4.38	1.64	6.40	1.06	3.60	1.76	3.61	1.54
	(-.15)		(-.56)		(-.65)		(-.03)		(.40)		(-.30)		(-.50)	
UPRIGHT	3.58	1.87	4.70	1.69	4.55	1.89	4.11	1.69	5.71	1.63	3.34	1.68	4.50	1.39
	(-.97)		(-.17)		(-.02)		(-.30)		(-.29)		(-.56)		(.39)	
URBAN	4.16	2.06	4.70	1.81	4.32	1.87	5.00	1.47	5.92	1.45	4.43	1.92	3.38	1.42
	(-.39)		(-.17)		(-.25)		(.59)		(-.08)		(.53)		(-.73)	
VET	4.81	2.26	4.88	2.21	4.95	1.95	3.82	1.74	5.30	1.81	3.54	1.79	4.07	1.36
	(.26)		(.01)		(.38)		(-.59)		(-.70)		(-.36)		(-.04)	
VOTE	3.85	2.07	5.27	2.01	4.23	1.78	4.43	1.74	6.47	1.05	3.94	1.98	4.07	1.64
	(-.70)		(.40)		(-.34)		(.02)		(.47)		(-.04)		(-.04)	
VOTER	5.44	1.83	4.86	2.09	5.02	1.75	4.50	1.46	6.41	.97	3.97	1.92	4.38	1.38
	(.89)		(-.01)		(.45)		(.09)		(.41)		(.07)		(.27)	
WAGE	4.39	2.19	3.88	2.18	4.37	1.93	4.79	1.84	6.02	1.65	3.33	1.70	4.46	1.73
	(-.16)		(-.99)		(-.20)		(.38)		(.02)		(-.57)		(.35)	
WALK	4.40	1.90	5.05	2.03	4.97	1.80	4.70	1.83	6.57	.76	3.79	1.80	5.12	1.32
	(-.15)		(.18)		(.40)		(.29)		(.57)		(-.11)		(1.01)	
WALTZ	4.69	2.04	4.94	2.06	5.72	1.72	4.33	1.62	5.27	1.93	3.85	1.82	4.38	1.65F
	(.07)		(.07)		(1.15)		(-.08)		(-.73)		(-.05)		(.27)	
WASH	4.20	1.81	4.98	1.86	4.17	1.88	5.11	1.67	6.59	.90	3.67	1.80	4.07	1.75
	(-.35)		(.11)		(-.40)		(.70)		(.59)		(-.23)		(-.04)	
WATCH	4.83	2.01	5.19	2.01	4.67	1.83	4.45	1.51	6.25	1.21	4.11	1.70	4.05	1.39
	(.28)		(.32)		(.10)		(.04)		(.25)		(.21)		(-.06)	
WATTS	4.58	2.11	4.22	2.07	4.57	1.93	3.68	1.98	5.36	1.78	3.18	1.65	3.86	1.83M
	(.03)		(-.65)		(.00)		(-.73)		(-.64)		(-.72)		(-.25)	
WAVE	4.88	2.00	5.36	2.02	4.88	1.70	4.02	1.82	5.92	1.48	3.25	1.54	4.95	1.24F
	(.33)		(.49)		(.31)		(-.39)		(-.08)		(-.65)		(.84)	
WEEK	3.79	2.13	4.75	2.14	5.48	1.72	4.46	2.00	6.51	1.08	3.64	1.94	3.81	1.38
	(-.76)		(-.12)		(.91)		(.05)		(.51)		(-.26)		(-.30)	
WEIGHT	4.58	1.83	5.15	1.77	4.39	1.69	4.57	1.74	6.52	1.15	3.97	1.94	3.41	1.49M
	(.03)		(.28)		(-.18)		(.16)		(.52)		(.07)		(-.70)	
WELL	4.63	2.13	5.16	1.69	4.47	2.01	4.18	1.48	6.24	1.15	3.59	1.50	4.41	1.46
	(.08)		(.29)		(-.10)		(-.23)		(.24)		(-.31)		(.30)	
WEST	4.03	2.09	3.98	1.99	5.17	2.01	4.17	1.80	6.41	1.08	3.64	1.90	5.19	1.34
	(-.52)		(-.89)		(.60)		(-.24)		(.41)		(-.26)		(1.08)	
WET	4.74	2.28	4.91	1.98	4.55	1.93	4.58	1.74	6.32	1.24	3.13	1.84	3.90	1.35
	(.19)		(.04)		(-.02)		(.17)		(.32)		(-.77)		(-.21)	
WIDE	3.44	1.96	4.71	1.96	4.53	1.83	5.20	1.61	6.30	1.32	3.43	1.83	3.90	1.66M
	(-1.11)		(-.16)		(-.04)		(.79)		(.30)		(-.47)		(-.21)	
WIND	5.48	1.53	5.29	1.88	4.53	1.89	5.13	1.79	6.66	1.03	3.44	1.57	4.23	1.67
	(.93)		(.42)		(-.04)		(.72)		(.66)		(-.46)		(.12)	
WINK	5.11	1.86	4.95	1.84	4.08	1.82	3.62	1.63	5.95	1.44	2.89	1.60	5.21	1.27
	(.56)		(.08)		(-.49)		(-.79)		(-.05)		(-1.01)		(1.10)	
WIZARD	4.69	2.33	5.45	1.75	4.65	1.96	4.10	1.79	5.47	1.75	4.13	1.54	4.85	1.59M
	(.14)		(.58)		(.08)		(-.31)		(-.53)		(.23)		(.74)	
WORK	3.98	2.14	4.52	2.15	4.43	1.58	5.58	1.75	6.77	.79	4.62	1.92	4.12	1.57
	(-.57)		(-.35)		(-.14)		(1.17)		(.77)		(.72)		(.01)	
WRAP	4.53	1.95	4.76	1.87	3.98	1.94	4.20	1.87	6.23	1.33	3.35	1.66	4.55	1.23F
	(-.02)		(-.11)		(-.59)		(-.21)		(.23)		(-.55)		(.44)	

	CON		IMG		CAT		MNG		FAM		NOA		PLS	
	M	SD	M	SD	M	SD	M	SD	M	SD	M	SD	M	SD
WRITE	4.42	2.11	5.42	1.84	5.40	1.78	4.92	1.76	6.34	1.42	5.02	1.67	4.71	1.43F
	(-.13)		(.55)		(.83)		(.51)		(.34)		(1.12)		(.60)	
YAWN	4.98	2.11	5.39	1.97	4.37	1.77	4.00	2.14	6.41	1.23	3.13	1.49	3.58	1.34
	(.43)		(.52)		(-.20)		(-.41)		(.41)		(-.77)		(-.53)	
YEAR	3.44	2.11	4.15	2.06	5.33	1.59	4.37	1.89	6.41	1.15	4.69	2.06	4.55	1.04
	(-1.11)		(-.72)		(.76)		(-.04)		(.41)		(.79)		(.44)	
YELL	4.35	2.07	4.95	1.92	4.55	1.62	4.52	1.74	5.83	1.45	3.11	1.64	3.32	1.53
	(-.20)		(.08)		(-.02)		(.11)		(-.17)		(-.79)		(-.79)	
YOUTH	4.18	2.12	4.82	1.72	5.02	1.75	5.61	1.52	6.45	1.02	4.95	1.60	5.62	1.42
	(-.37)		(-.05)		(.45)		(1.20)		(.45)		(1.05)		(1.51)	
ZONE	3.88	2.02	4.56	2.13	4.05	1.86	3.89	1.67	5.70	1.62	3.67	1.72	3.94	1.41
	(-.67)		(-.31)		(-.52)		(-.52)		(-.30)		(-.23)		(-.17)	

CLUSTER 7

	CON		IMG		CAT		MNG		FAM		NOA		PLS	
	M	SD	M	SD	M	SD	M	SD	M	SD	M	SD	M	SD
ACCORDION	5.72	1.99	5.31	2.02	5.43	2.10	3.52	1.90	4.83	1.98	3.61	1.86	4.05	1.16
	(.07)		(-.18)		(.09)		(-.53)		(-.91)		(.13)		(.35)	
ADMIRAL	5.00	2.17	4.89	1.94	5.66	1.86	3.81	1.84	4.98	1.94	3.66	2.01	3.69	1.72F
	(-.65)		(-.60)		(.32)		(-.24)		(-.76)		(.18)		(-.01)	
ALE	5.74	1.60	5.20	1.98	4.63	2.15	4.10	1.92	5.28	1.69	3.51	1.75	4.68	1.58M
	(.09)		(-.29)		(-.71)		(.05)		(-.46)		(.03)		(.98)	
ALLEY	5.53	1.79	5.66	1.70	5.25	1.76	4.18	1.56	6.00	1.49	3.92	1.64	3.47	1.29
	(-.12)		(.17)		(-.09)		(.13)		(.26)		(.44)		(-.23)	
ALLIGATOR	6.54	1.28	6.06	1.39	6.27	1.42	4.25	2.01	5.71	1.67	3.59	2.13	3.61	1.74M
	(.89)		(.57)		(.93)		(.20)		(-.03)		(.11)		(-.09)	
ALUMINUM	5.19	2.01	4.95	2.09	5.50	1.96	3.81	1.95	5.68	1.65	3.25	1.65	4.38	1.17M
	(-.46)		(-.54)		(.16)		(-.24)		(-.06)		(-.23)		(.68)	
AMBASSADOR	5.44	1.83	5.32	1.89	5.52	1.73	3.92	1.71	5.55	1.73	3.90	1.70	4.24	1.34F
	(-.21)		(-.17)		(.18)		(-.13)		(-.19)		(.42)		(.54)	
AMMONIA	5.59	1.97	5.30	2.02	5.47	1.76	3.43	1.73	5.98	1.40	2.70	1.48	2.60	1.36
	(-.06)		(-.19)		(.13)		(-.62)		(.24)		(-.78)		(-1.10)	
ANCHOR	5.91	1.62	5.55	1.82	5.14	1.66	3.90	1.66	5.32	1.80	3.56	1.63	4.51	1.29
	(.26)		(.06)		(-.20)		(-.15)		(-.42)		(.08)		(.81)	
ANT	6.00	1.92	6.07	1.67	6.40	1.43	4.15	2.03	6.15	1.70	3.16	1.83	2.95	1.44M
	(.35)		(.58)		(1.06)		(.10)		(.41)		(-.32)		(-.75)	
ARK	5.57	1.92	5.11	2.04	4.37	1.97	3.92	1.94	4.91	1.98	3.79	1.82	4.47	1.28
	(-.08)		(-.38)		(-.97)		(-.13)		(-.83)		(.31)		(.77)	
ARMOR	5.40	1.93	5.12	1.86	5.03	1.80	3.63	1.60	5.23	1.93	3.50	1.84	3.78	1.36
	(-.25)		(-.37)		(-.31)		(-.42)		(-.51)		(.02)		(.08)	
ARMY	5.24	2.12	5.49	1.85	5.27	1.97	5.15	1.93	6.22	1.60	4.14	2.03	2.38	1.57
	(-.41)		(.00)		(-.07)		(1.10)		(.48)		(.66)		(-1.32)	
ASH	5.41	2.06	5.62	1.87	5.05	1.71	3.50	1.48	5.82	1.58	3.30	1.70	3.85	1.56M
	(-.24)		(.13)		(-.29)		(-.55)		(.08)		(-.18)		(.15)	
ASPARAGUS	6.04	1.86	5.84	1.56	6.18	1.69	4.42	2.14	6.08	1.39	2.85	1.75	3.82	2.02
	(.39)		(.35)		(.84)		(.37)		(.34)		(-.63)		(.12)	
ASPHALT	5.79	1.71	5.63	1.51	5.10	1.87	3.85	1.73	5.62	1.68	3.17	1.89	3.07	1.32
	(.14)		(.14)		(-.24)		(-.20)		(-.12)		(-.31)		(-.63)	
ASPIRIN	5.70	1.97	5.36	2.11	5.85	1.56	4.45	1.90	6.20	1.28	3.10	1.77	3.35	1.46
	(.05)		(-.13)		(.51)		(.40)		(.46)		(-.38)		(-.35)	
AUDITORIUM	5.48	1.96	5.67	1.78	5.36	1.81	3.80	1.77	5.93	1.46	4.11	2.12	3.63	1.34
	(-.17)		(.18)		(.02)		(-.25)		(.19)		(.63)		(-.07)	
AXLE	5.51	2.04	5.54	1.72	5.15	1.91	3.57	1.91	5.56	1.74	3.14	1.80	3.40	1.24
	(-.14)		(.05)		(-.19)		(-.48)		(-.18)		(-.34)		(-.30)	
BACTERIA	5.62	1.85	4.80	1.92	5.48	1.95	4.37	1.89	5.56	1.41	4.74	1.63	2.90	1.21
	(-.03)		(-.69)		(.14)		(.32)		(-.18)		(1.26)		(-.80)	
BADGE	5.57	1.78	5.13	1.95	5.27	1.73	4.10	1.73	5.47	1.59	3.93	1.69	3.56	1.52
	(-.08)		(-.36)		(-.07)		(.05)		(-.27)		(.45)		(-.14)	
BAGPIPE	5.79	1.79	5.64	1.66	5.67	1.95	3.80	1.96	4.85	1.94	3.52	1.90	4.79	1.14
	(.14)		(.15)		(.33)		(-.25)		(-.89)		(.04)		(1.09)	
BANDAGE	6.35	1.13	5.48	1.85	5.33	1.78	4.82	1.72	6.20	1.34	3.13	1.44	2.87	1.36
	(.70)		(-.01)		(-.01)		(.77)		(.46)		(-.35)		(-.83)	
BANKER	5.16	2.03	5.53	1.51	5.90	1.55	4.27	1.91	6.03	1.44	4.14	2.13	3.84	1.55M
	(-.49)		(.04)		(.56)		(.22)		(.29)		(.66)		(.14)	
BARK	5.59	1.72	5.33	1.83	5.20	1.77	4.33	1.76	5.92	1.52	3.51	1.47	4.00	1.38M
	(-.06)		(-.16)		(-.14)		(.28)		(.18)		(.03)		(.30)	
BARREL	5.77	1.85	5.80	1.61	5.32	1.71	3.85	1.65	6.12	1.44	3.56	1.54	4.02	1.24
	(.12)		(.31)		(-.02)		(-.20)		(.38)		(.08)		(.32)	
BASEMENT	5.83	1.76	5.59	1.79	5.52	1.68	4.52	1.76	5.76	1.59	3.97	1.88	4.05	1.23
	(.18)		(.10)		(.18)		(.47)		(.02)		(.49)		(.35)	

	CON		IMG		CAT		MNG		FAM		NOA		PLS	
	M	SD	M	SD	M	SD	M	SD	M	SD	M	SD	M	SD
BASIN	5.93	1.61	5.52	1.91	5.18	1.65	4.05	1.79	5.65	1.67	3.52	1.75	3.78	1.28F
	(.28)		(.03)		(-.16)		(.00)		(-.09)		(.04)		(.08)	
BASKET	6.02	1.59	5.54	1.81	4.58	2.09	4.07	1.82	5.81	1.56	3.80	1.46	4.40	1.31F
	(.37)		(.05)		(-.76)		(.02)		(.07)		(.32)		(.70)	
BAT	5.60	2.01	5.80	2.00	6.30	1.41	4.12	2.02	5.88	1.61	3.34	1.94	3.06	1.55M
	(-.05)		(.31)		(.96)		(.07)		(.14)		(-.14)		(-.64)	
BATON	5.66	1.96	5.10	2.11	4.27	2.07	3.38	2.01	4.98	1.95	2.87	1.48	3.80	1.40
	(.01)		(-.39)		(-1.07)		(-.67)		(-.76)		(-.61)		(.10)	
BATTLE	5.60	1.53	5.91	1.60	4.97	1.53	4.95	1.62	6.11	1.38	4.41	1.66	2.93	1.76
	(-.05)		(.42)		(-.37)		(.90)		(.37)		(.93)		(-.77)	
BEAK	5.48	2.11	5.68	1.69	5.15	1.91	3.85	1.93	5.50	1.81	3.40	1.57	3.92	1.32
	(-.17)		(.19)		(-.19)		(-.20)		(-.24)		(-.08)		(.22)	
BEAN	6.00	1.67	5.32	1.75	5.77	1.71	3.71	1.85	6.23	1.29	3.69	1.77	4.03	1.11
	(.35)		(-.17)		(.43)		(-.34)		(.49)		(.21)		(.33)	
BEE	5.93	1.94	6.17	1.44	6.17	1.63	4.41	1.94	6.28	1.34	3.66	1.80	3.30	1.52
	(.28)		(.68)		(.83)		(.36)		(.54)		(.18)		(-.40)	
BEET	6.41	1.41	5.49	1.76	5.82	1.67	3.97	2.02	5.71	1.81	3.05	1.68	3.92	1.54
	(.76)		(.00)		(.48)		(-.08)		(-.03)		(-.43)		(.22)	
BEETLE	6.15	1.58	6.34	1.20	6.37	1.34	4.44	1.63	5.77	1.48	4.09	1.82	3.14	1.65M
	(.50)		(.85)		(1.03)		(.39)		(.03)		(.61)		(-.56)	
BEGGAR	5.12	1.96	5.93	1.52	5.40	1.59	4.72	1.55	5.76	1.54	4.27	1.90	2.88	1.60
	(-.53)		(.44)		(.06)		(.67)		(.02)		(.79)		(-.82)	
BELLY	6.26	1.07	5.70	1.75	5.73	1.54	4.40	1.59	5.60	1.78	3.62	1.67	3.70	1.56
	(.61)		(.21)		(.39)		(.35)		(-.14)		(.14)		(.00)	
BELT	5.98	1.54	4.88	2.08	5.57	1.72	3.98	1.66	6.24	1.13	3.49	1.68	3.84	1.12
	(.33)		(-.61)		(.23)		(-.07)		(.50)		(.01)		(.14)	
BERET	5.74	1.77	5.11	2.19	5.33	1.80	3.92	1.82	4.93	1.91	3.31	1.66	3.97	1.49F
	(.09)		(-.38)		(-.01)		(-.13)		(-.81)		(-.17)		(.27)	
BIB	5.44	1.97	4.82	2.01	4.95	1.88	3.57	1.62	4.44	2.18	2.82	1.60	3.59	1.36
	(-.21)		(-.67)		(-.39)		(-.48)		(-1.30)		(-.66)		(-.11)	
BILL	5.36	2.01	5.61	1.78	5.00	1.85	4.28	1.90	6.39	1.14	4.16	1.65	3.12	1.65
	(-.29)		(.12)		(-.34)		(.23)		(.68)		(.68)		(-.58)	
BINOCULARS	5.73	1.91	5.75	1.80	5.19	1.83	3.44	1.81	5.75	1.62	3.60	1.96	4.18	1.48
	(.08)		(.26)		(-.15)		(-.61)		(.01)		(.12)		(.48)	
BISHOP	5.83	1.78	5.18	1.67	5.45	1.71	4.37	1.76	5.41	1.73	3.82	1.88	4.05	1.55
	(.18)		(-.31)		(.11)		(.32)		(-.33)		(.34)		(.35)	
BLACK	4.66	2.11	5.90	1.72	5.42	2.16	4.93	1.97	6.58	1.06	3.13	2.12	3.49	1.66M
	(-.99)		(.41)		(.08)		(.88)		(.84)		(-.35)		(-.21)	
BLACKSMITH	5.90	1.72	5.55	1.91	5.27	1.89	3.69	1.90	5.48	1.90	4.00	1.92	3.90	1.50M
	(.25)		(.06)		(-.07)		(-.36)		(-.26)		(.52)		(.20)	
BLADE	5.80	1.82	5.70	1.71	4.72	1.79	4.23	1.73	5.87	1.51	3.39	1.72	3.50	1.51M
	(.15)		(.21)		(-.62)		(.18)		(.13)		(-.09)		(-.20)	
BLEACH	5.40	1.83	5.04	1.90	4.83	1.90	3.87	1.82	6.23	1.41	3.49	1.60	3.50	1.47M
	(-.25)		(-.45)		(-.51)		(-.18)		(.49)		(.01)		(-.20)	
BLOOD	6.55	.99	5.67	1.77	5.72	1.63	4.67	1.86	6.02	1.41	4.20	1.85	2.89	1.30M
	(.90)		(.18)		(.38)		(.62)		(.28)		(.72)		(-.81)	
BOAR	5.54	1.96	5.18	2.09	5.40	1.98	3.85	1.76	5.29	1.82	3.44	1.81	2.82	1.40F
	(-.11)		(-.31)		(.06)		(-.20)		(-.45)		(-.04)		(-.88)	
BOARD	5.39	2.01	5.98	1.43	4.84	1.78	3.89	1.74	6.00	1.43	3.43	1.78	3.97	1.19
	(-.26)		(.49)		(-.50)		(-.16)		(.26)		(-.05)		(.27)	
BOLT	5.27	1.95	5.88	1.56	4.92	1.70	4.00	1.67	5.79	1.49	3.69	1.64	3.75	1.46
	(-.38)		(.39)		(-.42)		(-.05)		(.05)		(.21)		(.05)	
BOMB	5.91	1.79	6.00	1.50	5.77	1.57	4.97	1.97	6.40	1.17	4.52	1.79	2.22	1.52M
	(.26)		(.51)		(.43)		(.92)		(.66)		(1.04)		(-1.48)	

	CON		IMG		CAT		MNG		FAM		NOA		PLS	
	M	SD	M	SD	M	SD	M	SD	M	SD	M	SD	M	SD
BONE	5.84	1.85	5.61	1.61	5.55	1.80	4.18	1.80	6.15	1.57	4.02	1.61	3.64	1.30
	(.19)		(.12)		(.21)		(.13)		(.41)		(.54)		(-.06)	
BOOTH	5.64	1.66	5.28	1.98	4.45	1.71	4.08	1.54	5.92	1.42	3.58	1.51	4.04	1.25
	(-.01)		(-.21)		(-.89)		(.03)		(.18)		(.10)		(.34)	
BOW	5.78	1.65	5.26	1.86	4.60	1.91	4.48	1.70	5.70	1.58	3.87	1.65	3.71	1.53
	(.13)		(-.23)		(-.74)		(.43)		(-.04)		(.39)		(.01)	
BOWL	5.34	1.97	5.66	1.67	5.66	1.64	4.47	1.68	6.20	1.17	3.21	1.76	4.13	1.44
	(-.31)		(.17)		(.32)		(.42)		(.46)		(-.27)		(.43)	
BRAKE	5.22	2.01	5.05	1.91	4.72	1.92	4.37	1.69	6.25	1.37	3.25	1.51	3.57	1.47
	(-.43)		(-.44)		(-.62)		(.32)		(.51)		(-.23)		(-.13)	
BRASS	5.61	1.71	5.09	1.86	5.33	1.73	3.77	1.80	5.65	1.67	3.44	1.60	4.47	1.25
	(-.04)		(-.40)		(-.01)		(-.28)		(-.09)		(-.04)		(.77)	
BRICK	5.97	1.70	5.69	1.77	5.72	1.61	3.98	1.83	6.13	1.40	3.16	1.79	3.98	1.18M
	(.32)		(.20)		(.38)		(-.07)		(.39)		(-.32)		(.28)	
BROOM	6.09	1.61	6.02	1.62	6.05	1.43	4.44	1.76	6.21	1.30	3.25	1.63	3.28	1.30
	(.44)		(.53)		(.71)		(.39)		(.47)		(-.23)		(-.42)	
BRUSH	5.66	1.92	5.50	1.75	5.37	1.83	4.52	1.75	6.22	1.32	3.68	1.33	4.33	1.11
	(.01)		(.01)		(.03)		(.47)		(.48)		(.20)		(.63)	
BUCKET	5.90	1.88	5.81	1.75	5.45	1.69	4.02	1.69	6.19	1.23	3.44	1.66	3.71	1.12F
	(.25)		(.32)		(.11)		(-.03)		(.45)		(-.04)		(.01)	
BUCKLE	5.64	1.86	5.81	1.55	5.05	1.66	3.66	1.68	5.95	1.47	3.62	1.64	3.75	1.17
	(-.01)		(.32)		(-.29)		(-.39)		(.21)		(.14)		(.05)	
BURLAP	5.79	1.60	4.70	2.12	5.12	2.16	3.52	1.56	5.31	1.74	3.10	1.68	3.98	1.21
	(.14)		(-.79)		(-.22)		(-.53)		(-.43)		(-.38)		(.28)	
BUSH	5.78	1.91	5.10	1.94	5.52	1.68	3.82	1.76	5.90	1.80	3.41	1.66	4.26	1.34
	(.13)		(-.39)		(.18)		(-.23)		(.16)		(-.07)		(.56)	
BUTTON	6.00	1.66	5.48	1.90	5.65	1.54	3.87	1.67	6.29	.98	3.48	1.60	4.22	1.20
	(.35)		(-.01)		(.31)		(-.18)		(.55)		(.00)		(.52)	
CABBAGE	6.07	1.60	5.84	1.55	6.13	1.38	3.97	1.82	5.71	1.62	3.06	1.49	3.88	1.61
	(.42)		(.35)		(.79)		(-.08)		(-.03)		(-.42)		(.18)	
CABLE	5.40	1.94	4.63	2.07	4.55	1.74	3.68	1.49	5.66	1.52	3.34	1.53	3.79	1.19
	(-.25)		(-.86)		(-.79)		(-.37)		(-.08)		(-.14)		(.09)	
CAGE	5.88	1.77	6.07	1.56	5.28	1.82	4.46	1.82	5.77	1.83	3.69	1.84	2.43	1.58
	(.23)		(.58)		(-.06)		(.41)		(.03)		(.21)		(-1.27)	
CAMEL	5.93	1.68	5.39	2.03	6.13	1.66	3.72	1.85	5.64	1.67	3.80	1.97	4.06	1.19
	(.28)		(-.10)		(.79)		(-.33)		(-.10)		(.32)		(.36)	
CANARY	5.73	1.96	5.27	2.10	6.20	1.33	3.82	1.65	4.85	1.97	3.90	1.88	4.16	1.60M
	(.08)		(-.22)		(.86)		(-.23)		(-.89)		(.42)		(.46)	
CANCER	6.11	1.64	5.61	1.64	5.64	1.79	4.92	1.82	6.10	1.40	4.64	2.08	1.73	1.30
	(.46)		(.12)		(.30)		(.87)		(.36)		(1.16)		(-1.97)	
CANNON	6.00	1.66	5.82	1.76	5.88	1.26	4.43	1.85	5.72	1.65	3.92	1.94	3.04	1.68
	(.35)		(.33)		(.54)		(.38)		(-.02)		(.44)		(-.66)	
CANON	5.37	2.01	4.87	2.11	4.80	1.97	4.10	1.70	4.98	2.14	3.75	1.58	3.16	1.36M
	(-.28)		(-.62)		(-.54)		(.05)		(-.76)		(.27)		(-.54)	
CANOPENER	5.88	1.87	5.91	1.62	5.50	1.85	3.45	2.01	5.90	1.69	3.17	1.87	3.67	1.14
	(.23)		(.42)		(.16)		(-.60)		(.16)		(-.31)		(-.03)	
CANTEEN	5.81	1.82	5.21	2.07	5.67	1.71	4.08	1.71	5.71	1.68	3.64	1.66	4.73	1.30
	(.16)		(-.28)		(.33)		(.03)		(-.03)		(.16)		(1.03)	
CAPE	5.77	1.87	5.60	1.88	5.33	1.78	4.27	1.76	5.95	1.48	3.26	1.61	3.94	1.29
	(.12)		(.11)		(-.01)		(.22)		(.21)		(-.22)		(.24)	
CAPSULE	5.36	2.05	5.88	1.73	4.92	1.72	4.23	1.68	5.79	1.42	3.81	1.84	4.07	1.33
	(-.29)		(.39)		(-.42)		(.18)		(.05)		(.33)		(.37)	
CAPTAIN	5.30	1.82	4.91	2.07	5.70	1.53	4.38	1.68	5.72	1.82	4.38	1.94	4.15	1.34F
	(-.35)		(-.58)		(.36)		(.33)		(-.02)		(.90)		(.45)	

	CON		IMG		CAT		MNG		FAM		NOA		PLS	
	M	SD	M	SD	M	SD	M	SD	M	SD	M	SD	M	SD
CARBON	5.07	2.16	4.39	2.13	5.00	1.94	3.52	1.85	5.44	1.61	3.08	1.50	3.67	1.14
	(-.58)		(-1.10)		(-.34)		(-.53)		(-.30)		(-.40)		(-.03)	
CARD	5.61	1.86	5.72	1.70	4.87	1.82	4.47	1.66	6.17	1.29	3.95	1.64	4.03	1.51
	(-.04)		(.23)		(-.47)		(.42)		(.43)		(.47)		(.33)	
CARDINAL	5.96	1.66	5.25	2.07	5.55	1.88	4.00	1.80	5.25	1.90	3.95	1.87	4.37	1.60
	(.31)		(-.24)		(.21)		(-.05)		(-.49)		(.47)		(.67)	
CAROL	5.31	1.93	4.93	2.04	5.34	1.91	4.02	2.02	5.63	1.65	3.42	1.77	5.06	1.43
	(-.34)		(-.56)		(.00)		(-.03)		(-.11)		(-.06)		(1.36)	
CARP	6.09	1.55	5.33	2.03	5.78	1.87	3.72	1.92	5.13	1.94	3.69	1.84	3.24	1.68
	(.44)		(-.16)		(.44)		(-.33)		(-.61)		(.21)		(-.46)	
CARPET	5.77	1.68	5.22	1.94	5.19	1.85	4.03	1.39	6.02	1.48	3.67	1.57	4.44	1.36
	(.12)		(-.27)		(-.15)		(-.02)		(.28)		(.19)		(.74)	
CASKET	6.09	1.62	5.82	1.73	5.37	1.74	4.33	1.73	5.40	1.80	3.56	1.68	2.45	1.57
	(.44)		(.33)		(.03)		(.28)		(-.34)		(.08)		(-1.25)	
CATFISH	5.98	1.81	5.71	1.76	6.15	1.76	3.56	1.96	5.52	1.91	3.60	2.04	3.80	1.73M
	(.33)		(.22)		(.81)		(-.49)		(-.22)		(.12)		(.10)	
CAULIFLOWER	6.38	1.59	5.61	1.94	6.20	1.55	3.90	1.79	5.36	1.79	3.25	2.04	4.21	1.67
	(.73)		(.12)		(.86)		(-.15)		(-.38)		(-.23)		(.51)	
CAVE	5.88	1.70	5.95	1.43	4.77	2.04	4.78	1.60	6.00	1.51	3.58	1.76	3.90	1.53
	(.23)		(.46)		(-.57)		(.73)		(.26)		(.10)		(.20)	
CEILING	6.02	1.58	5.51	1.77	5.45	1.83	4.39	1.79	6.05	1.37	3.13	1.49	3.73	1.12
	(.37)		(.02)		(.11)		(.34)		(.31)		(-.35)		(.03)	
CELL	5.09	2.06	5.62	1.59	5.30	1.78	4.69	1.97	5.95	1.49	4.07	1.98	3.41	1.72
	(-.56)		(.13)		(-.04)		(.64)		(.21)		(.59)		(-.29)	
CELLAR	5.41	2.04	5.27	1.76	5.08	1.75	4.38	1.62	5.88	1.53	3.79	1.70	3.84	1.44M
	(-.24)		(-.22)		(-.26)		(.33)		(.14)		(.31)		(.14)	
CEMENT	6.42	1.32	5.72	1.56	5.72	1.49	4.23	1.75	5.90	1.47	3.39	1.69	3.42	1.14M
	(.77)		(.23)		(.38)		(.18)		(.16)		(-.09)		(-.28)	
CENT	5.41	1.95	5.79	1.78	6.02	1.53	4.34	1.96	6.13	1.52	3.03	1.77	4.32	1.47
	(-.24)		(.30)		(.68)		(.29)		(.39)		(-.45)		(.62)	
CENTS	4.92	1.82	5.39	1.67	5.52	1.70	4.69	1.80	6.53	1.10	3.20	1.80	4.07	1.43
	(-.73)		(-.10)		(.18)		(.64)		(.79)		(-.28)		(.37)	
CEREBRUM	5.00	2.18	5.46	1.97	5.50	1.85	3.53	1.94	5.24	1.71	3.48	1.84	3.66	1.53
	(-.65)		(-.03)		(.16)		(-.52)		(-.50)		(.00)		(-.04)	
CHAIN	5.94	1.56	5.37	1.95	4.57	1.94	4.61	1.71	6.07	1.26	3.72	1.69	3.17	1.61M
	(.29)		(-.12)		(-.77)		(.56)		(.33)		(.24)		(-.53)	
CHALK	6.30	1.26	5.95	1.38	5.13	1.89	4.33	1.82	6.34	1.17	2.92	1.66	3.56	1.44
	(.65)		(.46)		(-.21)		(.28)		(.60)		(-.56)		(-.14)	
CHESTNUT	5.96	1.80	5.96	1.43	6.00	1.62	4.08	1.95	5.97	1.33	3.02	1.71	4.30	1.78F
	(.31)		(.47)		(.66)		(.03)		(.23)		(-.46)		(.60)	
CHICKENPOX	5.78	1.68	5.68	1.69	6.42	1.11	3.72	1.98	5.45	1.76	3.35	2.10	1.99	1.27
	(.13)		(.19)		(1.08)		(-.33)		(-.29)		(-.13)		(-1.71)	
CHINCHILLA	5.54	2.03	5.24	2.19	6.00	1.82	3.22	1.93	4.67	2.01	3.42	2.04	4.18	1.52
	(-.11)		(-.25)		(.66)		(-.83)		(-1.07)		(-.06)		(.48)	
CHISEL	5.93	1.68	5.61	1.75	5.38	1.96	4.08	1.83	5.43	1.74	3.30	1.58	3.51	1.43
	(.28)		(.12)		(.04)		(.03)		(-.31)		(-.18)		(-.19)	
CHOPSTICK	5.96	1.70	5.68	1.67	5.62	1.81	4.25	1.95	5.36	1.67	2.82	1.68	4.50	1.16
	(.31)		(.19)		(.28)		(.20)		(-.38)		(-.66)		(.80)	
CIGAR	5.64	2.02	5.95	1.64	5.84	1.35	3.95	1.77	6.07	1.39	3.38	1.79	3.51	1.92M
	(-.01)		(.46)		(.50)		(-.10)		(.33)		(-.10)		(-.19)	
CIGARETTE	6.03	1.68	6.39	1.40	5.48	1.72	4.61	1.73	6.47	1.20	3.44	1.84	2.91	2.06
	(.38)		(.90)		(.14)		(.56)		(.73)		(-.04)		(-.79)	
CINDER	5.75	1.73	5.43	1.55	4.60	1.77	3.79	1.74	5.38	1.70	2.93	1.55	3.69	1.77
	(.10)		(-.06)		(-.74)		(-.26)		(-.36)		(-.55)		(-.01)	

	CON		IMG		CAT		MNG		FAM		NOA		PLS	
	M	SD	M	SD	M	SD	M	SD	M	SD	M	SD	M	SD
CLAM	5.60	2.07 (-.05)	5.35	1.85 (-.14)	5.57	1.88 (.23)	3.92	1.77 (-.13)	5.60	1.69 (-.14)	3.68	1.79 (.20)	4.23	1.71M (.53)
CLAMPS	5.88	1.56 (.23)	4.82	1.80 (-.67)	4.35	1.97 (-.99)	3.78	1.78 (-.27)	5.47	1.83 (-.27)	3.10	1.58 (-.38)	3.37	1.09 (-.33)
CLAMS	6.35	1.36 (.70)	6.11	1.34 (.62)	5.97	1.74 (.63)	4.28	1.70 (.23)	5.66	1.74 (.03)	3.51	1.62 (.03)	4.27	1.57 (.57)
CLARINET	6.29	1.58 (.64)	5.87	1.60 (.38)	5.82	1.89 (.48)	4.28	1.73 (.23)	5.42	1.83 (-.32)	3.46	1.92 (-.02)	4.44	1.36 (.74)
CLOAK	5.39	2.00 (-.26)	5.12	1.92 (-.37)	5.38	1.73 (.04)	4.10	1.67 (.05)	5.23	1.67 (-.51)	3.08	1.53 (-.40)	3.97	1.37 (.27)
CLOSET	5.95	1.68 (.30)	5.19	1.92 (-.30)	5.13	1.84 (-.21)	4.15	1.78 (.10)	6.14	1.36 (.40)	3.89	1.74 (.41)	3.81	1.20 (.11)
COAL	5.56	1.89 (-.09)	5.74	1.38 (.25)	5.90	1.51 (.56)	3.77	1.80 (-.28)	5.79	1.73 (.05)	3.59	1.83 (.11)	3.61	1.23 (-.09)
COCKPIT	5.72	1.77 (.07)	5.88	1.63 (.39)	5.22	1.74 (-.12)	3.46	2.03 (-.59)	5.55	1.85 (-.19)	4.08	1.97 (.60)	3.91	1.50M (.21)
COFFIN	5.91	1.79 (.26)	6.00	1.56 (.51)	5.55	1.72 (.21)	4.53	1.88 (.48)	6.05	1.48 (.31)	3.42	1.85 (-.06)	2.28	1.47M (-1.42)
COLLAR	6.18	1.38 (.53)	5.76	1.66 (.27)	5.25	1.92 (-.09)	4.00	1.77 (-.05)	5.83	1.57 (.09)	3.46	1.44 (-.02)	4.16	1.13 (.46)
COLONEL	5.19	1.91 (-.46)	5.46	1.74 (-.03)	5.85	1.40 (.51)	3.67	1.82 (-.38)	5.56	1.78 (-.18)	3.41	1.74 (-.07)	3.70	1.53 (.00)
CONCRETE	5.58	2.01 (-.07)	5.58	1.70 (.09)	5.34	1.82 (.00)	4.27	1.66 (.22)	6.02	1.48 (.28)	3.53	1.74 (.05)	3.58	1.58M (-.12)
CONVENT	5.33	2.14 (-.32)	5.53	1.64 (.04)	4.78	1.79 (-.56)	3.97	1.74 (-.08)	5.32	1.81 (-.42)	3.61	1.68 (.13)	3.26	1.58 (-.44)
COPPER	5.05	2.12 (-.60)	5.33	1.63 (-.16)	5.93	1.42 (.59)	3.50	1.71 (-.55)	5.64	1.73 (-.10)	3.49	1.85 (.01)	4.21	1.12 (.51)
CORAL	5.69	1.81 (.04)	5.60	1.97 (.11)	5.67	1.62 (.33)	3.37	1.78 (-.68)	5.52	1.65 (-.22)	3.90	1.69 (.42)	4.67	1.73F (.97)
CORD	5.33	1.95 (-.32)	5.14	2.00 (-.35)	4.53	1.72 (-.81)	3.81	1.71 (-.24)	5.85	1.48 (.11)	3.16	1.53 (-.32)	3.90	1.03 (.20)
CORK	6.04	1.60 (.39)	6.25	1.46 (.76)	5.37	1.85 (.03)	4.29	1.92 (.24)	6.18	1.47 (.44)	2.70	1.39 (-.78)	4.43	1.46 (.73)
CORNER	4.89	2.03 (-.76)	5.20	1.86 (-.29)	4.70	1.84 (-.64)	3.75	1.75 (-.30)	6.25	1.35 (.51)	3.19	1.51 (-.29)	3.60	.98 (-.10)
CRABS	6.34	1.31 (.69)	6.22	1.19 (.73)	6.05	1.49 (.71)	3.95	1.73 (-.10)	5.75	1.64 (.01)	4.20	1.63 (.72)	2.97	1.74 (-.73)
CROCODILE	5.79	2.04 (.14)	5.95	1.66 (.46)	6.33	1.46 (.99)	3.87	1.88 (-.18)	5.30	1.83 (-.44)	3.59	2.01 (.11)	3.60	1.59 (-.10)
CROQUET	5.55	1.87 (-.10)	5.33	1.67 (-.16)	5.38	1.71 (.04)	3.48	1.93 (-.57)	4.92	2.05 (-.82)	3.51	1.73 (.03)	4.33	1.05 (.63)
CROW	5.49	2.07 (-.16)	5.67	1.75 (.18)	6.33	1.32 (.99)	3.75	1.84 (-.30)	5.84	1.53 (.10)	3.83	1.81 (.35)	3.69	1.53 (-.01)
CROWD	5.42	1.74 (-.23)	5.42	1.92 (-.07)	4.93	1.69 (-.41)	5.15	1.62 (1.10)	5.97	1.53 (.23)	4.72	1.69 (1.24)	3.11	1.45 (-.59)
CRUCIFIX	5.79	1.93 (.14)	5.55	2.02 (.06)	4.95	1.75 (-.39)	4.31	1.88 (.26)	5.16	1.79 (-.58)	3.40	1.80 (-.08)	3.09	1.97 (-.61)
CRUMB	5.37	1.74 (-.28)	4.91	1.78 (-.58)	4.50	1.73 (-.84)	3.85	1.51 (-.20)	5.98	1.44 (.24)	3.08	1.43 (-.40)	3.37	1.21 (-.33)
CUBE	5.13	1.89 (-.52)	5.69	1.93 (.20)	5.62	1.57 (.28)	4.17	1.71 (.12)	5.91	1.48 (.17)	3.57	1.76 (.09)	3.95	1.09 (.25)
CUP	5.35	1.89 (-.30)	5.52	1.82 (.03)	5.59	1.52 (.25)	4.33	1.81 (.28)	6.33	1.18 (.59)	3.49	1.75 (.01)	3.82	1.21 (.12)

	CON M	SD	IMG M	SD	CAT M	SD	MNG M	SD	FAM M	SD	NOA M	SD	PLS M	SD
CUPBOARDS	5.82	1.80	5.71	1.57	4.98	1.65	4.41	1.64	6.13	1.60	3.85	1.51	3.74	1.28
	(.17)		(.22)		(-.36)		(.36)		(.39)		(.37)		(.04)	
CURB	5.73	1.95	5.50	1.78	4.33	1.61	4.03	1.62	6.00	1.39	3.38	1.41	3.87	1.38
	(.08)		(.01)		(-1.01)		(-.02)		(.26)		(-.10)		(.17)	
CURLER	5.96	1.71	5.15	2.27	5.00	1.79	3.87	2.00	5.75	1.65	3.38	1.58	3.39	1.49
	(.31)		(-.34)		(-.34)		(-.18)		(.01)		(-.10)		(-.31)	
CUSTARD	5.45	1.90	5.09	1.94	5.40	1.61	3.13	1.56	5.34	1.80	3.08	1.47	4.03	1.53M
	(-.20)		(-.40)		(.06)		(-.92)		(.01)		(-.40)		(.33)	
CYMBAL	5.09	2.18	4.88	2.15	5.45	1.87	3.08	1.91	4.49	2.12	2.50	1.39	4.25	1.34
	(-.56)		(-.61)		(.11)		(-.97)		(-1.25)		(-.98)		(.55)	
DAGGER	5.72	2.02	5.75	1.63	5.58	1.72	4.40	1.69	5.54	1.76	3.44	1.58	2.94	1.70
	(.07)		(.26)		(.24)		(.35)		(-.20)		(-.04)		(-.76)	
DAME	5.24	1.89	5.24	1.71	4.97	1.87	4.98	1.71	5.46	1.74	3.93	2.01	3.70	2.13M
	(-.41)		(-.25)		(-.37)		(.93)		(-.28)		(.45)		(.00)	
DANDRUFF	5.42	2.14	5.48	1.67	5.27	1.78	3.85	1.75	5.69	1.64	2.61	1.38	2.30	1.29
	(-.23)		(-.01)		(-.07)		(-.20)		(-.05)		(-.87)		(-1.40)	
DENTIST	6.03	1.49	6.16	1.56	6.18	1.49	4.46	1.67	6.37	1.06	4.28	1.92	2.78	1.63
	(.38)		(.67)		(.84)		(.41)		(.63)		(.80)		(-.92)	
DESK	5.79	2.01	5.68	1.75	5.63	1.80	4.21	1.87	6.57	.89	3.94	1.79	3.65	1.20
	(.14)		(.19)		(.29)		(.16)		(.83)		(.46)		(-.05)	
DESTROYER	5.09	2.20	5.02	1.91	5.37	1.82	3.88	1.78	5.22	1.74	4.57	1.92	2.29	1.46
	(-.56)		(-.47)		(.03)		(-.17)		(-.52)		(1.09)		(-1.41)	
DIAL	5.33	1.82	5.35	1.85	4.42	1.83	4.30	1.82	6.40	1.11	3.02	1.19	3.91	1.39
	(-.32)		(-.14)		(-.92)		(.25)		(.66)		(-.46)		(.21)	
DIAPERS	6.30	1.35	6.02	1.30	5.62	1.80	4.18	1.94	5.59	1.86	2.90	1.77	2.65	1.31
	(.65)		(.53)		(.28)		(.13)		(-.15)		(-.58)		(-1.05)	
DIMPLE	5.43	1.76	5.12	2.05	4.97	1.73	3.17	1.57	5.16	1.74	2.58	1.39	4.91	1.31
	(-.22)		(-.37)		(-.37)		(-.88)		(-.58)		(-.90)		(1.21)	
DISHWASHERS	5.73	1.66	5.52	1.94	5.29	1.81	3.57	1.92	5.81	1.44	4.20	1.91	3.53	1.64
	(.08)		(.03)		(-.05)		(-.48)		(.07)		(.72)		(-.17)	
DITCH	5.35	1.96	5.41	1.75	4.72	1.66	4.16	1.76	6.08	1.42	3.37	1.65	3.20	1.49M
	(-.30)		(-.08)		(-.62)		(.11)		(.34)		(-.11)		(-.50)	
DOE	5.75	2.02	5.26	2.04	5.33	2.14	3.51	1.88	5.38	1.85	3.25	1.83	5.31	1.63F
	(.10)		(-.23)		(-.01)		(-.54)		(-.36)		(-.23)		(1.61)	
DOLL	5.52	2.03	5.27	2.02	5.36	1.83	4.49	1.72	6.00	1.51	4.16	1.75	4.13	1.54F
	(-.13)		(-.22)		(.02)		(.44)		(.26)		(.68)		(.43)	
DOME	5.13	2.13	5.51	1.66	4.71	1.86	3.34	1.60	5.78	1.58	3.32	1.65	4.35	1.12
	(-.52)		(.02)		(-.63)		(-.71)		(.04)		(-.16)		(.65)	
DOOR	6.04	1.70	5.91	1.62	5.42	1.88	4.87	1.65	6.77	.74	3.52	1.84	3.70	1.49
	(.39)		(.42)		(.08)		(.82)		(1.03)		(.04)		(.00)	
DOORMAN	5.76	1.79	5.66	1.79	5.79	1.75	3.19	1.73	5.73	1.58	3.82	1.87	4.03	1.15F
	(.11)		(.17)		(.45)		(-.86)		(-.01)		(.34)		(.33)	
DORM	5.68	2.00	5.73	1.80	5.13	1.87	4.66	1.92	6.38	1.47	4.03	1.87	3.34	1.55
	(.03)		(.24)		(-.21)		(.61)		(.64)		(.55)		(-.36)	
DOUGH	6.32	1.09	5.35	1.80	4.93	1.74	4.23	1.73	5.64	1.69	3.74	1.44	4.61	1.23F
	(.67)		(-.14)		(-.41)		(.18)		(-.10)		(.26)		(.91)	
DRESSER	5.56	1.93	5.50	1.75	5.32	1.69	3.85	1.88	6.00	1.40	3.57	1.53	4.08	1.05
	(-.09)		(.01)		(-.02)		(-.20)		(.26)		(.09)		(.38)	
DRILL	5.12	2.04	5.65	1.68	4.70	1.81	3.70	1.36	5.71	1.56	3.92	1.69	2.84	1.49
	(-.53)		(.16)		(-.64)		(-.35)		(-.03)		(.44)		(-.86)	
DRIZZLE	5.54	1.51	5.76	1.58	4.83	1.60	4.84	1.51	5.90	1.51	3.25	1.52	3.93	1.65
	(-.11)		(.27)		(-.51)		(.79)		(.16)		(-.23)		(.23)	
DUCHESS	5.64	1.78	5.19	1.69	5.15	1.88	3.67	1.85	4.90	2.05	3.74	2.02	4.33	1.51
	(-.01)		(-.30)		(-.19)		(-.38)		(-.84)		(.26)		(.63)	

	CON		IMG		CAT		MNG		FAM		NOA		PLS	
	M	SD	M	SD	M	SD	M	SD	M	SD	M	SD	M	SD
DUKE	5.04	1.96	4.74	2.05	5.16	1.78	3.67	1.77	5.31	1.71	3.70	1.77	4.11	1.33
	(-.61)		(-.75)		(-.18)		(-.38)		(-.43)		(.22)		(.41)	
DUNGEON	5.58	2.04	5.73	1.58	5.27	1.87	4.30	1.48	5.02	1.89	3.80	1.78	2.35	1.56
	(-.07)		(.24)		(-.07)		(.25)		(-.72)		(.32)		(-1.35)	
DUST	5.23	2.07	5.14	1.95	4.75	1.79	4.03	1.76	6.25	1.37	3.03	1.47	3.26	1.40
	(-.42)		(-.35)		(-.59)		(-.02)		(.28)		(-.45)		(-.44)	
DYE	5.25	1.99	5.12	1.80	4.55	1.95	4.11	1.80	6.02	1.35	3.25	1.65	3.72	1.46
	(-.40)		(-.37)		(-.79)		(.06)		(.51)		(-.23)		(.02)	
EARTHWORM	6.02	1.82	5.63	1.71	6.15	1.45	3.57	1.80	5.82	1.76	3.23	1.85	3.25	1.46M
	(.37)		(.14)		(.81)		(-.48)		(.08)		(-.25)		(-.45)	
EASEL	5.76	1.69	5.26	2.01	5.07	1.89	4.05	1.87	5.06	1.78	3.41	1.69	4.74	1.25
	(.11)		(-.23)		(-.27)		(.00)		(-.68)		(-.07)		(1.04)	
EEL	6.30	1.50	5.46	2.01	5.93	1.73	3.50	2.05	5.07	1.87	2.69	1.87	2.71	1.62
	(.65)		(-.03)		(.59)		(-.55)		(-.67)		(-.79)		(-.99)	
EGG	5.88	1.76	5.57	1.77	5.71	1.71	4.23	1.92	6.54	1.01	3.38	1.62	4.29	1.37
	(.23)		(.08)		(.37)		(.18)		(.80)		(-.10)		(.59)	
ENVELOPE	5.75	1.83	5.48	1.92	5.28	1.75	3.48	1.52	6.16	1.19	3.30	1.65	4.24	1.25
	(.10)		(-.01)		(-.06)		(-.57)		(.42)		(-.18)		(.54)	
FAN	5.53	1.94	5.76	1.71	5.08	1.70	4.25	1.83	5.94	1.46	3.98	1.75	4.42	1.47
	(-.12)		(.27)		(-.26)		(.20)		(.20)		(.50)		(.72)	
FANG	5.70	1.78	5.53	1.67	4.93	1.89	4.05	1.98	5.24	1.86	3.10	1.58	3.22	1.51M
	(.05)		(.04)		(-.41)		(.00)		(-.50)		(-.38)		(-.48)	
FENCE	5.93	1.71	6.05	1.28	5.18	1.85	4.31	1.72	6.03	1.30	3.74	1.56	3.81	1.25
	(.28)		(.56)		(.18)		(.26)		(.29)		(.26)		(.11)	
FIDDLE	5.80	1.74	5.29	2.01	5.17	2.00	4.52	1.92	5.75	1.48	3.67	1.41	3.90	1.74
	(.15)		(-.20)		(-.17)		(.47)		(.01)		(.19)		(.20)	
FISHHOOK	5.77	1.80	5.66	1.80	5.71	1.76	3.65	1.88	5.53	1.59	3.25	1.83	3.71	1.59M
	(.12)		(.17)		(.37)		(-.40)		(-.21)		(-.23)		(.01)	
FLAG	6.20	1.37	5.98	1.48	5.13	1.92	4.48	1.74	6.41	1.19	4.11	1.72	3.81	1.53
	(.55)		(.49)		(-.21)		(.43)		(.67)		(.63)		(.11)	
FLANNEL	5.70	1.76	5.14	1.85	5.35	1.91	4.02	1.57	5.73	1.33	3.18	1.54	4.80	1.27F
	(.05)		(-.35)		(.01)		(-.03)		(-.01)		(-.30)		(1.10)	
FLASHBULBS	6.10	1.52	6.26	1.45	5.72	1.49	3.85	1.82	5.92	1.61	3.28	1.80	3.79	1.36
	(.45)		(.77)		(.38)		(-.20)		(.18)		(-.20)		(.09)	
FLEA	6.21	1.44	6.00	1.69	6.25	1.27	3.93	1.83	5.89	1.61	3.60	1.75	2.50	1.35
	(.56)		(.51)		(.91)		(-.12)		(.15)		(.12)		(-1.20)	
FLEAS	5.81	1.87	5.67	1.79	6.10	1.35	3.82	1.95	5.61	1.65	3.72	2.03	2.49	1.51
	(.16)		(.18)		(.76)		(-.23)		(-.13)		(.24)		(-1.21)	
FLOOD	5.32	1.79	5.89	1.59	4.98	1.90	4.79	1.50	6.03	1.37	3.92	1.70	2.36	1.35
	(-.33)		(.40)		(-.36)		(.74)		(.29)		(.44)		(-1.34)	
FLOOR	5.55	1.94	5.38	1.95	5.16	1.72	4.02	1.75	6.25	1.31	3.51	1.63	3.72	1.21
	(-.10)		(-.11)		(-.18)		(-.03)		(.51)		(.03)		(.02)	
FOG	5.52	2.04	6.00	1.58	4.92	1.97	4.85	1.83	6.20	1.31	2.87	1.44	3.72	1.78
	(-.13)		(.51)		(-.42)		(.80)		(.46)		(-.61)		(.02)	
FOOT	5.54	1.74	5.88	1.68	6.05	1.36	4.35	1.88	6.34	1.18	3.77	1.82	3.91	1.47
	(-.11)		(.39)		(.71)		(.30)		(.60)		(.29)		(.21)	
FORCEPS	5.81	1.78	5.47	1.88	5.52	1.67	3.66	1.54	4.76	1.85	3.09	1.54	2.94	1.36
	(.16)		(-.02)		(.18)		(-.98)		(-.60)		(-.39)		(-.76)	
FORK	5.58	2.17	5.71	1.91	6.02	1.41	4.12	1.90	6.24	1.33	3.11	1.57	3.54	1.25M
	(-.07)		(.22)		(.68)		(.07)		(.50)		(-.37)		(-.16)	
FOXTROT	4.36	1.79	4.72	2.06	5.65	1.82	3.42	1.97	4.77	2.05	3.00	1.63	3.86	1.54
	(-1.29)		(-.77)		(.31)		(-.63)		(-.97)		(-.48)		(.16)	
FRECKLES	6.00	1.68	5.63	1.74	5.05	1.75	3.95	1.87	5.83	1.56	2.63	1.26	4.86	1.53F
	(.35)		(.14)		(-.29)		(-.10)		(.09)		(-.85)		(1.16)	

	CON		IMG		CAT		MNG		FAM		NOA		PLS	
	M	SD	M	SD	M	SD	M	SD	M	SD	M	SD	M	SD
FREIGHT	5.20	2.07	5.33	1.77	4.53	1.62	3.80	1.73	5.69	1.46	4.02	1.57	3.65	1.33
	(-.45)		(-.16)		(-.81)		(-.25)		(-.05)		(.54)		(-.05)	
FROWN	4.50	2.03	5.83	1.45	4.95	1.82	4.55	1.82	5.76	1.51	3.31	1.63	2.53	1.37
	(-1.15)		(.34)		(-.39)		(.50)		(.02)		(-.17)		(-1.17)	
FUEL	5.55	1.71	5.15	1.79	5.32	1.65	4.59	1.84	6.08	1.43	4.00	1.82	3.67	1.22
	(-.10)		(-.34)		(-.02)		(.54)		(.34)		(.52)		(-.03)	
GALLON	4.84	2.00	5.19	1.77	5.42	1.72	3.94	1.92	5.93	1.44	3.08	1.73	3.66	1.20
	(-.81)		(-.30)		(.08)		(-.11)		(.19)		(-.40)		(-.04)	
GARBAGE	5.68	1.84	5.90	1.46	5.52	1.65	5.25	1.58	6.28	1.28	5.02	1.86	2.64	1.46
	(.03)		(.41)		(.18)		(1.20)		(.54)		(1.54)		(-1.06)	
GARDENIA	5.72	1.99	5.58	1.89	5.60	2.06	4.19	1.83	5.46	1.66	3.21	1.81	4.78	1.81
	(.07)		(.09)		(.26)		(.14)		(-.28)		(-.27)		(1.08)	
GARLIC	6.32	1.39	5.59	1.78	5.92	1.60	4.30	1.99	5.83	1.51	2.77	1.51	3.66	1.85
	(.67)		(.10)		(.58)		(.25)		(.09)		(-.71)		(-.04)	
GASKET	5.21	2.18	4.81	2.22	4.85	1.90	3.05	1.93	5.02	1.89	3.54	1.66	3.48	1.23M
	(-.44)		(-.68)		(-.49)		(-1.00)		(-.72)		(.06)		(-.22)	
GASOLINE	6.05	1.65	5.45	1.61	5.85	1.48	4.60	1.81	6.19	1.34	4.03	1.84	3.74	1.43
	(.40)		(-.04)		(.51)		(.55)		(.45)		(.55)		(.04)	
GATE	5.69	1.86	5.39	1.76	5.13	1.85	4.44	1.67	6.18	1.39	3.25	1.48	3.89	1.44
	(.04)		(-.10)		(-.21)		(.39)		(.44)		(-.23)		(.19)	
GAVEL	5.54	2.13	5.33	1.99	4.70	1.99	3.94	2.11	4.57	2.15	3.13	1.58	3.49	1.42
	(-.11)		(-.16)		(-.64)		(-.11)		(-1.17)		(-.35)		(-.21)	
GINGER	5.18	1.70	4.24	2.07	5.14	1.85	3.33	1.61	5.29	1.52	2.93	1.60	4.82	1.32F
	(-.47)		(-1.25)		(-.20)		(-.72)		(-.45)		(-.55)		(1.12)	
GIRDLE	5.66	2.02	5.53	1.91	5.15	1.73	4.00	1.68	5.62	1.80	3.15	1.30	2.90	1.41M
	(.01)		(.04)		(-.19)		(-.12)		(-.12)		(-.33)		(-.80)	
GNAT	5.25	2.03	5.44	1.93	6.05	1.64	3.38	1.74	5.14	1.93	2.98	1.94	2.63	1.42
	(-.40)		(-.05)		(.71)		(-.67)		(-.60)		(-.50)		(-1.07)	
GOAT	6.32	1.61	5.79	1.61	6.18	1.55	4.02	1.75	5.61	1.76	3.90	1.88	3.98	1.30
	(.67)		(.30)		(.84)		(-.03)		(-.13)		(.42)		(.28)	
GRAPH	5.49	1.62	5.29	1.83	5.03	1.60	3.85	1.73	5.98	1.35	4.23	1.60	3.85	1.49
	(-.16)		(-.20)		(-.31)		(-.20)		(.24)		(.75)		(.15)	
GRASSHOPPER	6.56	1.04	6.24	1.45	6.13	1.52	4.55	1.79	5.81	1.47	3.69	2.00	3.45	1.65
	(.91)		(.75)		(.79)		(.50)		(.07)		(.21)		(-.25)	
GRAVE	5.27	1.85	6.23	1.05	4.68	1.92	4.85	1.58	5.89	1.53	3.77	1.76	2.07	1.55
	(-.38)		(.74)		(-.66)		(.80)		(.15)		(.29)		(-1.63)	
GRAVEL	5.83	1.80	5.63	1.85	5.45	1.57	3.95	1.65	5.76	1.72	3.41	1.58	2.76	1.35
	(.18)		(.14)		(.11)		(-.10)		(.02)		(-.07)		(-.94)	
GRAY	4.67	2.25	5.35	1.72	5.72	1.82	4.37	1.68	6.05	1.38	2.79	1.50	3.52	1.58
	(-.98)		(-.14)		(.38)		(.32)		(.31)		(-.69)		(-.18)	
GROCER	5.72	1.81	5.74	1.43	5.42	1.61	4.21	1.97	6.08	1.31	3.89	1.77	4.02	1.32
	(.07)		(.25)		(.08)		(.16)		(.34)		(.41)		(.32)	
GROIN	5.02	2.16	5.10	1.94	5.54	1.80	3.70	1.82	5.60	1.63	3.17	1.60	3.34	1.62
	(-.63)		(-.39)		(.20)		(-.35)		(-.14)		(-.31)		(-.36)	
GUN	6.08	1.75	5.88	1.60	5.72	1.80	5.05	1.74	6.28	1.56	4.48	1.78	1.98	1.35M
	(.43)		(.39)		(.38)		(1.00)		(.54)		(1.00)		(-1.72)	
GUTTER	4.94	2.18	5.00	2.17	4.55	1.86	3.27	1.49	5.41	1.79	2.83	1.45	2.48	1.36
	(-.71)		(-.49)		(-.79)		(-.78)		(-.33)		(-.65)		(-1.22)	
HAILSTONE	5.72	1.89	5.56	1.89	5.29	1.65	3.24	1.78	5.22	1.91	3.13	1.65	3.36	1.41
	(.07)		(.07)		(-.05)		(-.81)		(-.52)		(-.35)		(-.34)	
HAIRPIN	5.71	1.93	5.46	1.81	5.32	1.78	3.89	2.00	5.40	2.02	3.00	1.75	4.08	1.20
	(.06)		(-.03)		(-.02)		(-.16)		(-.34)		(-.48)		(.38)	
HALL	5.36	1.96	5.14	1.86	4.72	1.82	4.21	1.60	6.58	1.06	3.58	1.76	3.78	1.56
	(-.29)		(-.35)		(-.62)		(.16)		(.84)		(.10)		(.08)	

	CON	IMG	CAT	MNG	FAM	NOA	PLS
	M SD	M SD	M SD	M SD	M SD	M SD	M SD
HALLWAY	5.71 1.78 (.06)	5.77 1.38 (.28)	4.73 1.82 (-.61)	4.24 1.67 (.19)	6.16 1.50 (.42)	3.74 1.81 (.26)	3.59 1.33 (-.11)
HAMMER	5.94 1.85 (.29)	6.04 1.72 (.55)	6.26 1.32 (.92)	4.35 1.93 (.30)	6.28 1.17 (.54)	3.65 1.65 (.17)	3.88 1.32 (.18)
HAMSTER	5.95 1.73 (.30)	5.75 1.77 (.26)	6.32 1.37 (.98)	4.18 1.96 (.13)	5.41 1.64 (-.33)	3.61 2.02 (.13)	4.35 1.67F (.65)
HANDGRENADE	5.88 2.00 (.23)	5.79 1.89 (.30)	5.63 1.80 (.29)	4.05 2.06 (.00)	5.15 2.11 (-.59)	3.50 2.01 (.02)	2.44 1.86M (-1.26)
HANDLEBARS	5.95 1.75 (.30)	5.44 1.98 (-.05)	5.33 1.96 (-.01)	3.92 1.99 (-.13)	6.03 1.50	2.86 1.58 (-.62)	4.48 1.36 (.78)
HARDWARE	5.56 1.75 (-.09)	5.70 1.61 (.21)	5.08 1.81 (-.26)	4.34 1.71 (.29)	5.70 1.68 (-.04)	4.84 1.72 (1.36)	3.44 1.26 (-.26)
HARE	6.05 1.51 (.40)	5.50 1.91 (.01)	6.17 1.53 (.83)	4.07 1.80 (.02)	5.31 1.61 (-.43)	3.89 1.92 (.41)	4.30 1.34F (.60)
HARNESS	5.33 1.92 (-.32)	5.21 1.83 (-.28)	4.52 1.87 (-.82)	3.08 1.58 (-.97)	5.63 1.62 (-.11)	3.34 1.72 (-.14)	3.26 1.35 (-.44)
HARPOON	5.88 1.87 (.23)	5.25 1.90 (-.24)	5.33 1.72 (-.01)	3.56 1.88 (-.49)	4.97 1.94 (-.77)	3.08 1.66 (-.40)	3.02 1.55M (-.68)
HATCHET	6.03 1.59 (.38)	5.21 1.80 (-.28)	5.45 1.73 (.11)	3.97 1.50 (-.08)	5.41 1.65 (-.33)	3.44 1.51 (-.04)	3.10 1.62M (-.60)
HAZE	5.05 1.83 (-.60)	5.15 1.88 (-.34)	4.50 1.57 (-.84)	4.23 1.71 (.18)	5.58 1.49 (-.16)	3.18 1.47 (-.30)	3.63 1.65 (-.07)
HEADBOARD	6.32 1.43 (.67)	5.34 1.88 (-.15)	5.20 1.75 (-.14)	3.58 1.90 (-.47)	5.58 1.88 (-.16)	3.03 1.43 (-.45)	4.22 1.11 (.52)
HEEL	5.75 1.92 (.10)	5.91 1.75 (.42)	5.38 1.67 (.04)	4.08 1.80 (.03)	5.98 1.31 (.24)	3.38 1.58 (-.10)	3.42 1.24 (-.28)
HELMET	5.98 1.71 (.33)	6.14 1.49 (.65)	5.52 1.53 (.18)	4.36 1.75 (.31)	6.02 1.48 (.28)	3.75 1.78 (.27)	3.94 1.70M (.24)
HERMIT	5.04 2.04 (-.61)	5.27 1.91 (-.22)	4.93 2.12 (-.41)	3.95 1.58 (-.10)	5.30 1.65 (-.44)	3.98 1.87 (.50)	4.09 1.65M (.39)
HEROIN	6.34 1.23 (.69)	5.45 1.56 (-.04)	6.12 1.60 (.78)	5.23 1.63 (1.18)	5.88 1.60 (.14)	3.95 2.14 (.47)	2.87 1.94M (-.83)
HERRING	5.93 1.63 (.28)	4.93 2.12 (-.56)	5.88 1.68 (.54)	3.61 1.99 (-.44)	4.98 1.74 (-.76)	3.22 1.79 (-.26)	3.68 1.66 (-.02)
HEXAGON	5.55 1.93 (-.10)	5.21 1.83 (-.28)	5.50 1.94 (.16)	3.90 1.94 (-.15)	5.34 1.82 (-.40)	2.61 1.86 (-.87)	3.36 1.46 (-.34)
HOE	5.33 2.04 (-.32)	5.19 1.83 (-.30)	5.79 1.53 (.45)	3.56 1.83 (-.49)	5.63 1.73 (-.11)	2.77 1.56 (-.71)	3.75 1.32 (.05)
HOG	5.77 1.96 (.12)	5.21 2.18 (-.28)	6.32 1.28 (.98)	4.52 1.51 (.47)	6.02 1.48 (.28)	4.02 1.82 (.54)	3.03 1.74M (-.67)
HOOD	5.43 1.94 (-.22)	5.52 1.80 (.03)	4.92 1.77 (-.42)	4.30 1.66 (.25)	5.84 1.64 (.10)	3.94 1.68 (.46)	3.57 1.35F (-.13)
HOOK	5.21 1.99 (-.44)	5.35 1.86 (-.14)	4.65 1.80 (-.69)	3.45 1.69 (-.60)	5.71 1.56 (-.03)	3.34 1.58 (-.14)	3.12 1.33M (-.58)
HORN	6.09 1.46 (.44)	5.53 1.75 (.04)	5.43 1.76 (.09)	4.23 1.96 (.18)	5.90 1.48 (.16)	3.59 1.76 (.11)	3.77 1.25 (.07)
HOSTAGE	5.10 1.81 (-.49)	5.24 1.76 (-.25)	4.82 1.66 (-.52)	4.38 1.78 (.33)	5.72 1.68 (-.02)	3.86 1.78 (.38)	2.37 1.54 (-1.33)
HURRICANE	5.84 1.78 (.19)	6.09 1.70 (.60)	6.13 1.32 (.79)	4.93 1.90 (.88)	6.10 1.43 (.36)	4.67 1.88 (1.19)	3.00 1.84F (-.70)
HUT	5.85 1.76 (.20)	5.54 1.79 (.05)	5.12 1.98 (-.22)	4.15 1.91 (.10)	5.60 1.82 (-.14)	3.48 1.41 (.00)	4.00 1.38 (.30)
ICEBOX	5.54 1.89 (-.11)	5.70 1.61 (.21)	5.48 1.60 (.14)	3.97 1.73 (-.08)	5.74 1.75 (.00)	3.60 1.86 (.12)	4.44 1.43 (.74)

	CON		IMG		CAT		MNG		FAM		NOA		PLS	
	M	SD	M	SD	M	SD	M	SD	M	SD	M	SD	M	SD
ICICLE	5.65	1.92	5.20	2.26	4.78	2.08	3.53	1.90	5.24	2.06	2.80	1.45	5.11	1.39F
	(.00)		(-.29)		(-.56)		(-.52)		(-.50)		(-.68)		(1.41)	
INCENSE	4.95	2.02	5.49	1.67	4.59	1.75	3.52	1.69	5.78	1.51	2.98	1.60	4.08	1.78
	(-.70)		(.00)		(-.75)		(-.53)		(.04)		(-.50)		(.38)	
INK	6.26	1.45	5.67	1.70	5.27	1.80	4.15	1.83	5.83	1.67	3.34	1.62	4.05	1.15
	(.61)		(.18)		(-.07)		(.10)		(.09)		(-.14)		(.35)	
IRON	5.55	1.83	5.41	1.71	5.70	1.63	3.88	1.84	6.03	1.39	3.62	1.82	3.37	1.35
	(-.10)		(-.08)		(.36)		(-.17)		(.29)		(.14)		(-.33)	
IVY	5.63	1.80	5.45	1.83	5.85	1.46	3.97	1.44	5.53	1.69	3.41	1.87	4.70	1.59F
	(-.02)		(-.04)		(.51)		(-.08)		(-.21)		(-.07)		(1.00)	
JACK	5.20	2.12	4.97	2.18	4.55	2.13	3.40	1.97	5.60	1.83	3.37	1.83	3.69	1.32
	(-.45)		(-.52)		(-.79)		(-.65)		(-.14)		(-.11)		(-.01)	
JAIL	6.02	1.77	6.02	1.56	5.55	1.68	5.06	1.78	6.46	.92	4.07	1.81	2.28	1.79
	(.37)		(.53)		(.21)		(1.01)		(.72)		(.59)		(-1.42)	
JAM	5.59	1.87	5.63	1.77	5.10	1.95	4.48	1.79	6.03	1.47	3.26	1.58	4.16	1.58F
	(-.06)		(.14)		(-.24)		(.43)		(.29)		(-.22)		(.46)	
JAR	5.77	1.84	5.53	1.74	5.30	1.82	4.26	2.07	6.25	1.27	3.87	1.63	3.62	.96
	(.12)		(.04)		(-.04)		(.21)		(.51)		(.39)		(-.08)	
JAW	6.14	1.46	5.84	1.50	5.50	1.66	4.18	1.89	6.26	1.30	3.51	1.67	3.82	1.25M
	(.49)		(.35)		(.16)		(.13)		(.52)		(.03)		(.12)	
JELLY	5.38	2.09	5.67	1.77	5.59	1.61	3.93	1.82	6.08	1.41	3.75	1.67	4.47	1.30
	(-.27)		(.18)		(.25)		(-.12)		(.34)		(.27)		(.77)	
JELLYFISH	6.04	1.88	5.89	1.49	6.38	1.28	3.38	1.98	5.53	1.88	3.90	2.05	3.23	1.79
	(.39)		(.40)		(1.04)		(-.67)		(-.21)		(.42)		(-.47)	
JITTERBUG	4.68	1.98	4.67	1.91	5.29	1.99	3.41	1.77	5.14	2.05	3.19	1.79	4.16	1.49
	(-.97)		(-.82)		(-.05)		(-.64)		(-.60)		(-.29)		(.46)	
JOCKEY	5.53	1.96	6.00	1.49	5.30	1.67	3.84	1.88	5.67	1.63	3.84	1.58	4.21	1.29
	(-.12)		(.51)		(-.04)		(-.21)		(-.07)		(.36)		(.51)	
JUGGLER	5.32	1.95	5.16	1.70	5.38	1.66	3.49	1.75	5.59	1.59	3.72	1.74	4.24	1.18
	(-.33)		(-.33)		(.04)		(-.56)		(-.15)		(.24)		(.54)	
KERNEL	5.55	1.83	5.36	1.66	5.12	1.80	3.68	1.74	5.51	1.72	3.00	1.62	3.62	1.44
	(-.10)		(-.13)				(-.37)		(-.23)		(-.48)		(-.08)	
KEROSENE	6.03	1.54	5.33	1.91	5.70	1.61	3.64	1.89	5.48	1.63	3.18	1.78	3.51	1.39
	(.38)		(-.16)		(.36)		(-.41)		(-.26)		(-.30)		(-.19)	
KETTLE	5.93	1.77	5.81	1.65	5.77	1.65	4.50	1.77	5.95	1.62	3.31	1.57	3.90	1.43
	(.28)		(.32)		(.43)		(.45)		(.21)		(-.17)		(.20)	
KNIFE	6.08	1.73	6.27	1.27	5.98	1.26	4.66	1.83	6.21	1.32	3.72	1.87	3.13	1.40
	(.43)		(.78)		(.64)		(.61)		(.47)		(.24)		(-.57)	
KNOB	5.82	1.53	5.48	1.78	4.62	2.03	4.26	1.69	6.08	1.43	3.07	1.44	3.76	1.35
	(.17)		(-.01)		(-.72)		(.21)		(.34)		(-.41)		(.06)	
KNUCKLE	5.67	2.00	4.95	1.90	5.18	1.96	3.37	1.70	5.81	1.49	2.87	1.67	3.49	1.27
	(.02)		(-.54)		(-.16)		(-.68)		(.07)		(-.61)		(-.21)	
LAP	5.51	1.95	5.43	1.82	4.70	1.83	3.92	1.55	6.21	1.34	3.18	1.60	4.51	1.58
	(-.14)		(-.06)		(-.64)		(-.13)		(.47)		(-.30)		(.81)	
LARD	5.13	2.17	4.85	2.19	5.00	1.71	3.57	1.83	5.32	1.82	2.80	1.54	2.75	1.25
	(-.52)		(-.64)		(-.34)		(-.48)		(-.42)		(-.68)		(-.95)	
LARK	5.69	1.94	5.50	1.58	5.70	1.77	3.79	1.73	5.52	1.68	3.45	1.75	5.03	1.53
	(.04)		(.01)		(.36)				(-.26)		(-.03)		(1.33)	
LENS	5.52	1.93	5.39	1.85	4.66	1.94	3.85	1.91	6.12	1.37	3.70	1.61	4.23	1.08
	(-.13)		(-.10)		(-.68)		(-.20)		(.38)		(.22)		(.53)	
LEVER	5.68	1.71	5.09	1.83	4.39	1.99	4.11	1.80	5.92	1.43	3.41	1.70	3.72	1.24
	(.03)		(-.40)		(-.95)		(.06)		(.18)		(-.07)		(.02)	
LICE	5.29	2.16	5.16	1.90	5.91	1.37	3.86	1.72	5.38	1.85	3.38	1.79	2.02	1.62M
	(-.36)		(-.33)		(.57)		(-.19)		(-.36)		(-.10)		(-1.68)	

	CON		IMG		CAT		MNG		FAM		NOA		PLS	
	M	SD	M	SD	M	SD	M	SD	M	SD	M	SD	M	SD
LIEUTENANT	5.75	1.77	5.46	1.79	5.86	1.66	4.63	1.85	5.53	1.71	3.89	2.00	3.59	1.57
	(.10)		(-.03)		(.52)		(.58)		(-.21)		(.41)		(-.11)	
LINEN	5.75	1.86	5.45	1.75	5.32	1.78	4.15	1.85	6.12	1.25	3.35	1.52	4.39	1.45
	(.10)		(-.04)		(-.02)		(.10)		(.38)		(-.13)		(.69)	
LINT	5.33	2.02	5.07	1.92	4.60	1.85	3.10	1.36	5.53	1.70	2.71	1.54	3.05	1.19
	(-.32)		(-.42)		(-.74)		(-.95)		(-.21)		(-.77)		(-.65)	
LIVER	6.11	1.67	6.02	1.41	6.12	1.43	3.87	1.77	5.76	1.47	3.62	1.95	3.21	1.81
	(.46)		(.53)		(.78)		(-.18)		(.02)		(.14)		(-.49)	
LIZARD	5.84	1.87	6.26	1.28	6.38	1.36	4.03	1.97	5.57	1.84	4.34	2.01	3.12	1.54
	(.19)		(.77)		(1.04)		(-.02)		(-.17)		(.86)		(-.58)	
LOCKER	5.75	1.81	5.35	1.86	4.59	1.98	4.03	1.70	6.31	1.26	3.07	1.46	3.55	1.43
	(.10)		(-.14)		(-.75)		(-.02)		(.57)		(-.41)		(-.15)	
LOOT	5.38	1.86	5.73	1.58	4.45	1.81	4.48	1.67	5.44	1.69	3.52	1.57	4.10	1.72M
	(-.27)		(.24)		(-.89)		(.43)		(-.30)		(.04)		(.40)	
LUMBER	6.07	1.62	5.67	1.58	5.57	1.78	4.47	1.77	5.93	1.50	3.97	1.79	4.05	1.32
	(.42)		(.18)		(.23)		(.42)		(.19)		(.49)		(.35)	
LUNG	5.65	1.83	5.70	1.69	5.78	1.78	4.35	1.93	6.20	1.47	3.80	1.86	4.02	1.28
	(.00)		(.21)		(.44)		(.30)		(.46)		(.32)		(.32)	
MAGNET	5.46	2.04	5.37	1.73	4.97	1.82	3.65	1.93	6.00	1.57	3.11	1.47	3.85	1.17
	(-.19)		(-.12)		(-.37)		(-.40)		(.26)		(-.37)		(.15)	
MAHOGANY	5.09	2.07	4.94	1.98	6.10	1.32	3.33	1.71	5.25	1.85	3.29	1.89	4.98	1.44
	(-.56)		(-.55)		(.76)		(-.72)		(-.49)		(-.19)		(1.28)	
MALLET	6.19	1.47	5.51	1.68	4.98	1.87	3.48	1.82	4.62	1.99	2.92	1.61	3.89	1.24
	(.54)		(.02)		(-.36)		(-.57)		(-1.12)		(-.56)		(.19)	
MANE	5.50	1.94	5.22	1.97	4.77	1.89	3.77	1.75	4.90	1.93	3.23	1.61	3.87	1.77
	(-.15)		(-.27)		(-.57)		(-.28)		(-.84)		(-.25)		(.17)	
MANURE	6.40	1.35	5.28	2.09	5.57	1.71	4.53	1.90	5.32	2.04	3.33	1.75	2.73	1.62M
	(.75)		(-.21)		(.23)		(.48)		(-.42)		(-.15)		(-.97)	
MARE	5.45	1.97	5.23	1.81	5.38	1.96	4.26	1.80	5.34	1.76	3.62	1.98	4.61	1.52
	(-.20)		(-.26)		(.04)		(.21)		(-.40)		(.14)		(.91)	
MAROON	4.82	2.32	4.97	2.07	5.50	1.81	3.94	1.73	5.66	1.71	2.90	1.59	4.06	1.58
	(-.83)		(-.52)		(.16)		(-.11)		(-.08)		(-.58)		(.36)	
MARSHALL	5.53	1.69	5.16	1.82	4.73	1.96	4.05	1.76	5.38	1.79	3.87	1.64	3.94	1.41
	(-.12)		(-.33)		(-.61)		(.00)		(-.36)		(.39)		(.24)	
MAST	5.53	1.81	4.98	1.94	4.76	1.99	3.03	1.64	5.42	1.73	3.17	1.58	4.13	1.40
	(-.12)		(-.51)		(-.58)		(-1.02)		(-.32)		(-.31)		(.43)	
MAT	5.09	2.03	5.31	1.77	4.66	1.78	3.63	1.41	5.64	1.79	3.10	1.47	3.80	.97
	(-.56)		(-.18)		(-.68)		(-.42)		(-.10)		(-.38)		(.10)	
MAYOR	4.82	2.21	4.96	2.15	6.02	1.68	3.93	1.78	5.62	1.84	3.73	2.02	3.48	1.42M
	(-.83)		(-.53)		(.68)		(-.12)		(-.12)		(.25)		(-.22)	
MAZE	5.09	1.92	5.48	1.76	4.57	1.93	4.08	1.77	5.32	1.75	3.79	1.81	3.94	1.69
	(-.56)		(-.01)		(-.77)		(.03)		(-.42)		(.31)		(.24)	
MEASLES	5.64	1.85	5.76	1.90	6.53	1.11	3.98	1.94	5.61	1.86	3.19	1.96	2.00	1.37
	(-.01)		(.27)		(1.19)		(-.07)		(-.13)		(-.29)		(-1.70)	
MEDAL	5.67	1.73	5.23	2.06	5.25	1.66	4.20	1.74	5.68	1.57	3.72	1.72	4.37	1.58
	(.02)		(-.26)		(-.09)		(.15)		(-.06)		(.24)		(.67)	
MERCURY	5.33	1.89	5.15	1.80	5.52	1.85	3.33	1.86	5.41	1.76	3.39	1.81	3.75	1.41F
	(-.32)		(-.34)		(.18)		(-.72)		(-.33)		(-.09)		(.05)	
METAL	5.85	1.57	4.96	1.81	5.02	2.02	4.66	1.73	6.23	1.25	4.20	2.01	3.62	1.45M
	(.20)		(-.53)		(-.32)		(.49)		(.49)		(.72)		(-.08)	
MILE	4.78	2.03	5.11	2.01	5.77	1.67	3.98	1.90	6.15	1.38	3.03	1.74	4.19	1.31
	(-.87)		(-.38)		(.43)		(-.07)		(.41)		(-.45)		(.49)	
MINER	5.47	2.04	5.63	1.62	5.23	1.96	3.97	1.95	5.95	1.55	3.78	1.75	4.25	1.42
	(-.18)		(.14)		(-.11)		(-.08)		(.21)		(.30)		(.55)	

	CON		IMG		CAT		MNG		FAM		NOA		PLS	
	M	SD	M	SD	M	SD	M	SD	M	SD	M	SD	M	SD
MINNOW	6.17	1.73	5.59	1.88	5.85	1.83	4.20	1.74	5.10	2.00	3.46	1.89	4.58	1.41
	(.52)		(.10)		(.51)		(.15)		(-.64)		(-.02)		(.88)	
MISSILE	6.09	1.54	5.98	1.63	5.67	1.73	4.82	1.95	5.93	1.54	4.69	1.89	3.16	1.84
	(.44)		(.49)		(.33)		(.77)		(.19)		(1.21)		(-.54)	
MOLE	5.86	1.88	5.61	1.83	5.57	1.76	3.72	1.95	5.58	1.74	3.75	1.56	3.01	1.39
	(.21)		(.12)		(.23)		(-.33)		(-.16)		(.27)		(-.69)	
MONASTERY	5.60	1.94	5.44	1.76	4.92	1.93	4.16	2.05	5.35	1.77	4.21	2.03	3.82	1.29
	(-.05)		(-.05)		(-.42)		(.11)		(-.39)		(.73)		(.12)	
MONSOON	4.77	2.15	4.90	1.87	5.72	1.55	3.45	1.70	4.75	2.05	3.54	1.88	3.46	1.65F
	(-.88)		(-.59)		(.38)		(-.60)		(-.99)		(.06)		(-.24)	
MORGUE	5.80	1.79	5.95	1.58	5.05	1.92	4.52	1.87	5.48	1.74	3.56	1.98	1.87	1.45
	(.15)		(.46)		(-.29)		(.47)		(-.26)		(.08)		(-1.83)	
MORPHINE	5.76	1.80	5.44	1.98	6.45	.93	4.33	1.78	5.20	1.71	3.61	1.96	3.16	1.77
	(.11)		(-.05)		(1.11)		(.28)		(-.54)		(.13)		(-.54)	
MOSQUITO	5.93	1.79	6.02	1.70	6.48	1.27	4.22	2.01	6.22	1.35	3.84	2.03	2.34	1.55
	(.28)		(.53)		(1.14)		(.17)		(.48)		(.36)		(-1.36)	
MOSS	5.60	1.87	5.32	1.93	5.62	1.55	3.73	1.71	5.53	1.64	3.52	1.72	4.81	1.28
	(-.05)		(-.17)		(.28)		(-.32)		(-.21)		(.04)		(1.11)	
MOTH	5.46	2.06	5.71	1.71	5.88	1.82	3.98	1.74	5.70	1.66	3.59	1.87	3.23	1.62M
	(-.19)		(.22)		(.54)		(-.07)		(-.04)		(.11)		(-.47)	
MOUSE	6.12	1.75	6.07	1.52	6.20	1.63	4.26	1.85	6.12	1.72	3.86	1.80	3.46	1.54M
	(.47)		(.58)		(.86)		(.21)		(.38)		(.38)		(-.24)	
MOUTHPIECE	6.04	1.56	5.43	1.71	4.78	1.93	4.00	1.93	5.69	1.73	3.23	1.49	3.71	1.80M
	(.39)		(-.06)		(-.56)		(-.05)		(-.05)		(-.25)		(.01)	
MUCUS	5.61	1.98	5.64	1.77	4.47	1.98	3.66	1.87	5.21	1.95	3.10	1.71	2.51	1.69
	(-.04)		(.15)		(-.87)		(-.39)		(-.53)		(-.38)		(-1.19)	
MUD	6.02	1.68	5.79	1.67	5.05	1.81	4.72	1.58	6.05	1.31	3.05	1.36	3.56	1.69
	(.37)		(.30)		(-.29)		(.67)		(.31)		(-.43)		(-.14)	
MULE	5.46	2.10	5.89	1.34	6.47	.96	4.08	1.49	5.85	1.56	4.11	1.93	3.72	1.33
	(-.19)		(.40)		(1.13)		(.03)		(.11)		(.63)		(.02)	
MURDER	4.68	1.99	5.43	1.74	5.13	1.87	5.36	1.51	6.08	1.39	4.27	1.98	1.75	1.31
	(-.97)		(-.06)		(-.21)		(1.31)		(.34)		(.79)		(-1.95)	
MUSTARD	5.91	1.91	5.93	1.49	6.16	1.34	3.88	2.04	6.06	1.42	3.06	1.54	4.11	1.46
	(.26)		(.44)		(.82)		(-.17)		(.32)		(-.42)		(.41)	
MUTTON	5.34	2.03	4.63	2.02	4.87	2.13	3.34	1.96	4.50	1.88	3.16	1.42	3.49	1.64
	(-.31)		(-.86)		(-.47)		(-.71)		(-1.24)		(-.32)		(-.21)	
NAIL	5.77	1.79	5.46	1.96	5.62	1.72	4.03	1.80	6.17	1.34	3.33	1.59	3.60	1.42
	(.12)		(-.03)		(.28)		(-.02)		(.43)		(-.15)		(-.10)	
NAPKIN	5.44	2.05	5.76	1.76	5.22	1.94	3.57	1.57	6.08	1.46	2.94	1.57	3.89	1.13
	(-.21)		(.27)		(-.12)		(-.48)		(.34)		(-.54)		(.19)	
NAVAL	5.15	1.83	5.29	1.90	5.08	1.66	4.07	1.74	5.50	1.80	3.51	1.60	3.95	1.37
	(-.50)		(-.20)		(-.26)		(.02)		(-.24)		(.03)		(.25)	
NAVEL	5.79	1.58	5.40	1.74	5.23	1.82	4.37	1.87	5.59	1.73	3.39	1.75	4.40	1.31
	(.14)		(-.09)		(-.11)		(.32)		(-.15)		(-.09)		(.70)	
NEEDLE	6.04	1.79	6.07	1.42	5.22	1.82	4.35	1.69	6.09	1.42	3.38	1.70	3.41	1.47
	(.39)		(.58)		(-.12)		(.30)		(.35)		(-.10)		(-.29)	
NET	5.46	2.15	5.14	2.14	4.80	2.06	3.94	1.76	6.07	1.55	3.13	1.52	3.69	1.18
	(-.19)		(-.35)		(-.54)		(-.11)		(.33)		(-.35)		(-.01)	
NOODLE	5.84	1.69	5.24	1.88	5.60	1.52	3.85	1.86	5.73	1.49	2.97	1.66	4.11	1.48F
	(.19)		(-.25)		(.26)		(-.20)		(-.01)		(-.51)		(.41)	
NUN	5.82	1.83	6.00	1.71	5.80	1.67	4.35	1.97	5.88	1.68	3.66	2.08	4.13	1.62M
	(.17)		(.51)		(.46)		(.30)		(.14)		(.18)		(.43)	
OAR	5.68	2.05	5.86	1.57	5.35	1.77	3.77	1.87	5.70	1.65	3.02	1.57	4.43	1.41M
	(.03)		(.37)		(.01)		(-.28)		(-.04)		(-.46)		(.73)	

	CON		IMG		CAT		MNG		FAM		NOA		PLS	
	M	SD	M	SD	M	SD	M	SD	M	SD	M	SD	M	SD
OAT	5.49	1.96	4.93	1.90	5.75	1.75	3.57	1.66	5.58	1.58	3.20	1.69	4.28	1.14
	(-.16)		(-.56)		(.41)		(-.48)		(-.16)		(-.28)		(.58)	
OATMEAL	5.48	2.16	5.75	1.77	5.84	1.51	3.46	1.95	5.91	1.56	3.11	1.61	3.88	1.40
	(-.17)		(.26)		(.50)		(-.59)		(.17)		(-.37)		(.18)	
OBESE	4.88	2.02	5.57	1.65	4.68	2.09	5.35	1.54	4.98	1.98	3.67	1.83	2.52	1.58
	(-.77)		(.08)		(-.66)		(1.30)		(-.76)		(.19)		(-1.18)	
OBOE	5.82	1.85	4.89	2.18	5.07	2.36	3.74	2.09	4.59	2.20	3.03	1.78	4.10	1.66
	(.17)		(-.60)		(-.27)		(-.31)		(-1.15)		(-.45)		(.40)	
OFFICE	5.65	1.88	4.89	1.98	5.17	1.74	4.25	1.60	6.31	1.24	4.36	1.74	3.66	1.44
	(.00)		(-.60)		(-.17)		(.20)		(.57)		(.88)		(-.04)	
OIL	5.60	1.81	5.21	1.79	5.28	1.71	4.13	1.85	6.23	1.10	4.26	2.01	3.55	1.49M
	(-.05)		(-.28)		(-.06)		(.08)		(.49)		(.78)		(-.15)	
OLIVE	6.14	1.56	5.88	1.59	5.82	1.56	3.51	1.79	5.85	1.48	3.31	1.52	4.17	1.44
	(.49)		(.39)		(.48)		(-.54)		(.11)		(-.17)		(.47)	
ONION	6.16	1.71	6.26	1.25	6.30	1.50	4.52	2.07	6.41	1.27	3.25	1.80	3.78	1.80
	(.51)		(.77)		(.96)		(.47)		(.67)		(-.23)		(.08)	
OPAL	5.29	2.14	4.84	2.23	5.62	1.85	3.05	1.88	4.92	1.99	3.33	1.86	4.91	1.52F
	(-.36)		(-.65)		(.28)		(-1.00)		(-.82)		(-.15)		(1.21)	
OPIUM	5.42	2.23	5.02	2.03	5.27	2.07	4.13	1.91	5.60	1.79	4.14	2.05	3.67	1.91M
	(-.23)		(-.47)		(-.07)		(.08)		(-.14)		(.66)		(-.03)	
OREGANO	5.39	2.26	4.91	2.17	5.77	1.67	3.98	2.07	5.10	2.08	2.57	1.27	4.46	1.55F
	(-.26)		(-.58)		(.43)		(-.07)		(-.64)		(-.91)		(.76)	
OVEN	5.70	1.98	5.72	1.77	5.54	1.68	4.07	1.92	6.35	1.13	3.66	1.80	4.13	1.43
	(.05)		(.23)		(.20)		(.02)		(.61)		(.18)		(.43)	
OYSTER	5.69	1.94	5.15	1.93	5.93	1.74	3.66	1.76	5.27	1.82	3.59	1.69	4.44	1.49F
	(.04)		(-.34)		(.59)		(-.39)		(-.47)		(.11)		(.74)	
PAGE	5.85	1.72	5.72	1.63	4.52	1.84	3.80	1.86	6.29	1.27	3.47	1.69	3.91	1.03
	(.20)		(.23)		(-.82)		(-.25)		(.55)		(-.01)		(.21)	
PAIL	5.34	2.13	5.02	2.12	4.62	2.00	3.54	1.71	5.27	2.02	3.16	1.43	3.55	1.20
	(-.31)		(-.47)		(-.72)		(-.51)		(-.47)		(-.32)		(-.15)	
PAN	5.82	1.78	5.26	2.10	5.33	1.84	4.51	1.99	6.40	1.34	3.05	1.72	3.61	1.27
	(.17)		(-.23)		(-.01)		(.46)		(.66)		(-.43)		(-.09)	
PANS	5.55	2.01	4.81	2.21	4.82	1.97	3.69	1.91	5.77	1.72	3.18	1.57	3.59	1.32
	(-.10)		(-.68)		(-.52)		(-.36)		(.03)		(-.30)		(-.11)	
PAPER	5.96	1.72	5.84	1.72	5.02	2.13	4.60	1.83	6.61	1.20	3.51	1.95	4.09	1.56
	(.31)		(.35)		(-.32)		(.55)		(.87)		(.03)		(.39)	
PASTE	5.49	1.90	5.23	1.63	4.15	1.84	4.27	1.70	6.03	1.45	3.20	1.47	3.54	1.26
	(-.16)		(-.26)		(-1.19)		(.22)		(.29)		(-.28)		(-.16)	
PASTOR	5.63	1.85	4.82	2.09	5.47	1.71	3.67	1.68	5.35	1.88	3.85	1.95	3.89	1.54
	(-.02)		(-.67)		(.13)		(-.38)		(-.39)		(.37)		(.19)	
PATCH	5.54	1.76	5.23	1.93	4.12	1.75	4.23	1.79	6.02	1.31	3.52	1.67	3.68	1.43
	(-.11)		(-.26)		(-1.22)		(.18)		(.28)		(-.04)		(-.02)	
PAUL	5.20	2.16	4.34	2.47	5.53	2.05	3.57	2.25	5.60	1.94	3.13	2.17	4.48	1.36F
	(-.45)		(-1.15)		(.19)		(-.48)		(-.14)		(-.35)		(.78)	
PEA	6.10	1.64	5.62	1.82	5.78	1.85	3.85	1.91	5.98	1.50	2.92	1.69	3.85	1.34
	(.45)		(.13)		(.44)		(-.20)		(.24)		(-.56)		(.15)	
PEDAL	6.04	1.48	5.49	1.74	4.90	1.82	4.11	1.70	6.12	1.47	3.43	1.40	4.04	1.49
	(.39)		(.00)		(-.44)		(.06)		(.38)		(-.05)		(.34)	
PEG	5.33	2.01	5.32	1.82	4.51	1.70	3.38	1.71	5.36	1.67	2.77	1.33	3.91	1.14
	(-.32)		(-.17)		(-.83)		(-.67)		(-.38)		(-.71)		(.21)	
PELT	5.31	2.16	5.09	1.86	4.87	1.85	3.46	1.73	4.60	2.04	3.58	1.52	3.72	1.66M
	(-.34)		(-.40)		(-.47)		(-.59)		(-1.14)		(.10)		(.02)	
PEN	5.67	2.00	5.70	1.72	5.76	1.70	4.25	1.85	6.28	1.35	3.71	2.05	3.92	1.20
	(.02)		(.21)		(.42)		(.20)		(.54)		(.23)		(.22)	

	CON		IMG		CAT		MNG		FAM		NOA		PLS	
	M	SD	M	SD	M	SD	M	SD	M	SD	M	SD	M	SD
PENICILLIN	5.86	1.90	4.95	1.85	5.47	2.07	4.55	2.09	5.68	1.76	3.83	1.91	4.21	1.71
	(.21)		(-.54)		(.13)		(.50)		(-.06)		(.35)		(.51)	
PEPPER	5.61	1.96	5.72	1.50	5.69	1.65	3.78	1.85	6.02	1.43	2.95	1.50	4.04	1.39
	(-.04)		(.23)		(.35)		(-.27)		(.28)		(-.53)		(.34)	
PETAL	5.82	1.62	5.02	1.97	4.75	2.06	3.97	1.65	5.40	1.87	3.69	1.59	4.98	1.53F
	(.17)		(-.47)		(-.59)		(-.08)		(-.34)		(.21)		(1.28)	
PEW	5.38	2.21	5.45	2.05	4.55	2.05	3.59	1.94	5.03	1.87	2.86	1.55	3.54	1.82
	(-.27)		(-.04)		(-.79)		(-.46)		(-.71)		(-.62)		(-.16)	
PIER	5.84	1.83	5.39	1.72	4.58	2.05	3.80	1.69	5.10	1.94	3.55	1.66	4.81	1.37F
	(.19)		(-.10)		(-.76)		(-.25)		(-.64)		(.07)		(1.11)	
PIGEON	5.77	1.97	6.05	1.43	5.83	1.75	4.11	1.75	5.92	1.72	3.72	1.99	4.14	1.56
	(.12)		(.56)		(.49)		(.06)		(.18)		(.24)		(.44)	
PIMPLE	5.75	1.74	6.11	1.50	5.25	1.66	4.39	1.97	6.31	1.25	3.27	1.88	1.81	1.09
	(.10)		(.62)		(-.09)		(.34)		(.57)		(-.21)		(-1.89)	
PIN	5.81	1.82	5.43	1.74	5.07	1.71	4.25	1.78	5.76	1.59	3.33	1.65	3.73	1.60
	(.16)		(-.06)		(-.27)		(.20)		(.02)		(-.15)		(.03)	
PINT	4.79	2.19	4.81	1.74	5.55	1.73	4.18	1.89	6.10	1.23	2.60	1.62	4.54	1.32M
	(-.86)		(-.68)		(.21)		(.13)		(.36)		(-.88)		(.84)	
PLATE	5.91	1.69	5.21	2.03	5.48	1.55	4.60	1.65	6.30	1.24	3.43	1.82	4.31	1.10
	(.26)		(-.28)		(.14)		(.55)		(.56)		(-.05)		(.61)	
PLATTER	5.89	1.83	5.70	1.61	5.74	1.45	3.90	1.57	5.52	1.73	3.33	1.56	4.03	1.36
	(.24)		(.21)		(.40)		(-.15)		(-.22)		(-.15)		(.33)	
PLIERS	6.41	1.28	5.82	1.55	5.48	1.90	4.08	1.88	5.73	1.69	3.36	1.75	3.89	1.42
	(.76)		(.33)		(.14)		(.03)		(-.01)		(-.12)		(.19)	
PLOW	5.77	1.86	5.63	1.79	5.12	1.64	4.27	1.97	5.75	1.57	3.44	1.72	4.00	1.38
	(.12)		(.14)		(-.22)		(.22)		(.01)		(-.04)		(.30)	
PLUM	6.28	1.52	6.05	1.54	6.17	1.64	4.70	1.92	6.21	1.33	3.18	1.89	3.66	1.69
	(.63)		(.56)		(.83)		(.65)		(.47)		(-.30)		(-.04)	
POCKET	5.59	1.97	5.61	1.68	5.38	1.76	4.13	1.93	6.37	1.23	3.29	1.68	4.38	1.08
	(-.06)		(.12)		(.04)		(.08)		(.63)		(-.19)		(.68)	
PODIUM	5.42	2.07	5.02	2.28	4.72	1.90	3.67	1.79	5.29	1.65	3.27	1.50	3.93	1.37F
	(-.23)		(-.47)		(-.62)		(-.38)		(-.45)		(-.21)		(.23)	
POLE	5.59	1.82	5.68	1.64	4.78	1.87	4.20	1.73	6.05	1.28	3.34	1.62	3.85	1.21M
	(-.06)		(.19)		(-.56)		(.15)		(.31)		(-.14)		(.15)	
POLIO	5.51	1.78	5.55	1.64	6.37	.99	3.97	1.86	5.37	1.74	3.65	1.83	1.99	1.60
	(-.14)		(.06)		(1.03)		(-.08)		(-.37)		(.17)		(-1.71)	
POLLEN	5.80	1.66	5.20	1.96	5.78	1.46	4.21	1.71	5.62	1.53	3.86	1.93	3.24	1.69F
	(.15)		(-.29)		(.44)		(.16)		(-.12)		(.38)		(-.46)	
POLO	4.91	2.13	5.18	1.79	5.08	1.83	3.05	1.87	5.20	1.85	3.30	1.63	4.67	1.41
	(-.74)		(-.31)		(-.26)		(-1.00)		(-.54)		(-.18)		(.97)	
POPE	5.89	1.65	5.70	1.68	5.58	1.81	4.36	1.95	5.63	1.70	3.74	2.02	3.69	1.55
	(.24)		(.21)		(.24)		(.31)		(-.11)		(.26)		(-.01)	
PORK	5.81	1.97	5.16	1.91	5.67	1.69	4.35	1.68	6.12	1.49	3.24	1.61	3.80	1.66
	(.16)		(-.33)		(.33)		(.30)		(.38)		(-.24)		(.10)	
POTS	5.71	1.91	5.27	1.93	5.47	1.86	4.42	2.08	5.95	1.71	3.84	1.72	3.85	1.39M
	(.06)		(-.22)		(.13)		(.37)		(.21)		(.36)		(.15)	
PROJECTOR	5.44	1.93	5.78	1.61	5.16	1.68	3.18	1.55	5.51	1.67	4.00	1.81	3.82	1.21
	(-.21)		(.29)		(-.18)		(-.87)		(-.23)		(.52)		(.12)	
PROPELLER	5.89	1.95	5.93	1.47	5.47	1.56	3.95	1.95	5.65	1.78	3.19	1.73	3.95	1.50M
	(.24)		(.44)		(.13)		(-.10)		(-.09)		(-.29)		(.25)	
PUDDLE	6.00	1.54	5.56	1.75	5.12	1.76	4.30	1.79	5.95	1.34	3.15	1.55	4.31	1.20
	(.35)		(.07)		(-.22)		(.25)		(.25)		(-.33)		(.61)	
PULPIT	5.58	1.89	5.45	1.95	4.50	2.02	3.70	1.85	4.89	2.00	3.14	1.63	3.63	1.37
	(-.07)		(-.04)		(-.84)		(-.35)		(-.85)		(-.34)		(-.07)	

	CON M SD	IMG M SD	CAT M SD	MNG M SD	FAM M SD	NOA M SD	PLS M SD
PUMP	5.29 1.94 (-.36)	5.81 1.68 (.32)	4.77 1.74 (-.57)	3.89 1.52 (-.16)	5.81 1.55 (.07)	3.78 1.73 (.30)	3.88 1.50 (.18)
PUPIL	5.66 1.93 (.01)	5.34 1.78 (-.15)	4.98 1.85 (-.36)	5.02 1.72 (.97)	6.08 1.32 (.34)	4.27 1.85 (.79)	3.72 1.38 (.02)
PURSE	5.68 1.88 (.03)	5.61 1.69 (.12)	5.55 1.61 (.21)	4.33 1.73 (.28)	6.07 1.40 (.33)	4.17 1.80 (.69)	3.81 1.22 (.11)
PYTHON	6.00 1.72 (.35)	5.77 1.85 (.28)	5.03 2.31 (-.31)	3.64 1.95 (-.41)	4.27 1.98 (-1.47)	3.44 1.77 (-.04)	3.14 1.74 (-.56)
QUART	5.00 2.15 (-.65)	5.39 1.70 (-.10)	5.63 1.73 (.29)	4.31 1.89 (.26)	6.42 1.00 (.68)	3.08 1.67 (-.40)	4.07 1.02M (.37)
QUILL	5.91 1.72 (.26)	5.24 1.84 (-.25)	4.77 1.77 (-.57)	3.59 1.99 (-.46)	4.83 2.04 (-.91)	3.02 1.84 (-.46)	4.39 1.33 (.69)
RABBI	5.68 1.86 (.03)	5.51 1.91 (.02)	5.72 1.73 (.38)	4.30 2.25 (.25)	5.89 1.52 (.15)	3.89 2.11 (.41)	3.91 1.78 (.21)
RACQUET	5.09 2.20 (-.56)	5.16 2.09 (-.33)	5.13 1.89 (-.21)	3.97 1.99 (-.08)	5.54 1.76 (-.20)	3.79 1.60 (.31)	4.52 1.42 (.82)
RAIL	5.36 2.04 (-.29)	5.50 1.87 (.01)	4.50 1.74 (-.84)	3.85 1.73 (-.20)	5.79 1.50 (.05)	3.49 1.73 (.01)	3.59 1.20 (-.11)
RAINCOATS	6.25 1.39 (.60)	5.94 1.39 (.45)	5.75 1.63 (.41)	4.16 1.90 (.11)	5.69 1.60 (-.05)	3.56 1.70 (.08)	4.06 1.24F (.36)
RAINHAT	5.69 1.91 (.04)	5.07 1.98 (-.42)	5.27 1.83 (-.07)	3.30 1.91 (-.75)	4.95 2.22 (-.79)	2.92 1.65 (-.56)	3.48 1.13 (-.22)
RAKE	5.74 1.98 (.09)	5.61 1.75 (.12)	5.33 1.68 (-.01)	3.80 1.83 (-.25)	5.87 1.60 (.13)	3.49 1.51 (.01)	2.82 1.24 (-.88)
RAM	5.37 1.88 (-.28)	5.40 1.75 (-.09)	5.03 2.15 (-.31)	3.84 1.95 (-.21)	5.42 1.78 (-.32)	3.35 1.40 (-.35)	4.05 1.53 (.35)
RAMP	5.34 2.12 (-.31)	5.21 1.69 (-.28)	4.07 1.91 (-1.27)	3.44 1.89 (-.61)	5.78 1.56 (.04)	2.90 1.25 (-.58)	3.84 .97M (.14)
RAPE	4.68 2.11 (-.97)	5.59 1.52 (.10)	5.10 1.75 (-.24)	4.68 1.75 (.63)	6.29 1.37 (.55)	4.20 1.99 (.72)	2.40 1.76M (-1.30)
RASH	5.19 1.86 (-.46)	5.14 2.09 (-.35)	4.35 1.77 (-.99)	4.03 1.48 (-.02)	5.59 1.64 (-.15)	3.70 1.71 (.22)	2.46 1.39 (-1.24)
RAT	6.20 1.46 (.55)	5.82 1.81 (.33)	6.48 1.08 (1.14)	4.68 1.77 (.63)	6.22 1.26 (.48)	3.80 1.74 (.32)	2.50 1.55M (-1.20)
RATTLESNAKE	5.82 1.96 (.17)	6.05 1.76 (.56)	6.02 1.79 (.68)	3.77 1.87 (-.28)	5.67 1.71 (-.07)	3.86 1.92 (.38)	2.54 1.54M (-1.16)
RECTANGLE	5.50 1.73 (-.15)	5.84 1.65 (.35)	6.16 1.34 (.82)	4.40 1.96 (.35)	6.00 1.44 (.26)	2.24 1.51 (-1.24)	3.86 1.15 (.16)
REED	5.31 2.08 (-.34)	5.08 1.91 (-.41)	4.40 1.82 (-.94)	3.44 1.75 (-.61)	5.18 1.80 (-.56)	3.36 1.64 (-.12)	4.16 1.15 (.46)
REFEREE	5.50 1.98 (-.15)	5.58 1.65 (.09)	4.95 1.77 (-.39)	4.65 1.68 (.60)	6.08 1.42 (.34)	3.64 1.70 (.16)	3.72 1.44 (.02)
RHINESTONES	5.79 1.71 (.14)	5.07 2.22 (-.42)	5.85 1.72 (.51)	4.07 1.83 (.02)	4.86 1.95 (-.88)	3.51 1.89 (.03)	4.46 1.54 (.76)
RIB	5.95 1.56 (.30)	5.80 1.44 (.31)	5.57 1.73 (.23)	4.34 1.96 (.29)	6.10 1.39 (.36)	3.03 1.53 (-.45)	3.90 1.61 (.20)
RIFLE	6.04 1.70 (.39)	5.61 1.88 (.12)	5.75 1.62 (.41)	4.53 1.59 (.48)	5.98 1.53 (.24)	4.05 1.87 (.57)	3.02 1.66M (-.68)
ROCKER	5.79 1.58 (.14)	5.14 1.83 (-.35)	5.22 1.75 (-.12)	3.88 1.57 (-.17)	5.48 1.61 (-.26)	3.75 1.58 (.27)	4.59 1.56F (.89)
ROD	6.15 1.58 (.50)	5.52 1.70 (.03)	4.83 1.82 (-.51)	4.16 1.83 (.11)	5.62 1.63 (-.12)	3.33 1.67 (-.15)	3.76 1.44M (.06)
ROOT	5.54 1.91 (-.11)	5.59 1.68 (.10)	5.17 1.69 (-.17)	4.43 1.78 (.38)	6.28 1.23 (.54)	3.38 1.57 (-.10)	4.29 1.56 (.59)

	CON		IMG		CAT		MNG		FAM		NOA		PLS	
	M	SD	M	SD	M	SD	M	SD	M	SD	M	SD	M	SD
ROPE	5.96	1.86	6.00	1.53	5.17	1.91	4.41	1.69	6.42	1.14	3.36	1.62	4.08	1.26M
	(.31)		(.51)		(-.17)		(.36)		(.68)		(-.12)		(.38)	
ROSARY	5.31	2.08	4.58	2.22	4.81	1.83	3.52	1.95	4.84	2.02	3.72	1.65	4.21	1.33
	(-.34)		(-.91)		(-.53)		(-.53)		(-.90)		(.24)		(.51)	
ROWBOAT	5.49	2.02	5.89	1.42	6.07	1.55	4.07	1.79	5.99	1.39	3.49	1.71	4.36	1.66
	(-.16)		(.40)		(.73)		(.02)		(-.15)		(.01)		(.66)	
RUDDER	5.68	1.96	5.14	1.54	4.88	1.94	3.57	1.83	5.10	1.90	3.38	1.66	4.05	1.15
	(.03)		(-.35)		(-.46)		(-.48)		(-.64)		(-.10)		(.35)	
RUSTY	5.02	1.81	5.76	1.56	4.18	1.69	4.23	1.61	5.87	1.48	3.45	1.58	3.29	1.35F
	(-.63)		(.27)		(-1.16)		(.18)		(.13)		(-.03)		(-.41)	
SACK	5.78	1.67	5.42	1.75	4.45	1.93	4.47	1.72	6.13	1.45	3.52	1.69	3.85	1.20
	(.13)		(-.07)		(-.89)		(.42)		(.39)		(.04)		(.15)	
SALT	5.69	1.97	5.54	1.65	6.03	1.52	3.97	2.02	6.44	1.07	2.93	1.81	4.37	1.27
	(.04)		(.05)		(.69)		(-.08)		(.70)		(-.55)		(.67)	
SAPPHIRE	5.68	1.90	5.54	1.78	5.53	2.07	3.77	1.91	4.54	2.00	3.13	1.60	5.24	1.31F
	(.03)		(.05)		(.19)		(-.28)		(-1.20)		(-.35)		(1.54)	
SARDINE	6.02	1.68	5.87	1.61	6.38	1.21	4.03	1.98	5.08	1.97	3.38	1.76	3.63	1.74
	(.37)		(.38)		(1.04)		(-.02)		(-.66)		(-.10)		(-.07)	
SAUCER	6.02	1.67	5.38	1.88	5.37	1.57	4.25	1.95	6.07	1.31	3.43	1.71	3.76	1.65
	(.37)		(-.11)		(.03)		(.20)		(.33)		(-.05)		(.06)	
SAUERKRAUT	6.00	1.75	5.79	1.75	5.92	1.66	3.39	1.92	5.00	2.05	3.02	1.74	3.48	1.80
	(.35)		(.30)		(.58)		(-.66)		(-.74)		(-.46)		(-.22)	
SCAB	5.55	1.94	5.67	1.68	4.80	1.77	4.24	1.88	5.98	1.50	3.18	1.55	2.64	1.57
	(-.10)		(.18)		(-.54)		(.19)		(.24)		(-.30)		(-1.06)	
SCALLOPS	5.87	1.97	5.52	1.63	5.58	1.73	4.23	1.96	5.36	1.80	3.18	1.67	4.10	1.59F
	(.22)		(.03)		(.24)		(.18)		(-.38)		(-.30)		(.40)	
SCAPEL	5.18	2.24	4.81	2.13	4.95	2.14	3.69	2.02	4.43	2.09	3.08	1.78	3.28	1.64
	(-.47)		(-.68)		(-.39)		(-.36)		(-1.31)		(-.40)		(-.42)	
SCAR	5.48	1.88	5.59	1.84	4.93	1.80	4.16	1.95	6.03	1.54	3.43	1.64	2.62	1.33M
	(-.17)		(.10)		(-.41)		(.11)		(.29)		(-.05)		(-1.08)	
SCARLET	5.08	1.91	5.63	1.59	5.22	2.02	4.53	1.91	5.30	1.86	3.00	1.68	4.75	1.45
	(-.57)		(.14)		(-.12)		(.48)		(-.44)		(-.48)		(1.05)	
SCISSORS	5.92	1.73	6.21	1.33	5.81	1.50	4.05	1.63	6.35	1.13	3.14	1.52	3.54	1.27
	(.27)		(.72)		(.47)		(.00)		(.61)		(-.34)		(-.16)	
SCOOTER	5.61	1.92	5.63	1.55	5.35	1.68	3.74	1.82	5.42	1.84	3.89	1.86	4.21	1.27
	(-.04)		(.14)		(.01)		(-.31)		(-.32)		(.41)		(.51)	
SCULL	5.49	2.04	5.09	2.18	4.95	2.11	3.48	2.16	4.65	1.99	3.52	1.92	3.42	1.52F
	(-.16)		(-.40)		(-.39)		(-.57)		(-1.09)		(.04)		(-.28)	
SEAL	5.44	1.92	4.98	1.98	5.47	1.85	3.98	1.84	5.97	1.38	3.85	1.61	4.40	1.24
	(-.21)		(-.51)		(.13)		(-.07)		(.23)		(.37)		(.70)	
SEAM	5.34	1.92	5.49	1.91	4.85	1.70	3.98	1.82	6.21	1.29	3.38	1.62	3.74	1.19
	(-.31)		(.00)		(-.49)		(-.07)		(.47)		(-.10)		(.04)	
SEAMAN	5.59	1.86	4.75	2.14	5.48	1.69	3.80	1.69	5.23	1.85	4.38	1.82	4.58	1.35
	(-.06)		(-.74)		(.14)		(-.25)		(-.51)		(.90)		(.88)	
SEAT	5.51	1.86	5.36	1.96	5.02	1.73	4.69	1.79	6.58	.87	3.60	1.80	4.07	1.12
	(-.14)		(-.13)		(-.32)		(.64)		(.84)		(.12)		(.37)	
SEAWEED	5.89	1.82	5.84	1.60	5.35	1.78	3.84	1.97	5.52	1.74	3.19	1.82	3.95	1.59F
	(.24)		(.35)		(.01)		(-.21)		(-.22)		(-.29)		(.25)	
SECRETARY	5.74	1.84	5.53	1.81	5.42	1.80	4.11	1.79	6.05	1.38	4.48	1.91	3.98	1.63M
	(.09)		(.04)		(.08)		(.06)		(.31)		(1.00)		(.28)	
SEMEN	5.46	2.01	4.88	2.08	4.65	2.06	4.13	1.90	5.03	1.87	3.44	1.89	4.43	1.50
	(-.19)		(-.61)		(-.69)		(.08)		(-.71)		(-.04)		(.73)	
SERGEANT	5.07	2.02	5.43	1.86	5.50	1.91	3.65	1.78	5.54	1.59	3.30	1.85	2.93	1.53
	(-.58)		(-.06)		(.16)		(-.40)		(-.20)		(-.18)		(-.77)	

	CON		IMG		CAT		MNG		FAM		NOA		PLS	
	M	SD	M	SD	M	SD	M	SD	M	SD	M	SD	M	SD
SEWER	5.60	1.89	5.32	1.74	4.53	1.87	3.74	1.91	5.63	1.70	3.43	1.56	2.34	1.38M
	(-.05)		(-.17)		(-.81)		(-.31)		(-.11)		(-.05)		(-1.36)	
SHARK	6.07	1.71	5.96	1.63	6.52	1.05	4.23	1.74	5.90	1.43	4.05	1.86	3.01	1.48F
	(.42)		(.47)		(1.18)		(.18)		(.16)		(.57)		(-.69)	
SHAWL	5.93	1.70	5.47	1.73	5.25	1.87	4.32	2.02	5.51	1.56	3.25	1.65	3.69	1.54
	(.28)		(-.02)		(-.09)		(.27)		(-.23)		(-.23)		(-.01)	
SHEEP	6.18	1.69	6.09	1.57	5.98	1.82	4.44	2.09	6.26	1.37	3.61	2.05	3.83	1.75
	(.53)		(.60)		(.64)		(.39)		(.52)		(.13)		(.13)	
SHEEPSKIN	6.12	1.44	5.41	1.94	5.48	1.67	3.82	2.02	5.47	1.79	3.62	1.89	4.12	1.60
	(.47)		(-.08)		(.14)		(-.23)		(.14)		(.14)		(.42)	
SHELL	5.93	1.64	5.75	1.64	5.02	1.88	4.15	1.69	5.98	1.35	4.22	1.66	4.24	1.62F
	(.28)		(.26)		(-.32)		(.10)		(.24)		(.74)		(.54)	
SHILLING	5.18	1.95	4.50	2.05	5.74	1.70	3.20	1.93	4.32	2.10	2.87	1.64	4.34	1.67
	(-.47)		(-.99)		(.40)		(-.85)		(-1.42)		(-.61)		(.64)	
SHOT	4.63	1.94	5.29	1.80	4.65	1.76	4.33	1.58	6.05	1.35	3.22	1.47	2.39	1.48
	(-1.02)		(-.20)		(-.69)		(.28)		(.31)		(-.26)		(-1.31)	
SHOVEL	5.77	1.74	5.32	1.97	5.64	1.84	4.18	1.64	6.02	1.41	3.35	1.63	3.48	1.18
	(.12)		(-.17)		(.30)		(.13)		(.28)		(-.13)		(-.22)	
SIDEWALK	5.93	1.82	5.25	2.11	5.33	1.82	4.25	1.67	6.60	.90	3.67	1.82	4.14	1.20
	(.28)		(-.24)		(-.01)		(.20)		(.86)		(.19)		(.44)	
SILK	5.34	2.07	5.04	2.05	5.57	1.80	3.68	1.76	5.56	1.81	3.81	1.65	5.05	1.56
	(-.31)		(-.45)		(.23)		(-.37)		(-.18)		(.33)		(1.35)	
SINK	5.88	1.76	6.04	1.40	5.37	1.60	4.18	1.88	6.34	1.23	3.42	1.58	3.17	1.35
	(.23)		(.55)		(.03)		(.13)		(.60)		(-.06)		(-.53)	
SKATE	5.58	1.72	5.57	1.79	4.90	1.82	4.13	1.79	6.08	1.49	3.20	1.57	4.12	1.39
	(-.07)		(.08)		(-.44)		(.08)		(.34)		(-.28)		(.42)	
SKILLET	5.72	1.89	5.83	1.59	5.73	1.60	4.50	1.85	5.71	1.76	3.11	1.68	3.75	1.27
	(.07)		(.34)		(.39)		(.45)		(-.03)		(-.37)		(.05)	
SKULL	5.44	2.05	6.00	1.48	6.14	1.29	4.00	1.68	5.88	1.52	4.19	2.16	3.42	1.37
	(-.21)		(.51)		(.80)		(-.05)		(.14)		(.71)		(-.28)	
SKUNK	6.44	1.19	6.46	1.12	6.62	1.04	4.46	1.81	5.93	1.50	3.92	2.02	3.04	1.59F
	(.79)		(.97)		(1.28)		(.41)		(.19)		(.44)		(-.66)	
SLEET	5.34	2.01	5.41	1.68	5.15	1.81	4.07	1.64	5.53	1.55	2.89	1.50	3.51	1.51
	(-.31)		(-.08)		(-.19)		(.02)		(-.21)		(-.59)		(-.19)	
SLEEVE	5.61	1.89	5.27	1.90	5.25	1.78	4.21	1.94	6.17	1.30	3.26	1.47	4.15	1.05
	(-.04)		(-.22)		(-.09)		(.16)		(.43)		(-.22)		(.45)	
SLIME	5.32	1.99	5.27	1.74	3.98	1.70	3.84	1.86	5.42	1.71	3.67	1.64	2.66	1.56M
	(-.33)		(-.22)		(-1.36)		(-.21)		(-.32)		(.19)		(-1.04)	
SLIPPER	5.74	1.88	5.72	1.47	5.60	1.73	4.18	1.71	5.72	1.61	3.08	1.65	4.49	1.04
	(.09)		(.23)		(.26)		(.13)		(-.02)		(-.40)		(.79)	
SLUSH	5.63	1.76	5.32	1.94	4.30	1.66	4.15	1.69	5.40	1.72	3.15	1.57	3.56	1.50
	(-.02)		(-.17)		(-1.04)		(.10)		(-.34)		(-.33)		(-.14)	
SNAIL	5.75	1.99	5.71	1.75	6.15	1.47	3.46	1.68	5.63	1.84	3.54	1.97	3.51	1.35M
	(.10)		(.22)		(.81)		(-.59)		(-.11)		(.06)		(-.19)	
SNAKE	6.48	1.23	6.04	1.37	6.03	1.66	4.58	1.80	5.92	1.56	4.00	1.75	3.16	1.73M
	(.83)		(.55)		(.69)		(.53)		(.18)		(.52)		(-.54)	
SNEEZE	5.59	1.80	5.56	1.66	4.82	1.83	3.82	1.97	6.18	1.23	2.74	1.41	3.61	1.37
	(-.06)		(.07)		(-.52)		(-.23)		(.44)		(-.74)		(-.09)	
SOCK	5.46	1.92	4.91	2.10	4.95	2.05	3.78	1.68	6.17	1.33	3.15	1.70	3.67	1.16
	(-.19)		(-.58)		(-.39)		(-.27)		(.43)		(-.33)		(-.03)	
SOD	5.65	1.85	4.61	2.01	4.66	2.01	3.82	1.67	5.07	1.94	2.90	1.54	3.49	1.54
	(.00)		(-.88)		(-.23)		(-.23)		(-.67)		(-.58)		(-.21)	
SODIUM	5.07	2.15	4.17	2.19	5.42	2.14	3.31	2.08	4.77	2.06	2.89	1.51	3.62	1.39
	(-.58)		(-1.32)		(.08)		(-.74)		(-.97)		(-.59)		(-.08)	

	CON		IMG		CAT		MNG		FAM		NOA		PLS	
	M	SD	M	SD	M	SD	M	SD	M	SD	M	SD	M	SD
SOLDIER	5.68	1.89	5.71	1.58	5.15	2.07	4.97	1.71	6.13	1.68	4.65	1.78	2.43	1.48M
	(.03)		(.22)		(-.19)		(.92)		(.39)		(1.17)		(-1.27)	
SOOT	5.59	1.76	5.25	2.04	4.47	1.87	3.85	1.89	4.64	1.99	3.07	1.74	2.84	1.48
	(-.06)		(-.24)		(-.87)		(-.20)		(-1.10)		(-.41)		(-.86)	
SOW	5.00	2.13	4.73	2.17	4.68	1.95	3.67	1.74	5.02	2.00	3.05	1.43	3.52	1.44
	(-.65)		(-.76)		(-.66)		(-.38)		(-.72)		(-.43)		(-.18)	
SPADE	5.61	1.89	5.72	1.61	5.40	1.66	4.36	1.49	5.87	1.59	3.48	1.40	3.01	1.54
	(-.04)		(.23)		(.06)		(.31)		(.13)		(.00)		(-.69)	
SPATULA	5.82	1.83	5.11	1.87	5.52	2.03	3.33	1.56	4.81	1.76	3.07	1.64	3.82	1.05
	(.17)		(-.38)		(.18)		(-.72)		(-.93)		(-.41)		(.12)	
SPEAR	5.80	1.61	5.39	1.95	5.37	1.46	4.03	1.77	5.87	1.37	3.73	1.52	3.10	1.57M
	(.15)		(-.10)		(.03)		(-.02)		(.13)		(.25)		(-.60)	
SPHERE	4.85	2.24	5.56	1.60	5.40	1.74	4.26	1.70	5.31	1.80	3.26	1.74	4.35	1.15
	(-.80)		(-.07)		(.06)		(.21)		(-.43)		(-.22)		(.65)	
SPIDER	6.03	1.85	5.92	1.68	6.19	1.56	3.92	1.78	6.36	1.14	3.95	1.91	2.69	1.49M
	(.38)		(.43)		(.85)		(-.13)		(.62)		(.47)		(-1.01)	
SPIKE	5.55	1.97	5.63	1.69	4.50	1.66	4.05	2.03	5.70	1.71	3.11	1.51	2.78	1.61M
	(-.10)		(.19)		(-.84)		(.00)		(-.04)		(-.37)		(-.92)	
SPINACH	5.85	2.03	5.95	1.64	5.82	1.75	3.84	1.76	5.67	1.77	3.14	1.75	3.48	1.71
	(.20)		(.46)		(.48)		(-.21)		(-.07)		(-.34)		(-.22)	
SPONGE	5.93	1.96	5.71	1.66	5.53	1.68	3.87	1.79	6.12	1.39	3.20	1.56	3.92	1.23M
	(.28)		(.22)		(.19)		(-.18)		(.38)		(-.28)		(.22)	
SPOOL	5.61	2.03	5.46	1.86	4.52	1.83	3.47	1.84	5.73	1.72	3.06	1.52	4.02	1.23F
	(-.04)		(-.03)		(-.82)		(-.58)		(-.01)		(-.42)		(.32)	
SPOON	6.05	1.73	5.38	2.05	5.95	1.47	4.25	1.95	6.53	1.07	2.89	1.48	4.29	1.06
	(.40)		(-.11)		(.61)		(.20)		(.79)		(-.59)		(.59)	
SQUARE	5.15	1.99	6.10	1.48	5.43	1.74	5.19	1.49	6.25	1.20	3.11	1.81	3.79	1.21
	(-.50)		(.61)		(.14)		(1.14)		(.51)		(-.37)		(.09)	
STAIR	5.54	1.96	5.45	1.84	5.05	1.93	4.28	1.73	6.34	1.14	3.44	1.69	3.95	1.09
	(-.11)		(-.04)		(-.29)		(.23)		(.60)		(-.04)		(.25)	
STAKE	5.36	1.82	5.00	2.04	4.05	1.71	3.72	1.48	5.34	1.61	3.11	1.70	2.90	1.17
	(-.29)		(-.49)		(-1.29)		(-.33)		(-.40)		(-.37)		(-.80)	
STARCH	5.65	1.43	5.09	1.86	4.82	1.65	3.85	1.64	5.63	1.63	3.51	1.62	3.29	1.30
	(.00)		(-.40)		(-.52)		(-.20)		(-.11)		(.03)		(-.41)	
STEAM	5.66	1.53	5.98	1.49	4.93	1.84	4.33	1.75	6.32	1.16	3.65	1.66	4.34	1.45
	(.01)		(.49)		(-.41)		(.28)		(.58)		(.17)		(.64)	
STEEL	5.82	1.94	5.28	1.94	5.53	1.57	4.34	1.91	6.27	1.36	3.66	1.70	3.85	1.30M
	(.17)		(-.21)		(.19)		(.29)		(.53)		(.18)		(.15)	
STEEPLE	5.28	2.01	5.20	1.90	4.77	2.04	3.70	1.62	4.97	1.88	3.61	1.60	4.40	1.35F
	(-.37)		(-.29)		(-.57)		(-.35)		(-.77)		(.13)		(.70)	
STEM	5.52	1.90	5.41	1.73	4.98	1.75	4.45	1.75	6.05	1.32	3.33	1.45	3.72	1.45F
	(-.13)		(-.08)		(-.36)		(.40)		(.31)		(-.15)		(.02)	
STICK	6.00	1.52	5.11	1.88	5.07	1.87	5.03	1.52	6.02	1.45	3.57	1.80	3.77	1.00
	(.35)		(-.38)		(-.27)		(.98)		(.28)		(.09)		(.07)	
STOCKING	5.47	1.97	5.49	1.76	5.23	1.68	3.90	1.87	5.90	1.48	3.43	1.64	4.32	1.17
	(-.18)		(.00)		(-.11)		(-.15)		(.16)		(-.05)		(.62)	
STOMACH	6.13	1.70	5.73	1.61	5.82	1.74	4.57	1.77	6.07	1.50	4.10	1.96	3.39	1.03
	(.48)		(.24)		(.48)		(.52)		(.33)		(.62)		(-.31)	
STOOL	5.66	1.82	5.75	1.78	5.07	1.74	3.74	1.78	5.66	1.57	3.44	1.55	3.54	1.21
	(.01)		(.26)		(-.27)		(-.31)		(-.08)		(-.04)		(-.16)	
STRAW	5.91	1.68	5.58	1.75	5.18	1.78	4.36	1.81	6.07	1.51	3.05	1.40	4.75	1.28
	(.26)		(.09)		(-.16)		(.31)		(.33)		(-.43)		(1.05)	
STRING	5.48	1.87	5.15	2.16	5.41	1.61	4.43	1.81	6.34	1.15	3.49	1.79	4.10	1.10
	(-.17)		(-.34)		(.07)		(.38)		(.60)		(.01)		(.40)	

	CON		IMG		CAT		MNG		FAM		NOA		PLS	
	M	SD	M	SD	M	SD	M	SD	M	SD	M	SD	M	SD
SUIT	5.41	2.06	5.30	1.78	5.18	1.95	4.52	1.96	6.17	1.39	3.98	1.66	4.05	1.19
	(-.24)		(-.19)		(-.16)		(.47)		(.43)		(.50)		(.35)	
SUITE	5.40	1.69	4.73	1.96	4.77	2.00	3.62	1.40	5.40	1.75	3.52	1.76	4.57	1.42
	(-.25)		(-.76)		(-.57)		(-.43)		(-.34)		(.04)		(.87)	
SULPHUR	6.02	1.75	5.38	1.80	5.65	1.80	3.70	2.00	5.38	1.75	2.84	1.69	2.82	1.50
	(.37)		(-.11)		(.31)		(-.35)		(-.36)		(-.64)		(-.88)	
SWEAT	5.65	1.78	5.54	1.90	4.63	1.84	4.57	1.58	6.19	1.27	3.46	1.69	3.29	1.61M
	(.00)		(.05)		(-.71)		(.52)		(.45)		(-.02)		(-.41)	
SWORD	5.32	2.17	5.98	1.43	5.33	1.69	3.87	1.62	5.44	1.73	3.23	1.50	3.81	1.54
	(-.33)		(.49)		(-.01)		(-.18)		(-.30)		(-.25)		(.11)	
SYNAGOGUE	5.41	2.03	4.92	2.05	5.10	2.09	4.30	2.09	5.05	1.95	3.63	2.04	3.75	1.45
	(-.24)		(-.57)		(-.24)		(.25)		(-.69)		(.15)		(.05)	
TABLE	6.09	1.65	5.43	2.03	6.07	1.47	4.23	1.62	6.35	1.23	3.56	1.78	3.97	.78
	(.44)		(-.06)		(.73)		(.18)		(.61)		(.08)		(.27)	
TACK	5.64	2.04	5.56	1.87	4.77	1.92	3.58	1.83	5.68	1.52	2.66	1.29	3.03	1.29
	(-.01)		(.07)		(-.57)		(-.47)		(-.06)		(-.82)		(-.67)	
TAIL	6.09	1.43	5.45	1.84	5.32	1.91	4.73	1.69	6.07	1.41	3.64	1.39	3.90	1.57
	(.44)		(-.04)		(-.02)		(.68)		(.33)		(.16)		(.20)	
TANK	5.71	1.89	5.27	1.76	5.18	1.91	4.02	1.58	5.75	1.52	4.25	1.61	3.06	1.69
	(.06)		(-.22)		(-.16)		(-.03)		(.01)		(.77)		(-.64)	
TAR	5.93	1.78	5.44	2.03	4.87	1.80	3.46	1.88	5.65	1.64	2.86	1.45	2.76	1.28
	(.28)		(-.05)		(-.47)		(-.59)		(-.09)		(-.62)		(-.94)	
TEA	6.05	1.54	5.93	1.55	5.80	1.68	4.49	1.84	6.46	.99	3.23	1.61	4.01	1.74
	(.40)		(.44)		(.46)		(.44)		(.72)		(-.25)		(.31)	
TEST TUBE	6.03	1.85	6.07	1.61	5.82	1.47	4.05	1.84	5.89	1.51	3.30	1.79	3.44	1.54
	(.39)		(.59)		(.49)		(.00)		(.15)		(-.18)		(-.26)	
THERMOMETER	6.02	1.77	5.83	1.65	5.42	1.74	4.43	1.93	5.80	1.65	3.25	1.84	4.00	1.22
	(.37)		(.34)		(.08)		(.38)		(.06)		(-.23)		(.30)	
THIEF	5.09	1.81	5.22	1.79	5.39	1.77	4.80	1.55	6.05	1.48	4.14	1.93	2.50	1.51
	(-.57)		(-.27)		(.04)		(.75)		(.31)		(.66)		(-1.20)	
THIMBLE	5.25	2.19	5.64	1.82	5.26	1.63	3.60	1.70	5.44	1.72	2.89	1.48	3.97	1.27
	(-.40)		(.15)		(-.09)		(-.45)		(-.30)		(-.59)		(.27)	
THREAD	6.04	1.62	5.49	1.63	4.83	1.66	4.43	1.85	6.10	1.50	3.02	1.37	3.82	1.48F
	(.39)		(.00)		(-.51)		(.38)		(.36)		(-.46)		(.12)	
THREE	4.35	2.22	4.89	2.16	5.95	1.56	3.98	2.18	6.55	1.08	2.40	1.51	3.84	1.17
	(-1.30)		(-.60)		(.61)		(-.07)		(.81)		(-1.08)		(.14)	
THROAT	5.74	1.92	5.55	1.89	6.24	1.38	3.88	1.90	6.22	1.42	4.11	1.83	3.83	1.21
	(.09)		(.06)		(.90)		(-.17)		(.48)		(.63)		(.13)	
THUNDER	5.43	1.90	5.43	1.97	5.10	1.66	4.67	1.78	6.21	1.24	3.43	1.83	4.53	1.81F
	(-.22)		(-.01)		(-.24)		(.62)		(.47)		(-.05)		(.83)	
TICKET	5.84	1.75	5.09	1.95	5.22	1.91	4.43	1.52	6.24	1.32	4.13	1.82	3.90	1.50
	(.19)		(-.40)		(-.12)		(.38)		(.50)		(.65)		(.20)	
TIE	5.64	1.91	5.45	1.84	5.05	2.11	4.32	1.70	6.33	1.30	3.16	1.54	3.28	1.36
	(-.01)		(-.04)		(-.29)		(.27)		(.59)		(-.32)		(-.42)	
TIRE	5.59	1.77	5.05	2.03	5.39	1.72	4.00	1.70	6.20	1.34	3.69	1.83	3.81	1.37M
	(-.06)		(-.44)		(.05)		(-.05)		(.46)		(.21)		(.11)	
TOAD	5.64	1.96	5.85	1.59	6.29	1.47	4.15	1.65	5.90	1.72	3.79	1.72	3.08	1.63M
	(-.01)		(.36)		(.95)		(.10)		(.16)		(.31)		(-.62)	
TOAST	5.70	1.79	5.62	1.77	5.81	1.53	4.02	1.77	6.12	1.34	3.48	1.75	4.31	1.30
	(.05)		(.13)		(.47)		(-.03)		(.38)		(.00)		(.61)	
TOASTER	5.75	1.87	5.74	1.78	6.05	1.48	3.65	1.81	6.00	1.44	3.54	1.62	4.25	1.12
	(.10)		(.25)		(.71)		(-.40)		(.26)		(.06)		(.55)	
TOBACCO	6.16	1.63	5.95	1.52	5.62	1.92	4.44	1.93	6.30	1.12	3.92	1.82	3.27	1.88
	(.51)		(.46)		(.28)		(.39)		(.56)		(.44)		(-.43)	

	CON		IMG		CAT		MNG		FAM		NOA		PLS	
	M	SD	M	SD	M	SD	M	SD	M	SD	M	SD	M	SD
TOILET	5.82	1.86	5.97	1.63	5.47	1.67	4.30	1.85	6.41	1.19	3.62	1.95	3.18	1.16
	(.17)		(.48)		(.13)		(.25)		(.67)		(.14)		(-.52)	
TOMB	5.62	1.93	5.93	1.39	5.20	1.62	4.42	1.75	5.73	1.73	4.08	1.77	2.67	1.67M
	(-.03)		(.44)		(-.14)		(.37)		(-.01)		(.60)		(-1.03)	
TON	5.16	2.05	4.79	2.13	5.15	2.15	4.77	1.87	6.11	1.45	2.64	1.63	3.09	1.56M
	(-.49)		(-.70)		(-.19)		(.72)		(.37)		(-.84)		(-.61)	
TORNADO	6.40	1.25	5.85	1.51	5.92	1.46	4.92	1.76	5.58	1.77	3.87	2.09	2.50	1.73
	(.75)		(.36)		(.58)		(.87)		(-.16)		(.39)		(-1.20)	
TORTOISE	5.98	1.80	5.44	1.74	6.10	1.61	4.03	1.86	5.46	1.67	3.87	1.77	4.39	1.18
	(.33)		(-.05)		(.76)		(-.02)		(-.28)		(.39)		(.69)	
TRAILER	5.93	1.71	5.81	1.68	5.41	1.64	3.63	1.84	6.02	1.33	4.40	1.90	4.00	1.37M
	(.28)		(.32)		(.07)		(-.42)		(.28)		(.92)		(.30)	
TRAPEZE	6.05	1.75	5.46	1.85	4.78	1.86	4.05	1.75	5.43	1.92	2.93	1.53	4.00	1.71
	(.40)		(-.03)		(-.56)		(.00)		(-.31)		(-.55)		(.30)	
TRAPEZOID	4.90	2.22	5.12	2.09	5.27	2.06	3.59	1.87	4.85	1.90	2.51	1.79	3.57	1.55F
	(-.75)		(-.37)		(-.07)		(-.46)		(-.89)		(-.97)		(-.13)	
TRASH	5.84	1.70	5.93	1.52	4.92	1.92	4.98	1.81	6.15	1.40	4.28	1.85	2.24	1.41
	(.19)		(.44)		(-.42)		(.93)		(.41)		(.80)		(-1.06)	
TRAY	5.86	1.78	5.44	1.89	5.32	1.62	4.50	1.90	6.32	1.19	3.16	1.56	3.90	.97
	(.21)		(-.05)		(-.02)		(.45)		(.58)		(-.32)		(.20)	
TREASURER	5.53	1.93	4.87	1.83	5.23	1.60	4.17	1.94	5.85	1.68	4.20	2.03	4.52	1.41
	(-.12)		(-.62)		(-.11)		(.12)		(.11)		(.72)		(.82)	
TRIANGLE	5.19	1.98	5.91	1.71	6.02	1.61	4.25	1.91	6.06	1.52	2.42	1.62	3.94	1.45F
	(-.46)		(.42)		(.68)		(.20)		(.32)		(-1.06)		(.24)	
TRIPOD	5.66	1.84	5.49	1.83	5.25	1.59	3.38	1.72	5.00	2.01	3.03	1.65	3.76	1.22
	(.01)		(.00)		(-.09)		(-.67)		(-.74)		(-.45)		(.06)	
TROLLEY	5.75	2.04	5.79	1.62	5.28	1.74	3.68	1.97	5.23	1.86	3.70	1.72	4.56	1.49M
	(.10)		(.30)		(-.06)		(-.37)		(-.51)		(.22)		(.86)	
TROMBONE	6.02	1.82	5.73	1.75	6.47	1.19	4.17	2.06	5.55	1.84	3.41	2.08	4.20	1.29
	(.37)		(.24)		(1.13)		(.12)		(-.19)		(-.07)		(.50)	
TROUSER	5.75	1.84	5.92	1.54	5.85	1.51	4.75	1.59	5.65	1.60	3.48	1.78	3.74	1.18
	(.10)		(.43)		(.51)		(.70)		(-.09)		(.00)		(.04)	
TUBE	5.77	1.62	5.58	1.72	4.54	1.98	4.16	1.78	6.13	1.24	3.05	1.73	3.87	1.49
	(.12)		(.09)		(-.80)		(.11)		(.39)		(-.43)		(.17)	
TUBERCULOSIS	5.15	1.92	4.20	2.27	6.27	1.21	3.92	1.98	5.35	1.74	3.19	2.03	1.87	1.37
	(-.50)		(-1.29)		(.93)		(-.13)		(-.29)		(-.29)		(-1.83)	
TUNIC	5.41	1.80	4.73	2.09	4.57	2.04	3.55	1.70	4.54	1.96	3.15	1.69	4.10	1.21
	(-.24)		(-.76)		(-.77)		(-.50)		(-1.20)		(-.33)		(.40)	
TUNNEL	5.51	1.97	5.72	1.88	5.36	1.63	3.93	1.91	6.15	1.44	3.79	1.68	4.54	1.32M
	(-.14)		(.23)		(.02)		(-.12)		(.41)		(.31)		(.84)	
TURPENTINE	6.00	1.74	5.81	1.66	5.68	1.46	3.68	2.15	5.57	1.85	3.14	1.81	3.33	1.35M
	(.35)		(.32)		(.34)		(-.37)		(-.17)		(-.34)		(-.37)	
TUSK	5.76	1.70	5.32	2.05	4.98	1.96	3.38	1.67	5.07	1.88	3.10	1.76	4.20	1.25
	(.11)		(-.17)		(-.36)		(-.67)		(-.67)		(-.38)		(.50)	
TWEEZER	5.36	2.19	5.81	1.41	5.27	1.68	3.56	1.95	5.70	1.60	2.79	1.51	3.54	1.36M
	(-.29)		(.32)		(-.07)		(-.49)		(-.04)		(-.69)		(-.16)	
TWIG	5.55	1.89	5.49	1.73	5.24	1.76	4.20	1.70	5.67	1.65	3.35	1.73	4.40	1.51F
	(-.10)		(.00)		(-.10)		(.15)		(-.07)		(-.13)		(.70)	
TWIRLER	5.15	1.94	5.74	1.55	4.43	1.84	3.57	1.81	5.20	1.87	3.30	1.57	4.38	1.60M
	(-.50)		(.25)		(-.91)		(-.48)		(-.54)		(-.18)		(.68)	
TYPEWRITER	5.91	1.85	6.26	1.23	5.97	1.54	4.15	2.03	6.32	1.23	3.92	1.91	3.66	1.31
	(.26)		(.77)		(.63)		(.10)		(.58)		(.44)		(-.04)	
UMBRELLA	5.95	1.84	5.49	1.95	5.55	1.75	4.00	1.78	5.90	1.51	3.31	1.52	4.21	1.20
	(.30)		(.00)		(.21)		(-.05)		(.16)		(-.17)		(.51)	

	CON		IMG		CAT		MNG		FAM		NOA		PLS	
	M	SD	M	SD	M	SD	M	SD	M	SD	M	SD	M	SD
UMPIRE	5.77	1.90	5.66	1.88	5.72	1.65	4.82	2.03	6.16	1.34	3.67	1.82	3.42	1.44
	(.12)		(.17)		(.38)		(.77)		(.42)		(.19)		(-.28)	
VASE	5.79	1.61	5.23	1.88	5.46	1.50	3.88	1.68	5.67	1.57	3.52	1.71	4.56	1.19F
	(.14)		(-.26)		(.12)		(-.17)		(-.07)		(.04)		(.86)	
VAULT	5.46	2.10	5.44	1.82	4.77	1.71	3.95	1.71	5.19	1.90	3.79	1.98	3.81	1.42
	(-.19)		(-.05)		(-.57)		(-.10)		(-.55)		(.31)		(.11)	
VEAL	5.24	2.21	5.13	1.85	6.02	1.46	3.85	1.67	5.39	1.85	3.63	1.73	4.14	1.74M
	(-.41)		(-.36)		(.68)		(-.20)		(-.35)		(.15)		(.44)	
VEIL	5.48	1.90	4.96	1.93	4.52	1.80	3.79	1.63	5.15	1.90	3.38	1.66	4.15	1.40
	(-.17)		(-.53)		(-.82)		(-.26)		(-.59)		(-.10)		(.45)	
VEIN	5.49	1.83	5.40	1.78	5.37	1.64	4.51	1.81	5.70	1.74	3.90	1.63	3.84	1.63F
	(-.16)		(-.09)		(.03)		(.46)		(-.04)		(.42)		(.14)	
VEST	5.69	1.89	5.52	1.85	5.28	1.75	3.78	1.77	5.77	1.62	3.32	1.55	4.12	1.24
	(.04)		(.03)		(-.06)		(-.27)		(.03)		(-.16)		(.42)	
VINEGAR	6.41	1.33	5.56	1.74	5.08	1.85	3.61	1.87	5.42	1.90	3.20	1.65	3.14	1.47
	(.76)		(.07)		(-.26)		(-.44)		(-.32)		(-.28)		(-.56)	
VIOLET	5.20	1.99	5.41	1.98	5.62	1.97	4.03	1.71	5.88	1.43	2.74	1.55	4.94	1.48F
	(-.45)		(-.08)		(.28)		(-.02)		(.14)		(-.74)		(1.24)	
VOLCANO	5.95	1.76	6.24	1.41	5.42	1.65	4.31	1.96	5.88	1.58	4.10	1.94	3.84	1.57M
	(.30)		(.75)		(.08)		(.26)		(.14)		(.62)		(.14)	
WAFER	5.32	1.90	4.93	1.94	4.90	1.69	3.70	1.76	5.23	1.87	3.15	1.42	3.76	1.25
	(-.33)		(-.56)		(-.44)		(-.35)		(-.51)		(-.33)		(.06)	
WAIST	5.66	1.69	5.11	1.86	5.38	1.75	4.02	1.74	6.00	1.33	3.13	1.52	4.06	1.38
	(.01)		(-.38)		(.04)		(-.03)		(.26)		(-.35)		(.36)	
WALL	5.85	1.96	5.84	1.57	5.42	1.84	4.39	1.77	6.38	1.19	3.56	1.80	3.41	1.22
	(.20)		(.35)		(.08)		(.34)		(.64)		(.08)		(-.29)	
WALRUS	6.25	1.57	5.84	1.72	6.27	1.45	4.20	1.98	5.80	1.60	3.31	2.10	4.14	1.53
	(.60)		(.35)		(.93)		(.15)		(.06)		(-.17)		(.44)	
WAX	5.55	1.84	5.43	1.77	5.41	1.51	3.92	1.77	6.03	1.48	3.17	1.71	3.76	1.14
	(-.10)		(-.06)		(.07)		(-.13)		(.29)		(-.31)		(.06)	
WEB	5.57	1.94	5.96	1.59	4.92	1.66	3.74	1.78	5.90	1.57	3.97	1.62	3.93	1.54M
	(-.08)		(.47)		(-.42)		(-.31)		(.16)		(.49)		(.23)	
WEED	5.96	1.58	5.90	1.63	5.82	1.62	4.85	1.76	6.16	1.29	3.92	1.83	3.38	2.02M
	(.31)		(.41)		(.48)		(.80)		(.42)		(.44)		(-.32)	
WHIP	5.35	1.98	5.69	1.84	4.93	1.78	4.54	1.74	6.10	1.43	3.57	1.58	3.07	1.67
	(-.30)		(.20)		(-.41)		(.49)		(.36)		(.09)		(-.63)	
WHISKER	5.56	2.07	5.59	1.83	4.53	1.91	3.79	1.56	5.90	1.62	3.21	1.64	3.93	1.58M
	(-.09)		(.10)		(-.81)		(-.26)		(.16)		(-.27)		(.23)	
WIG	6.14	1.52	5.81	1.70	5.28	1.45	4.23	1.81	5.92	1.51	3.50	1.76	2.94	1.36
	(.49)		(.32)		(-.06)		(.18)		(.18)		(.02)		(-.76)	
WIRE	5.81	2.04	5.58	1.82	5.42	1.65	3.78	1.65	6.30	1.32	3.35	1.61	3.74	1.30M
	(.16)		(.09)		(.08)		(-.27)		(.56)		(-.13)		(.04)	
WITCH	5.52	1.82	5.64	1.88	5.54	1.75	4.65	1.69	6.16	1.33	4.03	2.01	3.07	1.61
	(-.13)		(.15)		(.20)		(.60)		(.42)		(.55)		(-.63)	
WRECK	4.88	1.76	6.19	1.25	4.45	1.75	4.88	1.58	6.24	1.20	4.08	1.70	2.28	1.38
	(-.77)		(.70)		(-.89)		(.83)		(.50)		(.60)		(-1.42)	
YOKE	5.38	2.11	5.08	1.89	4.63	1.92	3.52	1.67	5.15	1.83	3.17	1.52	3.48	1.30
	(-.27)		(-.41)		(-.71)		(-.59)		(-.59)		(-.31)		(-.22)	
YOLK	5.89	1.86	5.24	2.01	5.36	1.89	3.73	2.03	5.45	1.98	3.15	1.66	3.24	1.51
	(.24)		(-.25)		(.02)		(-.32)		(-.29)		(-.33)		(-.46)	
ZIPPER	5.95	1.71	6.26	1.22	5.52	1.36	4.02	1.86	6.30	1.35	3.73	1.78	4.04	1.40
	(.30)		(.77)		(.18)		(-.03)		(.56)		(.25)		(.34)	

	CON		IMG		CAT		MNG		FAM		NOA		PLS	
	M	SD	M	SD	M	SD	M	SD	M	SD	M	SD	M	SD
ACROBAT	5.74	1.76	5.43	1.68	5.32	1.94	4.20	1.84	5.54	1.76	4.10	1.91	4.94	1.27
	(-.09)		(-.42)		(-.44)		(-.55)		(-.68)		(-.11)		(.08)	
ADULT	4.88	1.97	5.20	1.82	5.42	1.72	5.43	1.60	6.64	.85	5.34	1.88	4.67	1.36
	(-.95)		(-.65)		(-.34)		(.68)		(.42)		(1.13)		(-.19)	
ALCOHOL	6.45	1.30	5.79	1.74	5.85	1.74	5.35	1.57	6.27	1.28	4.59	1.88	4.09	1.56M
	(.62)		(-.06)		(.09)		(.60)		(.05)		(.38)		(-.77)	
ANIMALS	5.65	1.89	5.82	1.58	5.66	1.84	5.39	1.77	6.54	1.03	5.75	1.79	5.09	1.73F
	(-.18)		(-.03)		(-.10)		(.64)		(.32)		(1.54)		(.23)	
APARTMENT	5.77	1.82	5.87	1.58	5.35	1.80	4.90	1.69	6.42	1.02	5.18	1.83	4.53	1.52F
	(-.06)		(.02)		(-.41)		(.15)		(.20)		(.97)		(-.33)	
APE	6.50	1.16	6.10	1.53	6.18	1.62	5.38	1.61	6.21	1.34	4.00	2.13	3.66	1.89M
	(.67)		(.25)		(.42)		(.63)		(-.01)		(-.21)		(-1.20)	
APPLE	6.21	1.63	6.43	1.13	6.45	1.41	4.51	1.93	6.51	1.09	3.57	1.93	5.37	1.52F
	(.38)		(.58)		(.69)		(-.24)		(.29)		(-.64)		(.51)	
ARM	5.69	1.88	5.61	1.83	6.34	1.07	4.28	2.16	6.41	1.10	4.00	2.01	4.25	1.24
	(-.14)		(-.24)		(.58)		(-.47)		(.19)		(-.21)		(-.61)	
ARTIST	5.65	1.71	6.25	1.32	5.45	1.88	5.28	1.72	6.21	1.29	4.97	1.74	5.42	1.31
	(-.18)		(.40)		(-.31)		(.53)		(-.01)		(.76)		(.56)	
AUNT	5.79	1.59	5.57	1.77	5.67	1.71	4.98	1.77	6.46	1.03	3.43	2.16	5.00	1.52
	(-.04)		(-.28)		(-.09)		(.23)		(.24)		(-.78)		(.14)	
BABY	5.85	1.68	5.80	1.67	5.72	1.89	5.73	1.47	6.61	.86	5.07	1.87	4.87	1.90
	(.02)		(-.05)		(-.04)		(.98)		(.39)		(.86)		(.01)	
BALL	6.08	1.65	6.25	1.21	5.48	1.49	5.15	1.82	6.42	1.19	4.33	2.02	5.01	1.52M
	(.25)		(.40)		(-.28)		(.40)		(.20)		(.12)		(.15)	
BALLOON	6.19	1.73	5.75	1.79	5.48	1.92	3.94	2.06	5.81	1.52	3.31	1.85	5.32	1.36F
	(.36)		(-.10)		(-.10)		(-.81)		(-.41)		(-.90)		(.46)	
BANANA	6.29	1.44	6.38	1.21	6.62	1.11	4.49	1.79	6.50	1.10	3.28	1.66	5.18	1.53F
	(.46)		(.53)		(.86)		(-.26)		(.28)		(-.93)		(.32)	
BAND	6.00	1.43	5.44	1.84	5.30	1.74	4.77	1.64	5.93	1.70	4.38	1.74	4.94	1.24
	(.17)		(-.41)		(-.46)		(.02)		(-.29)		(.17)		(.08)	
BANK	5.69	1.80	5.54	1.88	5.57	1.66	4.65	1.74	6.47	.99	4.62	1.80	4.10	1.44
	(-.14)		(-.31)		(-.19)		(-.10)		(.25)		(.41)		(-.76)	
BAR	5.43	2.01	5.80	1.60	5.38	1.90	5.00	1.88	6.75	.60	4.16	1.71	4.56	1.63M
	(-.40)		(-.05)		(-.38)		(.25)		(.53)		(-.05)		(-.30)	
BASEBALL	5.93	1.91	5.98	1.68	6.33	1.50	4.46	2.12	6.26	1.32	4.56	2.22	4.42	1.42M
	(.10)		(.13)		(.57)		(-.29)		(.04)		(.35)		(-.44)	
BASKETBALL	5.96	1.76	6.17	1.67	6.38	1.27	4.55	2.19	6.19	1.32	4.08	2.13	4.48	1.58M
	(.13)		(.32)		(.62)		(-.20)		(-.03)		(-.13)		(-.38)	
BASS	5.43	1.83	5.38	1.89	5.92	1.55	4.21	1.80	6.14	1.25	3.68	1.67	4.67	1.42M
	(-.40)		(-.47)		(.16)		(-.54)		(-.08)		(-.53)		(-.19)	
BATH	5.90	1.68	6.18	1.32	4.85	1.81	4.77	1.78	6.39	1.31	3.73	1.72	5.45	1.37
	(.07)		(.33)		(-.91)		(.02)		(.17)		(-.48)		(.59)	
BEACH	6.08	1.49	6.61	.77	5.58	1.65	5.18	1.61	6.27	1.40	4.78	1.72	5.81	1.41F
	(.25)		(.76)		(-.18)		(.43)		(.05)		(.57)		(.95)	
BEAR	5.81	1.93	5.60	1.80	6.14	1.64	4.08	1.71	6.07	1.55	4.22	1.69	4.36	1.54M
	(-.02)		(-.25)		(.38)		(-.67)		(-.15)		(.01)		(-.50)	
BEARD	5.76	1.71	6.24	1.19	5.64	1.45	4.34	1.85	6.12	1.34	4.08	1.72	4.33	1.58
	(-.07)		(.39)		(-.12)		(-.41)		(-.10)		(-.13)		(-.53)	
BEAVER	5.81	1.96	6.03	1.56	6.35	1.38	4.12	1.91	6.02	1.51	3.77	2.03	5.38	1.20M
	(-.02)		(.18)		(.59)		(-.63)		(-.20)		(-.44)		(.52)	
BED	6.68	.89	6.23	1.38	5.72	1.62	5.45	1.58	6.54	.99	4.41	1.86	5.61	1.41
	(.85)		(.38)		(-.04)		(.70)		(.32)		(.20)		(.75)	
BEEF	6.33	1.28	6.19	1.33	6.32	1.44	5.31	1.64	6.72	.69	3.92	1.73	5.26	1.53
	(.50)		(.34)		(.56)		(.56)		(.50)		(-.29)		(.40)	

	CON	IMG	CAT	MNG	FAM	NOA	PLS
	M SD	M SD	M SD	M SD	M SD	M SD	M SD
BEER	5.83 1.98 (.00)	5.92 1.81 (.07)	6.08 1.60 (.32)	4.60 1.82 (-.15)	6.78 .52 (.56)	3.60 1.97 (-.61)	4.77 1.75M (-.09)
BELL	6.16 1.48 (.33)	6.04 1.53 (.19)	5.43 1.75 (-.33)	4.50 1.91 (-.25)	6.25 1.23 (.03)	3.78 1.74 (-.43)	4.23 1.40 (-.63)
BERRY	5.56 1.70 (-.27)	5.20 1.87 (-.65)	5.51 1.77 (-.25)	4.48 1.83 (-.27)	5.63 1.53 (-.59)	3.77 1.76 (-.44)	5.03 1.40 (.17)
BIBLE	5.81 1.98 (-.02)	5.95 1.72 (.10)	5.78 1.87 (.02)	4.89 1.98 (.14)	6.28 1.51 (.06)	4.65 2.13 (.44)	4.43 1.50 (-.43)
BIRCH	6.16 1.41 (.33)	5.55 1.64 (-.30)	5.68 1.71 (-.08)	4.48 1.89 (-.27)	5.92 1.42 (-.30)	3.66 1.64 (-.55)	4.57 1.72 (-.29)
BIRD	5.94 1.65 (.11)	6.14 1.33 (.29)	6.19 1.47 (.43)	5.19 1.86 (.44)	6.33 1.30 (.11)	5.02 1.86 (.81)	5.32 1.45 (.46)
BISCUIT	5.70 1.94 (-.13)	5.65 1.96 (-.20)	5.98 1.33 (.22)	3.97 1.85 (-.78)	5.95 1.46 (-.27)	3.56 1.63 (-.65)	4.61 1.35 (-.25)
BLANKET	6.21 1.59 (.38)	5.44 1.83 (-.41)	5.38 1.64 (-.38)	4.49 1.64 (-.26)	6.30 1.31 (.08)	3.36 1.61 (-.85)	5.10 1.11 (.24)
BLONDE	4.98 1.97 (-.85)	6.02 1.59 (.17)	5.52 1.73 (-.24)	4.63 1.86 (-.12)	6.37 1.19 (.15)	3.57 1.88 (-.64)	5.21 1.54M (.35)
BLOSSOM	5.44 1.69 (-.39)	6.02 1.36 (.17)	4.75 1.80 (-1.01)	4.93 1.70 (.18)	5.85 1.52 (-.37)	4.60 1.67 (.39)	5.91 1.17 (1.05)
BLOUSE	6.36 1.33 (.53)	5.89 1.60 (.04)	5.68 1.91 (-.08)	5.30 1.30 (.55)	6.36 1.28 (.14)	3.75 1.69 (-.46)	4.82 1.55M (-.04)
BLUE	4.55 2.06 (-1.28)	5.66 1.74 (-.19)	5.81 1.70 (.05)	4.46 2.01 (-.29)	6.41 1.13 (.19)	3.31 1.68 (-.90)	5.10 1.50 (.24)
BLUEJAY	5.89 1.70 (.06)	5.89 1.53 (.04)	6.53 1.16 (.77)	4.10 1.84 (-.65)	5.87 1.55 (-.35)	3.89 2.11 (-.32)	5.22 1.43 (.36)
BOAT	6.33 1.58 (.50)	6.25 1.48 (.40)	5.63 1.97 (-.13)	5.42 1.55 (.67)	6.58 1.01 (.36)	4.57 2.00 (.36)	4.72 1.60 (-.14)
BOATING	4.90 2.11 (-.93)	5.27 1.79 (-.58)	5.63 1.60 (-.13)	4.60 1.72 (-.15)	5.93 1.35 (-.29)	4.33 1.99 (.12)	5.19 1.52 (.33)
BODY	5.45 1.91 (-.38)	5.93 1.51 (.08)	5.51 1.75 (-.25)	5.43 1.36 (.68)	6.44 1.10 (.22)	5.48 1.75 (1.27)	5.19 1.57 (.33)
BOOK	6.09 1.73 (.26)	5.60 1.90 (-.25)	5.70 1.83 (-.06)	5.82 1.49 (1.07)	6.78 .61 (.56)	5.08 1.84 (.87)	5.02 1.50 (.16)
BOOT	5.71 1.91 (-.12)	5.73 1.82 (-.12)	6.16 1.41 (.40)	4.40 1.71 (-.35)	6.20 1.44 (-.02)	4.11 1.82 (-.10)	4.11 1.34M (-.75)
BOULDER	5.97 1.83 (.14)	6.36 1.22 (.51)	6.05 1.57 (.29)	5.51 1.61 (.76)	6.59 .85 (.37)	5.00 1.76 (.79)	5.16 1.61 (.30)
BOUQUET	5.62 1.79 (-.21)	5.57 1.54 (-.28)	4.75 1.81 (-1.01)	4.23 1.84 (-.52)	5.41 1.78 (-.81)	3.84 1.64 (-.37)	5.38 1.34F (.52)
BOURBON	5.66 2.06 (-.17)	6.00 1.62 (.15)	6.18 1.63 (.42)	4.65 1.95 (-.10)	6.05 1.46 (-.17)	3.29 1.90 (-.17)	4.52 1.74 (-.34)
BOX	5.91 1.83 (.08)	6.00 1.38 (.15)	5.30 1.92 (-.46)	4.82 1.87 (.07)	6.62 .98 (.40)	4.00 1.77 (-.21)	3.84 1.44M (-1.02)
BOY	6.23 1.54 (.40)	6.11 1.25 (.26)	5.97 1.75 (.21)	5.43 1.71 (.68)	6.36 1.31 (.14)	4.82 2.40 (.61)	4.84 1.32F (-.02)
BRA	6.25 1.68 (.42)	6.18 1.55 (.33)	5.80 1.73 (.04)	5.15 1.84 (.40)	6.49 1.07 (.27)	3.15 1.84 (-1.06)	4.32 1.88M (-.54)
BRACELET	5.98 1.75 (.15)	6.00 1.44 (.15)	6.00 1.31 (.24)	4.61 1.58 (-.14)	6.21 1.36 (.14)	4.16 1.92 (-.05)	4.97 1.23F (.11)
BRAIN	5.48 2.06 (-.35)	5.63 1.71 (-.22)	6.14 1.29 (.38)	4.94 1.91 (.19)	6.36 1.15 (.14)	5.37 2.08 (1.16)	5.09 1.32 (.23)
BRANDY	5.91 1.69 (.08)	5.84 1.55 (-.01)	5.88 1.65 (.12)	5.19 1.66 (.44)	6.16 1.28 (-.06)	3.43 1.84 (-.78)	5.40 1.56 (.54)

	CON M SD	IMG M SD	CAT M SD	MNG M SD	FAM M SD	NOA M SD	PLS M SD
BREAD	6.18 1.51 (.35)	6.38 1.32 (.53)	6.02 1.40 (.26)	4.84 1.52 (.09)	6.52 1.05 (.30)	4.19 1.57 (-.02)	5.30 1.31 (.44)
BREAST	5.74 1.93 (-.09)	5.52 1.93 (-.33)	5.40 1.94 (-.36)	4.98 1.83 (.23)	6.33 1.35 (.11)	4.19 1.64 (-.02)	5.20 1.44M (.34)
BROTHER	6.00 1.66 (.17)	5.75 1.79 (-.10)	5.93 1.66 (.17)	5.69 1.84 (.94)	6.79 .71 (.57)	4.72 2.12 (.51)	5.49 1.61 (.63)
BUBBLE	5.39 1.85 (-.44)	6.11 1.16 (.26)	4.52 1.78 (-1.24)	4.15 1.61 (-.60)	6.05 1.31 (-.17)	3.51 1.66 (-.70)	4.99 1.40F (.13)
BUILDING	6.00 1.67 (.17)	5.86 1.48 (.01)	5.08 1.93 (-.68)	5.03 1.85 (.28)	6.54 1.06 (.32)	4.85 2.06 (.64)	3.89 1.33M (-.97)
BURRO	6.14 1.62 (.31)	6.32 1.45 (.47)	6.35 1.40 (.59)	4.32 1.94 (-.43)	5.49 1.76 (-.73)	3.85 1.80 (-.36)	4.91 1.50F (.05)
BUTTER	6.24 1.35 (.41)	5.47 1.79 (-.38)	6.10 1.36 (.34)	4.66 1.99 (-.09)	6.41 .98 (.19)	3.11 1.47 (-1.10)	4.49 1.27 (-.37)
BUTTERFLY	5.91 1.68 (.08)	6.18 1.48 (.33)	6.47 1.29 (.71)	4.24 2.06 (-.51)	5.95 1.56 (.38)	4.59 1.95 (.03)	5.89 1.38F (1.03)
CABIN	5.96 1.73 (.13)	5.47 1.91 (-.38)	5.83 1.59 (.07)	4.88 1.63 (.13)	6.15 1.37 (-.07)	4.80 1.75 (.59)	5.40 1.43F (.54)
CAFE	5.64 1.81 (-.19)	6.19 1.23 (.34)	5.35 1.74 (-.41)	4.79 1.65 (.04)	6.05 1.41 (-.17)	4.71 1.75 (.50)	5.06 1.38 (.20)
CAKE	6.11 1.64 (.28)	6.23 1.35 (.38)	5.97 1.67 (.21)	4.73 2.00 (-.02)	6.60 .92 (.38)	3.86 1.80 (-.35)	5.38 1.25 (.52)
CALF	5.88 1.93 (.05)	5.59 1.76 (-.26)	6.27 1.52 (.51)	4.15 1.73 (-.60)	5.85 1.45 (-.37)	3.89 1.92 (-.32)	4.82 1.36 (-.04)
CAMERA	6.23 1.18 (.40)	5.70 1.69 (-.15)	5.88 1.44 (.12)	4.72 1.78 (-.03)	6.24 1.18 (.02)	4.80 1.90 (.59)	4.87 1.40 (.01)
CAMP	5.78 1.63 (-.05)	5.51 1.70 (-.34)	4.48 1.92 (-1.28)	4.84 1.76 (.09)	6.26 1.29 (.04)	4.03 1.84 (-.18)	4.82 1.70 (-.04)
CANDLE	5.61 2.00 (-.22)	5.88 1.65 (.03)	5.21 1.81 (-.55)	3.93 1.76 (-.82)	6.18 1.30 (-.04)	3.70 1.74 (-.51)	4.94 1.52F (.08)
CANDY	6.33 1.55 (.50)	5.72 1.73 (-.13)	5.70 1.71 (-.06)	5.03 1.77 (.28)	6.13 1.43 (-.09)	4.54 1.91 (.33)	5.03 1.46F (.17)
CAPITOL	5.25 1.94 (-.58)	5.39 1.93 (-.46)	5.50 1.70 (-.26)	4.87 1.97 (.12)	6.03 1.64 (-.19)	4.79 1.99 (.58)	4.08 1.51 (-.78)
CAR	6.35 1.41 (.52)	6.22 1.53 (.37)	5.93 1.69 (.17)	5.53 1.64 (.78)	6.80 .68 (.58)	5.74 1.71 (1.53)	5.09 1.60 (.23)
CARNATION	6.21 1.53 (.38)	6.05 1.50 (.20)	6.10 1.62 (.34)	4.66 1.81 (-.09)	5.64 1.66 (-.58)	3.52 1.88 (-.69)	5.73 1.13 (.87)
CARROT	6.18 1.47 (.35)	5.71 1.80 (-.14)	6.31 1.39 (.55)	4.25 2.00 (-.50)	6.41 1.02 (.19)	3.15 1.87 (-1.06)	4.37 1.19 (-.49)
CARS	6.08 1.65 (.25)	6.14 1.47 (.29)	6.17 1.36 (.41)	5.25 1.68 (.50)	6.54 1.09 (.32)	5.64 1.78 (1.43)	4.41 1.59M (-.45)
CAT	6.30 1.59 (.47)	5.91 1.55 (.06)	6.20 1.58 (.44)	4.87 1.83 (.12)	6.36 1.23 (.14)	4.30 2.05 (.09)	4.48 1.72 (-.38)
CATERPILLAR	5.75 2.08 (-.08)	6.27 1.27 (.42)	6.21 1.42 (.45)	3.87 1.86 (-.88)	5.88 1.58 (-.34)	4.52 1.81 (.31)	4.38 1.35 (-.48)
CATHEDRAL	5.49 1.97 (-.34)	5.93 1.44 (.08)	5.14 1.81 (-.68)	4.48 1.76 (-.27)	5.14 1.99 (-1.08)	4.26 1.73 (.05)	4.97 1.43F (.11)
CEREAL	6.33 1.15 (.50)	5.70 1.70 (-.15)	5.80 1.71 (.04)	4.49 1.69 (-.26)	6.17 1.21 (-.05)	4.34 1.84 (.13)	4.66 1.14 (-.20)
CHAIR	6.12 1.60 (.29)	5.89 1.57 (.04)	5.97 1.40 (.21)	4.46 1.74 (-.29)	6.65 .91 (.43)	3.90 1.92 (-.31)	4.24 1.22F (-.62)
CHAPEL	5.91 1.72 (.08)	5.55 1.72 (-.30)	5.47 1.86 (-.29)	4.45 1.88 (-.30)	5.58 1.78 (-.64)	4.20 1.91 (-.01)	4.60 1.58F (-.26)

	CON		IMG		CAT		MNG		FAM		NOA		PLS	
	M	SD	M	SD	M	SD	M	SD	M	SD	M	SD	M	SD
CHEEKS	5.96	1.46	5.59	1.82	5.48	1.58	3.98	1.67	6.20	1.21	3.61	1.46	4.87	1.24
	(.13)		(-.26)		(-.28)		(-.77)		(-.02)		(-.60)		(.01)	
CHEESE	6.14	1.56	5.56	1.86	6.18	1.50	5.02	1.80	6.66	.76	4.61	1.93	4.95	1.62F
	(.31)		(-.29)		(.42)		(.27)		(.44)		(.40)		(.09)	
CHERRY	5.95	1.76	5.61	1.72	6.15	1.64	4.97	1.69	6.15	1.28	3.49	1.73	5.44	1.02
	(.12)		(-.24)		(.39)		(.22)		(-.07)		(-.72)		(.58)	
CHEST	5.76	1.54	5.50	1.61	5.67	1.60	4.53	1.45	6.17	1.26	3.93	1.57	4.52	1.20
	(-.07)		(-.35)		(-.09)		(-.22)		(.05)		(-.28)		(-.34)	
CHICKEN	5.88	1.88	6.02	1.55	6.47	.96	4.62	1.81	6.31	1.19	4.00	1.88	3.84	1.57
	(.05)		(.17)		(.71)		(-.13)		(.09)		(-.21)		(-1.02)	
CHILD	5.72	1.94	6.17	1.30	5.78	1.65	5.84	1.37	6.40	1.14	4.61	2.00	5.31	1.51
	(-.11)		(.32)		(.02)		(1.09)		(.18)		(.40)		(.45)	
CHILDREN	5.78	1.81	5.93	1.66	5.75	1.83	6.08	1.26	6.64	.88	5.03	1.98	5.03	1.71F
	(-.05)		(.08)		(.02)		(1.33)		(.42)		(.82)		(.17)	
CHILI	5.93	1.84	6.26	1.36	6.02	1.55	4.44	1.81	6.20	1.57	3.64	1.60	4.91	1.62F
	(.10)		(.41)		(.26)		(-.31)		(-.02)		(-.57)		(.05)	
CHINA	5.74	1.84	5.91	1.48	6.17	1.52	4.74	1.78	5.81	1.56	5.36	1.73	4.52	1.45
	(-.09)		(.06)		(.41)		(-.01)		(-.41)		(1.15)		(-.34)	
CHIPMUNK	6.07	1.84	6.03	1.68	6.17	1.63	4.42	1.84	6.03	1.46	4.00	2.09	4.88	1.58
	(.24)		(.18)		(.41)		(-.33)		(-.19)		(-.21)		(.02)	
CHOCOLATE	5.72	1.73	6.05	1.19	6.26	1.21	4.77	1.94	6.34	1.11	3.86	1.90	5.14	1.68F
	(-.11)		(.20)		(.50)		(.02)		(.12)		(-.35)		(.28)	
CHOIR	5.63	1.89	5.61	1.71	5.00	1.68	4.18	1.85	6.00	1.65	3.88	1.69	4.67	1.34
	(-.20)		(-.24)		(-.76)		(-.57)		(-.22)		(-.33)		(-.19)	
CHURCH	5.91	1.59	5.98	1.61	5.70	1.86	5.20	1.73	6.32	1.23	4.46	1.99	4.10	1.95
	(.08)		(.13)		(-.06)		(.45)		(.10)		(.25)		(-.76)	
CINNAMON	5.95	1.73	5.65	1.96	5.92	1.58	3.80	1.92	5.89	1.40	3.16	1.53	5.18	1.43F
	(.12)		(-.20)		(.16)		(-.95)		(-.33)		(-1.05)		(.32)	
CIRCLE	5.14	1.92	5.97	1.46	5.48	1.82	4.74	1.65	6.48	1.08	3.11	1.94	4.44	1.13
	(-.69)		(.12)		(-.28)		(-.01)		(.26)		(-1.10)		(-.42)	
CIRCUS	5.31	1.98	5.68	1.53	5.17	1.93	4.90	1.76	5.78	1.58	5.10	1.84	5.11	1.65F
	(-.52)		(-.17)		(-.59)		(.15)		(-.44)		(.89)		(.25)	
CITY	5.48	2.17	5.95	1.62	5.81	1.48	5.60	1.70	6.83	.53	5.59	1.70	4.10	1.52
	(-.35)		(.10)		(.05)		(.85)		(.61)		(1.38)		(-.76)	
CLOTH	5.76	1.92	5.41	1.78	5.13	1.85	4.75	1.56	6.35	1.26	4.10	1.73	4.64	1.20F
	(-.07)		(-.44)		(-.63)		(.00)		(.13)		(-.11)		(-.22)	
CLOUD	5.50	1.98	5.89	1.63	5.35	1.63	4.54	1.84	6.27	1.39	4.21	1.68	5.10	1.63
	(-.33)		(.04)		(-.41)		(-.21)		(.05)		(.00)		(.24)	
CLOVER	5.50	1.92	6.00	1.47	5.23	1.92	3.97	1.85	5.60	1.59	3.49	1.49	5.30	1.42F
	(-.33)		(.15)		(-.53)		(-.78)		(-.62)		(-.72)		(.44)	
CLOWN	6.23	1.43	5.83	1.63	5.75	1.41	4.72	1.70	5.93	1.63	4.38	1.81	4.98	1.54F
	(.40)		(-.02)		(-.01)		(-.03)		(-.29)		(.17)		(.12)	
COAST	5.51	1.93	5.84	1.57	4.90	1.65	4.93	1.80	6.02	1.35	3.97	1.76	4.99	1.70
	(-.32)		(-.01)		(-.86)		(.18)		(-.20)		(-.24)		(.13)	
COAT	5.83	1.74	5.38	1.81	5.85	1.47	4.55	1.62	6.47	1.01	3.89	1.54	4.29	1.21F
	(.00)		(-.47)		(.09)		(-.20)		(.25)		(-.32)		(-.57)	
COCKTAIL	5.72	1.79	5.98	1.37	5.93	1.52	4.88	1.91	5.85	1.74	4.49	1.88	4.92	1.73
	(-.11)		(.15)		(.17)		(.13)		(-.37)		(.28)		(.06)	
COFFEE	6.43	1.35	5.79	1.76	5.82	1.73	4.40	2.02	6.39	1.23	3.75	1.82	4.73	1.52F
	(.60)		(-.06)		(.06)		(-.35)		(.17)		(-.46)		(-.13)	
COIN	5.70	2.03	5.86	1.53	5.65	1.81	5.03	1.77	6.51	.92	4.03	1.69	4.62	1.20
	(-.13)		(.01)		(-.11)		(.28)		(.29)		(-.18)		(-.24)	
COKE	5.76	1.82	6.17	1.53	6.12	1.33	4.47	1.89	6.59	1.05	3.81	1.72	4.61	1.77M
	(-.07)		(.32)		(.36)		(-.28)		(.37)		(-.40)		(-.25)	

	CON		IMG		CAT		MNG		FAM		NOA		PLS	
	M	SD	M	SD	M	SD	M	SD	M	SD	M	SD	M	SD
COLOR	4.63	2.15	5.41	1.91	4.93	2.08	5.34	1.88	6.60	1.03	4.85	1.99	5.22	1.51F
	(-1.20)		(-.44)		(-.83)		(.59)		(.38)		(.64)		(.36)	
COOKIE	6.30	1.26	5.94	1.61	6.02	1.59	5.02	1.60	6.59	.78	3.66	1.68	5.26	1.49
	(.47)		(.09)		(.26)		(.27)		(.37)		(-.55)		(.40)	
CORN	5.59	1.94	5.84	1.57	6.38	1.06	4.28	1.89	5.93	1.55	4.10	1.65	4.37	1.33
	(-.24)		(-.01)		(.62)		(-.47)		(-.29)		(-.11)		(-.49)	
COTTAGE	5.93	1.78	5.93	1.55	5.71	1.63	4.82	1.62	5.59	1.60	4.46	1.60	5.53	1.31F
	(.10)		(.08)		(-.05)		(.07)		(-.63)		(.25)		(.67)	
COTTON	6.28	1.36	5.67	1.61	5.80	1.49	4.31	1.79	5.62	1.78	3.87	1.68	4.48	1.35
	(.45)		(-.18)		(.04)		(-.44)		(-.60)		(-.34)		(-.38)	
COUCH	5.74	1.83	5.30	1.97	5.85	1.73	4.73	1.58	5.95	1.38	3.74	1.76	4.56	1.42
	(-.09)		(-.55)		(.09)		(-.02)		(-.27)		(-.47)		(-.30)	
COUNTRY	4.54	1.95	5.14	1.76	5.27	1.84	5.95	1.33	6.57	.89	5.57	1.65	5.54	1.27
	(-1.29)		(-.71)		(-.49)		(1.20)		(.35)		(1.36)		(.68)	
COW	6.17	1.58	6.26	1.33	6.48	1.33	4.74	1.98	6.35	1.28	3.77	2.12	4.43	1.55
	(.34)		(.41)		(.72)		(-.01)		(.13)		(-.44)		(-.43)	
CRADLE	5.78	1.73	5.85	1.67	5.83	1.44	4.30	1.67	5.70	1.67	3.79	1.54	4.59	1.38F
	(-.05)		(.00)		(.07)		(-.45)		(-.52)		(-.42)		(-.27)	
CRANBERRY	5.92	1.83	6.43	1.14	6.40	1.14	3.93	1.89	5.57	1.64	3.38	2.02	4.78	1.79F
	(.09)		(.58)		(.64)		(-.82)		(-.65)		(-.83)		(-.08)	
CRAYONS	6.12	1.64	6.00	1.74	5.85	1.68	4.38	1.72	5.87	1.59	4.06	1.92	4.66	1.49F
	(.29)		(.15)		(.09)		(-.37)		(-.35)		(-.15)		(-.20)	
CREAM	6.17	1.33	5.51	1.87	5.23	1.60	4.70	1.86	5.88	1.45	3.64	1.45	5.05	1.30
	(.34)		(-.34)		(-.53)		(-.05)		(-.34)		(-.57)		(.19)	
CROWN	5.82	1.82	5.96	1.59	5.22	1.73	4.63	1.65	6.05	1.51	3.70	1.48	4.80	1.50
	(-.01)		(.11)		(-.54)		(-.12)		(-.17)		(-.51)		(-.06)	
CRUISER	5.67	1.81	5.47	1.50	4.77	1.60	4.68	2.01	5.64	1.45	4.38	1.81	4.71	1.66
	(-.16)		(-.38)		(-.99)		(-.07)		(-.58)		(.17)		(-.15)	
CRYSTAL	5.83	1.64	5.73	1.63	5.17	1.53	3.73	1.65	5.84	1.50	4.03	1.82	4.91	1.52
	(.00)		(-.12)		(-.59)		(-1.02)		(-.38)		(-.18)		(.05)	
CUCUMBER	6.49	1.39	6.17	1.39	6.22	1.51	4.28	2.03	6.10	1.31	3.18	1.75	4.65	1.89
	(.66)		(.32)		(.46)		(-.47)		(-.12)		(-1.03)		(-.21)	
DAFFODILS	5.95	1.89	5.80	1.61	6.17	1.53	4.47	2.03	5.84	1.50	3.54	1.84	5.21	1.76F
	(.12)		(-.05)		(.41)		(-.28)		(-.38)		(-.67)		(.35)	
DAISY	6.09	1.46	5.67	1.71	5.85	1.59	4.31	1.84	5.93	1.51	3.57	2.04	5.48	1.17F
	(.26)		(-.18)		(.09)		(-.44)		(-.29)		(-.64)		(.62)	
DANCE	4.98	1.96	5.04	1.95	5.52	1.69	4.77	1.54	6.24	1.19	4.44	1.60	5.51	1.33F
	(-.85)		(-.81)		(-.24)		(.02)		(.02)		(.23)		(.65)	
DANCER	5.54	1.95	5.45	1.90	5.70	1.68	4.58	1.52	6.09	1.35	4.64	1.75	5.32	1.38
	(-.29)		(-.40)		(-.06)		(-.17)		(-.13)		(.43)		(.46)	
DANDELION	5.54	2.11	5.73	1.94	6.50	1.13	4.22	1.87	5.87	1.69	4.19	1.72	4.74	1.73F
	(-.29)		(-.12)		(.74)		(-.53)		(-.35)		(-.02)		(-.12)	
DATE	5.45	1.75	5.29	1.95	4.80	1.87	5.02	1.71	6.54	1.19	4.33	1.71	5.12	1.77M
	(-.38)		(-.56)		(-.96)		(.27)		(.32)		(.12)		(.26)	
DAWN	4.98	2.03	5.29	1.89	4.97	1.68	4.52	1.51	6.02	1.42	4.20	1.60	5.79	1.37
	(-.85)		(-.56)		(-.79)		(-.23)		(-.20)		(-.01)		(.93)	
DAY	4.73	1.98	5.20	1.83	5.37	1.81	5.05	1.83	6.69	.75	5.13	1.94	5.15	1.40
	(-1.10)		(-.65)		(-.39)		(.30)		(.47)		(.92)		(.29)	
DEER	6.27	1.48	6.40	1.48	6.55	1.10	4.77	1.75	6.13	1.40	4.09	1.93	5.85	1.16
	(.44)		(.55)		(.79)		(.02)		(-.09)		(-.12)		(.99)	
DIAMOND	6.21	1.54	6.26	1.52	6.13	1.46	4.70	1.73	5.97	1.45	3.93	1.75	5.21	1.47
	(.38)		(.41)		(.37)		(-.05)		(-.25)		(-.28)		(.35)	
DIME	5.78	2.03	5.84	1.67	5.97	1.90	4.72	2.03	6.60	.96	2.84	1.42	4.70	1.13
	(-.05)		(-.01)		(.21)		(-.03)		(.38)		(-1.37)		(-.16)	

	CON M SD	IMG M SD	CAT M SD	MNG M SD	FAM M SD	NOA M SD	PLS M SD
DINNER	5.38 2.19 (-.45)	5.65 1.75 (-.20)	5.53 2.05 (-.23)	5.39 1.57 (.64)	6.82 .62 (.60)	4.59 2.10 (.38)	5.53 1.28 (.67)
DIVING	5.43 1.76 (-.40)	5.92 1.34 (.07)	4.90 1.76 (-.86)	4.33 1.88 (-.42)	5.80 1.61 (-.42)	4.16 1.75 (-.05)	5.22 1.20 (.36)
DOCTOR	5.75 1.74 (-.08)	5.87 1.64 (.02)	5.93 1.62 (.69)	5.44 1.55 (.69)	6.59 1.16 (.37)	5.13 1.77 (.92)	4.09 1.81 (-.77)
DOG	5.84 1.91 (.01)	6.15 1.63 (.30)	6.64 1.00 (.88)	5.53 1.49 (.78)	6.54 1.04 (.32)	5.00 1.95 (.79)	5.29 1.76F (.43)
DOLLAR	5.76 1.84 (-.07)	6.02 1.77 (.17)	6.36 1.24 (.60)	4.92 1.97 (.17)	6.63 .97 (.41)	4.38 2.07 (.17)	4.89 1.58M (.03)
DOUGHNUT	6.02 1.72 (.19)	5.93 1.58 (.08)	5.98 1.44 (.22)	4.11 2.03 (-.64)	6.40 1.25 (.18)	3.33 1.69 (-.88)	5.13 1.32 (.27)
DRESS	5.91 1.66 (.02)	5.61 1.71 (-.24)	5.78 1.49 (.02)	5.02 1.69 (.27)	6.25 1.32 (.03)	4.85 1.92 (.64)	4.86 1.44 (.00)
DRUM	5.98 1.50 (.15)	5.93 1.48 (.08)	6.10 1.39 (.34)	4.31 1.74 (-.44)	5.87 1.55 (-.35)	4.00 1.78 (-.21)	4.47 1.25 (-.39)
DUCK	5.76 1.90 (-.07)	6.35 1.36 (.50)	6.48 1.21 (.72)	4.73 1.68 (-.02)	6.10 1.38 (-.12)	4.18 1.65 (-.03)	4.62 1.52 (-.24)
EAGLE	6.12 1.58 (.29)	6.10 1.71 (.25)	6.68 .89 (.92)	4.57 1.88 (-.18)	5.87 1.58 (-.35)	3.87 1.98 (-.34)	5.53 1.63 (.67)
EAR	6.36 1.49 (.53)	5.91 1.71 (.06)	5.95 1.75 (.19)	4.62 1.96 (-.13)	6.22 1.38 (.00)	3.79 2.10 (-.42)	4.00 1.33 (-.86)
EARRINGS	6.00 1.68 (.17)	5.81 1.55 (-.04)	5.73 1.83 (-.03)	4.37 1.76 (-.38)	6.39 1.13 (.17)	3.79 1.84 (-.42)	4.59 1.58 (-.27)
EARTH	5.77 1.67 (-.06)	5.61 1.76 (-.24)	5.79 1.52 (.03)	5.15 2.02 (.40)	6.33 1.15 (.11)	5.32 2.11 (1.11)	5.25 1.36F (.39)
EAT	4.82 2.07 (-1.01)	5.57 1.72 (-.28)	5.07 1.84 (-.69)	5.00 1.86 (.25)	6.03 1.60 (-.19)	4.38 1.98 (.17)	5.16 1.53 (.30)
EATING	4.81 2.15 (-1.02)	5.75 1.67 (-.10)	4.75 1.77 (-1.01)	5.52 1.56 (.77)	6.71 .95 (.49)	4.92 1.89 (.71)	5.21 1.63M (.35)
ELEPHANT	6.53 1.27 (.70)	5.74 1.83 (-.11)	6.08 1.67 (.32)	4.40 1.91 (-.35)	5.73 1.72 (-.49)	3.69 2.06 (-.52)	4.75 1.30M (-.11)
ELM	5.22 2.08 (-.61)	5.32 1.80 (-.53)	6.32 1.35 (.56)	3.92 1.93 (-.83)	5.68 1.73 (-.54)	3.85 1.92 (-.36)	4.80 1.29 (-.06)
EMERALD	6.09 1.62 (.26)	5.96 1.63 (.11)	6.02 1.68 (.26)	4.28 1.82 (-.47)	5.31 1.75 (-.91)	3.15 1.61 (-1.06)	5.44 1.33F (.58)
ENGINE	5.88 1.84 (.05)	5.84 1.74 (-.01)	5.75 1.54 (-.01)	4.90 1.79 (.15)	6.39 1.04 (.17)	5.26 1.97 (1.05)	4.16 1.57 (-.70)
ESTATE	5.37 1.85 (-.46)	4.68 2.27 (-1.17)	5.57 1.60 (-.19)	4.95 1.37 (.20)	5.72 1.50 (-.50)	4.94 1.58 (.63)	4.77 1.50 (-.09)
EYE	6.28 1.37 (.45)	5.89 1.72 (.04)	6.12 1.45 (.36)	4.83 1.76 (.08)	6.63 .81 (.41)	5.31 1.63 (1.10)	4.94 1.41 (.08)
FACE	5.76 1.60 (-.07)	5.65 1.49 (-.20)	5.36 1.67 (-.40)	4.88 1.86 (.13)	6.41 1.15 (.19)	5.46 1.67 (1.25)	4.72 1.25 (-.14)
FARM	5.61 1.87 (-.22)	5.54 1.87 (-.31)	5.80 1.58 (.04)	5.32 1.47 (.57)	6.38 1.09 (.16)	5.28 1.77 (1.07)	4.77 1.69 (-.09)
FATHER	5.90 1.84 (.07)	6.40 1.25 (.55)	6.17 1.42 (.41)	5.54 1.68 (.79)	6.65 1.03 (.43)	4.68 2.01 (.47)	5.78 1.52 (.92)
FAWN	5.47 1.94 (-.36)	5.60 1.89 (-.25)	5.97 1.54 (.21)	3.77 1.60 (-.98)	5.63 1.60 (-.59)	3.49 1.94 (-.72)	5.42 1.47F (.56)
FEET	6.38 1.36 (.55)	6.09 1.32 (.24)	5.93 1.69 (.17)	4.63 1.94 (-.12)	6.67 .91 (.45)	4.38 1.86 (.17)	4.10 1.36 (-.76)
FERRY	5.72 2.02 (-.11)	5.97 1.59 (.12)	5.73 1.60 (-.03)	3.92 1.89 (-.83)	5.40 1.82 (-.82)	3.92 1.84 (-.29)	4.62 1.69F (-.24)

	CON		IMG		CAT		MNG		FAM		NOA		PLS	
	M	SD	M	SD	M	SD	M	SD	M	SD	M	SD	M	SD
FILM	6.00	1.53 (.17)	5.56	1.87 (-.29)	5.17	1.93 (-.59)	5.61	1.32 (.86)	6.52	.83 (.30)	4.59	1.99 (.38)	5.41	1.33 (.55)
FINGERS	6.40	1.43 (.57)	5.88	1.75 (.03)	5.80	1.91 (.04)	4.80	1.81 (.05)	6.67	.82 (.45)	3.59	1.92 (-.62)	4.76	1.55 (-.10)
FIRE	6.13	1.47 (.47)	6.32	1.42 (.47)	4.90	2.13 (-.86)	5.33	1.76 (.58)	6.33	1.41 (.11)	4.22	1.86 (.01)	3.55	1.87 (-1.31)
FISH	5.93	1.65 (.10)	6.09	1.51 (.24)	6.31	1.33 (.55)	4.73	1.77 (-.02)	6.16	1.35 (-.06)	5.06	1.81 (.85)	4.53	1.60 (-.33)
FISHING	5.05	1.69 (-.78)	5.93	1.60 (.08)	5.40	1.63 (-.36)	4.15	1.71 (-.60)	6.06	1.37 (-.16)	4.10	1.76 (-.11)	5.18	1.68 (.32)
FLAME	5.81	1.85 (-.02)	5.76	1.73 (-.09)	5.08	1.60 (-.68)	4.89	1.75 (.14)	6.23	1.32 (.01)	3.84	1.34 (-.37)	4.62	1.50 (-.24)
FLOWER	5.71	2.00 (-.12)	6.10	1.41 (.25)	5.87	1.70 (.11)	5.29	1.72 (.54)	6.50	1.12 (.28)	5.06	1.95 (.85)	5.70	1.44 (.84)
FLUTE	5.83	1.99 (.00)	5.75	1.81 (-.10)	6.29	1.35 (.53)	4.36	1.92 (-.39)	5.70	1.69 (-.52)	3.69	1.84 (-.52)	5.09	1.54F (.23)
FLY	5.21	1.88 (-.62)	5.76	1.75 (-.09)	6.07	1.35 (.31)	4.60	1.79 (-.15)	6.11	1.50 (-.11)	4.83	1.88 (.62)	3.88	2.05 (-.98)
FOOD	5.93	1.67 (.10)	5.33	1.91 (-.52)	5.63	1.98 (-.13)	5.88	1.51 (1.13)	6.53	1.02 (.31)	5.80	1.64 (1.59)	4.98	1.71 (.12)
FOOTBALL	5.75	2.01 (-.08)	5.68	1.80 (-.17)	6.23	1.33 (.47)	4.88	1.87 (.13)	6.40	1.36 (.18)	4.79	2.02 (.58)	4.73	1.59 (-.13)
FOREST	6.46	1.32 (.63)	6.30	1.45 (.45)	5.80	1.75 (.04)	5.20	1.80 (.45)	6.03	1.49 (-.19)	5.34	1.93 (1.13)	5.74	1.48 (.88)
FOX	5.80	2.00 (-.03)	5.61	1.83 (-.24)	6.25	1.36 (.49)	4.30	1.85 (-.45)	6.24	2.13 (.02)	4.10	1.86 (-.11)	4.81	1.37 (-.05)
FRIEND	4.40	2.15 (-1.43)	5.63	1.67 (-.22)	4.82	1.75 (-.94)	5.38	1.69 (.63)	6.50	1.19 (.28)	5.36	1.76 (1.15)	6.16	1.33F (1.30)
FROG	6.21	1.53 (.38)	6.04	1.60 (.19)	6.20	1.60 (.44)	4.66	1.73 (-.09)	6.05	1.53 (-.17)	4.03	2.10 (-.18)	3.87	1.60 (-.99)
FROST	6.24	1.35 (.41)	5.71	1.58 (-.14)	5.33	1.47 (-.43)	4.52	1.78 (-.23)	6.00	1.44 (-.22)	3.56	1.52 (-.65)	4.97	1.56 (.11)
FRUIT	6.09	1.42 (.26)	5.93	1.71 (.08)	5.98	1.64 (.22)	5.41	1.42 (.66)	6.41	1.38 (.19)	5.28	1.60 (1.07)	5.73	1.29F (.87)
FUR	6.23	1.55 (.40)	5.77	1.68 (-.08)	5.77	1.64 (.01)	4.54	1.78 (-.21)	6.05	1.41 (-.17)	4.23	1.69 (.02)	5.00	1.64 (.14)
GALLERY	5.75	1.55 (-.08)	5.45	1.92 (-.40)	5.02	1.41 (-.74)	4.20	1.69 (-.55)	5.75	1.49 (-.47)	4.30	1.67 (.09)	4.71	1.56 (-.15)
GAME	4.72	1.85 (-1.11)	5.42	1.67 (-.51)	5.25	1.73 (-.51)	5.03	1.71 (.28)	6.24	1.30 (.02)	5.62	1.43 (1.41)	4.72	1.55 (-.14)
GARDEN	5.92	1.72 (.09)	6.23	1.43 (.38)	5.55	1.71 (-.21)	5.51	1.55 (.76)	6.53	.94 (.31)	5.00	1.68 (.79)	6.07	1.20 (1.21)
GAS	5.50	1.73 (-.33)	5.41	1.81 (-.44)	5.88	1.31 (.12)	4.38	1.78 (-.37)	6.50	1.10 (.28)	4.30	2.01 (.09)	3.80	1.40M (-1.06)
GEM	5.73	1.74 (-.10)	5.32	1.73 (-.53)	5.42	1.72 (-.34)	4.42	1.60 (-.33)	5.39	1.80 (-.83)	4.61	1.80 (.40)	4.99	1.53 (.13)
GIFT	5.36	1.96 (-.47)	5.42	1.64 (-.43)	5.17	1.61 (-.59)	5.15	1.40 (.40)	6.46	1.01 (.24)	4.83	2.11 (.62)	5.49	1.40 (.63)
GIN	6.35	1.45 (.52)	5.49	1.80 (-.36)	6.23	1.50 (.47)	5.25	1.83 (.50)	5.95	1.51 (-.27)	3.85	1.90 (-.36)	4.03	1.84M (-.83)
GIRL	6.05	1.96 (.22)	6.31	1.20 (.46)	6.13	1.63 (.37)	5.87	1.63 (1.12)	6.85	.48 (.63)	5.22	2.00 (1.01)	5.20	1.68M (.34)
GLASS	6.31	1.32 (.48)	5.79	1.53 (-.06)	5.65	1.69 (-.11)	4.94	1.59 (.19)	6.85	.40 (.63)	3.97	1.91 (-.24)	4.61	1.42 (-.25)

	CON		IMG		CAT		MNG		FAM		NOA		PLS	
	M	SD	M	SD	M	SD	M	SD	M	SD	M	SD	M	SD
GLASSES	6.02	1.91	6.02	1.63	5.35	2.00	5.02	1.58	6.57	.93	4.29	1.79	3.87	1.48
	(.19)		(.17)		(-.41)		(.27)		(.35)		(.08)		(-.99)	
GLOBE	5.57	1.85	5.70	1.96	4.98	1.73	4.52	1.65	5.75	1.54	4.24	1.97	4.97	1.30M
	(-.26)		(-.15)		(-.78)		(-.23)		(-.47)		(.03)		(.11)	
GLOVE	6.14	1.47	5.89	1.77	5.88	1.70	4.90	1.64	6.46	.94	3.59	1.81	4.27	1.43
	(.31)		(.04)		(.12)		(.15)		(.24)		(-.62)		(-.59)	
GOLD	5.68	1.78	5.70	1.66	5.67	1.91	4.56	2.01	6.03	1.56	3.94	2.07	5.27	1.54M
	(-.15)		(-.15)		(-.09)		(-.19)		(-.19)		(-.27)		(.41)	
GORILLA	6.16	1.58	6.28	1.21	6.25	1.40	4.69	1.78	6.28	1.29	3.82	2.07	3.67	1.67
	(.33)		(.43)		(.49)		(-.06)		(.06)		(-.39)		(-1.19)	
GOWN	5.82	1.85	5.72	1.75	5.42	1.78	4.87	1.69	5.89	1.74	3.54	1.66	5.09	1.72
	(-.01)		(-.13)		(-.34)		(.12)		(-.33)		(-.67)		(.23)	
GRAPE	5.85	1.94	5.86	1.62	6.07	1.54	4.03	1.89	6.35	1.25	3.32	1.63	4.90	1.40
	(.02)		(.01)		(.31)		(-.72)		(.13)		(-.89)		(.04)	
GRAPEFRUIT	6.32	1.36	6.18	1.34	6.08	1.57	4.31	1.97	6.33	1.17	3.16	1.69	4.68	1.78F
	(.49)		(.33)		(.32)		(-.44)		(.11)		(-1.05)		(-.18)	
GRASS	6.02	1.63	5.73	1.84	6.15	1.30	5.12	1.63	6.57	.95	3.98	1.75	5.70	1.42F
	(.19)		(-.12)		(.39)		(.37)		(.35)		(-.23)		(.84)	
GREEN	4.31	2.13	5.81	1.80	6.13	1.63	5.02	1.92	6.19	1.35	3.16	2.01	4.98	1.45
	(-1.52)		(-.04)		(.37)		(.27)		(-.03)		(-1.05)		(.12)	
GYM	5.93	1.61	6.07	1.52	5.03	1.89	4.62	1.77	6.21	1.28	4.33	1.82	4.74	1.59
	(.10)		(.22)		(-.73)		(-.13)		(-.01)		(.12)		(-.12)	
HAIR	5.79	1.98	5.74	1.79	5.74	1.59	4.55	1.96	6.49	1.17	4.45	1.97	4.74	1.49
	(-.04)		(-.11)		(-.02)		(-.20)		(.27)		(.24)		(-.12)	
HAM	5.50	2.04	5.64	1.87	6.41	.99	4.30	1.87	6.10	1.31	3.47	1.70	4.44	1.68
	(-.33)		(-.21)		(.65)		(-.45)		(-.12)		(-.74)		(-.42)	
HAND	6.00	1.72	6.15	1.36	6.08	1.44	4.87	1.78	6.59	1.10	4.42	1.93	4.69	1.48F
	(.17)		(.30)		(.32)		(.12)		(.37)		(.21)		(-.17)	
HANDS	6.37	1.48	6.37	1.20	6.18	1.27	5.00	1.82	6.60	1.17	5.03	1.64	4.88	1.41
	(.54)		(.52)		(.42)		(.25)		(.38)		(.82)		(.02)	
HAT	5.97	1.68	5.56	1.77	5.67	1.72	4.78	1.86	6.55	.95	3.87	1.82	3.80	1.20
	(.14)		(-.29)		(-.09)		(.03)		(.33)		(-.34)		(-1.06)	
HAWK	6.19	1.77	5.85	1.49	6.23	1.50	4.67	1.67	5.78	1.57	4.03	2.01	4.52	1.53M
	(.36)		(.00)		(.47)		(-.08)		(-.44)		(-.18)		(-.34)	
HEAD	6.16	1.45	6.15	1.35	6.05	1.38	5.05	1.59	6.34	1.20	5.28	1.56	4.19	1.29
	(.33)		(.30)		(.29)		(.30)		(.12)		(1.07)		(-.67)	
HEART	6.02	1.50	6.09	1.31	5.97	1.64	5.38	1.58	6.37	1.13	5.41	1.52	5.16	1.56F
	(.19)		(.24)		(.21)		(.63)		(.15)		(1.20)		(.30)	
HERB	5.54	1.84	4.96	2.03	5.42	1.90	4.45	1.75	5.88	1.42	4.05	1.72	4.98	1.48F
	(-.29)		(-.89)		(-.34)		(-.30)		(-.34)		(-.16)		(.12)	
HIGHWAY	5.95	1.68	6.07	1.55	6.00	1.44	4.89	1.87	6.65	.92	3.91	2.04	4.16	1.33M
	(.12)		(.22)		(.24)		(.14)		(.43)		(-.30)		(-.70)	
HOCKEY	5.31	2.01	5.87	1.59	6.48	1.00	3.94	2.01	5.88	1.62	4.44	2.08	4.52	1.62M
	(-.52)		(.02)		(.72)		(-.81)		(-.34)		(.23)		(-.34)	
HOME	5.39	1.73	5.64	1.57	5.08	2.04	5.68	1.65	6.84	.76	5.52	1.95	5.61	1.60
	(-.44)		(-.21)		(-.68)		(.93)		(.62)		(1.31)		(.75)	
HONEY	5.91	1.88	5.93	1.60	5.62	1.83	4.97	1.64	6.41	1.24	3.69	1.68	5.75	1.60
	(.08)		(.08)		(-.14)		(.22)		(.19)		(-.52)		(.89)	
HONEYMOON	5.11	1.97	5.57	1.75	5.35	1.86	5.37	1.87	6.15	1.33	4.80	2.03	5.46	1.98
	(-.72)		(-.28)		(-.41)		(.62)		(-.07)		(.59)		(.60)	
HORSE	6.31	1.53	6.05	1.53	5.92	1.79	4.71	1.81	6.17	1.35	4.07	1.98	4.94	1.50
	(.48)		(.20)		(.16)		(-.04)		(-.05)		(-.14)		(.08)	
HOSPITAL	5.72	2.02	5.91	1.68	5.93	1.59	5.03	1.74	6.21	1.31	5.30	2.00	3.33	1.54
	(-.11)		(.06)		(.17)		(.28)		(-.01)		(1.09)		(-1.53)	

	CON M SD	IMG M SD	CAT M SD	MNG M SD	FAM M SD	NOA M SD	PLS M SD
HOTEL	5.88 1.72 (.05)	6.00 1.50 (.15)	5.28 1.91 (-.48)	4.54 1.71 (-.21)	6.47 1.05 (.25)	4.16 1.91 (-.05)	4.62 1.29 (-.24)
HOUSE	6.21 1.60 (.38)	5.79 1.58 (-.06)	5.98 1.50 (.22)	5.06 1.70 (.31)	6.34 1.13 (.12)	5.31 1.99 (1.10)	5.08 1.27F (.22)
HUSBAND	5.45 1.83 (-.38)	5.24 1.89 (-.61)	5.55 1.55 (-.21)	4.92 1.99 (.17)	6.12 1.39 (.50)	4.71 2.17 (1.10)	4.14 1.60 (-.72)
ICECREAM	5.93 1.76 (.10)	6.45 1.13 (.60)	6.32 1.20 (.56)	4.71 2.02 (-.04)	6.49 1.19 (.27)	4.38 1.94 (.17)	5.66 1.59F (.80)
INDIAN	6.18 1.47 (.35)	5.74 1.92 (-.11)	5.80 1.73 (.04)	5.24 1.87 (.49)	6.20 1.24 (-.02)	4.83 2.01 (.62)	4.54 1.57 (-.32)
INSECT	5.78 1.75 (-.05)	5.79 1.70 (-.06)	6.18 1.47 (.42)	4.97 1.77 (.22)	6.26 1.16 (.04)	4.97 1.95 (.76)	3.24 1.61 (-1.62)
IRIS	5.85 1.93 (.02)	6.00 1.46 (.15)	5.75 1.87 (-.01)	4.39 1.91 (-.36)	5.67 1.79 (-.55)	3.33 1.68 (-.88)	4.55 1.76 (-.31)
IVORY	5.67 1.86 (-.16)	5.23 1.86 (-.62)	5.52 1.73 (-.24)	3.75 1.67 (-1.00)	5.86 1.20 (-.36)	3.36 1.61 (-.85)	5.19 1.37F (.33)
JACKET	6.31 1.41 (.48)	6.05 1.55 (.20)	6.17 1.54 (.41)	5.64 1.49 (.89)	6.70 .64 (.48)	4.26 1.98 (.05)	4.77 1.35 (-.09)
JEEP	6.18 1.60 (.35)	6.53 1.17 (.68)	6.57 1.05 (.81)	4.77 1.94 (.02)	6.38 1.01 (.16)	4.47 2.07 (.26)	5.25 1.49 (.39)
JELLO	5.93 1.83 (.10)	5.98 1.43 (.13)	5.71 1.70 (-.05)	3.95 1.98 (-.80)	6.20 1.44 (-.02)	3.60 1.77 (-.61)	4.66 1.59 (-.20)
JET	5.76 1.89 (-.07)	5.79 1.94 (-.06)	5.87 1.57 (-.11)	5.13 1.63 (.38)	6.57 .77 (.35)	4.89 1.81 (.68)	4.80 1.48M (-.06)
JEWEL	5.73 1.66 (-.10)	6.05 1.11 (.20)	5.30 1.65 (-.46)	5.02 1.77 (.27)	6.23 1.40 (.01)	4.70 1.75 (.49)	5.19 1.40 (.33)
JUICE	6.00 1.46 (.17)	5.80 1.55 (-.05)	5.45 1.77 (-.31)	4.10 1.80 (-.65)	6.17 1.35 (-.05)	3.83 1.72 (-.38)	5.18 1.40 (.32)
KEY	6.08 1.62 (.25)	6.12 1.45 (.27)	5.40 1.84 (-.36)	4.30 1.86 (-.45)	6.67 .75 (.45)	3.60 1.83 (-.61)	4.54 1.22 (-.32)
KID	5.32 2.03 (-.51)	5.19 1.83 (-.66)	5.05 1.79 (-.71)	4.97 1.56 (.22)	6.33 1.28 (.11)	4.30 1.72 (.09)	4.43 1.48 (-.43)
KING	5.62 1.86 (-.21)	5.67 1.66 (-.18)	5.85 1.61 (.09)	4.95 1.67 (.20)	6.00 1.50 (-.22)	4.92 1.79 (.71)	4.46 1.61 (-.40)
KISS	5.86 1.58 (.03)	6.22 1.45 (.37)	5.17 1.74 (-.59)	5.13 1.97 (.38)	6.63 1.00 (.41)	4.86 1.79 (.65)	6.18 1.15 (1.32)
KITE	5.88 1.96 (.05)	6.18 1.44 (.33)	5.37 1.63 (-.39)	4.08 1.85 (-.67)	5.95 1.41 (-.27)	3.79 1.67 (-.42)	5.34 1.37 (.48)
KITTEN	5.81 1.90 (-.02)	6.28 1.37 (.43)	6.53 .86 (.77)	4.47 1.92 (-.28)	6.41 1.02 (.19)	4.83 1.77 (.62)	4.84 1.86F (-.02)
KNIGHT	5.75 1.71 (-.08)	6.02 1.48 (.17)	5.90 1.39 (.14)	4.38 1.76 (-.37)	5.79 1.59 (-.43)	3.61 1.85 (-.60)	4.54 1.58 (-.32)
LADY	5.58 1.49 (-.25)	5.52 1.88 (-.33)	5.45 1.96 (-.31)	5.58 1.53 (.83)	6.25 1.37 (.03)	5.27 1.58 (1.06)	5.00 1.68M (.14)
LAKE	5.78 1.76 (-.05)	5.98 1.63 (.13)	5.86 1.71 (.10)	4.97 1.71 (.22)	6.43 1.05 (.21)	3.90 1.84 (-.31)	5.74 1.29 (.88)
LAMB	6.24 1.50 (.41)	5.88 1.65 (.03)	6.12 1.54 (.36)	4.45 1.80 (-.30)	5.77 1.61 (-.45)	3.92 1.93 (-.29)	5.38 1.19F (.52)
LAMP	6.18 1.40 (.35)	5.50 1.98 (-.35)	5.85 1.46 (.09)	4.42 1.52 (-.33)	6.41 1.05 (.19)	3.95 1.79 (-.26)	4.34 1.14 (-.52)
LAND	6.16 1.55 (.33)	5.64 1.59 (-.21)	5.72 1.53 (-.04)	5.08 1.73 (.33)	6.22 1.28 (.00)	5.13 1.95 (.92)	4.82 1.32 (-.04)
LANTERN	6.26 1.49 (.43)	5.65 1.58 (-.20)	5.52 1.62 (-.24)	4.48 1.79 (-.27)	5.64 1.82 (-.58)	3.85 1.65 (-.36)	4.61 1.16 (-.25)

	CON		IMG		CAT		MNG		FAM		NOA		PLS	
	M	SD	M	SD	M	SD	M	SD	M	SD	M	SD	M	SD
LAWN	5.79	1.78	5.91	1.29	5.33	1.62	4.60	1.65	6.30	1.17	3.98	1.88	5.18	1.51
	(-.04)		(.06)		(-.43)		(-.15)		(.08)		(-.23)		(.32)	
LAWYER	5.66	1.78	5.64	1.63	5.95	1.55	4.57	1.72	6.32	1.30	4.54	1.88	4.42	1.43
	(-.17)		(-.21)		(.19)		(-.18)		(.10)		(.33)		(-.44)	
LEAF	5.89	1.89	6.02	1.33	6.05	1.42	4.37	1.90	6.27	1.33	4.06	1.71	5.18	1.43
	(.06)		(.17)		(.29)		(-.38)		(.05)		(-.15)		(.32)	
LEATHER	5.71	1.89	5.80	1.70	5.53	1.64	4.34	1.80	6.45	.88	3.83	1.57	4.77	1.35
	(-.12)		(-.05)		(-.23)		(-.41)		(.23)		(-.38)		(-.09)	
LEG	6.22	1.51	5.95	1.62	6.07	1.76	5.03	1.76	6.66	1.06	3.67	1.88	4.28	1.54
	(.39)		(.10)		(.31)		(.28)		(.44)		(-.54)		(-.58)	
LEMON	5.98	1.65	6.15	1.53	6.48	1.11	4.70	1.83	6.21	1.25	3.63	1.89	4.49	1.46F
	(.15)		(.30)		(.72)		(-.05)		(-.01)		(-.58)		(-.37)	
LEMONADE	6.36	1.42	5.92	1.45	5.92	1.55	4.58	1.72	5.92	1.59	3.39	1.76	5.65	1.21
	(.53)		(.07)		(.16)		(-.17)		(-.30)		(-.82)		(.79)	
LETTER	5.31	2.05	5.46	1.91	5.53	1.58	4.33	1.84	6.48	.91	4.71	1.73	5.05	1.53
	(-.52)		(-.39)		(-.23)		(-.42)		(.26)		(.50)		(.19)	
LETTERS	5.52	1.86	5.69	1.74	5.10	1.85	5.21	1.60	6.75	.65	4.46	2.00	5.37	1.54F
	(-.31)		(-.16)		(-.66)		(.46)		(.53)		(.25)		(.51)	
LETTUCE	5.75	1.96	6.02	1.48	6.52	.88	4.23	1.88	6.39	1.16	3.44	1.73	4.71	1.53F
	(-.08)		(.17)		(.76)		(-.52)		(.17)		(-.77)		(-.15)	
LIBRARY	5.38	1.95	5.36	1.81	5.36	2.02	4.53	1.69	6.31	1.13	5.18	1.86	4.63	1.43
	(-.45)		(-.49)		(-.40)		(-.22)		(.09)		(.97)		(-.23)	
LIGHT	5.46	1.62	5.24	1.82	4.93	1.95	5.33	1.59	6.42	1.16	4.94	1.89	5.03	1.42
	(-.37)		(-.61)		(-.83)		(.58)		(.20)		(.73)		(.17)	
LILY	5.96	1.65	5.46	1.94	5.88	1.59	4.17	1.96	5.53	1.56	3.38	1.60	5.26	1.54F
	(.13)		(-.39)		(.12)		(-.58)		(-.69)		(-.83)		(.40)	
LIMB	5.86	1.71	5.66	1.58	5.37	1.81	4.56	1.80	6.22	2.14	4.22	1.56	4.21	1.32
	(.03)		(-.19)		(-.39)		(-.19)		(.00)		(.01)		(-.65)	
LIME	5.97	1.62	5.87	1.61	6.23	1.39	4.00	1.83	5.89	1.39	3.54	1.84	4.48	1.61F
	(.14)		(.02)		(.47)		(-.75)		(-.33)		(-.67)		(-.38)	
LIMOUSINE	6.20	1.38	5.89	1.69	6.00	1.55	5.05	1.66	5.79	1.70	4.30	2.05	3.85	1.88M
	(.37)		(.04)		(.24)		(.30)		(-.43)		(.09)		(-1.01)	
LION	6.14	1.63	6.22	1.44	6.45	1.45	4.98	1.86	6.30	1.27	3.88	2.19	4.90	1.79
	(.31)		(.37)		(.69)		(.23)		(.08)		(-.33)		(.04)	
LIPS	6.60	1.15	6.05	1.46	5.83	1.70	4.42	1.92	6.21	1.42	5.18	1.86	5.66	1.32
	(.77)		(.20)		(.07)		(-.33)		(-.01)		(.15)		(.80)	
LIQUOR	6.26	1.36	5.93	1.59	6.05	1.56	5.38	1.61	6.25	1.29	5.18	1.88	4.39	1.55M
	(.43)		(.08)		(.29)		(.63)		(.03)		(.97)		(-.47)	
LOBSTER	5.84	1.90	6.35	1.19	6.10	1.54	4.07	1.93	6.08	1.45	4.21	1.81	4.93	1.80M
	(.01)		(.50)		(.34)		(-.68)		(-.14)		(.00)		(.07)	
LUNCH	5.46	1.70	6.00	1.35	5.48	1.76	4.85	1.82	6.50	1.39	4.88	1.58	5.24	1.36
	(-.37)		(.15)		(-.28)		(.10)		(.28)		(.67)		(.38)	
MACARONI	6.62	1.13	6.21	1.48	6.22	1.46	4.59	2.05	6.18	1.41	3.16	1.70	4.54	1.60
	(.79)		(.36)		(.46)		(-.16)		(-.04)		(-1.05)		(-.32)	
MAGAZINE	5.91	1.93	5.65	1.83	6.08	1.51	4.93	1.75	6.15	1.49	5.33	1.78	5.19	1.25F
	(.08)		(-.20)		(.32)		(.18)		(-.07)		(1.12)		(.33)	
MAGICIAN	5.56	1.96	5.63	1.54	5.97	1.50	4.12	1.75	6.02	1.33	4.74	1.96	5.24	1.20
	(-.27)		(-.22)		(.21)		(-.63)		(-.20)		(.53)		(.38)	
MALE	5.56	1.79	5.93	1.62	5.65	1.95	5.33	1.81	6.48	1.25	4.52	1.99	4.93	1.58
	(-.27)		(.08)		(-.11)		(.58)		(.26)		(.31)		(.07)	
MAN	6.14	1.49	5.41	1.95	6.00	1.54	6.07	1.25	6.74	.71	5.49	1.96	4.84	1.52F
	(.31)		(-.44)		(.24)		(1.32)		(.52)		(1.28)		(-.02)	
MANSION	5.75	1.82	6.22	1.36	5.97	1.47	4.90	1.60	5.63	1.62	4.41	2.02	4.85	1.24
	(-.08)		(.37)		(.21)		(.15)		(-.59)		(.20)		(-.01)	

	CON M	CON SD	IMG M	IMG SD	CAT M	CAT SD	MNG M	MNG SD	FAM M	FAM SD	NOA M	NOA SD	PLS M	PLS SD
MAP	5.61	1.99	5.81	1.68	5.10	1.92	4.60	1.74	6.43	1.32	4.21	2.16	4.38	1.23
	(-.22)		(-.04)		(-.66)		(-.15)		(.21)		(.00)		(-.48)	
MAPLE	5.30	1.65	5.05	1.68	5.84	1.58	4.13	1.81	5.92	1.46	3.79	1.75	5.20	1.60F
	(-.53)		(-.80)		(.08)		(-.62)		(-.30)		(-.42)		(.34)	
MARIJUANA	6.24	1.70	6.21	1.58	6.33	1.16	5.72	1.72	6.48	1.26	4.41	2.14	4.96	1.94M
	(.41)		(.36)		(.57)		(.97)		(.26)		(.20)		(.10)	
MARSHMALLOWS	6.43	1.35	5.61	1.71	5.57	1.84	4.15	1.97	5.86	1.48	2.98	1.61	5.24	1.26
	(.60)		(-.24)		(-.19)		(-.60)		(-.36)		(-1.23)		(.38)	
MATTRESS	6.36	1.25	5.95	1.51	5.53	1.59	4.50	1.76	5.98	1.47	3.90	1.66	5.11	1.26
	(.53)		(.10)		(-.23)		(-.25)		(-.24)		(-.31)		(.25)	
MEAL	5.98	1.41	5.67	1.62	5.33	1.70	5.48	1.63	6.77	.76	4.74	1.68	5.43	1.36M
	(.15)		(-.18)		(-.43)		(.73)		(.55)		(.53)		(.57)	
MEAT	5.80	1.90	6.06	1.48	6.21	1.15	5.06	1.69	6.40	1.26	5.00	1.69	4.61	1.56
	(-.03)		(.21)		(.45)		(.31)		(.18)		(.79)		(-.25)	
MEN	6.09	1.71	5.88	1.76	5.87	1.87	6.16	1.36	6.85	.52	5.67	1.83	5.15	1.39F
	(.26)		(.03)		(.11)		(1.41)		(.63)		(1.46)		(.29)	
MERMAID	5.16	2.03	5.55	1.79	5.26	1.70	3.42	1.96	5.42	1.82	3.89	2.05	5.51	1.15
	(-.67)		(-.30)		(-.50)		(-1.33)		(-.80)		(-.32)		(.65)	
MICROSCOPE	5.82	1.94	6.09	1.47	5.87	1.52	3.89	1.96	5.92	1.65	4.13	1.99	4.23	1.27
	(-.01)		(.24)		(.11)		(-.86)		(-.30)		(-.08)		(-.63)	
MILK	6.66	.96	6.32	1.35	6.05	1.65	5.15	1.90	6.62	1.04	3.25	1.75	5.30	1.58
	(.83)		(.47)		(.29)		(.40)		(.40)		(-.96)		(.44)	
MINISTER	5.83	1.85	5.91	1.52	5.73	1.84	4.87	1.79	5.63	1.76	4.30	1.86	3.90	1.33
	(.00)		(.06)		(-.03)		(.12)		(-.59)		(.09)		(-.96)	
MINK	5.85	1.78	5.98	1.45	5.98	1.62	4.52	1.74	5.98	1.65	3.51	1.91	4.28	1.79M
	(.02)		(.13)		(.22)		(-.23)		(-.24)		(-.70)		(-.58)	
MINTS	5.63	1.91	5.62	1.58	5.62	1.73	4.35	1.80	6.10	1.50	3.57	1.71	5.16	1.54
	(-.20)		(-.23)		(-.14)		(-.40)		(-.12)		(-.64)		(.30)	
MIRROR	5.91	1.85	6.34	1.05	5.53	1.83	4.69	1.74	6.57	.83	3.75	1.77	4.54	1.38
	(.08)		(.49)		(-.23)		(-.06)		(.35)		(-.46)		(-.32)	
MIXER	5.70	1.64	5.30	1.88	4.77	1.80	4.50	1.75	6.26	1.08	4.33	1.60	4.42	1.58
	(-.13)		(-.55)		(-.99)		(-.25)		(.04)		(.12)		(-.44)	
MOCCASIN	6.07	1.74	5.67	1.73	6.00	1.70	4.36	1.78	5.49	1.73	3.61	1.99	4.74	1.24
	(.24)		(.24)		(.24)		(-.39)		(-.73)		(-.60)		(-.12)	
MONEY	5.77	1.75	6.32	1.40	5.47	1.79	5.36	1.58	6.55	1.11	4.20	1.85	4.96	1.82M
	(-.06)		(.47)		(-.29)		(.61)		(.33)		(-.01)		(.10)	
MONKEY	5.62	2.07	5.82	1.76	6.50	1.14	4.48	1.80	6.05	1.44	4.79	1.89	4.46	1.21F
	(-.21)		(-.03)		(.74)		(-.27)		(-.17)		(.58)		(-.40)	
MOON	5.77	1.80	5.72	1.80	5.34	1.98	4.42	1.98	6.26	1.28	4.22	1.92	5.48	1.45F
	(-.06)		(-.13)		(-.42)		(-.33)		(.04)		(.01)		(.62)	
MOOSE	6.12	1.48	5.98	1.70	6.58	1.14	4.20	1.92	5.92	1.41	3.72	1.86	4.65	1.55
	(.29)		(.13)		(.82)		(-.55)		(-.30)		(-.49)		(-.21)	
MORNING	5.11	1.90	5.80	1.56	5.36	1.64	5.10	1.75	6.57	1.18	3.98	2.04	5.29	1.68
	(-.72)		(-.05)		(-.40)		(.35)		(.35)		(-.23)		(.43)	
MOTHER	5.47	2.13	6.33	1.41	5.79	2.00	5.84	1.53	6.85	.52	5.17	1.81	5.84	1.42F
	(-.36)		(.48)		(.02)		(1.09)		(.63)		(.96)		(.98)	
MOUNTAIN	6.25	1.66	6.14	1.66	6.27	1.34	5.73	1.23	6.78	.64	5.83	1.61	6.09	1.39F
	(.42)		(.29)		(.51)		(.98)		(.56)		(1.62)		(1.23)	
MOUTH	5.64	2.00	6.07	1.57	6.36	1.17	4.98	1.84	6.46	1.15	4.59	1.79	4.49	1.50
	(-.19)		(.22)		(.60)		(.23)		(.24)		(.38)		(-.37)	
MOVIE	6.02	1.70	5.73	1.72	5.65	1.72	4.77	1.55	6.25	1.20	5.10	1.87	5.32	1.48F
	(.19)		(-.12)		(-.11)		(.02)		(.03)		(.89)		(.46)	
MUG	5.72	1.91	5.68	1.67	5.38	1.92	4.77	1.64	6.22	1.28	3.76	1.62	4.63	1.48
	(-.11)		(-.17)		(-.38)		(.02)		(.00)		(-.45)		(-.23)	

	CON		IMG		CAT		MNG		FAM		NOA		PLS	
	M	SD	M	SD	M	SD	M	SD	M	SD	M	SD	M	SD
MUSIC	5.15	1.80	5.30	2.24	5.38	1.89	5.69	1.65	6.77	.74	5.71	1.52	6.22	1.23
	(-.68)		(-.55)		(-.38)		(.94)		(.55)		(1.50)		(1.36)	
NECK	5.83	1.82	6.16	1.32	5.90	1.41	4.34	1.91	6.50	1.10	3.73	1.66	4.78	1.41
	(.00)		(.31)		(.14)		(-.41)		(.28)		(-.48)		(-.08)	
NECKLACE	6.29	1.49	6.00	1.70	6.07	1.45	4.57	1.85	6.10	1.46	4.26	1.88	4.80	1.49
	(.46)		(.15)		(.31)		(-.12)		(.05)		(.05)		(-.06)	
NEST	5.53	1.93	5.65	1.65	5.43	1.64	4.40	1.71	6.25	1.25	3.84	1.47	4.92	1.20
	(-.30)		(-.20)		(-.33)		(-.35)		(.03)		(-.37)		(.06)	
NICKEL	5.93	1.63	5.66	1.79	6.14	1.41	4.31	1.96	6.33	1.23	3.45	1.74	4.59	1.16
	(.10)		(-.19)		(.38)		(-.44)		(.11)		(-.76)		(-.27)	
NIGHT	4.91	2.06	5.82	1.60	5.29	1.90	5.33	1.64	6.71	.84	4.13	2.09	4.89	1.51
	(-.92)		(-.03)		(-.47)		(.58)		(.49)		(-.08)		(.03)	
NIGHTGOWN	6.40	1.21	5.58	1.83	5.88	1.51	4.52	1.80	5.80	1.60	3.75	1.90	4.94	1.56
	(.57)		(-.27)		(.12)		(-.23)		(-.42)		(-.46)		(.08)	
NOSE	6.26	1.47	6.01	1.51	5.97	1.58	4.72	1.77	6.23	1.43	3.85	1.82	4.09	1.27
	(.43)		(.16)		(.21)		(-.03)		(.01)		(-.36)		(-.77)	
NOVEL	5.34	1.89	5.09	1.87	5.52	1.73	4.76	1.75	6.16	1.22	4.60	1.84	4.83	1.48F
	(-.49)		(-.76)		(-.24)		(.01)		(-.06)		(.39)		(-.03)	
NURSE	5.95	1.74	6.07	1.35	6.18	1.21	4.52	1.56	6.21	1.25	4.06	1.84	4.51	1.62
	(.12)		(.22)		(.42)		(-.23)		(-.01)		(-.15)		(-.35)	
OAK	5.51	2.02	5.50	1.62	6.07	1.59	4.23	1.73	6.25	1.17	3.43	1.64	5.10	1.42
	(-.32)		(-.35)		(.31)		(-.52)		(.03)		(-.78)		(.24)	
OCEAN	5.80	1.73	6.04	1.51	6.12	1.42	5.22	1.69	6.28	1.18	5.37	1.98	5.69	1.72
	(-.03)		(.19)		(.36)		(.47)		(.06)		(1.16)		(.83)	
ORANGE	6.00	1.68	5.87	1.75	5.85	1.83	4.67	1.84	6.25	1.25	4.03	1.84	5.23	1.36F
	(.17)		(.02)		(.09)		(-.08)		(.03)		(-.18)		(.37)	
ORCHESTRA	5.87	1.89	5.97	1.43	5.58	1.54	4.77	1.72	5.97	1.50	4.81	1.98	5.21	1.20
	(.04)		(.12)		(-.18)		(.02)		(-.25)		(.60)		(.35)	
ORCHID	5.95	1.51	5.91	1.62	6.03	1.36	3.75	1.81	5.30	1.76	4.11	1.81	5.26	1.46
	(.12)		(.06)		(.27)		(-1.00)		(-.92)		(-.10)		(.40)	
ORGAN	5.89	1.65	5.70	1.84	6.03	1.33	4.55	1.65	5.93	1.39	5.10	1.77	4.31	1.53
	(.06)		(-.15)		(.27)		(-.20)		(-.29)		(.89)		(-.55)	
OWL	6.09	1.55	5.85	1.54	6.38	1.18	3.97	1.80	5.73	1.46	3.92	2.04	4.78	1.22
	(.26)		(.00)		(.62)		(-.78)		(-.49)		(-.29)		(-.08)	
PAINT	5.73	2.05	5.63	1.62	5.40	1.62	4.02	1.61	6.28	1.34	4.02	1.84	4.46	1.40
	(-.10)		(-.22)		(-.36)		(-.73)		(.06)		(-.19)		(-.40)	
PAJAMA	6.16	1.72	5.89	1.59	5.67	1.66	4.25	1.87	5.90	1.54	3.50	1.86	4.67	1.56F
	(.33)		(.04)		(-.09)		(-.50)		(-.32)		(-.71)		(-.19)	
PALACE	5.71	1.70	6.00	1.36	5.48	1.73	4.84	1.68	6.00	1.46	4.66	2.04	4.41	1.74
	(-.12)		(.15)		(-.28)		(.09)		(-.22)		(.45)		(-.45)	
PALM	5.85	1.85	5.36	1.64	5.05	1.89	4.21	1.66	5.93	1.45	3.86	1.47	4.69	1.22M
	(.02)		(-.49)		(-.71)		(-.54)		(-.29)		(-.35)		(-.17)	
PANTIES	5.93	1.64	5.68	1.65	5.68	1.60	4.71	1.67	5.72	1.79	3.64	1.86	4.59	1.63M
	(.10)		(-.17)		(-.08)		(-.04)		(-.50)		(-.57)		(-.27)	
PANTS	6.15	1.54	6.24	1.37	5.93	1.60	5.10	1.51	6.49	1.07	4.09	1.84	4.58	1.44
	(.32)		(.39)		(.17)		(.35)		(.27)		(-.12)		(-.28)	
PARADE	5.19	2.03	5.72	1.85	4.70	1.82	4.63	1.74	6.00	1.55	4.60	1.75	4.80	1.40
	(-.64)		(-.13)		(-1.06)		(-.12)		(-.22)		(.39)		(-.06)	
PARK	5.45	1.75	5.61	1.83	4.72	1.70	5.08	1.68	6.37	1.22	4.46	1.78	5.04	1.49
	(-.38)		(-.24)		(-1.04)		(.33)		(.15)		(.25)		(.18)	
PAWS	5.66	1.82	5.54	1.92	5.76	1.57	4.88	1.63	5.97	1.52	4.11	1.69	4.40	1.27
	(-.17)		(-.31)		(.00)		(.13)		(-.25)		(-.10)		(-.46)	
PEACH	6.24	1.55	5.77	1.84	5.98	1.53	4.59	1.65	6.20	1.19	3.59	1.54	5.50	1.32
	(.41)		(-.08)		(.22)		(-.16)		(-.02)		(-.62)		(.64)	

	CON		IMG		CAT		MNG		FAM		NOA		PLS	
	M	SD	M	SD	M	SD	M	SD	M	SD	M	SD	M	SD
PEAR	6.30	1.51	5.84	1.69	6.22	1.61	4.94	1.87	6.41	1.07	3.02	1.54	4.49	1.67
	(.47)		(-.01)		(.46)		(.19)		(.19)		(-1.19)		(-.37)	
PEARL	5.93	1.88	5.84	1.62	5.71	1.81	3.92	1.76	5.82	1.64	3.65	1.73	5.25	1.27
	(.10)		(-.01)		(-.05)		(-.83)		(-.40)		(-.56)		(.39)	
PENCIL	6.22	1.67	5.98	1.60	5.88	1.73	4.49	1.84	6.40	1.20	3.34	1.87	4.39	1.00
	(.39)		(.13)		(.12)		(-.26)		(.18)		(-.87)		(-.47)	
PENNY	5.92	1.75	6.13	1.57	6.38	1.18	4.70	1.83	6.52	1.12	2.84	1.76	4.35	1.44
	(.09)		(.28)		(.62)		(-.05)		(.30)		(-1.37)		(-.51)	
PEOPLE	5.51	2.02	5.36	1.92	4.92	2.05	6.12	1.43	6.72	.62	5.98	1.68	5.35	1.53F
	(-.32)		(-.49)		(-.84)		(1.37)		(.50)		(1.77)		(.49)	
PET	5.56	1.53	5.89	1.35	5.71	1.35	5.82	1.51	6.41	1.19	5.17	1.65	5.60	1.63F
	(-.27)		(.04)		(-.05)		(1.07)		(.19)		(.96)		(.74)	
PHONE	6.20	1.55	5.81	1.60	5.37	1.81	4.60	1.78	6.24	1.41	4.21	1.76	4.53	1.45
	(.37)		(-.04)		(-.39)		(-.15)		(.02)		(.00)		(-.33)	
PHOTOGRAPH	5.88	1.61	6.14	1.42	5.78	1.51	5.20	1.66	6.39	1.15	4.94	1.93	5.65	1.16
	(.05)		(.29)		(.02)		(.45)		(.17)		(.73)		(.79)	
PIANO	6.26	1.51	6.45	1.01	5.93	1.71	4.87	1.92	6.54	.98	4.39	1.94	4.60	1.80F
	(.43)		(.60)		(.17)		(.12)		(.32)		(.18)		(-.26)	
PICKLE	6.02	1.72	6.35	1.27	6.03	1.55	4.16	2.04	6.36	1.25	3.18	1.74	4.67	1.65F
	(.19)		(.50)		(.27)		(-.59)		(.14)		(-1.03)		(-.19)	
PIE	6.09	1.61	5.98	1.54	6.10	1.61	4.82	1.81	6.38	1.11	4.05	2.00	5.31	1.41
	(.26)		(.13)		(.34)		(.07)		(.16)		(-.16)		(.45)	
PILL	6.06	1.71	5.74	1.91	5.95	1.62	4.97	1.91	6.30	1.12	4.60	2.25	3.61	1.74M
	(.23)		(-.11)		(.19)		(.22)		(.08)		(.39)		(-1.25)	
PILLOW	6.21	1.51	6.29	1.31	5.88	1.67	4.71	1.82	6.67	.94	2.98	1.54	5.25	1.55F
	(.38)		(.44)		(.12)		(-.04)		(.45)		(-1.23)		(.39)	
PINE	5.88	1.60	6.11	1.40	5.77	1.83	4.87	1.98	6.31	1.31	3.67	1.74	5.01	1.58
	(.05)		(.26)		(.01)		(.12)		(.09)		(-.54)		(.15)	
PINEAPPLE	6.49	1.31	5.63	1.76	6.12	1.58	4.35	1.88	5.63	1.79	3.30	1.86	5.35	1.19
	(.66)		(-.22)		(.36)		(-.40)		(-.59)		(-.91)		(.49)	
PIPE	6.12	1.45	5.82	1.57	5.77	1.63	4.65	1.61	6.06	1.43	3.89	1.65	4.37	1.63
	(.29)		(-.03)		(.01)		(-.10)		(-.16)		(-.32)		(-.49)	
PLANE	5.31	1.92	5.50	1.91	5.73	1.68	4.72	1.51	6.32	1.18	4.58	1.97	4.85	1.53
	(-.52)		(-.35)		(-.03)		(-.03)		(.10)		(.37)		(-.01)	
PLANT	5.98	1.58	5.89	1.62	5.57	1.68	5.21	1.71	6.66	.93	5.06	1.79	5.50	1.47F
	(.15)		(.04)		(-.19)		(.46)		(.44)		(.85)		(.64)	
PONY	6.07	1.64	6.36	1.00	6.30	1.39	4.39	1.72	5.98	1.50	4.08	1.62	5.01	1.37F
	(.24)		(.51)		(.54)		(-.36)		(-.24)		(-.13)		(.15)	
POT	5.45	2.19	5.98	1.49	5.20	1.93	5.38	1.63	6.51	1.01	3.92	1.74	4.28	1.91M
	(-.38)		(.13)		(-.56)		(.63)		(.29)		(-.29)		(-.58)	
POTATO	6.56	1.13	6.16	1.56	6.30	1.51	4.84	2.03	6.44	1.12	3.51	1.83	4.49	1.47M
	(.73)		(.31)		(.54)		(.09)		(.22)		(-.70)		(-.37)	
PRESIDENT	5.40	1.92	6.25	1.53	6.23	1.36	5.16	1.87	6.40	1.29	4.54	2.04	3.49	1.61M
	(-.43)		(.40)		(.47)		(.41)		(.18)		(.33)		(-1.37)	
PRIEST	5.54	1.90	5.40	1.90	5.87	1.57	4.85	1.62	5.90	1.58	4.05	2.01	4.06	1.48F
	(-.29)		(-.45)		(.11)		(.10)		(-.32)		(-.16)		(-.80)	
PRINCE	5.38	1.99	6.00	1.43	5.98	1.41	4.97	1.70	5.80	1.58	4.09	1.80	4.63	1.55F
	(-.45)		(.15)		(.22)		(.22)		(-.42)		(-.12)		(-.23)	
PRINCESS	5.64	1.87	5.41	2.02	5.80	1.72	4.28	1.76	5.76	1.76	4.30	1.87	5.00	1.59
	(-.19)		(-.44)		(.04)		(-.47)		(-.46)		(.09)		(.14)	
PRINTS	5.76	1.67	5.82	1.69	4.80	1.78	4.56	1.65	6.18	1.24	4.38	1.57	4.43	1.53F
	(-.07)		(-.03)		(-.96)		(-.19)		(-.04)		(.17)		(-.43)	
PROFESSOR	5.63	1.81	6.23	1.25	6.05	1.50	5.23	1.36	6.48	1.00	4.69	1.90	4.38	1.26F
	(-.20)		(.38)		(.29)		(.48)		(.26)		(.48)		(-.48)	

	CON		IMG		CAT		MNG		FAM		NOA		PLS	
	M	SD	M	SD	M	SD	M	SD	M	SD	M	SD	M	SD
PUDDING	6.13	1.47	5.74	1.58	5.72	1.86	4.69	1.86	6.25	1.27	3.28	1.63	5.16	1.52
	(.30)		(-.11)		(-.04)		(-.06)		(.03)		(-.93)		(.30)	
PUP	5.40	2.12	6.18	1.31	5.15	1.98	4.84	1.73	6.05	1.50	4.27	1.88	5.51	1.62
	(-.43)		(.33)		(-.61)		(.09)		(-.17)		(.06)		(.65)	
QUAIL	6.04	1.74	5.67	1.66	5.88	1.76	4.05	1.85	5.20	1.82	3.49	1.89	4.92	1.26
	(.21)		(-.18)		(.12)		(-.70)		(-1.02)		(-.72)		(.06)	
QUARTER	5.90	1.74	5.71	1.61	5.83	1.54	4.50	1.69	6.21	1.36	3.75	1.72	4.50	1.34
	(.07)		(-.14)		(.07)		(-.25)		(-.01)		(-.46)		(-.36)	
QUEEN	5.05	2.11	5.94	1.47	6.03	1.53	4.56	1.75	5.74	1.55	4.48	1.82	4.41	1.49
	(-.78)		(.09)		(.27)		(-.19)		(-.48)		(.27)		(-.45)	
QUILT	6.09	1.57	5.48	1.76	5.38	1.85	4.44	1.62	5.64	1.55	4.33	1.80	5.52	1.36F
	(.26)		(-.37)		(-.38)		(-.31)		(-.58)		(.12)		(.66)	
RABBIT	6.22	1.69	5.80	1.80	6.60	1.11	4.33	1.81	6.05	1.48	3.72	2.13	4.48	1.46F
	(.39)		(-.05)		(.84)		(-.42)		(-.17)		(-.49)		(-.38)	
RAIN	5.85	1.68	5.89	1.52	6.03	1.45	4.75	1.86	6.43	1.14	4.21	1.82	5.23	1.41
	(.02)		(.04)		(.27)		(.00)		(.21)		(.00)		(.37)	
RASPBERRY	5.90	2.01	6.30	1.20	6.15	1.60	4.00	2.01	6.02	1.41	2.94	1.70	5.31	1.52F
	(.07)		(.45)		(.39)		(-.75)		(-.20)		(-1.27)		(.45)	
RED	4.97	1.86	5.88	1.75	5.45	2.15	4.45	1.85	6.55	1.03	3.25	1.98	4.80	1.40
	(-.86)		(.03)		(-.31)		(-.30)		(.33)		(-.96)		(-.06)	
REFRIGERATOR	5.48	2.11	5.91	1.82	5.98	1.34	3.95	1.93	6.16	1.67	4.54	1.93	4.58	1.42M
	(-.35)		(.06)		(.22)		(-.80)		(-.06)		(.33)		(-.28)	
REPTILE	5.80	1.78	5.76	1.71	5.97	1.63	4.87	1.82	5.82	1.72	4.63	1.89	3.44	1.59
	(-.03)		(-.09)		(.21)		(.12)		(-.40)		(.42)		(-1.42)	
RICE	6.04	1.66	5.00	2.05	6.40	1.06	4.58	1.79	6.22	1.29	3.61	1.62	4.78	1.30F
	(.21)		(-.85)		(.64)		(-.17)		(.00)		(-.60)		(-.08)	
RING	5.88	1.54	5.74	1.57	5.67	1.68	5.16	1.49	6.57	1.00	4.16	1.67	4.72	1.31F
	(.05)		(-.11)		(-.09)		(.41)		(.35)		(-.05)		(-.14)	
RIVER	5.83	1.77	6.35	1.06	5.90	1.57	5.21	1.48	6.37	1.13	4.90	1.58	5.49	1.43M
	(.00)		(.50)		(.14)		(.46)		(.15)		(.69)		(.63)	
ROAD	5.65	1.81	5.80	1.61	5.47	1.83	4.81	1.74	6.37	1.13	4.41	1.82	4.59	1.19
	(-.18)		(-.05)		(-.29)		(.06)		(.15)		(.20)		(-.27)	
ROBIN	6.32	1.22	5.96	1.98	6.30	1.25	4.31	1.78	5.84	1.61	3.65	1.86	5.32	1.43F
	(.49)		(.11)		(.54)		(-.44)		(-.38)		(-.56)		(.46)	
ROCK	6.03	1.45	6.13	1.47	5.82	1.49	4.82	1.70	6.45	1.08	3.65	1.86	4.53	1.50F
	(.20)		(.28)		(.06)		(.07)		(.23)		(-.56)		(-.33)	
ROCKET	6.41	1.17	6.06	1.61	5.67	1.65	4.78	1.74	5.93	1.48	4.70	2.06	4.11	1.62
	(.58)		(.21)		(-.09)		(.03)		(-.29)		(.49)		(-.75)	
ROOF	5.82	1.83	5.98	1.69	5.40	1.77	4.33	1.72	6.26	1.33	3.88	1.88	4.13	1.38
	(-.01)		(.13)		(-.36)		(-.42)		(.04)		(-.33)		(-.73)	
ROOM	5.45	1.94	5.34	1.84	5.53	1.65	4.95	1.73	6.48	1.05	4.87	1.72	4.22	1.17F
	(-.38)		(-.51)		(-.23)		(.20)		(.26)		(.66)		(-.64)	
ROSE	6.04	1.82	6.17	1.37	5.98	1.73	4.75	1.88	6.32	1.23	3.90	1.55	5.70	1.35
	(.21)		(.32)		(.22)		(.00)		(.10)		(-.31)		(.84)	
RUBY	5.75	1.94	5.47	1.79	5.73	1.65	4.05	1.96	5.62	1.67	3.38	1.52	5.00	1.43
	(-.08)		(-.38)		(-.03)		(-.70)		(-.60)		(-.83)		(.14)	
RUG	6.12	1.48	5.57	1.85	5.27	1.91	4.23	1.66	6.54	1.25	3.44	1.90	4.55	1.52
	(.29)		(-.28)		(-.49)		(-.52)		(.32)		(-.77)		(-.31)	
RUM	5.96	1.69	5.54	1.82	6.10	1.63	5.32	1.65	6.26	1.33	3.25	1.71	5.26	1.35
	(.13)		(-.31)		(.34)		(.57)		(.04)		(-.96)		(.40)	
SAIL	5.63	1.68	5.91	1.43	4.95	1.88	4.28	1.85	5.78	1.58	4.34	1.50	5.79	1.38
	(-.20)		(.06)		(-.81)		(-.47)		(-.44)		(.13)		(.93)	
SAILBOAT	6.15	1.74	6.41	1.22	6.25	1.41	4.59	1.64	6.03	1.44	4.29	1.97	5.78	1.34
	(.32)		(.56)		(.49)		(-.16)		(-.19)		(.08)		(.92)	

	CON		IMG		CAT		MNG		FAM		NOA		PLS	
	M	SD	M	SD	M	SD	M	SD	M	SD	M	SD	M	SD
SAND	6.25	1.50	6.06	1.42	5.33	1.73	4.63	1.71	6.31	1.12	2.98	1.65	4.74	1.77F
	(.42)		(.21)		(-.43)		(-.12)		(.09)		(-1.23)		(-.12)	
SANDAL	6.05	1.59	6.07	1.43	5.62	1.98	4.87	1.81	6.28	1.32	3.34	1.78	5.13	1.45F
	(.22)		(.22)		(-.14)		(.12)		(.06)		(-.87)		(.27)	
SATIN	5.90	1.84	6.02	1.54	5.88	1.47	4.38	1.62	5.71	1.55	3.24	1.78	4.84	1.57
	(.07)		(.17)		(.12)		(-.37)		(-.30)		(-.97)		(-.02)	
SAXOPHONE	6.18	1.56	6.00	1.54	5.97	1.80	4.24	2.00	5.92	1.55	3.87	1.98	4.64	1.64
	(.35)		(.15)		(.21)		(-.51)		(-.30)		(-.34)		(-.22)	
SCHOOL	5.49	1.84	5.72	1.61	5.79	1.60	5.17	1.89	6.47	1.16	5.13	1.90	3.84	1.59F
	(-.34)		(-.13)		(.03)		(.42)		(.25)		(.92)		(-1.02)	
SCOTCH	5.79	1.58	5.84	1.59	5.98	1.43	4.59	1.88	5.92	1.41	4.19	1.79	4.33	1.77M
	(-.04)		(-.01)		(.22)		(-.16)		(-.30)		(-.02)		(-.53)	
SCREWDRIVER	5.70	1.90	6.11	1.37	6.19	1.34	4.41	1.82	6.18	1.47	3.94	1.84	4.23	1.60M
	(-.13)		(.26)		(.43)		(-.34)		(-.04)		(-.27)		(-.63)	
SEA	6.07	1.65	5.73	1.81	5.50	1.71	5.29	1.78	6.24	1.33	5.16	1.99	5.57	1.60F
	(.24)		(-.12)		(-.26)		(.54)		(.02)		(.95)		(.71)	
SEED	6.07	1.45	5.36	1.73	5.10	1.63	4.67	1.80	5.88	1.52	4.10	1.80	4.53	1.17
	(.24)		(-.49)		(-.66)		(-.08)		(-.34)		(-.11)		(-.33)	
SEX	5.33	2.04	5.72	1.74	5.22	2.00	6.13	1.51	6.85	.66	5.65	1.60	6.02	1.15
	(-.50)		(-.13)		(-.54)		(1.38)		(.63)		(1.44)		(1.16)	
SHEETS	5.46	1.67	5.32	1.91	5.30	1.83	4.57	1.68	6.25	1.14	3.80	1.53	4.62	1.47
	(-.37)		(-.53)		(-.18)		(-.18)		(.03)		(-.41)		(-.24)	
SHIP	6.25	1.53	5.75	1.78	5.88	1.46	4.92	1.70	6.43	1.31	4.56	1.93	4.79	1.33
	(.42)		(-.10)		(.12)		(.17)		(.21)		(.35)		(-.07)	
SHIRT	6.05	1.77	6.12	1.42	6.17	1.48	5.47	1.68	6.69	.74	4.23	1.82	4.32	1.40
	(.22)		(.27)		(.41)		(.72)		(.47)		(.02)		(-.54)	
SHOE	5.96	1.88	5.95	1.51	6.00	1.38	4.85	1.96	6.43	1.23	3.86	1.88	4.23	1.19
	(.13)		(.10)		(.24)		(.10)		(.21)		(-.35)		(-.63)	
SHOULDER	5.67	1.88	5.67	1.56	6.12	1.26	4.08	1.92	6.02	1.37	3.70	1.64	4.70	1.31
	(-.16)		(-.18)		(.36)		(-.67)		(-.20)		(-.51)		(-.16)	
SHOWER	5.88	1.44	6.43	.96	4.97	1.88	4.54	1.80	6.56	1.00	4.06	1.85	5.57	1.27
	(.05)		(.58)		(-.79)		(-.21)		(.34)		(-.15)		(.71)	
SHRIMP	6.25	1.43	6.12	1.34	6.25	1.43	4.74	1.83	6.20	1.31	3.89	1.83	5.15	1.83
	(.42)		(.27)		(.49)		(-.01)		(-.02)		(-.32)		(.29)	
SILVER	5.36	2.00	5.68	1.79	6.03	1.48	4.31	1.93	6.13	1.31	3.49	1.79	5.30	1.37
	(-.47)		(-.17)		(.27)		(-.44)		(-.09)		(-.72)		(.44)	
SISTER	5.71	1.84	6.07	1.33	6.08	1.54	5.47	1.91	6.62	.95	4.93	1.90	5.17	1.71
	(-.12)		(.22)		(.32)		(.72)		(.40)		(.72)		(.31)	
SKI	5.86	1.77	6.09	1.38	5.77	1.70	5.00	1.96	6.25	1.31	4.72	1.91	5.85	1.41
	(.03)		(.24)		(.01)		(.25)		(.03)		(.51)		(.99)	
SKIING	5.27	1.99	5.64	1.83	5.85	1.64	4.92	1.97	6.46	1.13	5.13	1.83	5.38	1.68
	(-.56)		(-.21)		(.09)		(.17)		(.24)		(.92)		(.52)	
SKIN	6.31	1.62	6.61	.88	5.58	1.64	4.82	1.71	6.52	1.14	4.49	2.00	5.04	1.26
	(.48)		(.76)		(-.18)		(.07)		(.30)		(.28)		(.18)	
SKIRT	6.28	1.35	5.53	1.77	5.88	1.46	4.45	1.71	5.71	1.69	4.10	1.80	4.50	1.36
	(.45)		(-.32)		(.12)		(-.30)		(-.51)		(-.11)		(-.36)	
SKY	5.39	1.93	5.98	1.58	4.85	1.77	4.82	1.80	6.83	.50	4.59	1.98	5.76	1.40F
	(-.44)		(.13)		(-.91)		(.07)		(.61)		(.38)		(.90)	
SKYSCRAPER	6.14	1.54	5.71	1.59	5.92	1.70	4.90	1.56	5.63	1.59	4.87	1.92	3.71	1.59
	(.31)		(-.14)		(.16)		(.15)		(-.59)		(.66)		(-1.15)	
SLEIGH	6.09	1.60	6.02	1.44	5.18	1.94	4.55	1.90	6.05	1.42	3.51	1.71	4.88	1.81F
	(.26)		(.17)		(-.58)		(-.20)		(-.17)		(-.70)		(.02)	
SLOPE	5.09	1.69	5.72	1.55	4.82	1.53	4.75	1.41	6.37	1.08	3.92	1.52	5.06	1.24
	(-.74)		(-.13)		(-.94)		(.00)		(.15)		(-.29)		(.20)	

	CON		IMG		CAT		MNG		FAM		NOA		PLS	
	M	SD	M	SD	M	SD	M	SD	M	SD	M	SD	M	SD
SMILE	5.19	2.09	5.96	1.74	5.05	1.80	5.02	1.94	6.41	1.36	4.11	1.92	6.23	1.15
	(-.64)		(.11)		(-.71)		(.27)		(.19)		(-.10)		(1.37)	
SNOW	6.14	1.63	5.87	2.03	5.88	1.64	5.03	1.87	6.59	1.02	4.29	1.98	5.32	1.77
	(.31)		(.02)		(.12)		(.28)		(.37)		(.08)		(.46)	
SOAP	5.85	1.75	5.89	1.54	5.48	1.62	4.71	1.95	6.31	1.27	3.62	1.65	4.69	1.05F
	(.02)		(.04)		(-.28)		(-.04)		(.09)		(-.59)		(-.17)	
SOCCER	5.20	2.08	5.64	1.66	5.72	1.82	4.84	1.85	5.95	1.45	3.31	1.76	4.55	1.57
	(-.63)		(-.21)		(-.04)		(.09)		(-.27)		(-.90)		(-.31)	
SODA	5.96	1.57	5.38	1.93	5.92	1.49	4.70	1.60	6.10	1.50	3.82	1.59	5.02	1.37
	(.13)		(-.47)		(.16)		(-.05)		(-.12)		(-.39)		(.16)	
SOFA	6.25	1.52	5.91	1.55	5.77	1.75	4.95	1.77	6.38	.97	3.34	1.67	4.58	1.41
	(.42)		(.06)		(.01)		(.20)		(.16)		(-.87)		(-.28)	
SOIL	5.70	1.79	5.46	1.84	5.35	1.57	4.48	1.63	6.05	1.36	4.06	1.78	4.37	1.45
	(-.13)		(-.39)		(-.41)		(-.27)		(-.17)		(-.15)		(-.49)	
SONG	5.11	1.78	5.44	1.38	4.98	1.89	5.39	1.52	6.61	.82	4.61	1.96	5.63	1.72F
	(-.72)		(-.41)		(-.78)		(.64)		(.39)		(.40)		(.77)	
SOUP	6.11	1.61	5.98	1.33	5.90	1.70	4.35	1.92	6.50	1.10	3.98	2.11	4.41	1.23
	(.28)		(.13)		(.14)		(-.40)		(.28)		(-.23)		(-.45)	
SPARROW	6.25	1.49	5.77	1.55	5.92	1.86	4.70	1.88	5.97	1.44	3.44	1.95	4.65	1.52F
	(.42)		(-.08)		(.16)		(-.05)		(-.25)		(-.77)		(-.21)	
SPICE	5.86	1.54	5.86	1.49	5.30	1.82	4.52	1.82	5.92	1.52	4.32	1.79	5.21	1.21F
	(.03)		(.01)		(-.23)		(-.23)		(-.30)		(.11)		(.35)	
SPRING	5.20	1.76	5.79	1.72	5.87	1.52	5.45	1.59	6.62	.95	4.92	1.98	5.71	1.60F
	(-.63)		(-.06)		(.11)		(.70)		(.40)		(.71)		(.85)	
SPRUCE	5.64	2.07	5.26	1.87	5.95	1.68	4.48	1.83	5.73	1.66	3.86	1.48	5.52	1.22
	(-.19)		(-.59)		(.19)		(-.27)		(-.49)		(-.35)		(.66)	
SQUIRREL	6.08	1.75	6.36	1.17	6.27	1.35	3.97	1.89	6.20	1.30	3.84	1.90	5.39	1.31
	(.25)		(.51)		(.51)		(-.78)		(-.02)		(-.37)		(.53)	
STADIUM	5.65	1.96	5.80	1.85	5.16	1.97	4.13	1.81	6.00	1.43	4.13	1.98	4.41	1.35
	(-.18)		(-.05)		(-.60)		(-.62)		(-.22)		(-.08)		(-.45)	
STAR	5.67	1.93	6.11	1.44	5.57	1.84	4.90	1.66	6.53	1.00	4.76	1.71	5.48	1.51
	(-.16)		(.26)		(-.19)		(.15)		(.31)		(.55)		(.62)	
STATION	5.56	2.02	5.65	1.71	5.23	1.63	4.85	1.44	5.73	1.66	4.79	1.77	4.23	1.25
	(-.27)		(-.20)		(-.53)		(.10)		(-.49)		(.58)		(-.63)	
STEAK	6.57	1.27	6.45	1.44	6.18	1.53	5.33	1.79	6.57	.85	3.64	1.84	5.68	1.76M
	(.74)		(.60)		(.42)		(.58)		(.35)		(-.57)		(.82)	
STEW	5.88	1.70	5.90	1.47	5.65	1.61	4.65	1.81	6.08	1.28	4.15	1.79	4.96	1.63
	(.05)		(.05)		(-.11)		(-.10)		(-.14)		(-.06)		(.10)	
STONE	6.32	1.26	5.71	1.74	5.97	1.65	5.02	1.76	6.15	1.27	3.79	1.82	4.03	1.47
	(.49)		(-.14)		(.21)		(.27)		(-.07)		(-.42)		(-.83)	
STOVE	5.75	1.94	5.91	1.52	5.87	1.53	4.87	1.61	6.23	1.44	4.17	1.66	4.31	1.24
	(-.08)		(.06)		(.11)		(.12)		(.01)		(-.04)		(-.55)	
STRAWBERRY	6.21	1.65	6.18	1.36	6.15	1.62	4.65	1.93	6.40	1.24	3.48	1.80	5.50	1.61
	(.38)		(.33)		(.39)		(-.10)		(.18)		(-.73)		(.64)	
STREET	5.84	1.74	5.29	1.93	5.28	1.88	5.00	1.66	6.59	.91	4.44	1.86	4.05	1.11
	(.01)		(-.56)		(-.48)		(.25)		(.37)		(.23)		(-.81)	
STUDENT	5.51	1.94	5.87	1.44	5.92	1.28	5.49	1.40	6.71	.80	5.14	1.69	4.46	1.56
	(-.32)		(.02)		(.16)		(.74)		(.49)		(.93)		(-.40)	
SUBMARINE	5.68	1.99	5.88	1.62	6.24	1.11	4.03	1.75	5.69	1.62	4.50	2.02	3.97	1.53
	(-.15)		(.03)		(.48)		(-.72)		(-.53)		(.29)		(-.89)	
SUEDE	5.74	1.65	5.44	1.81	5.45	1.97	3.93	1.86	6.05	1.34	3.28	1.39	5.17	1.58F
	(-.09)		(-.41)		(-.31)		(-.82)		(-.17)		(-.93)		(.31)	
SUGAR	6.44	1.22	5.64	1.76	5.78	1.63	5.10	1.59	6.56	1.03	3.25	1.71	4.80	1.44
	(.61)		(-.21)		(.02)		(.35)		(.34)		(-.96)		(-.06)	

	CON M SD	IMG M SD	CAT M SD	MNG M SD	FAM M SD	NOA M SD	PLS M SD
SUN	6.23 1.44 (.40)	6.04 1.62 (.19)	6.22 1.52 (.46)	5.20 1.63 (.45)	6.85 .52 (.63)	4.43 1.99 (.22)	5.95 1.43F (1.09)
SUNSET	5.12 1.93 (-.71)	6.21 1.55 (.36)	4.57 1.86 (-1.19)	4.47 1.85 (-.28)	6.25 1.23 (.03)	4.73 2.15 (.52)	6.04 1.47F (1.18)
SUNTAN	5.40 1.77 (-.43)	5.81 1.75 (-.04)	4.79 1.78 (-.97)	4.22 1.92 (-.53)	6.08 1.46 (-.14)	3.91 1.92 (-.30)	5.07 1.69 (.21)
SUPPER	5.34 1.87 (-.49)	5.63 1.73 (-.22)	5.49 1.69 (-.27)	5.30 1.53 (.55)	6.47 .95 (.25)	4.43 1.90 (.22)	4.76 1.50 (-.10)
SURF	5.23 2.03 (-.60)	5.95 1.41 (.10)	4.90 1.96 (-.86)	4.35 1.76 (-.40)	6.00 1.39 (-.22)	4.26 1.83 (.05)	5.31 1.53 (.45)
SWIM	4.85 1.97 (-.98)	5.52 1.78 (-.33)	5.12 1.97 (-.64)	4.35 1.77 (-.40)	6.32 1.31 (.10)	3.90 1.58 (-.31)	5.26 1.42 (.40)
SWIMMING	5.44 2.05 (-.39)	6.29 1.07 (.44)	6.15 1.51 (.39)	5.02 1.93 (.27)	6.34 1.24 (.12)	4.89 1.81 (.68)	5.77 1.19F (.91)
TANGERINE	6.41 1.38 (.58)	6.19 1.47 (.34)	5.83 1.83 (.07)	4.45 1.70 (-.30)	5.69 1.67 (-.53)	3.67 2.00 (-.54)	5.66 1.16 (.80)
TAPE	5.62 1.86 (-.21)	6.22 1.15 (.37)	4.92 1.63 (-.84)	4.26 1.34 (-.49)	6.44 1.07 (.22)	4.09 1.75 (-.12)	4.14 1.39M (-.72)
TEACHER	5.54 1.81 (-.29)	5.69 1.68 (-.16)	5.50 1.66 (-.26)	5.45 1.47 (.70)	6.77 .59 (.55)	4.76 1.81 (.55)	4.44 1.34 (-.42)
TEAM	4.88 1.71 (-.95)	5.59 1.54 (-.26)	5.37 1.63 (-.39)	5.03 1.52 (.28)	6.12 1.38 (-.10)	4.78 1.80 (.57)	4.84 1.36 (-.02)
TEETH	6.14 1.82 (.31)	6.05 1.45 (.20)	5.80 1.85 (.04)	5.00 1.95 (.28)	6.67 .89 (.45)	3.34 1.90 (-.87)	4.20 1.68 (-.66)
TELEPHONE	6.15 1.60 (.32)	6.49 1.30 (.64)	5.68 1.61 (-.08)	4.67 1.84 (-.08)	6.60 .97 (.38)	4.06 1.88 (-.15)	4.20 1.37F (-.66)
TELESCOPE	5.88 1.67 (.05)	5.90 1.56 (.05)	5.60 1.73 (-.16)	4.10 1.88 (-.65)	6.08 1.23 (-.14)	4.25 1.88 (.04)	4.41 1.19 (-.45)
TENNIS	5.70 2.00 (-.13)	6.28 1.25 (.43)	6.13 1.51 (.37)	4.92 1.86 (.17)	6.02 1.57 (-.20)	4.18 2.05 (-.03)	5.40 1.54 (.54)
TENT	5.88 1.72 (.05)	5.59 1.53 (-.26)	5.60 1.68 (-.16)	4.52 1.60	6.22 1.12 (.00)	4.11 1.77 (-.10)	4.94 1.28F (.08)
TIGER	6.07 1.57 (.24)	6.00 1.50 (.15)	6.59 1.03 (.83)	4.33 1.75 (-.42)	5.87 1.47 (-.35)	4.10 1.98 (-.11)	4.69 1.37F (-.17)
TIMEPIECE	5.70 1.86 (-.13)	5.46 1.65 (-.39)	5.12 1.38 (-.64)	4.87 1.63 (.12)	5.47 1.78 (-.75)	4.77 1.87 (.56)	4.63 1.36 (-.23)
TOE	5.96 1.82 (.13)	6.28 1.31 (.43)	6.03 1.82 (.27)	4.69 1.78 (-.06)	6.58 .94 (.36)	3.16 1.77 (-1.05)	4.22 1.34 (-.64)
TOMATO	6.58 1.12 (.75)	6.04 1.72 (.19)	6.15 1.82 (.42)	4.89 1.98 (-.06)	6.48 1.09 (.26)	3.48 1.76 (-.73)	4.61 1.59 (-.25)
TONGUE	6.30 1.57 (.47)	6.15 1.25 (.30)	5.77 1.71 (.01)	4.38 1.97 (-.37)	6.05 1.44 (-.26)	3.67 1.83 (-.54)	4.40 1.50 (-.46)
TOOL	5.41 1.65 (-.42)	5.16 1.84 (-.69)	5.33 1.88 (-.43)	5.10 1.91 (.35)	5.98 1.56 (-.24)	4.74 1.92 (.53)	4.19 1.46 (-.67)
TOOTH	6.15 1.72 (.32)	6.18 1.48 (.33)	5.97 1.47 (.21)	4.36 1.80 (-.39)	6.52 .97 (.30)	3.84 1.92 (-.37)	3.84 1.43 (-1.02)
TOWN	5.52 2.04 (-.31)	5.47 2.15 (-.38)	5.58 1.82 (-.18)	5.65 1.60 (.90)	6.63 .84 (.41)	4.84 2.31 (.63)	4.65 1.27 (-.21)
TOY	5.32 1.86 (-.51)	5.36 1.69 (-.49)	5.16 1.68 (-.60)	5.05 1.76 (.30)	6.05 1.33 (-.17)	4.89 1.85 (.68)	4.60 1.34 (-.26)
TRACTOR	5.86 1.98 (.03)	5.79 1.78 (-.06)	6.20 1.30 (.44)	4.18 1.92 (-.57)	5.92 1.61 (-.30)	4.30 1.96 (.09)	4.02 1.48M (-.84)
TRAIN	5.88 2.06 (.05)	5.87 1.61 (.02)	5.93 1.57 (.17)	4.68 1.81 (-.07)	6.05 1.41 (-.17)	4.44 1.99 (.23)	4.66 1.19 (-.20)

	CON		IMG		CAT		MNG		FAM		NOA		PLS	
	M	SD	M	SD	M	SD	M	SD	M	SD	M	SD	M	SD
TREE	6.08 1.68 (.25)		6.03 1.57 (.18)		5.80 1.92 (.04)		4.89 1.77 (.14)		6.52 1.13 (.30)		4.53 2.05 (.32)		5.61 1.31 (.75)	
TRIP	4.51 2.22 (-1.32)		5.44 1.66 (-.41)		5.25 1.73 (-.51)		5.50 1.56 (.75)		6.49 1.12 (.27)		5.23 1.86 (1.02)		4.99 2.06F (.13)	
TROUT	5.93 1.73 (.10)		6.34 1.07 (.49)		6.62 .99 (.86)		4.30 2.02 (-.45)		5.87 1.48 (-.35)		4.06 1.77 (-.15)		4.94 1.62M (.08)	
TRUCKS	5.65 2.07 (-.18)		5.74 1.86 (-.11)		5.93 1.64 (.17)		4.37 1.72 (-.38)		5.98 1.59 (-.24)		4.84 1.90 (.63)		3.73 1.27M (-1.13)	
TRUMPET	6.17 1.75 (.34)		6.28 1.36 (.43)		5.97 1.78 (.21)		4.68 1.73 (-.07)		5.83 1.67 (-.39)		4.03 1.67 (-.18)		4.82 1.19 (-.04)	
TULIP	6.15 1.60 (.32)		6.35 1.24 (.50)		6.27 1.55 (.51)		4.70 2.02 (-.05)		6.20 1.45 (-.02)		3.48 1.79 (-.73)		5.43 1.62F (.57)	
TURTLE	6.40 1.25 (.57)		5.58 1.94 (-.27)		6.20 1.46 (.44)		4.31 1.82 (-.44)		5.83 1.68 (-.39)		3.92 1.97 (-.29)		4.50 1.29 (-.36)	
UNCLE	5.79 1.74 (-.04)		5.96 1.58 (-.24)		6.00 1.55 (.17)		4.55 1.89 (-.20)		6.31 1.24 (.09)		3.80 2.15 (-.73)		4.92 1.55F (.06)	
UNIVERSITY	5.49 1.97 (-.34)		5.86 1.75 (.01)		5.70 1.80 (-.06)		5.31 1.75 (.56)		6.82 .87 (.60)		5.39 1.97 (1.18)		4.22 1.57 (-.64)	
VALLEY	5.76 1.64 (-.07)		5.65 1.61 (-.20)		5.42 1.58 (-.34)		4.58 1.76 (-.17)		6.28 1.16 (.06)		4.02 1.86 (-.19)		5.01 1.66F (.15)	
VEGETABLE	6.15 1.27 (.32)		6.30 1.14 (.45)		6.02 1.60 (.26)		5.30 1.66 (.55)		6.34 1.17 (.12)		4.92 1.81 (.71)		4.70 1.68F (-.16)	
VELVET	5.76 1.79 (-.07)		5.63 1.67 (-.22)		5.86 1.54 (.10)		3.80 1.68 (-.95)		5.89 1.48 (-.33)		3.92 1.64 (-.29)		5.16 1.52F (.30)	
VILLAGE	5.70 1.63 (-.13)		5.32 1.66 (-.53)		5.75 1.61 (-.01)		5.28 1.44 (.53)		6.14 1.26 (-.08)		5.49 1.70 (1.28)		5.03 1.37F (.17)	
VIOLIN	6.22 1.52 (.39)		6.00 1.75 (.15)		6.17 1.53 (.41)		4.79 1.87 (.04)		6.03 1.39 (-.19)		3.77 1.99 (-.44)		4.18 1.90 (-.68)	
VODKA	5.72 2.13 (-.11)		6.07 1.46 (.22)		6.03 1.53 (.27)		4.85 1.94 (.10)		6.47 1.07 (.25)		3.49 1.83 (-.72)		4.40 1.80M (-.46)	
VOLLEYBALL	6.48 1.39 (.65)		6.20 1.28 (.35)		6.23 1.51 (.47)		5.08 1.97 (.33)		6.31 1.25 (.09)		3.41 2.02 (-.80)		5.19 1.34 (.33)	
WALKING	4.93 1.91 (-.90)		5.68 1.59 (-.17)		5.33 1.71 (-.43)		4.92 1.46 (.17)		6.33 1.19 (.11)		3.97 1.73 (-.24)		5.08 1.26F (.22)	
WALLET	5.80 1.83 (-.03)		6.11 1.41 (.26)		5.28 1.77 (-.49)		4.21 1.66 (-.54)		6.09 1.47 (-.13)		4.16 2.04 (-.05)		4.48 1.41M (-.38)	
WALNUT	6.38 1.48 (.55)		5.84 1.79 (-.01)		6.32 1.42 (.56)		4.68 1.93 (-.07)		6.12 1.49 (-.10)		3.43 1.69 (-.78)		4.71 1.57 (-.15)	
WATER	6.27 1.34 (.44)		6.25 1.60 (.40)		5.77 1.82 (.01)		5.48 1.61 (.73)		6.76 .90 (.54)		4.56 1.93 (.35)		5.38 1.59F (.52)	
WHALE	6.23 1.61 (.40)		6.26 1.37 (.41)		6.08 1.61 (.32)		4.74 1.90 (-.01)		5.95 1.59 (-.27)		4.54 1.99 (.33)		4.36 1.39 (-.50)	
WHEAT	5.72 1.96 (-.11)		5.78 1.76 (-.07)		5.91 1.51 (.15)		4.47 1.78 (-.28)		6.09 1.35 (-.13)		3.95 1.64 (-.26)		4.91 1.12 (.05)	
WHEEL	5.69 1.91 (-.14)		5.70 1.84 (-.15)		5.72 1.63 (-.04)		4.83 1.83 (.08)		6.34 1.23 (.12)		4.25 1.79 (.04)		4.38 1.18 (-.48)	
WHISKEY	6.00 1.86 (.17)		6.20 1.39 (.35)		5.85 1.63 (.09)		4.75 1.87 (.00)		6.60 .85 (.38)		3.67 1.80 (-.54)		4.44 1.74M (-.42)	
WHISTLE	5.75 1.70 (-.08)		5.81 1.66 (-.04)		4.92 1.63 (-.84)		4.20 1.64 (-.55)		6.22 1.25 (-.04)		3.68 1.74 (-.53)		4.72 1.53 (-.14)	
WHITE	4.68 2.11 (-1.15)		5.64 1.79 (-.21)		5.81 1.75 (.05)		4.64 2.10 (-.11)		6.37 1.29 (.15)		3.13 2.02 (-1.08)		4.82 1.40 (-.04)	
WIFE	5.57 1.68 (-.26)		5.28 1.98 (-.57)		5.45 1.79 (-.31)		5.27 1.60 (.52)		6.43 1.15 (.21)		5.33 1.93 (1.12)		4.66 1.78M (-.20)	

	CON		IMG		CAT		MNG		FAM		NOA		PLS	
	M	SD	M	SD	M	SD	M	SD	M	SD	M	SD	M	SD
WILLOW	5.76	1.75	5.54	1.71	5.97	1.43	3.95	1.94	5.18	1.73	3.63	1.72	5.25	1.50F
	(-.07)		(-.31)		(.21)		(-.80)		(-1.04)		(-.58)		(.39)	
WINDOW	6.27	1.30	6.14	1.41	5.63	1.63	5.07	1.83	6.66	.73	3.75	1.64	4.88	1.63F
	(.44)		(.29)		(-.13)		(.32)		(.44)		(-.46)		(.02)	
WINE	6.49	1.18	6.33	1.35	6.28	1.38	4.89	1.80	6.44	1.18	4.52	1.98	5.42	1.59
	(.66)		(.48)		(.52)		(.14)		(.22)		(.31)		(.56)	
WING	5.91	1.60	5.78	1.49	5.18	1.76	4.16	1.87	6.13	1.23	4.26	1.69	4.37	1.64
	(.08)		(-.07)		(-.58)		(-.59)		(-.09)		(.05)		(-.49)	
WOLF	5.91	1.87	6.04	1.48	6.27	1.53	4.55	2.00	6.11	1.48	3.87	2.05	3.93	1.66
	(.08)		(.19)		(.51)		(-.20)		(-.11)		(-.34)		(-.93)	
WOMAN	5.76	1.91	6.21	1.65	5.79	1.86	5.83	1.53	6.58	1.02	5.84	1.73	5.73	1.44M
	(-.07)		(.36)		(.03)		(1.08)		(.36)		(1.63)		(.87)	
WOMB	5.34	2.02	5.23	1.88	5.27	1.95	4.64	2.07	5.82	1.60	4.35	1.98	4.78	1.67
	(-.49)		(-.62)		(-.49)		(-.11)		(-.40)		(-.14)		(-.08)	
WOOD	5.89	1.67	5.42	1.89	5.61	1.84	5.05	1.72	6.46	1.01	4.28	2.00	4.85	1.52
	(.06)		(-.43)		(-.15)		(.30)		(.24)		(.07)		(-.01)	
WORLD	5.37	1.80	5.42	1.85	4.62	2.14	5.61	1.66	6.58	1.03	5.65	1.97	4.81	1.62
	(-.46)		(-.43)		(-1.14)		(.86)		(.36)		(1.44)		(-.05)	
YACHT	5.92	1.88	6.16	1.32	6.27	1.27	4.64	1.80	5.56	1.84	4.22	1.80	5.10	1.65
	(.09)		(.31)		(.51)		(-.11)		(-.66)		(.01)		(.24)	
YARD	5.23	2.07	5.82	1.53	5.45	1.64	4.82	1.63	5.97	1.52	4.15	1.76	4.62	1.20F
	(-.60)		(-.03)		(-.31)		(.07)		(-.25)		(-.06)		(-.24)	
YELLOW	5.33	1.97	6.18	1.35	6.22	1.36	4.33	2.22	6.30	1.19	3.19	2.03	4.62	1.67
	(-.50)		(.33)		(.46)		(-.42)		(.08)		(-1.02)		(-.24)	
ZOO	5.79	1.86	6.07	1.72	5.65	1.83	5.15	1.88	6.39	1.08	4.92	2.10	4.76	1.92F
	(-.04)		(.22)		(-.11)		(.40)		(.17)		(.71)		(-.10)	

References

Amster, H., & Battig, W. F. Effect of contextual meaningfulness on rated association value (m'), number of associations (m), and free recall. *Psychonomic Science,* 1965, *3,* 569–570.

Barrow, N. K. H. *Word affect and imagery effects in recognition and recall memory.* Unpublished doctoral dissertation, University of Colorado, 1976.

Battig, W. F. *Single-response free word associations for 300 most frequent four-letter English words.* Unpublished manuscript, 1964. (Available from Dept. of Psychology, University of Colorado, Boulder, Colo. 80309.)

Battig, W. F. *Rated number of features for words varying in rated frequency and imagery* (Tech. Rep. No. 46). Boulder: University of Colorado, Institute for the Study of Intellectual Behavior, September 1975. (a)

Battig, W. F. Within-individual differences in "cognitive" processes. In R. L. Solso (Ed.), *Information processing and cognition: The Loyola Symposium.* Hillsdale, N.J.: Lawrence Erlbaum Associates, 1975. (b)

Battig, W. F., & Montague, W. E. Category norms for verbal items in 56 categories. *Journal of Experimental Psychology Monograph Supplement,* 1969, *80*(3, P. 2).

Battig, W. F., & Spera, A. J. Rated association values of numbers from 0–100. *Journal of Verbal Learning and Verbal Behavior,* 1962, *1,* 200–202.

Bower, G. H. A multi-component theory of the memory trace. In K. W. Spence & J. T. Spence (Eds.), *The psychology of learning and motivation* (Vol. 1). New York: Academic Press, 1967.

Cartwright, D. S. *Concreteness–abstractness of verbal stimuli: Is it a dimension?* (Tech. Rep. No. 70) Boulder: University of Colorado, Institute for the Study of Intellectual Behavior, November 1977.

Ekstrand, B. R., Wallace, W. A., & Underwood, B. J. A frequency theory of verbal discrimination learning. *Psychological Review,* 1966, *73,* 566–578.

Galbraith, R. C., & Underwood, B. J. Perceived frequency of concrete and abstract words. *Memory and Cognition,* 1973, *1,* 56–60.

Kuder, G. F., & Richardson, M. W. The theory of the estimation of test reliability. *Psychometrika,* 1937, *2,* 151–160.

Locascio, D., & Ley, R. Scaled-rated meaningfulness of 319 CVCVC words and paralogs previously assessed for associative reaction time. *Journal of Verbal Learning and Verbal Behavior,* 1972, *11,* 243–250.

Maki, R. H. *Concreteness and the existence of a superordinate: What is their role in free recall?* Paper presented at the meetings of the Midwestern Psychological Association, Chicago, May 1975.

Neumann, P. G. An attribute frequency model for the abstraction of prototypes. *Memory and Cognition,* 1974, *2,* 241–248.

Noble, C. E. An analysis of meaning. *Psychological Review,* 1952, *59,* 421–430.

Paivio, A., Yuille, J. D., & Madigan, S. A. Concreteness, imagery, and meaningfulness values for 925 nouns. *Journal of Experimental Psychology: Monograph Supplement,* 1968, *76*(3, P. 2).

Palermo, D. S., & Jenkins, J. J. *Word association norms: Grade school through college.* Minneapolis: University of Minnesota Press, 1964.

Pellegrino, J. W., & Salzberg, P. M. Encoding specificity in associative processing tasks. *Journal of Experimental Psychology: Human Learning and Memory,* 1975, *1,* 538–548.

Perfetti, C. A., Lindsey, R., & Garson, B. *Association and uncertainty: Norms of association to ambiguous words.* Pittsburgh, Pa.: University of Pittsburgh, Learning Research and Development Center, 1971.

Postman, L., & Keppel, G. *Norms of word association.* New York: Academic Press, 1970.

Reder, L. M., Anderson, J. R., & Bjork, R. A. A semantic interpretation of encoding specificity. *Journal of Experimental Psychology,* 1974, *102,* 648–656.

Shapiro, S. I., & Palermo, D. S. Conceptual organization and class membership: Normative data for representatives of 100 categories. *Psychonomic Monograph Supplements,* 1970, *3*(No. 11, Whole No. 43), 107–127.

Spreen, O., & Schulz, R. W. Parameters of abstraction, meaningfulness, and pronunciability for 329 nouns. *Journal of Verbal Learning and Verbal Behavior,* 1966, *5,* 459–468.

Thorndike, E. L., & Lorge, I. *The teacher's word book of 30,000 words.* New York: Teachers College, Columbia University, 1944.

Tryon, R. C., & Bailey, D. E. *Cluster analysis.* New York: McGraw-Hill, 1970.

Underwood, B. J. Attributes of memory. *Psychological Review,* 1969, *76,* 559–573.

Underwood, B. J., & Richardson, J. Some verbal materials for the study of concept formation. *Psychological Bulletin,* 1956, *54,* 84–95.

Underwood, B. J., & Schulz, R. W. *Meaningfulness and verbal learning.* Philadelphia: Lippincott, 1960.

Author Index

Subject Index